Human–Computer Interaction Series

HCI is a multidisciplinary field focused on human aspects of the development of computer technology. As computer-based technology becomes increasingly pervasive—not just in developed countries, but worldwide—the need to take a human-centered approach in the design and development of this technology becomes ever more important. For roughly 30 years now, researchers and practitioners in computational and behavioral sciences have worked to identify theory and practice that influences the direction of these technologies, and this diverse work makes up the field of human-computer interaction. Broadly speaking it includes the study of what technology might be able to do for people and how people might interact with the technology. The HCI series publishes books that advance the science and technology of developing systems which are both effective and satisfying for people in a wide variety of contexts. Titles focus on theoretical perspectives (such as formal approaches drawn from a variety of behavioral sciences), practical approaches (such as the techniques for effectively integrating user needs in system development), and social issues (such as the determinants of utility, usability and acceptability).

Titles published within the Human–Computer Interaction Series are included in Thomson Reuters' Book Citation Index, The DBLP Computer Science Bibliography and The HCI Bibliography.

More information about this series at http://www.springer.com/series/6033

Tracy Hammond · Stephanie Valentine
Aaron Adler
Editors

Revolutionizing Education with Digital Ink

The Impact of Pen and Touch Technology on Education

Springer

Editors
Tracy Hammond
Sketch Recognition Lab
Department of Computer Science and Engineering
Texas A&M University
College Station, TX
USA

Aaron Adler
Raytheon BBN Technologies
Columbia, MD
USA

Stephanie Valentine
Sketch Recognition Lab
Department of Computer Science and Engineering
Texas A&M University
College Station, TX
USA

ISSN 1571-5035
Human–Computer Interaction Series
ISBN 978-3-319-31191-3 ISBN 978-3-319-31193-7 (eBook)
DOI 10.1007/978-3-319-31193-7

Library of Congress Control Number: 2016934202

Printed on acid-free paper

This Springer imprint is published by Springer Nature
The registered company is Springer International Publishing AG Switzerland

Foreword

The 2015 Workshop on the Impact of Pen and Touch Technology on Education was the ninth annual iteration of this conference. Researchers and practicing K-16 educators converged to the mutual benefit of each group. The conference content was a rich amalgam of keynote speakers, research papers, presentations by practicing teachers of classroom techniques that they found worthwhile, and hands-on You-Try-It sessions. People had ample opportunity to connect with one another to explore ideas and practices, yielding a stimulating cross-pollination in a diverse community.

Our tagline for the conference was "The Perfect Storm," carefully chosen to emphasize the converging conditions that provide opportunity as well as risks.

Many of us watched the initial excitement but subsequent malaise around the Microsoft Tablet PC, and felt that the tremendous impact that tablets could and should have on education—often testified to by WIPTTE researchers—wasn't being broadly realized. Some wondered when, or even if, it ever would be. But now—it may seem sudden but in reality developed over a couple of years—things are moving rapidly forward.

A perfect storm is the concurrency of multiple events that combine to create an extremely powerful weather phenomenon. We are seeing this same concurrence now around digital ink, much of it spurred by this year's host, Microsoft but also evident in a flurry of new tablets emphasizing the advantages of digital ink, including (after the conference) the Apple iPad Pro and Pencil.

Microsoft's rededication to software exploiting digital ink and touch in education was evident in sponsor's talks by the Office team that recently released OneNote Class Notebooks for O365—an application inspired by WIPTTE 2013 presentations followed by a lunch brainstorming meeting!—and the originators of education-oriented applications Sway and Mix. Wacom also described its innovations in a sponsor keynote address.

On the hardware side, the release of the Surface Pro 3 has captured the eye of the media as no ink-based tablet computer ever has. Other hardware vendors are following suit, exploring innovative, varied and very functional designs for systems supporting ink on devices that are increasingly affordable. Samsung is an alternative hardware platform with pen support. Wacom and the Surface Pro team gave sponsor talks on hardware design with education in mind.

Another development of potentially profound import is recent research showing the advantages in learning and problem-solving for students using digital pens in contrast to typing or even using traditional writing and sketching tools. The first two WIPTTE 2015 keynote speakers, Pam Mueller and Sharon Oviatt, presented their landmark research on this subject.

Abetting these developments is the shift toward new "twenty-first century" forms of pedagogy that rely on digital technology, and the building out of school infrastructure capable of supporting it. We at WIPTTE are contributing to all of these, and by showcasing best practices also support crucial professional development activity. Though much remains to be done, it is indeed a perfect storm, and one which bodes well for those in this community and in education at large who focus new developments.

The conference organizers are grateful to the many sponsors who have so generously funded us this year and without whom this whole affair would have been impossible. As Platinum level sponsors, we have Microsoft (Windows, OneNote, Surface Pro, Surface Hub, and Research), in addition to their support as host. Wacom is a Gold level sponsor. Fujitsu is a Silver level sponsor. Bronze sponsors are DyKnow, PDF Annotator, and the Sketch Recognition Lab of Texas A&M University. All were vital to the success of this conference.

We want to acknowledge here the hard work put in by all of the members of the organizing committee. Special praise goes to Tracy Hammond and her amazing students from Texas A&M. The conference would not have happened without them.

And last, thank you to all who attended. Every presentation, whether a keynote or a poster, represents many hours of work on the part of the presenter. Every attendee had to juggle other priorities to realize the opportunity to learn from and contribute to this community. Together, we will continue to push the capabilities of digital ink and touch technologies as powerful tools for education.

St. Louis, MO, USA
Redmond, WA, USA
January 2016

Mark Payton
Dr. Jonathan Grudin
WIPTTE 2015 Co-chairs

Mark Payton is the Director of Technology and Library Services for Whitfield School, an independent 6–12 school in St. Louis, MO. He is in his 17th year as an IT Director in independent schools, having been at schools in Vermont and Madaba, Jordan previously. He started his IT career working in the ski industry at Killington and as IT Director for Burton Snowboards. Between the industry and academic stints, he was a software developer. Self-taught as a programmer and IT person, his training is in early childhood education with a BA from the University of Kansas. He has taught subjects as varied as Introductory Programming and Christian Theology, and to students of every grade between Pre-K and the undergraduate university level. He has been interested in pen-based computing since the days of the GRiDpad and Windows for Pen Computing and has been a member of the WIPTTE steering committee since the conference's inception.

Jonathan Grudin is a Principal Researcher at Microsoft Research in the fields of human–computer interaction (HCI) and computer-supported cooperative work (CSCW). Grudin is a pioneer of the field of CSCW and one of its most prolific contributors, and was awarded the inaugural CSCW Lasting Impact Award in 2014 on the basis of his work. Grudin is currently also an Affiliate Professor at the Information School in the University of Washington. Previously, he was a Professor of Information and Computer Science at University of California Irvine. Grudin received his Ph.D. under Don Norman in Cognitive Psychology from the University of California San Diego.

Acknowledgements

We also thank the contributing authors and presenters, reviewers, students, and staff at the Microsoft Campus for the truly outstanding work that was done to produce, publish, present, and demonstrate at the conference, and in providing the behind-the-scenes work necessary to make it all possible. Thanks also to Anna Stephanova (Texas A&M University) and Jung In Koh (Texas A&M University).

The generous sponsorship of several corporations and organizations has been crucial to enabling WIPTTE to provide a high quality program at a very low cost to attendees. We would particularly like to thank our sponsors who have provided invaluable resources, both financial and in-kind. The 2015 Platinum and host sponsor was Microsoft. The 2015 Gold Sponsor was Wacom, with special thanks going to Sierra Modro and David Fleck. The 2015 Silver Sponsor was Fujitsu, with special thanks going to Mitsi Miller. The 2015 Bronze Sponsors included DyKnow, with special thanks to Anastasia Way and Michael Vasey; PDF Annotator, with special thanks to Oliver Grahl; and the Texas A&M University Sketch Recognition Lab, with special thanks to Dr. Tracy Hammond and Stephanie Valentine. Student volunteers included Laura Barretto (Sketch Recognition Lab, Vassar College), Seth Polsley (Sketch Recognition Lab, Texas A&M University), Raniero Lara-Garduno (Sketch Recognition Lab, Texas A&M University), and Paul Taele (Sketch Recognition Lab, Texas A&M University).

Organizing Committees

The chairs of WIPTTE 2015 were Dr. Jonathan Grudin (Microsoft) and Mark Payton (Whitfield School).

The paper chairs was Dr. Aaron Adler (BBN).

The poster chair was Dr. Jane Dong (California State University).

The high school chairs were Stephanie Valentine (Texas A&M University) and Cassandra Oduola (Texas A&M University).

The webmasters were Paul Taele (Texas A&M University) and David Turner (Texas A&M University).

Ex Officio members of the committee included Dr. Eric Hamilton (Pepperdine University), Dr. Tracy Hammond (Texas A&M University), and Dr. Joseph Tront (Virginia Tech).

Contents

Editors and Contributors

About the Editors

Tracy Hammond Director of the Sketch Recognition Lab and Associate Professor in the Department of Computer Science and Engineering at Texas A&M University, Dr. Hammond is an international leader in sketch recognition and human–computer interaction research. Dr. Hammond's publications on the subjects are widely cited and have well over 1500 citations, with Dr. Hammond having an h-index of 19, an h10-index of 29, and four papers with over 100 citations each. Her sketch recognition research has been funded by NSF, DARPA, Google, Microsoft, and many others, totaling over 3.6 million dollars in peer reviewed funding. She holds a Ph.D. in Computer Science and FTO (Finance Technology Option) from M.I.T., and four degrees from Columbia University: an M.S. in Anthropology, an M.S. in Computer Science, a B.A. in Mathematics, and a B.S. in Applied Mathematics. Prior to joining the TAMU CSE faculty, Dr. Hammond taught for 5 years at Columbia University and was a telecom analyst for 4 years at Goldman Sachs. Dr. Hammond is the 2011–2012 recipient of the Charles H. Barclay, Jr. '45 Faculty Fellow Award. The Barclay Award is given to professors and associate professors who have been nominated for their overall contributions to the engineering program through classroom instruction, scholarly activities, and professional service.

Stephanie Valentine is a Ph.D. student in the Department of Computer Science and Engineering at Texas A&M University. A Nebraska native, Valentine graduated Salutatorian of her class with a B.A. in Computer Science with a minor in Electronic Publishing from Saint Mary's University of Minnesota. Valentine is an NSF Graduate Fellow, winner of the Susan M. Arseven '75 Make-A-Difference Award, and Vice President of the CSE Departmental graduate student association. Valentine's research focuses around understanding how children communicate in online social networks and empowering children to have safe, healthy, and expressive digital friendships. Valentine is also the founding president of Wired Youth, Inc., a 501(c)3 nonprofit organization that works to educate the community about safe social networking for children as an active prevention strategy for cyberbullying, online predation, and other cyberthreats.

Aaron Adler is a Scientist at Raytheon BBN Technologies in Columbia, Maryland and Cambridge, Massachusetts. Dr. Adler has worked on variety of projects for DARPA and AFRL involving security, machine learning, robotics, artificial intelligence, and synthetic biology. Dr. Adler has a particular interest in creating intelligent user interfaces by automatically handling complexities to enable intuitive interfaces for users. He received his Ph.D. in Computer Science from M.I.T. where he also received his M.Eng. in Computer Science and Engineering and S.B. in Computer Science. His Ph.D. thesis centered on constructing multimodal interactive dialogues: combining speech recognition and sketch recognition for user input and generating speech and sketching for multimodal computer output. The system helps the user describe simple mechanical (Rube-Goldberg-like) devices by asking probing questions.

Contributors

Aaron Adler Information and Knowledge Technologies, Raytheon BBN Technologies, Columbia, MD, USA

Catherine Amelink College of Engineering, Virginia Tech, Blacksburg, VA, USA

Laura Barreto Sketch Recognition Lab, Computer Science and Engineering Department, Texas A&M University, College Station, TX, USA; Computer Science Department, Vassar College, New York, USA

Virginia Berninger Department of Educational Psychology, University of Washington, Seattle, WA, USA

Katya Borgos-Rodriguez Sketch Recognition Lab, Computer Science and Engineering Department, Texas A&M University, College Station, TX, USA; University of Puerto Rico at Mayaguez, Mayaguez, PR, USA

Nathaniel Bowditch Department of Computer Science, Brown University, Providence, RI, USA; Digital Results Group Inc., Boston, MA, USA

Bill Buxton Microsoft Research, Redmond, WA, USA

Nishesh Chalise School of Social Work, Augsburg College, Minneapolis, MN, USA

Samuel Cohen South Fayette High School, Mcdonald, PA, USA

Hannah Conrad Sketch Recognition Lab, Computer Science and Engineering Department, Texas A&M University, College Station, TX, USA

Tiffany Dinh Renton Preparatory Christian School, Renton, WA, USA

Jasmine Fernandez Renton Preparatory Christian School, Renton, WA, USA

George Foe-Aman Cabrillo High School, Long Beach, CA, USA

Lynette Foe-Aman Cabrillo High School, Long Beach, CA, USA

Julaine Fowlin Learning Sciences and Technologies, Virginia Tech, Blacksburg, VA, USA

Kayla Gonzalvo Renton Preparatory Christian School, Renton, WA, USA

Eric Hamilton Graduate School of Educational Psychology, Pepperdine University, Malibu, CA, USA

Tracy Hammond Sketch Recognition Lab, Department of Computer Science and Engineering, Texas A&M University, College Station, TX, USA

Michael Helms iDreem Lab at Georgia Institute of Technology, Atlanta, GA, USA

Ken Hinckley Microsoft Research, Redmond, WA, USA

Loide Kapenda Namibian Ministry of Education, Windhoek, Namibia

Richard Kassissieh University Prep, Seattle, WA, USA

Hiroo Kato Graduate School of Education and Psychology, Pepperdine University, Los Angeles, CA, USA

Kimberle Koile MIT Center for Educational Computing Initiatives, Cambridge, MA, USA

Radhir Kothuri University of Illinois at Urbana-Champaign, Champaign, IL, USA

Musik Kwon Samsung Electronics, Co., Ltd., Suwon-si, Gyeonggi-do, South Korea

Raniero Lara-Garduno Sketch Recognition Lab, Computer Science and Engineering Department, Texas A&M University, Texas, USA

Joseph J. LaViola Jr. Department of EECS, University of Central Florida, Orlando, FL, USA

Nancy Leslie Texas Brain and Spine Institute & Health Science Center, Texas A&M University, Bryan, Texas, USA

Angelica Leyva-McMurtry Sketch Recognition Lab, Computer Science and Engineering Department, Texas A&M University, College Station, TX, USA; Mills College, Oakland, CA, USA

Wayne Li Innovation and Design Collaborative, Georgia Institute of Technology, Atlanta, GA, USA

Julie Linsey iDreem Lab, Georgia Institute of Technology, Atlanta, GA, USA

Aurelio López-Malo Department of Chemical and Food Engineering, Center for Science, Engineering, and Technology Education, Universidad de las Americas Puebla, San Andres Cholula, Puebla, Mexico

Sara Mata Whitfield School, Creve Coeur, Mo, USA

Zachary Mbasu African Maths Initiative, Nairobi, Kenya

Helena Miranda University of Namibia, Ongwediva, Namibia

William Nagy School of Education, Seattle Pacific University, Seattle, WA, USA

Vaishali Nandy Learning Sciences and Technologies, Virginia Tech, Blacksburg, VA, USA

Trevor Nelligan Sketch Recognition Lab, Computer Science and Engineering Department, Texas A&M University, College Station, TX, USA

Elizabeth Ngololo Namibian Ministry of Education, Windhoek, Namibia

Scott Nguyen Renton Preparatory Christian School, Renton, WA, USA

Cassandra Oduola Sketch Recognition Lab, Computer Science and Engineering Department, Texas A&M University, College Station, TX, USA

Joseph Carilus Ogwel Kenyan Ministry of Education, Karen, Kenya

David Okoth Learning Sciences and Technologies, Virginia Tech, Blacksburg, VA, USA

Moses Okumu School of Social Work, University of Texas, Arlington, TX, USA

Sharon Oviatt Incaa Designs, Deer Harbor, WA, USA

Aileen Owens South Fayette High School, Mcdonald, PA, USA

Enrique Palou Department of Chemical and Food Engineering, Center for Science, Engineering, and Technology Education, Universidad de las Americas Puebla, San Andres Cholula, Puebla, Mexico

Audrey Lampe Ploesser Whitfield School, Saint Louis, MO, USA

Dale Pokorski College of Engineering, Virginia Tech, Blacksburg, VA, USA

Seth Polsley Sketch Recognition Lab, Computer Science and Engineering Department, Texas A&M University, College Station, TX, USA

Zaira Ramírez-Apud School of Biology, Benemerita Universidad Autonoma de Puebla, Puebla, Mexico

Nelly Ramírez-Corona Department of Chemical and Food Engineering, Center for Science, Engineering, and Technology Education, Universidad de las Americas Puebla, San Andres Cholula, Puebla, Mexico

Israel Ramirez-Gamez Spring Valley High School, Las Vegas, NV, USA

Jaideep Ray Sketch Recognition Lab, Computer Science and Engineering Department, Texas A&M University, College Station, TX, USA

Carla A. Romney Fordham College at Rose Hill, Fordham University, Bronx, NY, USA; Metropolitan College, Boston University, Boston, MA, USA

Andee Rubin TERC, Cambridge, MA, USA

Sandra Sarmonpal Pepperdine University, Malibu, CA, USA

Glenda Scales College of Engineering, Virginia Tech, Blacksburg, VA, USA

David Stern African Maths Initiative, Nairobi, Kenya

Paul Taele Sketch Recognition Lab, Computer Science and Engineering Department, Texas A&M University, College Station, TX, USA

Steven Tanimoto Department of Computer Science and Engineering, University of Washington, Seattle, WA, USA

Robert Thompson Department of Computer Science and Engineering, University of Washington, Seattle, WA, USA

Jeff Tillinghast University Prep, Seattle, WA, USA

Stephanie Valentine Sketch Recognition Lab, Department of Computer Science and Engineering, Texas A&M University, College Station, TX, USA

Guan Wang Department of Computer Science, Brown University, Providence, RI, USA

Nicholas Wilke South Fayette High School, Mcdonald, PA, USA

Leslie Williams Cary Academy, NC, Cary, USA

Blake Williford Innovation and Design Collaborative, Georgia Institute of Technology, Atlanta, GA, USA

Robert Zeleznik Brown University, Providence, RI, USA

Michelle Zimmerman Educational Design and Technology, Concordia University Wisconsin, Mequon, WI, USA; Renton Preparatory Christian School, Renton, WA, USA

Part I
Introductions and Welcome

Chapter 1
Introduction

Tracy Hammond, Aaron Adler, and Stephanie Valentine

Abstract Derived from contributions to the Workshop on Pen and Touch Technology on Education (WIPTTE) in 2015, this edited volume highlights recent developments for pen and tablet research within the education system with a particular focus on hardware and software developments, comprising the perspectives of teachers, school and university administrators, and researchers for educators at every level. Split into six distinct parts, the book explores topics like how classrooms are increasingly using sketch-based videos, created by teachers and students alike, and how the teaching of key skills such as literacy, languages, math, and art via pen and touch technologies within the classroom are leading to improvements in engagement, learning, and retention levels amongst students. Future perspectives of digital learning, as envisioned by current high school students, are also explored

1.1 Introduction

This monograph represents a collection of papers from the 2015 Workshop on the Impact of Pen and Touch Technology on Education (WIPTTE) held from April 28th through 30th on the Microsoft Campus in Redmond, Washington, USA. The workshop was chaired by Dr. Jonathan Grudin, Principal Researcher at Microsoft Researcher, and Mark Payton, Director at Technology and Library Resources at Whitfield School.

T. Hammond (✉) · S. Valentine
Sketch Recognition Lab, Department of Computer Science and Engineering, Texas A&M University, Mail Stop 3112, College Station, TX 77843-3112, USA
e-mail: thammond@gmail.com

S. Valentine
e-mail: valentine@cse.tamu.edu

A. Adler
Information and Knowledge Technologies, Raytheon BBN Technologies, 9861 Broken Land Parkway, Suite 400, Columbia, MD 21046, USA
e-mail: aadler@bbn.com

T. Hammond et al. (eds.), *Revolutionizing Education with Digital Ink*, Human–Computer Interaction Series, DOI 10.1007/978-3-319-31193-7_1

The 2015 WIPTTE marks the 9th annual instantiation of the workshop, organized first in 2006. Each year the workshop is held in a different location and has been growing stronger from year to year. In 2016, the workshop will be held on the Brown University Campus in Providence, RI, USA. In 2016, the WIPTTE will be updated to a conference status, with the new name being the Conference on Pen and Touch Technology in Education (CPTTE). It will be chaired by Andries van Dam, Professor of Computer Science at Brown University.

As highlighted in the Foreward by the workshop chairs, Jonathan Grudin and Mark Payton, this year marks a great amount of innovation for pen and tablet research, not only are software advances allowing computers to react more cleverly, but also great strides in hardware are making TabletPCs feel closer to traditional pen and paper, with frictionful pens and screens that provide an integrated experience. The workshop and this volume define how pen and touch computing are positively impacting modern education.

1.2 WIPTTE 2015—Keynotes

In 2015, the workshop had four keynote speakers: Pam Mueller, Dr. Sharon Oviatt, Anthony Salcito, and Dr. Richard Anderson. Keynote speakers were starting the opening session on each of the workshop days. Pam Mueller and Dr. Sharon Oviatt started off the workshop on Tuesday, the first day of the workshop. Anthony Salcito started off Wednesday, and Dr. Richard Anderson started off the last day of the workshop on Thursday.

Pam Mueller gave a talk entitled "The Pen is Mightier than the Keyboard" in which she discussed the advantages of taking notes with a pen over using a keyboard based on the data she collected during a recent study she conducted. Pam Mueller is a graduate student at Princeton University, and is working towards her Ph.D. in social psychology. She received her B.S. in psychology from Loyola University Chicago in 2002, and her J.D. from Harvard Law School in 2008. Prior to law school, she worked as a press secretary for Howard Dean's presidential campaign on Capitol Hill. Before entering graduate school, she practiced trademark, copyright, and false advertising law. She has published on a wide range of topics, from perceptions of knowledge and intentionality in legal cases to potential issues with the use of crowdsourcing websites for experimental data collection. Her research on laptop and longhand note taking was covered by many media outlets in the U.S. and abroad, including the New York Times, The Atlantic, NPR, the BBC, and the Sydney Morning Herald.

Dr. Sharon Oviatt gave a talk entitled "Computer Interfaces Can Stimulate or Undermine Students' Ability to Think" in which she talked about the advantages of using pens in the classroom setting. Sharon Oviatt is internationally known for her multidisciplinary work on human-centered interfaces, educational interfaces, multimodal and mobile interfaces, pen and speech interfaces, and technology design and evaluation. She has published over 150 scientific articles in a wide range of venues. She is an Associate Editor of the peer-reviewed journals and edited book collections in the field of human-centered interfaces, including the journals Human Computer Interaction and ACM Transactions on Intelligent Interactive Systems. She was the recipient of a National Science Foundation Special Creativity Award for pioneering research on mobile multimodal interfaces. She also received the inaugural ICMI Sustained Accomplishment Award for innovative, long-lasting, and influential contributions to defining the field of multimodal and multimedia interaction, interfaces, and system development. Sharon currently serves as President and Director of Incaa Designs Nonprofit. She originally received her Ph.D. in Experimental Psychology at the University of Toronto. For the most part of her career, she has served as a professor of Computer Science, as well as a faculty member and taught at Psychology and Linguistics departments. In 2013, Sharon published The Design of Future Educational Interfaces (Routledge). Her latest book, The Paradigm Shift to Multimodality in Contemporary Computer Interfaces (co-authored with Phil Cohen) will be published in 2016.

Anthony Salcito made a presentation entitled "Microsoft Worldwide Education Talk" in which he discussed Microsoft's impact on pen computing and K-12 education around the world after a Drum Cafe start-off. Anthony Salcito is Vice-President of Worldwide Education at Microsoft. Anthony's talk was a collocated talk with the E2 Global Educator Exchange, which hosted 300 educators from around the world.

Dr. Richard Anderson presented a talk entitled "Reflections of Classroom Presenter" describing the lasting impact of the Classroom Presenter application. Richard Anderson is a Professor from the University of Washington in the Computer Science and Engineering Department. Classroom Presenter is a TabletPC application developed to allow instructors more flexibility presenting the material during classes through the introduction of digital ink. The application achieved widespread use by early adopters of the TabletPC, and continues to be used in classrooms around the world. This talk described the history of Classroom Presenter, developed while the author worked at Microsoft, as well as a reflection on how the initial vision of Classroom Presenter could be applied today.

1.3 WIPTTE 2015—Socialization

One of the main benefits of the workshop is the networking opportunities that encourage university and high school pen and touch researchers to intermingle. WIPTTE is unique in that it blends perspectives from a wide variety of researchers, including high school teachers, technology administrators, college deans, university professors, and others interested in pen and touch technology and its impact in education.

Beyond the interactive lunches, talks, and other sessions, the workshop provided three socialization sessions. The first evening of the workshop (Tuesday) started off with a poster session at a welcome reception collocated with the E2 Global Educator Exchange (Fig. 1.1). The E2 consisted of three hundred educators from all over the world discussing innovative technology for the classroom. The combined event provided a unique opportunity for WIPTTE researchers to present their research to

Fig. 1.1 Laura Barreto and Seth Polsley presenting their posters on Maestoso and Mechanix at the E2 Global Educator Exchange Poster Session

a new group of educators. WIPTTE poster presenters were inundated with clever questions from hundreds of educators.

Wednesday evening provided a WIPTTE dinner cruise on the Argosy Spirit of Seattle as it cruised down Lake Washington, a 22-mile long deep freshwater ribbon lake situated between Seattle, Bellevue, and Redmond. WIPTTE researchers spent

Fig. 1.2 TAMU Sketch Recognition Lab researchers on the boat cruise at WIPTTE, from *left* to *right*: Cassandra Oduola, Blake Williford, Raniero Lara-Garduno, Seth Polsley, Lab Director Dr. Tracy Hammond, Andy Hurley, Laura Barreto, Stephanie Valentine, and Paul Taele

two hours in deep discussion on the day's riveting talks with a beautiful view of Seattle. Figure 1.2 shows a group of TAMU Sketch Recognition Lab researchers enjoying the view.

On Thursday evening the members of the workshop took a field trip to the Kent Technology Exposition. The Kent School District, south of Seattle, has over 40 schools and 25,000 students. Every year the students and staff organize a large technology integration showcase in an exposition hall in Kent. Kent, a diverse school district, for years has engaged in technology initiatives that have attracted recognition.

1.4 Monograph Organization

WIPTTE 2015 included four keynotes, seven emerging technology talks describing new technology in development, eleven technology-in-practice session describing research experiments in the classroom, nine You-Try-It sessions, and five highlights of previously published research at other peer-reviewed conferences. All paper submissions were peer-reviewed by 3–5 expert researchers in the field. Dr. Aaron Adler of BBN was the Paper Chair of the workshop, and handled the assignment of the paper reviews. Accepted papers were invited for resubmission as a chapter in this edited volume. Those papers are organized as follows:

1.4.1 Part I: Introduction

Jonathan Grudin and Mark Payton kick off this book with a foreword to both this book and the workshop.

1.4.2 Part II: Why We Pen and Touch

This section includes two papers that help to inspire us to do more research on pen and touch research. The first by Sharon Oviatt, "Computer Interfaces Can Stimulate or Undermine Students' Ability to Think" discusses the influence of computer input tools and various interfaces on human thought and performance. The chapter summarizes how and why the quality of a computer interface matters. To promote learning, students need high-quality interfaces that can support complex content creation activities and pen interfaces are especially good candidates for achieving this objective. Such interfaces are more expressively powerful than the keyboard, because they support people's ability to communicate information involving different representations, modalities, and linguistic codes. Oviatt describes a number of ways that pen input has been shown to be better than typing in recent literature: Hand-drawn diagrams help students view and interpret information. Students communicate more nonlinguistic content and produce a greater amount of ideation and variation in their scientific hypotheses. And students using a pen show greater fMRI activity than those using a keyboard. Additionally, the digital pen encouraged students to draw a greater number of diagrams, draw more correct diagrams, and make more correct interpretations than when using a regular pen. She highlights the battle pen researchers and educators are up against, as students still claim to prefer typing even being made aware that their grades dropped a full grade point when typing instead of hand-drawing.

The second chapter, by Microsoft Researchers Ken Hinckley and Bill Buxton, "Inking Outside the Box: How Context Sensing Affords More Natural Pen (and Touch) Computing" discusses the concept of "pen AND touch" interaction on touch-screens from different perspectives. They analyze how human manual activity. The user is holding the tablet, how the user is gripping the pen, and how each device is oriented and moving relative to the other, with all of these having the potential to considerably enrich interaction with tablets. Even when additional sensors are few, certain techniques allow for supporting richer, more natural, and more nuanced pen and touch interaction.

1.4.3 Part III: Novel Tutoring Systems and Intelligent Ink

Pen and touch have come a long way, with the digital pen not just laying down ink on a page, but also providing intelligence about the content sketched. Researchers combine techniques from artificial intelligence and other domains to allow for real-time tutoring or provide other high-level information based on the ink. Systems in this chapter range from teaching students how to write, math and algebra skills, engineering statics, how to draw, Asian languages, and music, as well as evaluating medical stroke effects.

In this section's first paper "Design Studies for Stylus and Finger-Based Interaction in Writing Instruction on Tablets," the authors Thompson, Tanimoto, Berniger, and Nagy present new instructional software HAWK (Help Agent for Writing Knowledge) for the essentials of writing, that runs on tablets. The lessons are designed to be used for typically developing oral and written language learners (OWLs) as well as children and youth with specific learning disabilities impairing subword letter writing (dysgraphia), word reading and spelling (dyslexia), and oral and written language syntax (OWL LD). The instructional material embedded in the HAWK software consists of 18 units called lessons. Each lesson is intended to be taken by a student in a single session of approximately two hours. The authors focused on providing graphical feedback to students in the context of a stylus and touch-based interface for the basic educational activity of learning to write letters of the alphabet. Each lesson provides a variety of activities, so that a student is sufficiently stimulated to continue and complete each lesson. In trials with an after school K-12 subject group, the use of the software improved the writing capabilities of most students.

In "Tablet-based Technology to Support Students' Understanding of Division," authors Koile and Rubin tested a new tablet-based tool designed to help upper elementary students develop a strong understanding of division in a 4th grade classroom. The tool provides an interactive visual model for the process of division and leverages students' understanding of the array as a model for multiplication. Their results indicate that the tool has helped students increase their understanding of division and multiplication.

In "A Tablet-Based Math Tutor for Beginning Algebra," authors Wang, Bowditch, Zelenik, Kwon, and LaViola provide a first version of an interactive mathematical tutor application that allows for a flexible, investigative approach that closely mimics the established method of solving an equation on paper. Mistakes found by the application are conveniently highlighted and explained to the student without any need for them to define what solution strategy they applied. When presented to a small group of students in a pilot study, results demonstrated that the application provided an enjoyable experience and helped students be more careful in their work.

In "Leveraging Trends in Student Interaction to Enhance the Effectiveness of Sketch-Based Educational Software," the authors Polsley, Ray, Nelligan, Helms, Linsey, and Hammond analyze student activities from using Mechanix—a sketch-based grading and tutoring system, primarily designed for engineering statics courses—in order to find trends that may be used to make the software a better tutor. The data showed a significant correlation between student performance and the amount of time students work on a problem before submitting, with students who submit their results too often performing worse than those who work on a problem longer. Another interesting conclusion was that there is a strong correlation between being willing to switch among problems and better performance. Overall, the authors conclude that student trends like these could be paired with machine learning techniques to make more intelligent educational tools.

In "PerSketchTivity: An Intelligent Pen-Based Educational Application for Design Sketching Instruction," Williford, Taele, Nelligan, Li, Linsey, and Hammond introduce PerSketchTivity, an intelligent pen-based computing educational application that teaches engineering students how to practice their design sketching skills through stylus-and-touchscreen interaction. This application provides feedback and improves motivation and self-regulated learning.

In "An Intelligent Sketch-Based Educational Interface for Learning Complex Written East Asian Phonetic Symbols," Taele and Hammond demonstrate preliminary results on an intelligent sketch-based educational interface developed specifically for assessing students' sketched input of complex East Asian languages phonetic symbols. After evaluating separately sketching data from novice and expert writers, the authors were able to achieve reasonably robust performance for both visual structure and technical correctness of our workbook interface.

In "A Stylus-Driven Intelligent Tutoring System for Music Education Instruction," Barreto, Taele, and Hammond present a stylus-driven intelligent tutoring system for music education instruction. The proposed system provides an accessible educational application Maestoso with an intelligent sketch user interface that is designed for novice students interested in learning music theory through a series of interactive music composition lessons and quizzes. The proposed system uses appropriate sketch and gesture recognition techniques to automatically understand the student's input and generates feedback. Novice students who tested the application reported that they were able to grasp introductory music theory concepts from a single session using Maestoso.

In "SmartStrokes: Digitizing Paper-Based Neuropsychological Tests," Lara-Garduno, Leslie, and Hammond introduce SmartStrokes, a testing suite that implements digital versions of common clinical neuropsychology pencil-and-paper tests, with the purpose of helping to automate and analyze patient sketches using the principles of sketch recognition. The tests include Trail Making test, Clock Drawing test and Rey-Osterrieth Complex Figure Test. Additionally, SmartStrokes includes a convenient Doctor-Patient confidential patient registration system. The current studies involve performing sketch recognition analysis on the two variations of the Trail-Making Test, that have allowed predicting user age based on broad age categories. Future work will focus on adding more neuropsychological tests into the testing suite in order to generate more sketch data that can be used to develop a more comprehensive prediction model.

1.4.4 Part IV: The Empowering Effects of Multimedia Generation

Classrooms are increasingly using sketch-based videos as part of the learning process. These videos are made not only by the teachers, but also by the students themselves. This section describes how multimedia generation is being integrated to motivate young children to communication online, to improve learning in math and other subjects both in the U.S. and in Africa.

In "The Digital Sash: A Sketch-Based Badge System in a Social Network for Children," Valentine, McMurtry, Borgos-Rodriguez, and Hammond describe a sketch-based reward system for promoting the practice of digital citizenship skills within a custom social network (KidGab) for children aged 7–12 years. To earn badges, children complete fun, creative sketching activities and short writing tasks. The authors give examples of the most popular badges and responses for each.

In "A Cyberensemble of Inversion, Immersion, Shared Knowledge Areas, Query, and Digital Media-Making in STEM Classrooms," Hamilton, Foe-Aman, Foe-Aman, and Ramirez-Gamez discuss the initial results on the use of digital ink in the flipped classroom approach in mathematics courses in the USA, Ghana, and Namibia. The authors discuss and analyze how a "cyberensemble" of various technologies can contribute to the learning environment and improve performance. The "cyberensemble" consists of the following elements: use of pen-based computing, "collaborative workspaces" allowing teachers and students to view each others' work in real time, video production for creativity, agent-based dialog and query system, flipped classroom, and low cost mobile devices. The initial design was guided by the following theoretical themes: learner engagement, question-asking and self-explaining, and the mathematical cognition theory of dualism, necessity, and repetition.

In "A Model and Research Agenda for Teacher and Student Collaboration using Pen-Based Tablets in Digital Media Making in Sub-Saharan Africa", Hamilton, Kapenda, Mbasu, Miranda, Ngololo, Ogwel, Sarmonpal, and Stern report their results on the introduction of pen-based mathematics video-making to both mathematics teachers and students in Kenya and Uganda in summer 2010 and early 2011. Interview data were collected in video recordings. The core digital making entails the use of pen-based tablet computers to create videos for teaching science and mathematics concepts in alignment with state and national curriculum. Results were visible along several dimensions: (1) Learners exhibited a high affective valence and enthusiasm for media-making with their teachers; (2) Important relational shifts occurred and were reported by both teachers and students; and (3) Students and teachers alike engaged in cognitive re-imagining and re-imaging of one another's roles and of subject matter. Some overarching themes in the responses of both teachers and students address the role of pen-based media making in nurturing personal creativity, building precision into mathematical and scientific expression, fostering deep and immersive engagement, promoting collaboration between students and teachers, and introducing new possibilities for more effective instructional approaches. The authors believe that collaborative instructional media-making may occupy an exceptionally promising role in helping to meet ideals for universal and effective, highly engaging education.

In "A System Dynamics Approach to Process Evaluation of Pen-Based Digital Media Making Projects," authors Okumu, Kato, and Chalise describe a study in which both qualitative and quantitative measurements are used to understand not only the effect of the pen-based experiences in the classroom but also how changes occur. The authors introduce novel metrics for quantitative evaluation through the coding of raw data using causal loop maps. The authors implement their method to evaluate a pen-based summer program that has been in place over the last three years at Pepperdine University, from which the authors concluded that active engagement of both teachers and students was crucial to improve the quality of the learning environment.

In "Student Producers: OneNote, Camtasia Studio, and the Authentic Project," Ploesser describes a classroom implementation of using multimedia in the classroom. The teachers and students at Whitfield School were using digital ink in OneNote notebooks in the 10th grade Modern World History: 1800-Present classroom. All students saw the benefits of using digital ink in OneNote in their daily homework assignments. At the end of the school year students were making educational videos for The Boeing Company. Using digital ink allowed for a unique approach to peer collaboration as well as teacher feedback throughout this project.

In "An Aqua Squiggle and Giggles: Pre-Teens as Researchers Influencing Little Lives through Inking and Touch Devices," Zimmerman describes a study on ink and touch devices used in middle school classrooms. The primary objective of this study was to analyze the human connection and touch screen laptop use in a cross-age mentoring model with middle school and preschool students in an urban independent school representing 27 ethnic groups. Non-traditional grouping of sixth- and seventh-graders in a 1:1 laptop environment utilized production and internet tools to facilitate their own data collection as they researched and tracked learning of the little buddy they mentored in literacy projects. The data showed students in this grouping becoming active pursuers of relational bonding with preschoolers and simultaneously developed a mindset parallel with that of adult teacher-researchers. Touch and inking unexpectedly became the tool that helped facilitate interpersonal conversational skills and social emotional development with English Language Learning.

1.4.5 Part V: Technology in the Wild: Classroom Perspectives

Pen and touch has been shown to improve retention and understanding in a number of studies. This section describes a number of classroom success stories where including inking in the classroom improves engagement, learning, and retention, in university, high school, middle school, and elementary schools in subjects such as math, chemical engineering, social studies.

Technology-enhanced instructional delivery is increasingly becoming the norm in the delivery of the engineering curriculum. In the first chapter on "Inking Pedagogy" the authors Pokorski, Okoth, Nandy, Fowlin, Amelink, and Scales reviewed the key developments that some signature engineering schools have undertaken to foster the use of inking technology in the last two decades. The studied schools include Virginia Tech, Georgia Tech, and University of Southern California. At Virginia Tech researchers studied the effect of the Tablet PC on instructional strategies for structured computer use in classrooms. They found that there are best practices that can be nurtured to realize the full potential of classroom technologies. Among the best practice examples were: collecting student generated content and classroom polling questions, which positively contributed to higher student engagement. Another group of researchers found that overall there was statistical significance and a positive relationship when student use of the Tablet PC was correlated with their learning behavior. The study also revealed that peer collaboration, metacognitive self-regulation, organization, and critical thinking were among the learning behaviors that were enhanced through exposure to inking technology in instruction. At Georgia Tech, there was a study conducted with the Tablet PC to evaluate students' attitudes about technology in pedagogy. The results indicated that interaction in class improved with the use of the technology whereby instructors made heavy use of the inking technology. The students' assessment of the Tablet PCs averaged 'Very Good' and 'Excellent' especially citing how the DyKnow software enabled them to scroll back to previous slides and interact/annotate the presentation as well as play-it-back after class. Researchers at California State University investigated the interactivity advantage of inking in education. The research picked up general educational affordances that inking provided the students, among them: spontaneous augmentation of prepared material, guided attention, natural pacing, and finally electronic archiving.

In “The Impact of Undergraduate Tablet PC Use on Retention in STEM Majors,” Romney studied the impact of a Tablet PC implementation in undergraduate college algebra and trigonometry (CAT) on student attendance, performance, learning outcomes, classroom evaluation, and retention in science, technology, engineering, and mathematics (STEM) majors. While a number of measures were increased for TabletPC classes, such as class attendance (96 % vs. 99 % for Tablet PC classes) student learning outcomes, and student evaluations, these differences were not significant. However, two increased measures were statistically significant; student retention in STEM was higher and average time to graduation was lower in the Tablet PC group.

In “Analysis of Student Perspectives on using Tablet PCs in Junior and Senior Level Chemical Engineering Classes,” Palou, Ramirez-Apud, Ramirez-Corona, and Lopez-Malo, used a previously developed How People Learn framework to redesign one junior-level chemical engineering course entitled Kinetics and Homogeneous Reactor Design as well as two senior-level courses, Catalysis and Heterogeneous Reactor Design and Process Dynamics and Control in Universidad de las Amricas Puebla in Mexico. The goal was to improve chemical engineering teaching and learning by creating high-quality learning environments that promote an interactive classroom while integrating formative assessments into classroom practices by means of Tablet PCs and associated technologies. In the studied courses, the authors mainly utilized three Tablet PC associated technologies, OneNote, InkSurvey, and Classroom Presenter to gauge student learning in real time, provide immediate feedback, and make real-time pedagogical adjustments as needed. To analyze how students evaluated the use of Tablet PCs and associated technologies, semi-structured interviews we conducted. Five overall themes emerged: student experience in using Tablet PCs (they found it very useful, and most of the students considered it to be a very enriching experience that enhanced their learning), impact on learning (was evaluated as favorable), potential of Tablet PCs and associated technologies (use of Tablet PCs allowed for a greater understanding of the topics discussed in class, increased students’ motivation and participation), formative assessments (real-time feedback allowed visualization of ideas and opportunity to revise immediately), as well as advantages and disadvantages of using the Tablet PC in studied classrooms (advantages are comfort of taking notes and increased level of participation, while connecting to network can be a distraction).

In “Student Demonstrations of Learning: Making Thinking Visible using Pen and Touch,” Kassissieh and Tillinghast describe how teachers and students at University Prep (Seattle, WA) used digital ink and virtual manipulation to increase the flexibility of formative assessment in a variety of subject areas. This paper describes the conceptual basis for work with a formative assessment and shares examples of student use of digital ink and virtual manipulation in different class settings, with middle school students using iPads and upper school students using touchscreen laptops. General purpose apps for writing, drawing, and making explainer videos have gained adoption more quickly at University Prep than subject specific learning apps that use a very specific pedagogical model.

In "The Integration of Inking, Touch, and Flipping within the Mathematics Middle School Classroom," Williams, a middle school math teacher, reports on her experience over the last eight years introducing inking technology and flipped classroom approach. The author started in 2008 with converting a textbook to a digital format. The major benefits of replacing notes, practice, and extra practice materials for one full semester included having all materials in one well-structured place that any instructor or student could easily use, and allowing students the tactile experience of writing in a versatile textbook. The electronic textbook and other resources were created over the period of three summers. The inking technology was used throughout the e-text to complete problems with verbal explanation while screencasting to create the videos. Now inking is used daily by students for taking notes, creating videos, and to build organizational and study skills, and the inking also helps keep students engaged in classroom activities. The flipped classroom model proved to be more efficient as evidenced by higher test scores but student feedback for flipping was mixed.

In "DYKNOW as a Tool for Differentiation: Exploring Alternative Ways to Assess in the Middle School Social Studies Classroom," Mata evaluated the DYKNOW software use for assessment in a middle school social studies classroom. DYKNOW software is a tool that is used to differentiate for students' learning needs by providing them with several multimedia options that allow them to utilize their computers to read, annotate, record, type, and ask for feedback from the teacher. DYKNOW allows teachers to monitor students progress in the class, monitor and limit Internet usage, as well as engage in teacher student communication during the class without making disruptions. The digital ink feature proved to be very beneficial as it provides clear immediate feedback about a student's written piece.

In "Personalizing Student Learning using the MyEduDecks Application through Teacher Supervision and Peer-to-Peer Networks," Kothuri, Cohen, Wilke, and Owens describes how the MyEduDecks platform was used to aid a class of third grade Technology Literacy in the South Fayette Intermediate School. The application is a pen-based digital flashcards program coded by several students at South Fayette High School over a development period of three years. The vision for MyEduDecks is that students will be able to make their own decks of flashcards, and practice the decks created by their teacher, as many times as necessary for students to fully understand the concept. The results showed that the MyEduDecks is an effective teaching tool for elementary instructors and personalizes the education of every student to fit their individualized needs.

1.4.6 Part VI: Voices of the Future: Student Perspectives

WIPTTE 2015 hosted the second WIPTTE High School Contest, with the first one held at WIPTTE 2014 on Texas A&M University Campus in College Station, TX. The contest was held on the first day of WIPTTE 2015, and was organized by TAMU Sketch Recognition Lab Ph.D. candidates Stephanie Valentine and Cassan-

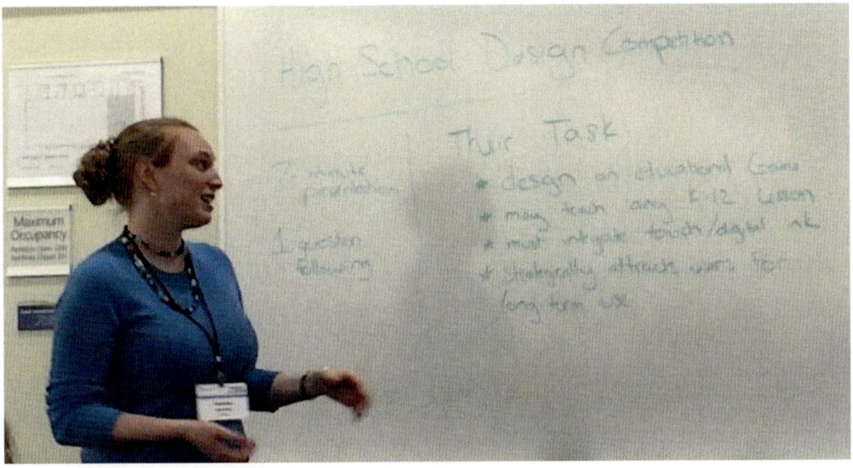

Fig. 1.3 Texas A&M University Sketch Recognition Lab Ph.D. Candidate and High School students Contest Chair Stephanie Valentine briefing the judges before the high school make their final presentations on Tuesday evening

dra Oduola. Four high school teams and nineteen students competed for top prizes. Figure 1.3 shows Stephanie Valentine briefing the judges before the high school students' final presentation. The first chapter in this section describes the contest in more detail and is followed by a paper written by four high school students' and their teacher, detailing their reflections from the workshop.

1.5 Conclusion

WIPTTE 2015 brought together diverse audiences of researchers, educators, and students from varying backgrounds. The major characteristic that unified these groups is an ongoing commitment to discovering ways to leverage digital ink and touch interfaces to support teaching and learning. The sharing of experiences and best practices during the workshops continues to provide the basis for a new community of tablets-in-education researchers, practitioners, and thought leaders.

Starting in 2016, the conference will be renamed to represent the growing presence of the community to CPTTE (Conference on Pen and Touch Technology in Education). To participate in this community and find out more, visit http://www.cptte.org.

Many other people contributed a great deal of time and energy to make these conferences successful. Thank you to all of the participants and other supporters.

Finally, we thank you, the reader, for your ongoing interest in trying to make education better through the intelligent application of digital ink and touch.

Part II
Why We Pen and Touch

Chapter 2
Computer Interfaces Can Stimulate or Undermine Students' Ability to Think

Sharon Oviatt

Abstract Computer input capabilities, such as a keyboard or pen, substantially influence basic cognitive abilities, including our ability to produce appropriate ideas, solve problems correctly, and make accurate inferences about information. Compared with keyboard interfaces, computer input tools that can be used to express information involving different *representations, modalities, and linguistic codes—or expressively powerful interfaces*—can directly stimulate human thought and performance. This chapter summarizes how and why the quality of a computer interface matters. It also discusses implications for establishing a new generation of digital tools that are far better at supporting thinking and reasoning, with special implications for designing more effective educational technologies.

2.1 Introduction

During the last decade, mobile devices that incorporate new input modes have eclipsed keyboard-based graphical interfaces as the dominant computer interface worldwide [20]. There likewise has been a shift toward expanding users' options for entering input to a computer, including using a digital stylus, gestures, multi-touch, speech, gaze, facial expressions, a multitude of sensors, and multimodal combinations of these input modes. These changes are expanding users' expressive power to create and manipulate digital information. They also are making it possible to select an input tool that is best matched for a particular task. These changes in computer interface design are enabling critical improvements in the design of new educational technologies.

In a very basic sense, any high-quality educational interface must be a rich communications interface, as illustrated in Fig. 2.1. From a communications perspective, expressively powerful interfaces support users' ability to convey information involving different modalities, representations, and linguistic codes. Since language is a carrier of thought, more expressively powerful interfaces are capable of directly and

S. Oviatt (✉)
Incaa Designs, P.O. Box 373, Deer Harbor, WA, USA
e-mail: Oviatt@incaadesigns.org

T. Hammond et al. (eds.), *Revolutionizing Education with Digital Ink*,
Human–Computer Interaction Series, DOI 10.1007/978-3-319-31193-7_2

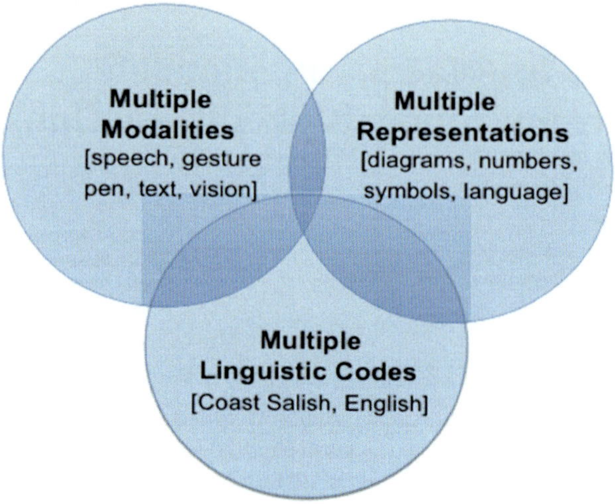

Fig. 2.1 Richly expressive communication interfaces that support multiple modalities, representations, and linguistic codes (copyright Lawrence Erlbaum Assoc., *source* [17] used with permission)

substantially stimulating human cognition. The aim of research on designing more expressively powerful computer interfaces is to develop a new generation of far more effective thinking tools [18].

2.2 Why Pen Interfaces Support Thinking and Learning

Educational interfaces need to be designed as rich communications interfaces that increase students' engagement, communicative activity, and related thinking and reasoning in the domains about which students are learning. One reason that pen interfaces are a promising input tool for facilitating active learning is that they support expression of a broad range of linguistic and nonlinguistic representational content, including numbers, symbols, diagrams, and words (Fig. 2.1, right side). They also provide a single input tool for easily shifting among different types of representation while working on a problem. For example, when given a geometry word problem, a student may first diagram the relation between objects, then generate algebraic expressions using symbols and numbers, and finally summarize their calculations using linguistic content. Such a flexible flow of expressions helps to preserve students' focus of attention and working memory resources while solving a problem. In an important respect, a digital pen that facilitates casting information in different representations, and translating among them, also supports perspective shifting in thinking about a problem.

Pen interfaces and the durable ink trace they create help students to view information, group related information, and retain it in memory—which facilitates reasoning about new domain content. The ability to use a pen to sketch or diagram information is considered to be a foundation for thinking and reasoning [8]. Diagramming objects and relations facilitates a more precise and elaborated understanding of the information depicted, and supports insight. It also deepens and improves students' transfer of learning to new contexts [15, 23, 24].

2.3 How Pen Interfaces Influence Communication and Cognition

Recent research has revealed that the same students accomplishing the same tasks communicate more when using a digital tool than an analogous non-digital one [22]. That is, digital tools elicit more total communicative fluency. This research also demonstrated that different input capabilities, such as a keyboard versus digital pen, have affordances that prime qualitatively different types of communicative content. Students expressed 44 % more nonlinguistic representational content (e.g., numbers, symbols, diagrams) when using pen interfaces. In contrast, when they used a keyboard the same students now expressed 36 % more linguistic content (e.g., words, abbreviations) and also more complete sentential constructions. These differences in communicative fluency generalized across tasks involving different types of thinking and reasoning, and were replicated in both low- and high-performing students [22].

These differences in communication pattern corresponded to striking changes in students' cognition. In particular, when students used the digital pen and wrote more nonlinguistic content, they generated 36 % more appropriate biology hypotheses. The regression analysis shown in Fig. 2.2 (left) reveals that knowledge of individual

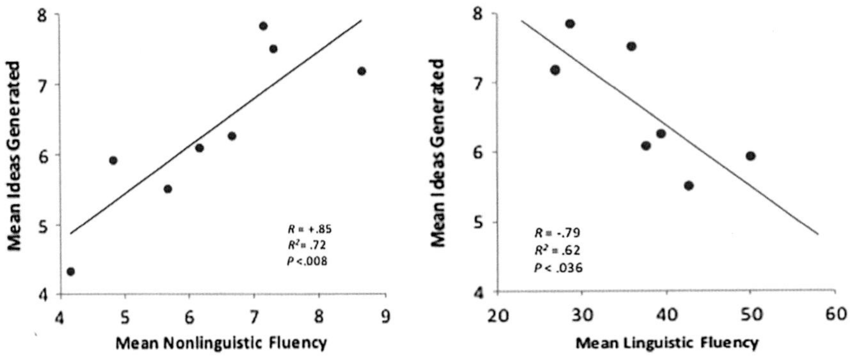

Fig. 2.2 Regression analysis showing positive relation between nonlinguistic communicative fluency and ideational fluency *left*; Regression showing negative relation between linguistic communicative fluency and ideational fluency *right* (copyright ACM, *source* [22] used with permission)

students' level of nonlinguistic fluency when using different interfaces accounted for 72 % of all the variance in their ability to produce appropriate biology hypotheses [22]. That is, interface support for expressing nonlinguistic content predicted most of the variance in students' ability to generate appropriate scientific ideas.

However, when the same students used the keyboard interface and communicated more linguistic content, the regression analysis shown in Fig. 2.2 (right) indicates that they experienced a substantial drop in science ideation. In this case, knowledge of students' level of linguistic communication had a negative predictive relation with their hypothesis generation. It accounted for 62 % of the variation in students' *inability* to produce science hypotheses.

In other tasks involving science problem solving, students using a digital pen rather than keyboard interface made more structured diagrams and elemental "thinking marks". Thinking marks are informal pen marks that students make, for example on text or visuals when they are preparing to solve a problem, in which they count, select, order, group, label, and mark up relations between problem elements so they can understand what the problem means. This type of elemental ink marking occurs at substantially higher rates in low-performing students, and it has been associated with 24.5 % more correct problem solutions [22]. Likewise, a higher rate of constructing diagrams in this research was associated with 36 % more correct problem solutions.

These results emphasize that pen input facilitates active marking, whether in the form of structured diagrams or more elemental ink marks. In this regard, pen interfaces are effective in helping students to externalize their thinking in spatial forms. Pen interfaces also lower the barrier for both low- and high-performing students to become actively engaged trying to solve problems. The spatial constructions that students produce in turn help them to understand and solve problems with substantially improved success.

2.4 Limitations of Keyboard Interfaces for Thinking Tasks

Keyboard interfaces were never designed as thinking tools. In fact, they constrict the representations, modalities, and linguistic codes that can be communicated when using computers [18]. For example, keyboards support textual information, but not multimodal transmission involving sketch, writing, speech, gesturing, body language, and other rich modalities. In addition, they support expressing language and numbers, but are poorly designed for constructing spatial representations like diagrams and symbols.

Keyboard interfaces also present a major handicap for expressing world languages that are not Roman alphabetic ones, which includes about 80 % of languages such as Mandarin, Hindi, and Japanese. Such languages can be complex, spatially intensive (e.g., diacritics, logograms), and include a large number of linguistic units that require many-to-one mappings with each key [4, 9]. Estimates indicate that less than 15 % of the world's 6,800 languages are supported by keyboard Unicode mappings, so most languages are not used on the Internet or computers at all [11, 25]. For all of the above reasons, keyboard interfaces are better suited for conducting relatively mechanical tasks, such as text processing, emailing, and searching the Internet. They are less well suited for completing extended thinking and reasoning tasks.

2.5 Neuroscience Findings on Writing Versus Typing

In the course of evolution, people's use of new physical tools has shaped related brain functions [27]. For example, the advent of stylus implements 6,000 years ago stimulated writing and reading skills that launched literacy and modern education. The manual action of writing symbols, and then reading them, led to structural specialization of the brain region for visual object recognition [3, 14]. The visual cortex reorganized in response to reading activity, creating the visual word form area (VWFA) that now supports literacy.

In both children and adults, actively writing letters has been shown in fMRI studies to increase brain activation to a greater extent than passively viewing, naming, or typing them [6, 7, 10, 12, 13].

Compared with typing, writing letter shapes also improves the accuracy of subsequent letter recognition, a prerequisite for successful comprehension and reading. These studies have been replicated in children learning their first language, and in adults learning a second one. They also have been replicated in Roman alphabetic languages (e.g., French, English) and in Asian languages that are not Roman alphabetic ones (e.g., Bengali, Mandarin).

This research has emphasized that physical activities directly prime perception and comprehension of related content. This action-perception loop represents an Embodied Cognition theoretical view of learning [1]. Writing complex letter shapes creates a long-term sensori-motor memory, which is part of an integrated "reading neural circuit" [16]. This writing activity leads to a more elaborated and durable ability to recognize letters later when we read them. Further research has documented the impact of writing versus typing on spelling and other aspects of written composition, as well as on the content of ideas expressed during written composition [2, 5].

2.6 How Digital Tools Can Facilitate Thinking

As introduced in Sect. 2.3, people communicate at higher levels when using a digital tool than an analogous non-digital one. In one study, the same students solved the same problems about science, but used an Anoto-based digital pen and paper for half their tasks, and a regular pen and paper for the other half. The physical tools that students used (i.e., pen and paper) looked nearly identical in both cases, but they understood that the digital pen was a small computer that could transmit and process their input. Perhaps surprisingly, when using the digital pen to complete inference tasks, students drew more total diagrams and more correct Venn diagrams. They also

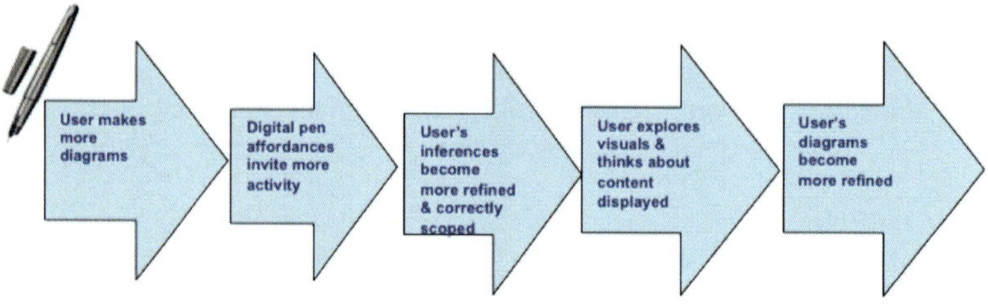

Fig. 2.3 Chain of activity—ideation refinement, in which pen interface elicited more diagramming, more correctly formed diagrams, and more accurate inferences about the displayed content than an analogous non-digital pen (copyright ACM, *source* [22], used with permission)

made more accurate inferences about the related domain content [22]. When using the digital pen interface, compared with the regular pen, students constructed and visually explored the diagrams they had made, which stimulated thinking about the content and a higher level of inference accuracy.

The summary in Fig. 2.3 illustrates this enhanced chain of activity-ideation refinement. One implication is that non-digital materials (e.g., pen and paper) are not more optimal for supporting education than digital tools. In the research described, a digital pen analogue of non-digital materials elicited a higher level of communicating, which facilitated students' cognition and also improved their performance.

2.7 Students' Lack of Metacognitive Self-Awareness About Computer Interfaces

Although students often are adept at operating computers procedurally, many studies have shown that they are unaware of when and how to use computers to best support their own performance. This research has uncovered a *"Performance-Preference Paradox"*, or a mismatch between the computer input tool that students say they prefer to use and the one that best supported their performance during the study. During these studies, students first had the opportunity to use a variety of different interfaces. Then they were interviewed about which interface they preferred to use if they had to perform their best on a high-stakes Advanced Placement exam. All studies uncovered a mismatch between students' stated beliefs and the interface that actually supported their performance the best [19, 21, 22].

For example, students often reported a preference to use a keyboard-based interface, even though their performance dropped a whole grade point when using it compared with alternatives like a pen interface. Longitudinal studies have revealed that the Performance-Preference Paradox becomes more accentuated over time, rather than attenuating as students gain experience with different interfaces. The Performance-Preference Paradox has been observed in both high- and low-performers, although it is more prevalent in low-performing students whose meta-cognitive skills are weaker [26].

New technology fluency curricula in the schools could improve students' ability to evaluate technology critically and self-regulate their use of it. When technology classes are taught, too often they focus on basic procedural skills involving the use of elementary applications like Excel, rather than critical evaluation of technology, its features and design, and its impact on performance. The aims of technology fluency training should include dispelling unrealistic expectations about computer technology, and improving students' judgment, self control, and critical thinking skills so they can use it more productively.

2.8 Conclusions

To stimulate thinking and learning in students, high-quality interfaces are required that can support complex content creation activities, including students' ability to construct diagrams, complex letter shapes, and other forms related to curriculum goals. Pen interfaces, and multimodal ones that incorporate pen input, are especially good candidates for achieving this objective. Such interfaces are more expressively powerful than the keyboard, because they support people's ability to communicate information involving different representations, modalities, and linguistic codes. As discussed in this chapter, interfaces with these properties can directly stimulate human thought and performance, and they are especially well suited as educational technologies. Other promising directions for developing educational technologies include tangible interfaces, conversational interfaces, mobile interfaces, and hybrid interfaces that combine these properties. In the future, one major challenge will be to develop new technology fluency curricula that can teach students to critically evaluate technology, and also to self regulate their use of technology tools to better support their own performance.

References

1. Beilock SL, Lyons IM, Mattarella-Micke A, Nusbaum HC, Small SL (2008) Sports experience changes the neural processing of action language. Proc Natl Acad Sci 105(36):13269–13273
2. Berninger VW, Abbott RD, Augsburger A, Garcia N (2009) Comparison of pen and keyboard transcription modes in children with and without learning disabilities. Learn Disabil Q 32(3):123–141
3. Dehaene S (2011) The massive impact of literacy on the brain and its consequences for education. Human neuroplasticity and education. Pontifical Academy of Sciences, Vatican city, pp 19–32
4. Hamzah MD, Tano S, Iwata M, Hashiyama T (2006) Effectiveness of annotating by hand for non-alphabetical languages. In: Proceedings of the SIGCHI conference on human factors in computing systems, CHI '06. ACM, New York, pp 841–850

5. Hayes JR, Berninger VW (2010) Relationships between idea generation and transcription. Traditions of writing research. Taylor and Francis, New York, p 166
6. James KH (2010) Sensori-motor experience leads to changes in visual processing in the developing brain. Dev Sci 13(2):279–288
7. James KH, Engelhardt L (2012) The effects of handwriting experience on functional brain development in pre-literate children. Trends Neurosci Educ 1(1):32–42
8. Johnson-Laird P (1999) Space to think. In: Bloom P, Peterson M, Nadel L, Garrett M (eds) Language and space. MIT press, Cambridge, pp 437–462
9. Joshi A, Ganu A, Chand A, Parmar V, Mathur G (2004) Keylekh: a keyboard for text entry in Indic scripts. In: CHI '04 extended abstracts on human factors in computing systems, CHI EA '04. ACM, New York, pp 928–942
10. Kersey AJ, James KH (2013) Brain activation patterns resulting from learning letter forms through active self-production and passive observation in young children. Front Psychol 4:1
11. Lewis MP, Simons GF, Fennig CD (2009) Ethnologue: languages of the world, vol 9. SIL International, Dallas. Online version: http://www.ethnologue.com/
12. Longcamp M, Zerbato-Poudou MT, Velay JL (2005) The influence of writing practice on letter recognition in preschool children: a comparison between handwriting and typing. Acta Psychol 119(1):67–79
13. Longcamp M, Boucard C, Gilhodes JC, Anton JL, Roth M, Nazarian B, Velay JL (2008) Learning through hand or typewriting influences visual recognition of new graphic shapes: behavioral and functional imaging evidence. J Cogn Neurosci 20(5):802–815
14. McCandliss BD, Cohen L, Dehaene S (2003) The visual word form area: expertise for reading in the fusiform gyrus. Trends Cogn Sci 7(7):293–299
15. Mestre JP (2005) Transfer of learning from a modern multidisciplinary perspective. IAP, Charlotte
16. Nakamura K, Kuo WJ, Pegado F, Cohen L, Tzeng OJ, Dehaene S (2012) Universal brain systems for recognizing word shapes and handwriting gestures during reading. Proc Natl Acad Sci 109(50):20762–20767
17. Oviatt S (2012) Multimodal interfaces. In: Jacko JA (ed) Human computer interaction handbook: fundamentals, evolving technologies, and emerging applications. CRC Press, Boca Raton, pp 405–430
18. Oviatt S (2013) The design of future educational interfaces. Routledge, London
19. Oviatt SL, Cohen AO (2010) Toward high-performance communications interfaces for science problem solving. J Sci Educ Technol 19(6):515–531
20. Oviatt S, Cohen PR (2015) The paradigm shift to multimodality in contemporary computer interfaces. Morgan & Claypool, San Rafael
21. Oviatt S, Arthur A, Cohen J (2006) Quiet interfaces that help students think. In: Proceedings of the 19th annual ACM symposium on user interface software and technology, UIST '06. ACM, New York, pp 191–200
22. Oviatt S, Cohen A, Miller A, Hodge K, Mann A (2012) The impact of interface affordances on human ideation, problem solving, and inferential reasoning. ACM Trans Comput-Hum Interact 19(3):22:1–22:30
23. Schwartz DL, Heiser J (2006) Spatial representations and imagery in learning. Citeseer, Princeton
24. Schwartz DL, Varma S, Martin L (2008) Dynamic transfer and innovation. International handbook of research on conceptual change. Routledge, New York, pp 479–506
25. The unicode standard, version 6.0
26. Winne PH, Perry NE (2000) Measuring self-regulated learning. Handbook of self-regulation. Academic, Orlando, pp 531–566
27. Wynn T (2002) Archaeology and cognitive evolution. Behav Brain Sci 25(03):389–402

Chapter 3
Inking Outside the Box: How Context Sensing Affords More Natural Pen (and Touch) Computing

Ken Hinckley and Bill Buxton

Abstract The authors were invited to present a reprise of a recently-published paper on Sensing Techniques for Tablet + Stylus Interaction at the WIPTTE 2015 Workshop. The talk took the original contribution as a point of departure, because for the WIPTTE venue we felt that the most important role of the work was to illuminate and help the audience understand more deeply the interaction modalities of pen and touch—as well as their use in tandem. And in the process the authors felt like they came to understand the topic more deeply as well, hence the paper that follows.

One of the premises of the talk was that even a concept as seemingly straightforward as 'touch'—not to mention pen + touch, used together in complementary roles—is perhaps not as well understood as we might think it is.

In particular, we argue that beyond the standard idiom of touch (and multi-touch) interaction on touchscreens, there are many aspects of 'touch' that are rarely considered (much less actually sensed) by existing devices and interaction designs. We show how this surrounding context of manual activity—how the user is holding the tablet, how the user is gripping the pen, and how each device is oriented and moving relative to the other—have the potential to considerably enrich interaction with tablets, and thereby to re-define what we conceive of as 'natural' interaction with pen and touch.

3.1 Introduction

Pens seem like such a relic of the twentieth century, and even more antiquated epochs long before that. Isn't it 2015? Why are we still talking about pens?

Well, by way of simple illustration I thought it would be fun to visit the supply room of one of the largest technology companies on the planet. Surely one can go in

---

K. Hinckley (✉)
Microsoft Research, One Microsoft Way, Redmond, WA, USA
e-mail: kenh@microsoft.com

B. Buxton
Microsoft Research, Redmond, WA, USA
e-mail: bibuxton@microsoft.com

T. Hammond et al. (eds.), *Revolutionizing Education with Digital Ink*,
Human–Computer Interaction Series, DOI 10.1007/978-3-319-31193-7_3

Fig. 3.1 The supply room of one of the largest technology corporations on the planet. Contrary to what one might expect, close inspection reveals the contents are quite pedestrian and well stocked with writing instruments of every description. *Photo* © Ken Hinckley, 2014. Used by permission. All rights reserved

there and find all manner of technological contrivances. Since it's just down the hall from my office it was easy to snap a photo (see Fig. 3.1). Surely it should be stacked to the ceiling with fancy robot arms and 3D printers, or perhaps bins chock full of the legendary flux capacitor.

Sadly, this was not to be the case.

But it does reveal something about what actually goes on when knowledge workers retreat to their cubicles and try to think outside the box.

The first thing they do is grab a pen!

Now, while the above illustration is a slightly tongue-in-cheek way to make the point, it is only just slightly so - because the research bears this out.

The work of students and creative professionals typically involves heavy doses of reading. And this is not just ordinary recreational reading, but rather a very particular way that people have of digging deeply into documents and source texts. Such deep, purposeful engagement with content (often multiple pieces of content) is known in the literature as *active reading*.

What people are trying to do in active reading is to distill and crystallize knowledge from diverse sources.

The reader's tasks are typically complex, open-ended, ill defined, and intellectually challenging.

The reader may annotate, mark-up pages, take notes, sketch out ideas and connections, or formulate summaries and responses based on what they've read.

Active reading, perhaps more than anything else, is characterized by reading side-by-side with writing. Such tasks involve reading in combination with writing and typically span multiple documents (or working surfaces) as well, such as the canonical yellow writing pad used to jot down notes while reviewing a manuscript.

A great entrée to this literature is Sellen and Harper's classic book, *The Myth of the Paperless Office* [19], but many studies of this activity have been published [3, 12, 15, 17, 18, 20].

One of the key viewpoints that has emerged in recent years is that although these types of working patterns carry over to electronic document work as well, there are clearly significant opportunities to improve on current practice.

Another emerging viewpoint is the recognition that, in contrast to the pen-only devices of the past, if we have a screen that supports both a stylus and touch, then we have something very powerful indeed.

Certainly much more expressive than a device with touch alone.

A device that can – not only sense the human touch – but also our pre-existing skill for dexterous manipulation of a mechanical intermediary is emerging. It is a tool that has blazed a trail for many centuries with significant impact on science, education and human intellect. A tool that lends itself to freeform expression and the creation of content that lives beyond the confines of any single data type, ruled business form that one must fill in, or the strictures of a particular application.

The pen. The perfect tool for inking outside the box.

Tools can elevate human skill, and we should not lose sight of this in our fervor to pursue 'natural' interfaces. Natural interaction does not require barehanded interaction, and therefore a touchscreen, in and of itself, does not a natural user interface make.

3.2 Human Skilled Manipulation

Another way of looking at this is to back away from the technology and look again to the underlying human habits and behaviors.

But this time, rather than considering work-practices in general, let's zoom in—to the very particular details of the manual activities involved.

In fact, let's completely eschew technology for the moment and recruit my six-year-old daughter to the effort (see Fig. 3.2):

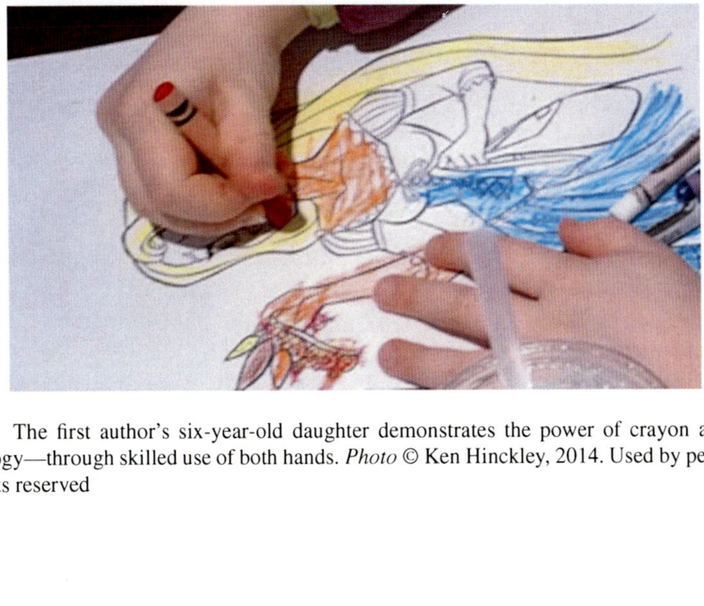

Fig. 3.2 The first author's six-year-old daughter demonstrates the power of crayon and touch technology—through skilled use of both hands. *Photo* © Ken Hinckley, 2014. Used by permission. All rights reserved

Now, of course she's using a crayon—a type of 'pen.'

But what we also see in this real-life example is that she's using 'touch' as well.

Not only is her preferred hand partially contacting and resting on the paper while holding the crayon, but also, prior to coloring this particular area of the page, she has positioned and oriented the sheet of paper as well, using her nonpreferred hand to optimize its placement for the action of the preferred hand.

A number of important lessons for pen and touch technology can be drawn from this simple illustration:

1. The nonpreferred hand manipulates the workspace with 'touch.'
2. The preferred hand articulates strokes with the crayon, which has an effect that is distinct from the fingers on the page. This stands in stark contrast to existing practice in many tablet applications, even today, where either a finger or the digital pen can be used interchangeably to leave marks on the page. In our view this is neither natural nor an effective use of pen and touch as distinct interaction modalities with unique affordances.
3. While the nonpreferred hand is *intentionally* positioning and orienting the page, at the same time the preferred hand may be *unintentionally* contacting the work surface. Here, it has no effect, but in a charcoal sketch (for example) this might produce undesired smudges—or it might be employed intentionally by a skilled artist to soften and blend pencil lines previously left on the page. As such, this hints that the very concept of 'palm rejection' on pen and touch displays is a misnomer—all touches are potentially valid, and can be put to good use by applications, so long as their nature can be understood and interpreted appropriately to the task and context.

Since one of the major themes of this paper is the ways in which close scrutiny of manual behavior—how people grip and manipulate objects such as tablets and pens—can inform interaction design, let's further unpack the first of the three statements above.

When we say that the *nonpreferred hand manipulates the workspace with touch*, what form does this take? What properties characterize this manipulation?

To answer this question and reveal the *oft seen, but seldom noticed* role of the nonpreferred hand in everyday interaction, the first author undertook an experiment in his Ph.D. thesis [7] that was inspired by a classic study of handwriting conducted by Yves Guiard [4].

In my variation of Guiard's experiment, the task required subjects to draw a 'perfect' circle that passed through tick marks at 90° intervals.

One diligent participant in the study produced the hand-drafted circles shown below, on the left-hand side of Fig. 3.3.

What the same participant *actually* drew, however, was the jumbled mess on the right.

Which is also a perfect circle.

There is a trick here, of course, which depends on your frame of reference.

The circles on the left show the strokes *relative to the sheet of paper*. This is the finished work product.

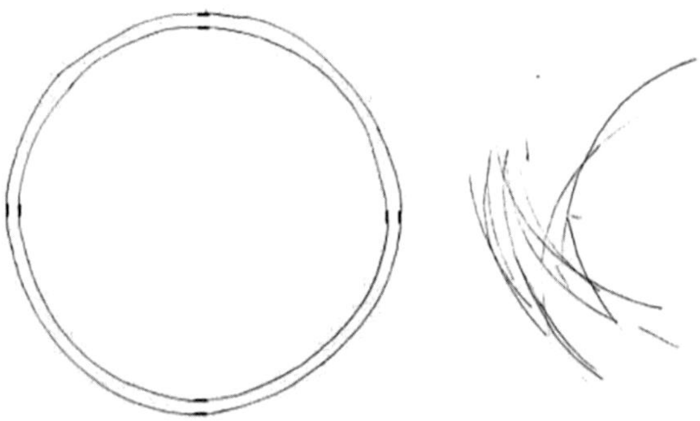

Fig. 3.3 When a circle is not a circle. *Left* Figure drawn by a participant. *Right* The strokes left behind on the desk blotter, which contained a hidden piece of carbon paper. The tightly clustered strokes demonstrate that the participant positioned and oriented the sheet of paper to make it easier, biomechanically, to draw the arcs comprising the full circle [7]. *Photo* © Ken Hinckley, 2014. Used by permission. All rights reserved

By contrast the strokes shown on the right are the strokes *relative to the desk surface*.

These were captured by placing a blotter on the work surface. The pen strokes on the paper passed through and were also recorded on the blotter underneath, which surreptitiously included a hidden layer of carbon paper. And as the user shifted and oriented the drawing, the resulting impressions reveal where on the desk the user actually drew the individual strokes comprising the circle.

What these crowded pen-stroke impressions reveal, is that the nonpreferred hand rotated the page to dynamically adjust the frame-of-reference to suit the action of the preferred hand: biomechanically it is far easier to draw smooth arcs in certain hand directions than in others.

This illustrates decisively that drawing a figure such as this circle—or as Guiard originally demonstrated, handwriting a page on dictation—is not, in fact a one-handed activity, but rather is the joint product of the activity of both hands:

The nonpreferred hand positioning and orienting the underlying page; Plus that of the preferred hand, which performs the actual micro-metric movements of the pen tip itself.

This simple illustration is ripe with lessons for interaction design in the context of pen and touch—and beyond.

It underscores that not only are there two hands, but that they play two distinct roles that are complementary.

And it further emphasizes that the same philosophy of thought can be applied to the input modality of the pen, as opposed to the input modality of touch, even though either hand can be used to make contact with the screen.

Guiard demonstrated that it is not helpful to ask, Which hand is best, left or right?

The correct question, rather, is one which frames the hands in a cooperative and complementary viewpoint:

What is the logic of the division of labor between the hands?

That is, which hand, left or right, should be used when assigning bimanual tasks to the preferred and nonpreferred hands?

Likewise, the question we should ask ourselves is not, which input modality is best, pen or touch?—but rather the following, which follows naturally from viewing pen and touch as cooperative and complementary input modalities:

What is the logic of the division of labor between pen and touch in interaction design?

3.3 Of 'Touch' Screens and Pens: A Tale of Two Modalities?

The question above has informed much of our own recent work exploring pen and touch interaction, such as our explorations of simultaneous pen and touch interaction [10, 11], or our explorations of how pen and touch can support more informal ways of working with electronic documents [12].

But to really delve more deeply into the issues this question raises, we must turn a more critical eye towards two of the interaction modalities that dwell at the heart of the WIPTTE moniker—the Workshop on the Impact of *Pen and Touch* Technology on Education—and challenge ourselves to think more deeply about what those two little words really mean.

Pen and touch.

Because they feel familiar and well-understood.

But neither of these terms are as well understood as you might think.

In particular, we want to raise some pointed questions about 'touch.' It's a term we often take for granted in the context of interaction with tablets.

A term rife with double-meanings and unintended consequences.

The foregoing discussion showed how a question as simple as "Which hand do you write (or draw circles) with" is in fact a loaded and ill-posed one. First off because it assumes that you write (draw) with only one hand, which is often not the case.

And second because inherent in that question is a worldview that one hand is "better" than the other, and that only our choice of task assignment to the preferred hand is what matters. Whereas, in real life, both hands play critical and complementary roles.

Taking this new perspective into account, and applying its lessons to pen and touch as interaction modalities, we can see hints of some fresh interpretations of 'touch' already:

Is the 'touch' articulated with one hand or two?

Is the touch made by the left hand or the right, or perhaps even by both in combination?

Going even further, we can take the scenario illustrated for 'crayon and touch' in Fig. 3.2 and carry it over to the digital context.

Here, if we look closely enough at manual interaction with pen and touch tablets (Fig. 3.4), further nuances and ambiguities rise to the fore.

The kneejerk reaction is that the participant illustrated in Fig. 3.4 is about to place his index finger on the touchscreen, and this is completely correct. However, if we

Fig. 3.4 What input modality is this? At first glance one might dismiss this as a straightforward illustration of a 'touch' interaction—a user about to put his index finger to the touchscreen. But a more careful look at the *oft seen, but seldom noticed* details of how the participant is using the tablet, and the stylus, with both hands suggests that the answer is not so simple. *Photo* © Ken Hinckley, 2014. Used by permission. All rights reserved

subject it to a discriminating eye for detail, a number of observations can be noted from the moment in time captured by the photograph:

1. **Touch: the obvious interpretation**, reflects nothing more than imminent intentional contact with the touchscreen, with a single finger—the index finger of the preferred hand.
2. **The intentional, but unavoidable, grip of the nonpreferred hand** plays another role here, namely to hold up and skillfully orient the tablet. And to do so, the nonpreferred hand clearly must grip the edge and a portion of the back surface of the device. This is 'touch' as well, albeit in a manner that is traditionally not sensed by existing tablets.
3. **The grasp of the pen**—although secondary to the interaction, with the stylus stowed in the preferred hand by palming—presents us with a third form of touch, albeit once again not traditionally sensed by electronic pens. This behavior of holding the pen at the ready hints that it was recently employed, and furthermore that the user anticipates writing with it again soon. In other words, it informs and situates the context of the interaction; and it distinguishes the impending touchscreen interaction as one performed with the pen-in-hand, as opposed to one performed bare-handed, or by the hand that is not holding the pen.
4. **The incidental, non-prehensile contact of the user's lap** with the bottom edge of the tablet shows yet another manifestation of 'touch' which helps to support the weight of the device. This aspect of touch is perhaps not one of much relevance for direct manipulation, but it does tell us something potentially important about the context of use: the tablet is partially resting on the user's lap, and the user's interactions will be necessarily constrained and encumbered by this situation. Although we leave this point as an exercise for future work, a cleverly designed application could very well take this information into account so as to better afford and accommodate this manner of interaction for its users.

5. **Inadvertent contact**: What about that pesky thumb of the hand gripping the tablet—not to mention the palm of the preferred hand? Accidental touch is a fifth form of touch that could be occurring (or about to occur) in this photograph. The thumb of the left hand rests on the front surface of the tablet, and as such rests perilously close to the touchscreen. What if the tablet had only a very thin screen bezel, none at all, or perhaps even one that curves around the edges of the device, as has recently come into commercial practice with mobile phones? Similarly, if the user is not careful, his knuckles or the palm of his hand could brush against the screen the next time he tries to write with that pen-at-the-ready. If the virtue of a touchscreen is that all you have to do is touch something to activate it, this fifth manifestation of touch shows that it has a dark side as well: all you have to do is touch something (by accident), and it might activate! Palm rejection and other related problems of incidental contact with touchscreens all stem from this inherent property of touch.
6. **Pen plus touch, and much more**. Note that we have not even begun to discuss more advanced forms of interaction, such as using the pen and touch in combination [1, 6, 11, 22], or the possibilities of sensing how the pen is oriented—and the tablet is tilted—as the user interacts with the devices in various ways. These, too, are aspects of touch—and pen—that could greatly enrich each modality, as well as their use in tandem.

Collectively, the six perspectives enumerated above show that there is much more to touch interaction than intentional contact with the touchscreen. And while wide-ranging, we make no claim that these six represent an exhaustive list, as we will discuss in more depth shortly in relation to point #3.

These perspectives also show that a holistic consideration of touch is not even limited to one implement: when writing on a tablet equipped with a pen, users necessarily must handle both devices. In this sense a pen is no more a peripheral to a tablet than a pencil is to a sheet of paper—each has an existence, and role, independent of the other, and we could just as easily say that the tablet is a peripheral to the pen.

Finally, and perhaps most importantly, the six perspectives identified above show that not all touches are intentional, or even desired. The user may not even be consciously aware that their hand or some other part of their body has come into contact with the tablet. Or the user may forget that they are even holding the pen at all.

Yet if we think about the interaction from the perspective of the tablet, which can only see what is going on in the very limited plane of the touchscreen, it should be clear that much of the information it needs to fully understand touch is impoverished, or missing altogether.

The same goes for its awareness of what the user is doing with the pen.

As such, there is great potential for additional sensors to augment the context of touch—broadly considered, across all six perspectives—such as to enable more intelligent, more nuanced, and more empowering pen and touch interactions in the future.

But first, by way of example, bear with us for a brief digression that goes deeper into one of these perspectives, namely how people hold the pen.

3.4 A Brief Look at Pen Grips During Pen + Touch Interaction

We just rattled off six ways to look at touch. One of our key points is that the surrounding user behaviors are often nuanced, dependent on task, and influenced by what the user has just done or what the user expects to do next.

To demonstrate this more concretely, we conducted an observational study of how people hold pens while working on electronic tablets with touchscreens. Full details of this study are reported elsewhere [14], but what matters is this:

Some thirty variations of grip and poses of the hand resulted.

For example, people often stow the pen in their hand while engaged in other tasks. This takes two primary forms: tucking the pen between the fingers; or palming the pen with their fingers wrapped around the barrel. Some people even exhibit both behaviors, depending on what exactly they are doing (see Fig. 3.5).

Taking this simple observation as a starting point, we can then go even deeper. From either grip, users will also extend their fingers to tap the screen, pinch to zoom, and perform other touch gestures. But certain common behaviors (such as tapping the screen with the middle finger, for example) were only ever observed from the *Tuck* form of the grip, and never from the *Palm* variation (see Fig. 3.6).

Hopefully this gives a sense of the richness of the human manual behaviors surrounding pen and touch interaction—as well as how much they can reveal about what the user is doing and how they are likely to interact with a device.

Fig. 3.5 Two common grips for stowing the pen. *Graphic* © Ken Hinckley, 2014. Used by permission. All rights reserved

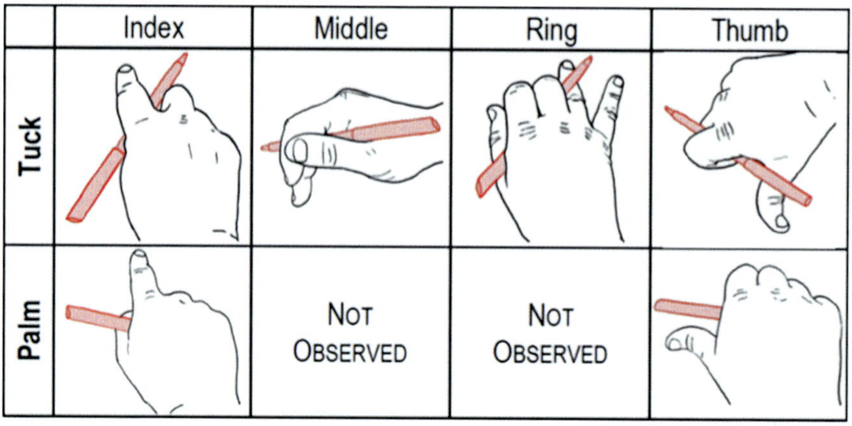

Fig. 3.6 Ways that users stow the pen while reaching out to touch the screen. We can get a sense of the richness of the user behaviors underlying even something as simple as gripping the pen by looking at how users extend a finger to touch the screen. We observed that the behavior exhibited depends on how the user prefers to stow the pen ('palm' vs. 'tuck') as well as the particular finger brought to bear on the task—which further derives from the particular manner in which that user grips the pen while writing. *Graphic* © Ken Hinckley, 2014. Used by permission. All rights reserved

But to be clear, our goal in the technical exploration which follows was never to recognize all of these grips. Rather, they served as a source of inspiration, while also representing variations in user behavior that our recognition techniques and interaction designs had to accommodate and otherwise take into account.

3.5 A Hard Look at the Context of Pen and Touch

By now our worldview should be clear. Our goal is to understand touch more deeply, as well as the many ways that people use the pen, so that we can make the combination of pen and touch on tablets richer, simpler, and more satisfying.

Indeed, many of the shortcomings of current pen and touch experiences—such as accidental contact of the hand with the screen while writing—can be viewed not as user error but rather as a result of the system's lack of awareness of what is really going on.

And by extending the tablet's aura of awareness beyond the confines of the screen itself, we can take some initial steps towards making experiences with technology feel more natural and complete.

Our hardware platform consists of two primary components, tablet and pen, each augmented by a similar array of sensors (Figs. 3.7 and 3.8).

The pen contains an accelerometer, gyroscope, and magnetometer. These represent the standard trio of sensors for detecting inertial motion. Each sensor has three degrees of freedom, such that inertial movement of the device can be fully

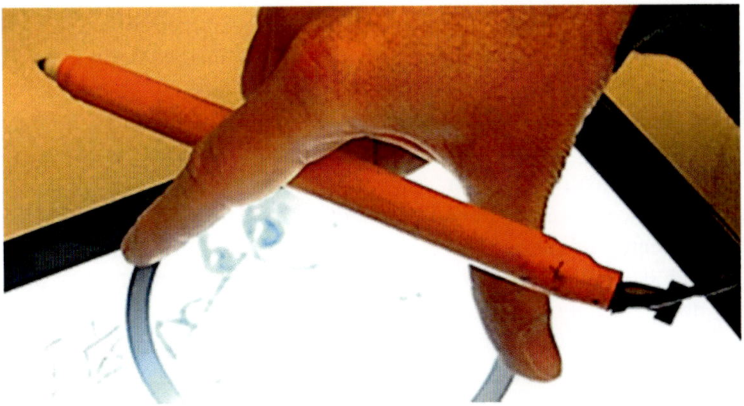

Fig. 3.7 Augmented stylus prototype in action. The current prototype is tethered, and somewhat bulky, but not so much so that it precludes interactions such as touching the screen while the pen is tucked between the fingers. *Photo* © Ken Hinckley, 2014. Used by permission. All rights reserved

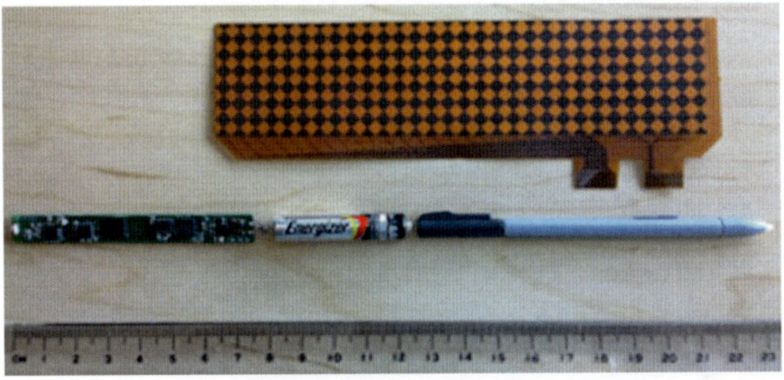

Fig. 3.8 The augmented stylus, unpacked. The green circuit board on the left contains all augmented sensors. The quad-A battery provides power, but due to the delicate nature of our mechanical prototype it is difficult to change the battery, and hence we reverted to a tether for power (as seen above in Fig. 3.7). The electronic pen sensed by the tablet digitizer is the Slim Pen from Wacom (MP200). The grip sensing is achieved by a flexible capacitive grid printed on Kapton, which we wrap around the barrel of the assembled stylus. *Photo* © Ken Hinckley, 2014. Used by permission. All rights reserved

characterized in three dimensions. We can determine only orientation from these sensors, not 3D position, but still this is enough to infer quite a bit about what is going on.

The entire barrel of the pen is furthermore wrapped in a flexible capacitive grid that provides full multi-touch sensing of the user's grip on the pen. To protect the sensor and provide mechanical stability, we currently sheathe the entire pen in shrink wrap, which adds some bulk and accounts for the garish orange color of our present prototype, but this simply a symptom of our early research prototype that could be done away with in a more meticulously crafted and engineered design.

The tablet itself is outfitted with a similar array of sensors (Fig. 3.9), which provide us with full motion sensing and grip sensing along most of the outer surfaces of the tablet (only the approximately half-inch wide outer bezel of the front surface—around the screen—is insensitive to touch.

Together, these sensor augmentations therefore give us a complete picture of how the pen is oriented relative to the screen of the tablet, as well as how the user is gripping both devices. Collectively these reveal a great deal about what the user is currently doing (or not doing, as the case may be).

Clearly, we went to some effort to construct this Frankensteinian vision of tablet computing. But it was with a clear sense of purpose to address the problems and missing nuances brought on by the lack of awareness suffered by present-day pen and touch interfaces. As such this effort, although a research endeavor, was completely consistent with the belief system and vision of pen computing set forth above—and which we believe will come to practical fruition in the (hopefully near) future, much as sensors have come to pervade everyday experiences with mobile devices and smartphones in the last 10 years [9].

In the following sections we now illustrate some of the ways in which such a sensing platform can address these problems, as well as to bring out greater expressiveness, which is really just greater respect for human manual and bi-manual skill, whether with the bare hand or through a mechanical intermediary, in pen and touch experiences for tablet computers.

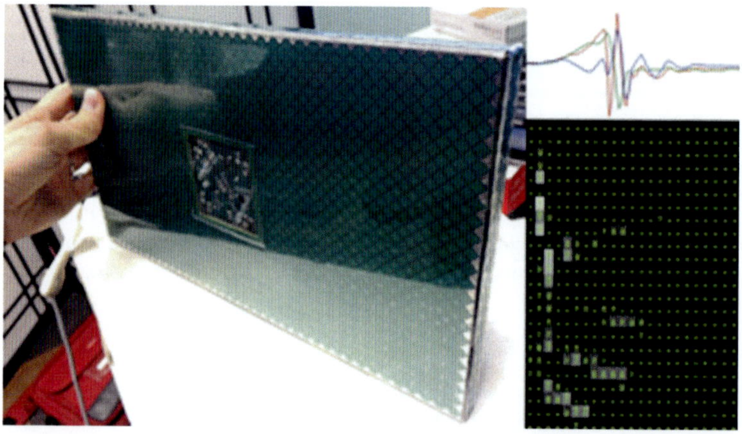

Fig. 3.9 The back surface of the grip-sensing tablet case. The tablet contains essentially the same circuitry as the pen, except that the grip sensing is integrated into a case which fits over the tablet itself. Grip can be sensed on all edges and the entire back, save for a roughly two square inch area that contains the circuitry. On the *right side* of the figure, examples of the motion (*top*) and grip (*bottom*) sensor data are provided. *Photo* © Ken Hinckley, 2014. Used by permission. All rights reserved

3.6 Sensing Techniques for Stylus + Touch Interaction

Given a new sensor—which is essentially a new input modality—often the first instinct for an interaction designer is to focus on the new types of gestures that modality can enable:

The new types of *intentional* gestures that one can make when the device is at the *foreground* of the user's attention.

However, while granting that new foreground gestures can have significant value, at least at the outset here we would like to focus on a different way of thinking about input to computers [2], in part because this way of thinking about interaction with technology is so often neglected by designers.

As we have hinted at in the six perspectives outlined above, when we think of 'touch' in its broadest sense, many of the problems and missing pieces result from the activity that surrounds the intentional touch gestures themselves. These are the less often considered aspects of 'touch' that may not even reach the user's conscious attention—the qualities of the interaction and manual habits in the *background*.

The missing context.

Context sensing, then, gives computers greater awareness of what is going on in the background, and the design of background interactions therefore seeks ways to leverage this additional context to automatically enhance and adapt the user experience.

What background sensing really boils down to is the following:

> There is tremendous potential to resolve ambiguity using sensors rather than foisting complexity on the user to establish the missing context.

We can see this perspective in the way that modern point and shoot cameras work, as one concrete example. The user attends to pointing the camera, while the camera senses the distance to the subject, the illumination levels, and many other properties. When the user shoots he need not be burdened by the manual configuration of these many settings.

Another example is the automatic screen rotation [9] now commonplace in mobile phones. The user simply holds the device in the desired posture, while the sensor detects the movement and automatically rotates the screen to the correct orientation.

Here we have adopted this perspective and used it to yield insights—and to design new experiences—for pen and touch interaction.

For example, we can employ our sensors to distinguish some types of intentional versus unintentional touch in the context of palm rejection. Incidental palm contact is inherent to the act of writing. Said another way, the act of writing is a hidden piece of context that could help to resolve the potential ambiguity of palm contact with the touchscreen.

And we can break this down further into a number of telling details that together can lead us towards a more satisfactory solution to this problem:

1. **Palm contact while writing typically results from the hand holding the pen**—that is, from the preferred hand—and not the other hand, which may be intentionally holding or moving objects, or manipulating the page itself.
2. **To write the user must hold the pen in a writing grip—as opposed to palming the pen, or tucking it between his fingers**. Hence the type of grip is a major clue as to whether the user is about to start writing—and whether a touch articulated by the preferred hand is consistent with intentional contact with the screen, or merely incident to the act of writing itself.
3. **The pen must be held at a certain orientation to write**. The orientation of the pen is not an unambiguous signal in and of itself, but it complements the information revealed by grip and provides another clue to user activity.
4. **Preferred hand motion and pen motion are necessarily correlated**. When the user moves, gestures, or touches the screen while the pen is held in hand, the pen moves too. When the hand makes contact with the screen, if we have good enough sensors and we maintain a high sampling rate, this subtle discontinuity in the movement can also be picked up by the motion sensors.

Specifically, when the user rests his or her palm on the screen, we can sense that the pen is held in a writing grip. And we can also sense the resulting bump signal produced by the hard-contact force of the palm with the display.

This then lets us associate the hand contact with the hand holding the pen, because the new touch reported by the touchscreen occurs at the same time as the bump signal sensed through the pen.

Meanwhile, an intentional bare-handed touch with the nonpreferred hand produces no such signal, since the pen doesn't move in a manner consistent with the nonpreferred hand's motion.

In this way we can screen out many incidental palm contacts while simultaneously allowing full bimanual interaction with both hands.

And we can still allow intentional preferred-hand touches, even while the pen is held tucked between the fingers, because such a grip (and the orientation of the pen) is not consistent with the user placing a hand on the screen to write.

We do not claim this approach to be perfect, as certain signals can still fool our straightforward signal-processing software, particularly if the palm contact is very light, but it does show how the palm-rejection problem can be re-cast as one of insufficient context.

And just as important, this approach allows us to *permit intentional touch* instead of solving the problem by discounting touches coincident with pen interaction altogether, that is a measure operating systems, device firmware, and applications often resort to. If we took such an approach, it would preclude the entire space of simultaneous pen + touch interaction.

However, these inferences potentially can allow pen and touch interfaces to do far more than handle incidental touch better. The four telling details listed above make clear that we can now distinguish touches with the pen-at-hand from other bare-handed touches, such as those produced by the nonpreferred hand.

Our prototype therefore employs this distinction to support fresh nuances of expression, such as seen in Fig. 3.10:

Fig. 3.10 Tapping the screen with the pen-at-hand brings up the pen tools. *Photo* © Ken Hinckley, 2014. Used by permission. All rights reserved

Tap the screen with the pen in hand to bring up the pen tools. A menu bar with different pen colors and thicknesses, as well as other pen tool modes such as lasso selection, the highlighter tool, an eraser tool, and so forth comes up when the user taps the screen with the preferred hand while the pen is tucked. Our reasoning was that it was only logical to bring up the tools associated with the pen when tapping the screen in this manner. The pen tucked between the fingers indicates that the user intends to use the pen again soon. This gives a simple and intuitive way to access all the tools, modes, and settings associated with the pen. Tapping with the (bare) nonpreferred hand, by contrast, produces an ordinary tap.

Nonpreferred hand: Full canvas zoom. As is the standard idiom in touch interfaces, the nonpreferred hand can be used to pinch to zoom (Fig. 3.11, left). However, in this case, the user can pinch-to-zoom even if the palm (of the preferred hand) is

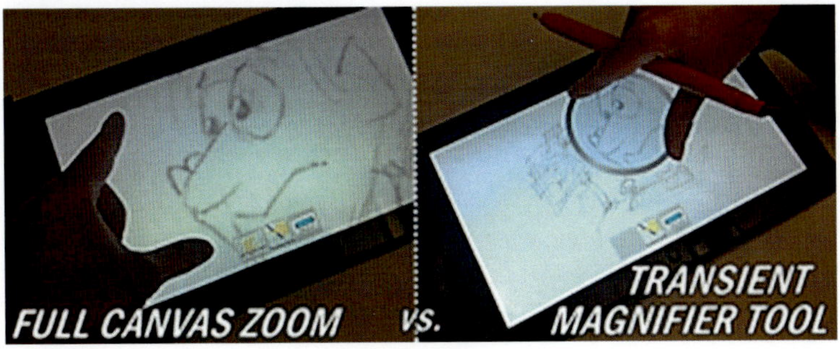

Fig. 3.11 Pinching with the nonpreferred hand zooms the full canvas, while a preferred hand pinch with the pen-in-hand brings up the transient magnifier tool. In this way we support a new class of multi-touch gesture which incorporates the context of *which had produces the touch* as well as *whether (and how) the pen is being gripped* at the time of the touchscreen contact. *Image* © Ken Hinckley, 2014. Used by permission. All rights reserved

resting on the screen preparatory to writing—because our sensors let us distinguish which touch is produced by which hand. Furthermore, this lets us entertain a design where a nonpreferred-hand pinch has a different function than one articulated by the preferred hand, as explored in the following.

Preferred hand: Transient magnifier tool. Touching down with two fingers while the pen is tucked-in-hand brings up the magnifier tool (Fig. 3.11, right). This provides localized zooming in one area of the canvas, which is ideal for detail work with the pen without disrupting the 'surround' of the workspace. Hence performing a pinch while the pen is at hand brings up another tool uniquely suited for the pen (much like the pen tools of Fig. 3.10).

Drafting tools suited to the writing grip. When the user is actively working with the pen, they often maintain a writing grip. We therefore use this to offer various drafting tools when the user taps the screen with the nonpreferred hand while the pen is held at the ready in the writing grip. For example, we provide a Compass tool (for drawing arcs) and an Airbrush tool in this mode (Fig. 3.12). The Airbrush tool, in particular, is interesting because it uses the additional degrees-of-freedom afforded by our pen's orientation sensing capabilities to provide a natural airbrush capability that allows the user to adjust the conic section of the spray that results by tilting the pen.

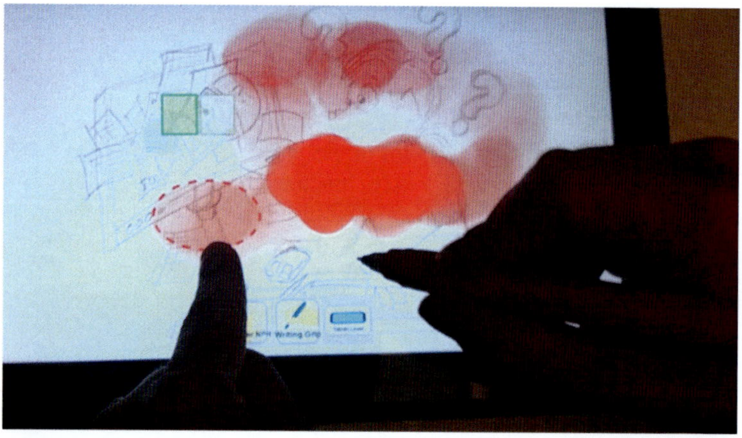

Fig. 3.12 The airbrush tool. A touch from the nonpreferred hand indicates where to airbrush, while the preferred hand orients the pen in 3D to control the conic section of the resulting spray. Note that the pen does not have to stay "within range" of the traditional 1 cm sensing range of the tablet digitizer during this interaction, because our augmented sensors provide the 3D orientation information. *Photo*

3.7 Tablet Grip Sensing

In the early going, we motivated our work by illustrating the many ways that users can 'touch' a tablet computer that are not respected as such by traditional touch-screen interaction. However, in the examples given above we primarily focused on interaction scenarios with the pen-in-hand, often in cases where both hands were interacting with the front of the device.

In part this is simply because even with fairly limited sensing we can do a lot. And because the techniques illustrated above do not necessarily depend on tablet grip sensing to realize.

But having said that, we believe the techniques above could be improved by more fully integrating the context of the current tablet grip into the interaction. That we have not yet done so and demonstrated more fully why it could valuable is more a symptom of limited time (and in some cases, perhaps limited imagination) than an inherent limitation of what is possible from the sensing modality. And indeed we hope that others will pick up this line of work and fill in the gaps, look for additional or alternative mappings for how these nuances of pen and touch can be leveraged in user interfaces, and generally advance this area in many other ways.

Nonetheless we have explored many other techniques that do rely on the tablet grip sensing, some of which appear in our earlier work that was the foundation for this paper [14], and in another forthcoming paper (accepted for publication [21]).

For example, we mentioned that pesky thumb on the front of the screen. One simple remediation we have experimented with is to discount thumb contact that occurs incident to gripping the tablet, such as when first picking it up (Fig. 3.13).

Fig. 3.13 Discounting thumb contact when initially gripping the device. The hand grip sensed on the back of the device tells us that the touch, immediately above on the front of the screen and near the edge, is necessarily associated with the thumb of the same hand. Controls near the edge of the screen initially appear semi-transparent and cannot be triggered by such incidental touches from the thumb. *Photo* © Ken Hinckley, 2014. Used by permission. All rights reserved

Another example is to sense when the user walks away while holding the tablet, but not the pen. This can be sensed in a straightforward manner by sensing the gait pattern of walking, while also noting that the pen is neither held (gripped) nor moving [13]. The user can then be reminded not to forget their pen. Since in pen computing it is always a matter of when, not if, the user will lose the pen, such a simple technique could be of considerable value to users.

A third example is to sense common ways of holding or using the tablet. For example, we observed that while reading books or paper documents, users pick up the material with both hands and angle it closer to themselves when deeply engaged in reading. This can be used to support an immersive reading mode, which automatically emphasizes the text while removing background distractions and ancillary screen controls, when the user grips their tablet in this manner.

A fourth example is to sense when the user passes their tablet to another user. People exhibit very distinctive patterns of grip and orienting the device when handing an object to another person. We have explored various techniques to sense this and to use it to support alternative semantics of "sharing" digital content with one another that are much more akin to physical sharing and therefore also very different than emailing an attachment, or placing a file in the cloud, for example.

Finally, we have explored how grip sensing can help a user to more effectively refer to and cross-reference information across multiple devices. Tablets and e-readers are increasingly being used as companion devices—often with multiple devices to support facile work with multiple documents and information sources, as repeatedly observed in natural information work with both paper and electronic reference materials [3, 15, 17, 19]. Sensing which devices the user is holding, therefore, and how they are gripping them therefore can potentially be a crucial piece of missing context in managing multi-device interaction [3, 5, 15, 16].

3.8 Summary, Conclusion, and Future Work

We have come a long way in this discussion. We have demonstrated how a keen eye for the *oft seen, but seldom noticed* role of manual (and bi-manual!) interaction in general—and in the behaviors manifested by users with pen and touch tablets in particular—lead to at least six perspectives of what it means to 'touch' a device. And there are likely many more beyond that.

We have argued that many of these missing perspectives in touch interaction are a symptom of missing context, and we set out to build sensor-augmented stylus and tablet devices to redress this. The prototype devices support inertial motion sensing as well as capacitive grip sensing, but certainly other sensors could be envisioned to accompany these modalities in the future. But even with a limited palette of additional sensors, we showed how we can detect a number of salient elements of context: how the user is gripping the pen, which hand is contacting the display, and what incidental motions are imparted to the devices during these interactions. We then presented techniques which illustrated how these sensors and contextual inferences allowed us to support richer, more natural, and more nuanced pen and touch interaction.

While the directions explored are hopefully provocative, and have been explored through implementing prototypes and by conducting observational studies as well as preliminary technological evaluations with test users, many of them remain speculative in the sense that their potential is not yet fully clear. Some of the techniques we propose may ultimately find broad acceptance, while others are likely to remain laboratory curiosities for the foreseeable future. And the truth of the matter is that—without the benefit of hindsight—it is often difficult to tell which is which. However, we take heart in some of our own early work on mobile sensing [2, 8, 9], which in some ways was indeed ahead of its time, but in other ways felt painfully similar to the present project. *Certainly such sensors are too expensive,* or so we heard from practically-minded people, *the power they demand too much, their interpretation too uncertain and too taxing of limited computational cycles.*

But here we are in 2015, and many of the techniques we proposed have come to fruition. And even if not always in the exact way we implemented it and anticipated it coming along, in several instances it was awfully close. We hope, and expect, that the same will be true of the techniques we have explored here for pen and touch, for stylus and tablet, some fifteen years from now—if not much sooner.

In the meantime we will continue to strive to go much further, and see how the new capabilities and nuances afforded by rich sensing capabilities may allow us to design interaction technologies, techniques, and experiences in new ways. Our goal remains to address latent and unmet needs—for freeform input, for more human ways of informally organizing information, and in the broadest sense for *inking outside the box*. Ultimately, we believe that such advances can help students, information workers, creative professionals, and educators to work together and to bring their efforts to fruition in a much deeper and more natural way.

Acknowledgments The work underlying this paper is the result of many years of study and prototyping by a large number of people. In particular we would like to acknowledge the efforts of Michel Pahud, Hrvoje Benko, Pourang Irani, Marcel Gavriliu, Francois Guimbretiere, Xiang 'Anthony' Chen, Fabrice Matulic, and Andy Wilson on our Stylus + Tablet Sensing Techniques paper [14] which prompted our invited presentation at WIPTTE (and hence, the present manuscript).

References

1. Brandl P, Forlines C, Wigdor D, Haller M, Shen C (2008) Combining and measuring the benefits of bimanual pen and direct-touch interaction on horizontal interfaces. In: Proceedings of the working conference on advanced visual interfaces, AVI '08. ACM, New York, NY, USA, pp 154–161

2. Buxton W (1995) Integrating the periphery and context: a new taxonomy of telematics. In: Proceedings of graphics interface, vol 95. Citeseer, pp 239–246
3. Chen N, Guimbretiere F, Sellen A (2012) Designing a multi-slate reading environment to support active reading activities. ACM Trans Comput-Hum Interact 19(3):18:1–18:35
4. Guiard Y (1987) Asymmetric division of labor in human skilled bimanual action: the kinematic chain as a model. J Mot Behav 19(4):486–517
5. Hamilton P, Wigdor DJ (2014) Conductor: enabling and understanding cross-device interaction. In: Proceedings of the SIGCHI conference on human factors in computing systems, CHI '14. ACM, New York, NY, USA, pp 2773–2782
6. Hamilton W, Kerne A, Robbins T (2012) High-performance pen + touch modality interactions: a real-time strategy game esports context. In: Proceedings of the 25th annual ACM symposium on user interface software and technology, UIST '12. ACM, New York, NY, USA, pp 309–318
7. Hinckley K (1996) Haptic issues for virtual manipulation. PhD thesis, University of Virginia
8. Hinckley K, Horvitz E (2001) Toward more sensitive mobile phones. In: Proceedings of the 14th annual ACM symposium on user interface software and technology, UIST '01. ACM, New York, NY, USA, pp 191–192
9. Hinckley K, Pierce J, Sinclair M, Horvitz E (2000) Sensing techniques for mobile interaction. In: Proceedings of the 13th annual ACM symposium on user interface software and technology, UIST '00. ACM, New York, NY, USA, pp 91–100
10. Hinckley K, Pahud M, Buxton B (2010) Direct display interaction via simultaneous pen + multi-touch input. In: SID symposium digest of technical papers, vol 41:1. Wiley Online Library, pp 537–540
11. Hinckley K, Yatani K, Pahud M, Coddington N, Rodenhouse J, Wilson A, Benko H, Buxton B (2010) Pen + touch = new tools. In: Proceedings of the 23rd annual ACM symposium on user interface software and technology, UIST '10. ACM, New York, NY, USA, pp 27–36
12. Hinckley K, Bi X, Pahud M, Buxton B (2012) Informal information gathering techniques for active reading. In: Proceedings of the SIGCHI conference on human factors in computing systems, CHI '12. ACM, New York, NY, USA, pp 1893–1896
13. Hinckley K, Chen XA, Benko H (2013) Motion and context sensing techniques for pen computing. In: Proceedings of graphics Interface 2013, GI '13. Canadian Information Processing Society, Toronto, Ont., Canada, pp 71–78
14. Hinckley K, Pahud M, Benko H, Irani P, Guimbretière F, Gavriliu M, Chen XA, Matulic F, Buxton W, Wilson A (2014) Sensing techniques for tablet+stylus interaction. In: Proceedings of the 27th annual ACM symposium on user interface software and technology, UIST '14. ACM, New York, NY, USA, pp 605–614
15. Hong M, Piper AM, Weibel N, Olberding S, Hollan J (2012) Microanalysis of active reading behavior to inform design of interactive desktop workspaces. In: Proceedings of the 2012 ACM international conference on interactive tabletops and surfaces, ITS '12. ACM, New York, NY, USA, pp 215–224
16. Marquardt N, Hinckley K, Greenberg S (2012) Cross-device interaction via micro-mobility and f-formations. In: Proceedings of the 25th annual ACM symposium on user interface software and technology, UIST '12. ACM, New York, NY, USA, pp 13–22
17. Morris MR, Meyers BR et al (2007) Reading revisited: evaluating the usability of digital display surfaces for active reading tasks. In: Second annual IEEE international workshop on horizontal interactive human-computer systems, TABLETOP '07. IEEE, pp 79–86
18. Schilit BN, Golovchinsky G, Price MN (1998) Beyond paper: supporting active reading with free form digital ink annotations. In: Proceedings of the SIGCHI conference on human factors in computing systems, CHI '98. ACM Press/Addison-Wesley, New York, NY, USA, pp 249–256
19. Sellen AJ, Harper RH (2002) The myth of the paperless office. MIT press, Cambridge
20. Tashman CS, Edwards WK (2011) Active reading and its discontents: the situations, problems and ideas of readers. In: Proceedings of the SIGCHI conference on human factors in computing systems, CHI '11. ACM, New York, NY, USA, pp 2927–2936
21. Yoon D, Hinckley K, Benko H, Guimbretire FV, Irani PP, Pahud M, Gavriliu M (2015) Sensing tablet grasp + micro-mobility for active reading. In: Proceedings of the 28th ACM user interface software and technology symposium, UIST. ACM, New York, NY, USA (Accepted)

22. Zeleznik R, Bragdon A, Adeputra F, Ko HS (2010) Hands-on math: a page-based multi-touch and pen desktop for technical work and problem solving. In: Proceedings of the 23rd annual ACM symposium on user interface software and technology, UIST '10. ACM, New York, NY, USA, pp 17–26

Part III
Novel Tutoring Systems and Intelligent Ink

Chapter 4
Design Studies for Stylus and Finger-Based Interaction in Writing Instruction on Tablets

Robert Thompson, Steven Tanimoto, Virginia Berninger, and William Nagy

Abstract HAWK (Help Agent for Writing Knowledge) is a new instructional software for the essentials of writing that runs on tablets. In trials with an after-school K-12 subject group, the use of the software showed improved writing capabilities of most students. One of the activities supported by the software involves students drawing letter shapes by tracing paths through scaffolded channels. Additionally, we detail the design studies we performed prior to implementing the full software package. We focused on how software can provide graphical feedback to students in the context of a stylus and touch-based interface for the basic educational activity of learning to write letters of the alphabet.

4.1 Introduction

4.1.1 Educational Need

Personalized instruction in basic writing is needed as part of diagnosing and overcoming learning disabilities and addressing shortcomings in achievement [2]. Students with dysgraphia, for example, have specific difficulty in the sequential finger movements that are needed for writing with pen and paper and keyboard [9].

R. Thompson · S. Tanimoto (✉)
Department of Computer Science and Engineering, University of Washington, Seattle, WA, USA
e-mail: tanimoto@cs.washington.edu

R. Thompson
e-mail: robthomp@cs.washington.edu

V. Berninger
Department of Educational Psychology, University of Washington, Seattle, WA 98195, USA
e-mail: vwb@uw.edu

W. Nagy
School of Education, Seattle Pacific University, Seattle, WA, USA
e-mail: wnagy@spu.edu

T. Hammond et al. (eds.), *Revolutionizing Education with Digital Ink*, Human–Computer Interaction Series, DOI 10.1007/978-3-319-31193-7_4

Mouse-based computing systems are not suitable as tools for learning the sensorimotor skills associated with handwriting. Tablet-based systems, however, are potentially helpful because of their pen-based and/or touch-based input capabilities.

4.1.2 Related Work

Previous work on the design of writing instruction includes both commercial and research systems. One of the research systems is the Clownware system of Berninger [3]. However, that system did not exploit stylus-based or touch-based technology. Our studies extend that approach by considering these technologies.

Several research and commercial systems have been developed that involve stylus technologies in children's writing. One of these is the CobWeb Interface [7], a research prototype that offered text-line scaffolding to primary-school writers, and whose objective was to evaluate the utility of handwriting-recognition software in writing environments for children.

In another research project by Janet Read, a system called Jabberwocky [7] was introduced which did not use tablets. However, it used a form of "digital ink" in which a pen outfitted with a digital camera captures stroke information in a manner sufficient to also render the writing on a computer screen. Like CobWeb and other systems, Jabberwocky is designed to work with software that automatically recognizes the user's writing, in order to be able to give feedback at a semantic level.

A recent study by Mann et al. [6] offered numerous insights into the possible uses of stylus technologies in children's writing including a methodology for evaluating handwriting quality. We used the same approach by offering interface prototypes for particular kinds of feedback.

4.1.3 Overview of the Paper

In the remainder of this paper, we first describe the overall software system we have built. Then we describe in some detail the design studies we performed relating particularly to the use of stylus and touch-based interaction for learning to write. Finally, we report on some of the lessons that we have learned so far during deployment of the software.

4.2 Overall Structure of the HAWK Software

Here we describe the structure of our software with the rationale for each major design decision we made. We call the software system HAWK, which stands for Help Agent for Writing Knowledge. Although the teaching of reading skills is also part of the educational mission of the project, our focus, from a technological point of view, has been on writing.

4.2.1 Pedagogical Background

The computerized lessons draw on two decades of instructional research with human teachers, which are adapted for use with computer teachers. The instructional approach is unique in that it aims to create functional systems for language by ear (listening), language by mouth (speaking), language by eye (reading), and language by hand (writing). Each functional language system is taught at multiple levels—subword, word, syntax, and text. The lessons are designed to be used for typically developing oral and written language learners (OWLs) as well as children and youth with specific learning disabilities impairing subword letter writing (dysgraphia), word reading and spelling (dyslexia), and oral and written language syntax (OWL LD).

Three studies to date (Study 1 [4]; Studies 2 and 3 [10]) have shown that both students with and without dysgraphia, dyslexia, and OWL LD improve from pre-test before the computer lessons to post-test after the computer lessons (effect sizes range from moderate to strong to very strong). Thus, the lessons can be used to provide differentiated instruction in the general education classroom.

A unique feature of the lessons is that students receive feedback from the computer teacher at the completion of most learning activities in each lesson, which they record on their response to instruction form. The forms provide visible feedback for evaluating progress across the lessons for both the students and teachers, and they can be used to supplement pre- and post-test changes based on normed tests.

4.2.2 Client-Server Structure

Although most software for the teaching of writing has been of the shrink-wrapped, desktop-computer or laptop computer variety, we opted to use a client-server architecture for our software, in order to take advantage of technology trends and better meet the goals of our research project. Figure 4.1 gives an overview of this structure in our case.

Some of the reasons for adopting the client-server structure were the following: facilitating rapid updating of the software, with no installation or reinstallation required on the client side; ease in collecting research data; and consistency with the trend towards more effective use of HTML5 and JavaScript technologies, which have proven effective for implementing rich internet applications, and which find increasingly powerful support in browsers.

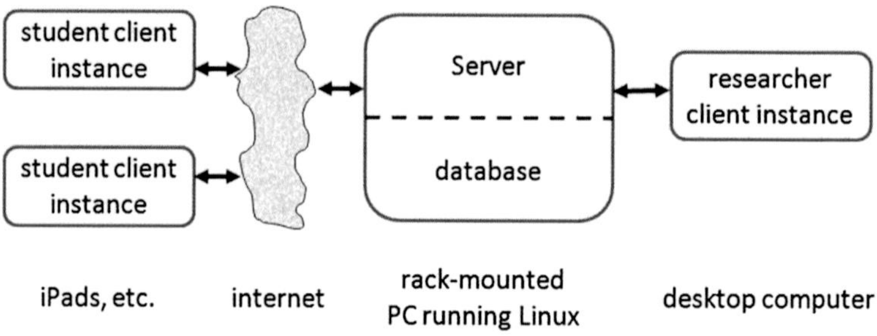

Fig. 4.1 The overall architecture for the HAWK system

4.2.3 The Student Client

Each student who uses HAWK interacts via a client interface. Although the client is browser-based and can therefore run on a wide variety of computers, we have optimized the client software to run on tablets. We chose tablets for three reasons: cost relative to that of laptops, support of stylus and touch-based interaction, and coolness factor, which is important for many students.

The particular tablet we chose is the iPad, due to its relative maturity and robustness, etc., at the time of our decision in 2011.

4.2.4 The Server

The server component of HAWK provides the content on a website. In addition, it manages student and researcher accounts, and it provides persistence for user activity records. The server employs standard computer hardware, a Linux operating system, a MYSQL database, and a collection of scripts written in PHP. It is maintained in a secure, air-conditioned machine room administered by the professional staff of the University of Washington's Department of Computer Science and Engineering. The server communicates with client instances via the HTTP protocol and AJAX methods.

4.3 Student Activity Organized into Lessons

The instructional material embedded in the HAWK software consists of 18 units called lessons. Each lesson is intended to be taken by a student in a single session of approximately 2 h. Each lesson provides a variety of activities, so that a student is sufficiently stimulated to continue and complete each lesson.

4.3.1 Division of Lessons into Modules

Each lesson has three main components. One addresses familiarity with the alphabet itself. A single software module supports the alphabet-oriented activities, and this module, as well as its activities, go under the name of "Letters In Motion." We discuss this particular module in detail later. The second component addresses knowledge about words. This knowledge includes spelling, the correspondence between phonetic and written representations, and the morphological structure of words including prefixes and suffixes. This component is called "Words in Motion." The third component concerns composition at the level of sentences and paragraphs. At this level, students express ideas to write personal narratives or take notes about source material and then write summaries based on the notes. This component is called "Minds In Motion."

The integration of these three kinds of knowledge and activities within each and every lesson helps reinforce to students the connectedness of these kinds of knowledge. Letters are parts of words, and words are parts of larger expressions. In each session, a student works on learning about components at different levels of this hierarchy, and by finishing each lesson with a composition, the student gets to put the knowledge about smaller components into practice.

4.3.2 Division of Modules into Activities

Within a module, and during the course of a single lesson, a student performs several activities. As an example, in the Words in Motion module, activities include the following: "Pattern Analyzer Through Ear" (students use their stylus or finger to tap the syllables of a word presented via audio); "Phoneme Pattern Analysis" (similar, but at the phoneme level); "Musical Rhythm of Language Through Stress Patterns" (students select and press a virtual button to indicate which syllable of a word is stressed); "Pattern Analyzer for Written Words" (letter sequences are presented, and students must distinguish those that could be words according to standard lexical patterns, and those that cannot); "Cross Code Talking Matrix: Single Spelling Sound Relationships and Different Sounds for the Same Spelling" (students repeat oral prompts while reading, and they press/touch to repeat or continue); "Exploding Word Families" (students watch and listen as words "explode"); "Exploding Word Part Bridges Between Spoken and Written Words" (similar style, with focus on suffixes); "Are They Real Fixes or Not?" (students determined whether a suffix or prefix is plausible in English). There are nine additional activity types for a total of 18 in Words in Motion.

The Minds in Motion activities focus on expression of ideas using multi-word constructions in phrases, clauses, and discourse units. There are 12 activity types in this module. The final activities in the module involve composition. In the composition activities, students write short pieces on the screen, using stylus, or touch or

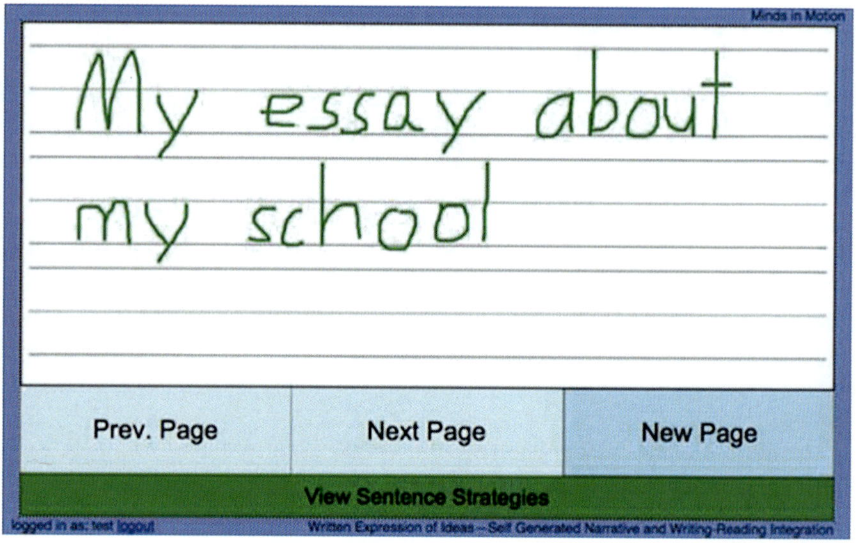

Fig. 4.2 Screenshot of a composition activity within the Minds In Motion portion of a lesson. Scaffolding here is limited to three guide lines per text line. Students can use any number of virtual pages within a fifteen-minute writing period

keyboard (depending on what condition they are assigned to). A typical composition is a short autobiography. The interface for the composition activities is illustrated in Fig. 4.2.

In most of these activities, the stylus or touch-based interactions are not essentially graphical, and keyboard interaction would suffice for tapping rhythms, selecting among choices or pressing the Done button. However, the graphical input of stylus or touch is essential for the Letters In Motion activities that we describe next.

4.3.3 The "Letters In Motion" Module

Each lesson in the Letters In Motion module involves the student in (a) observing the drawing of a letterform, (b) imitating the "computer teacher" in drawing the letterform by tracing with stylus or finger, (c) redrawing the letterform from memory, (d) identifying, by writing, the letter that comes before or after the given letter in the alphabet, and (e) for capital letters only, repeating steps a and b, but then writing capital letters at the beginning of provided sentences in handprinted or cursive format. In a given lesson, several different letters are covered. In addition, multiple modes are covered: lower-case handprinted, upper-case handprinted, lower-case cursive, and upper-case cursive. Each lesson begins with the introductory screen shown in Fig. 4.3, which indicates the mode to be used in current session.

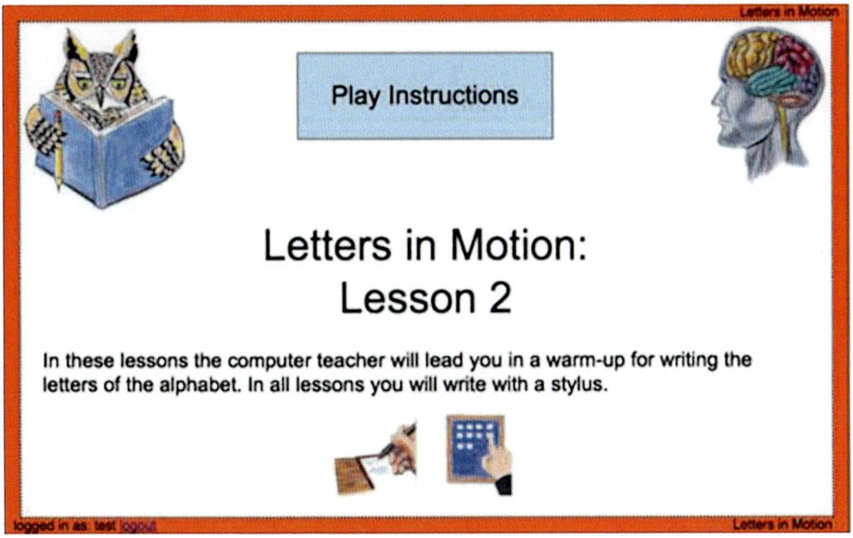

Fig. 4.3 Introductory screen for Letters In Motion

Of particular interest for stylus-based and touch-based interaction is the support for step (b). In this step, the software must both scaffold the student's drawing of the letterform and process what the student draws. We discuss these issues in the next section.

4.4 Design Studies for Letters In Motion

In this section, we discuss the issue of how to provide appropriate scaffolding to students who are learning to write, and how assessment can be done, for formative, summative and motivational purposes.

4.4.1 Presentation of the Handwriting Process

To support the above-mentioned step (a), before the student draws a letterform in any of the lessons of the Letters In Motion module, the drawing of the letterform is modeled by the HAWK software for the student with an animation of the "inking" of the strokes. This animation illustrates the separation of the drawing into strokes, the order in which the strokes are drawn, the direction in which each stroke moves within its channel, and roughly what the timing of drawing can be. A simple example for the letter O at the completion of the animation is shown below in Fig. 4.4.

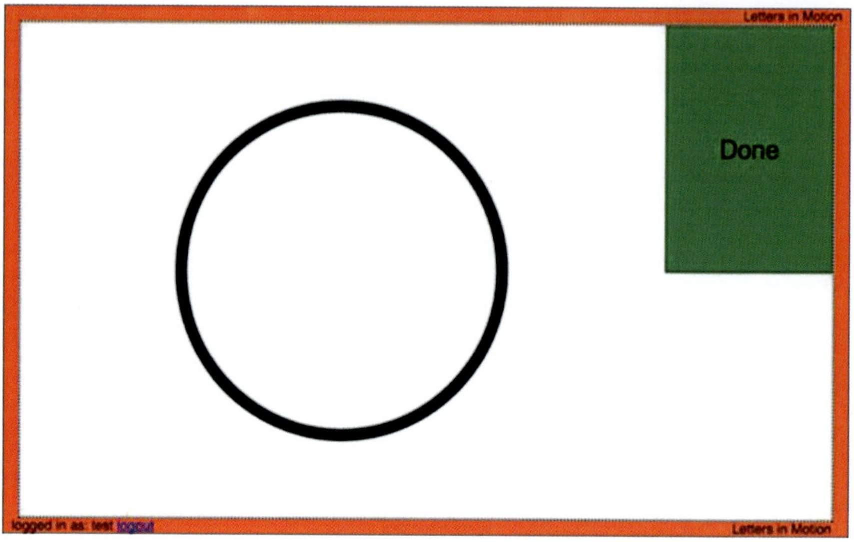

Fig. 4.4 After completion of the animation for the letter O, which consists of a single stroke

4.4.2 *Scaffolding the Handwriting Process*

Although animation was used to indicate the direction within each stroke's ductus as shown in Fig. 4.5, static visual cues provided additional scaffolding for direction as shown in Fig. 4.6.

In order to present clear distinctions among the separate strokes of multi-stroke letters of the alphabet, the animated presentation of the drawing process can use different colors for the strokes. This is shown in Fig. 4.7.

4.4.3 *Removing the Scaffolding*

In order to support step (c) of the activity described above, the student is prompted to redraw the strokes of the letterform; however, most or all of the scaffolding is removed for this step. Consequently, the student must remember each stroke's shape and relative position, its order within the stroke sequence, and the direction in which to draw it. Deciding where to begin the first stroke is also up to the student, at least to a certain extent.

In the first version of the software, no guide lines were provided in this step, and students could write anywhere on the screen. In the revised version, guide lines were provided as shown in Fig. 4.8, meaning the student was cued on where, vertically, to draw the letter, but not where, from left to right, to draw it.

Fig. 4.5 The modeled letter O, shown in *black*, superimposed on its ductus, shown in *light gray*. Display of the ductus is a form of instructional scaffolding

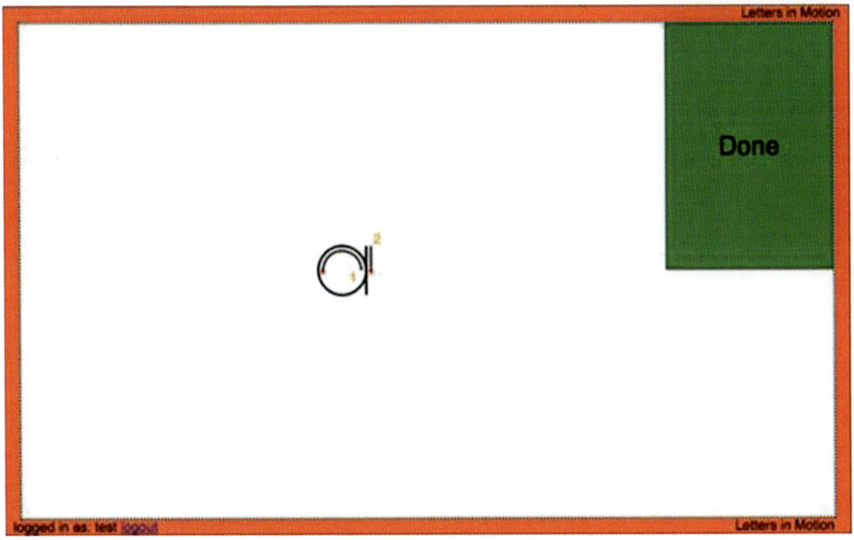

Fig. 4.6 Revised version of graphical presentation of letterform drawing process. Ducti have been removed, the size reduced, and stroke direction and numbering have been added. This example shows a lower-case letter a

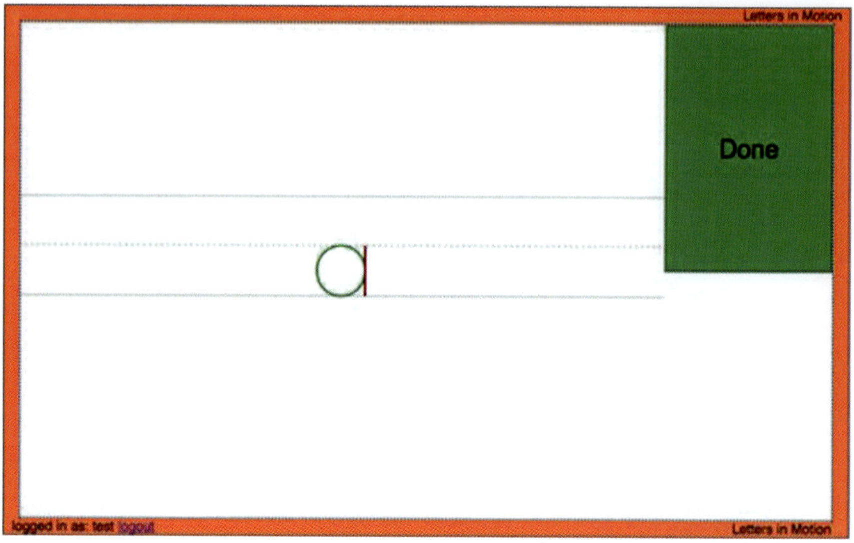

Fig. 4.7 Lower-case a with different colors for each stroke. This example also shows the use of text guide lines

Fig. 4.8 Scaffolding for step (c) in the revised design, guide lines are presented. We see an example of a student's letter a drawn within the *lines*

4.4.4 Assessment of Handwriting and Graphical Feedback

Perhaps the most interesting issue we addressed in the early stages of our software development was the design of alternative means of assessment for the Letters In Motion activities. We considered three categories of assessment: formative (to help students correct their drawing of letterforms), summative (to report progress in learning the letterforms and their relationships within the alphabet) and motivational (to provide excitement via a sense of challenge and to provide encouragement to continue).

We considered three methods of scoring the work of students in step (b) of the activity. The first we call crossings-based scoring. The second is distance-based scoring, and the third is timing-based scoring.

4.4.5 Crossings-Based Scoring

The ductus can be viewed as a very simple kind of maze. The basic rule for doing mazes with a pen or pencil is that you are not allowed to go through a wall. The student should only draw each stroke within its ductus on the screen. A student with dysgraphia might have difficulty simply staying within the ductus, particularly if he or she has a sensorimotor disability. Crossing-based scoring tallies error points, where one error point is given for moving the stylus or touch from inside the ductus to outside.

We implemented a form of graphical feedback related to crossings in which the student's inked trajectory changes color from green inside the ductus to red outside the ductus. (See Fig. 4.9.) This feedback makes crossing detection a kind of formative assessment. It is clear to the student that the computer "knows" that the drawn stroke went outside the bounds of the ductus, and the student can try again to draw the stroke without that error. By keeping track of the scores obtained by counting crossings, student progress can be tracked from activity to activity and lesson to lesson, for summative purposes.

Another type of error, easily detected by software is a stroke-order error. These come in several varieties. In general, there should be a one-to-one correspondence between modeled strokes and strokes drawn by the student. In one variety of error, a student has more than one drawn stroke for a single modeled stroke. (A case of this is shown in Fig. 4.10.) An inverse situation is where a student has no stroke that corresponds to a particular modeled stroke. The third variety of stroke-order error occurs when the student draws strokes that correspond, in permuted fashion, to the modeled strokes. A fourth type of stroke error is the drawing a stroke in the opposite direction to that of the modeled stroke. This is a bit different from the stroke-order errors, but is closely related; it typically represents a lack of knowledge of the correct drawing direction rather than any failure to perceive shape or trace within a ductus.

Fig. 4.9 Graphical feedback based on the crossings of the ductus boundary. The student's trajectory, in *green* and *red*, is shown superimposed upon the ductus and the modeled trajectory. The score for this performance is −2, based on the number of *red* segments

Fig. 4.10 When the student lifts the stylus, the current stroke is considered by the software to have been completed. The student's attempt to continue the stroke is marked as a stroke error and it is given a score of −1

Fig. 4.11 Graphical feedback in the revised software. It is left to the student to compare his or her letterform with the modeled one

In the revised version of the software, the actual feedback presented consisted of the modeled letterform with static scaffolding in juxtaposition with the student's letterform as shown in Fig. 4.11.

While the crossings-based and stroke-order-based assessment offers a simple scoring method with easily understandable scores, they do not measure the finer points of accuracy in drawing letterforms. Consequently, we explored the use of more continuous measurement methods.

4.4.6 Distance-Based Scoring

In order to measure the accuracy with which a student traces a letterform over a modeled example or within a series of ducti, we considered measures of distance between the student's trajectory and the prototype. These are typically computed per stroke, and we assume that a student is following the proper stroke order. Figures 4.12 and 4.13 below illustrate graphical feedback in which the student's trace is inked with a color that varies continuously between green (meaning "accurate") and red (meaning "inaccurate") according to the euclidean distance between trace point and a corresponding point on the model stroke. (The correspondence is computed parametrically based on arc length.) Figure 4.12 shows an example where the student has drawn inside the modeled O, and Fig. 4.13 shows one where the student is mostly outside, but crosses through the modeled O at the top. Distance-based scoring

Fig. 4.12 Distance-based graphical feedback example where the student drew inside the modeled letter O

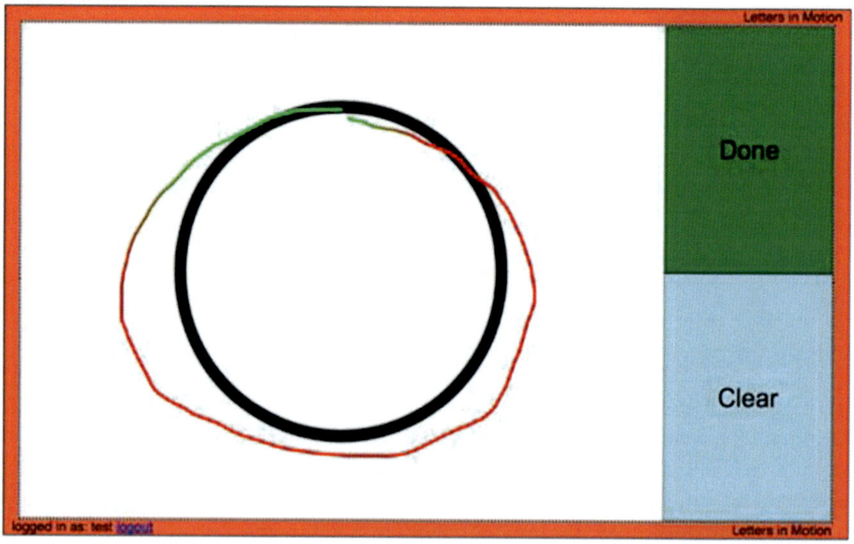

Fig. 4.13 Distance-based graphical feedback example where the student drew mostly outside the modeled O

could be performed in many different ways. For example the error at any point of the student's trace could be computed as the Euclidean distance from that point to the closest point on the modeled letter. Alternatively, another method we considered was dividing the drawing screen into multiple zones, and defining the accuracy, or rather the total error, based on which zones the pen entered while drawing. The zones around the modeled letter could be predefined to be weighted according to how seriously wrong entering that zone might be from an expert's judgment. For example, zones further from the ideal stroke would be weighted more, but also a zone might be predefined with a higher weight to be a more serious error when far away from an endpoint of a stroke than when far away from the midpoint of a stroke, where it perhaps does not need to meet up with another stroke. However, experts might prefer to evaluate shape than stretch the fine points of distance-based scoring. We did not pursue either shape analysis or the more sophisticated kind of analysis pursued by researchers who work to exploit automatic handwriting recognition technology (e.g., [7]).

4.4.7 Timing-Based Scoring

A limitation of the distance-based assessment methods, in addition to their relative insensitivity to shape features, is that they do not take dynamics of the drawing process into account. A student who traces a letter in fits and starts might achieve the same score as he or she would if smoothly drawing the same path. Consequently, we explored means of assessing the student drawing process in a way that could reward accuracy in timing.

Our timing method involves a special prompt consisting of an animated dot that is both modeling the drawing process and serving as a reference for the evaluation. The animated blue dot showed the student where his or her cursor should be at each moment during the drawing process. The software then renders the student's stroke with a color that shows how close to, or far from, the student's cursor was in relation to the reference dot. (See Fig. 4.14.)

A limitation of our implementation is that only one speed of writing was available to the student. While this could easily be remedied with a choice or just a presented sequence of examples of increasing speed, one can question the value of this form of assessment. It may be appropriate for a particular sort of student who is struggling to write smooth and consistent strokes, but inappropriate for most students for whom timing is at most a minor issue.

4.4.8 Support for Cursive

Although the teaching of cursive writing today is debated among educators and the public, there remain good arguments for it. Alstad et al. showed that cursive contributed uniquely to spelling and composing in each grade 4–7, probably because the connecting strokes link letters into words and increase speed of spelling during composing [1].

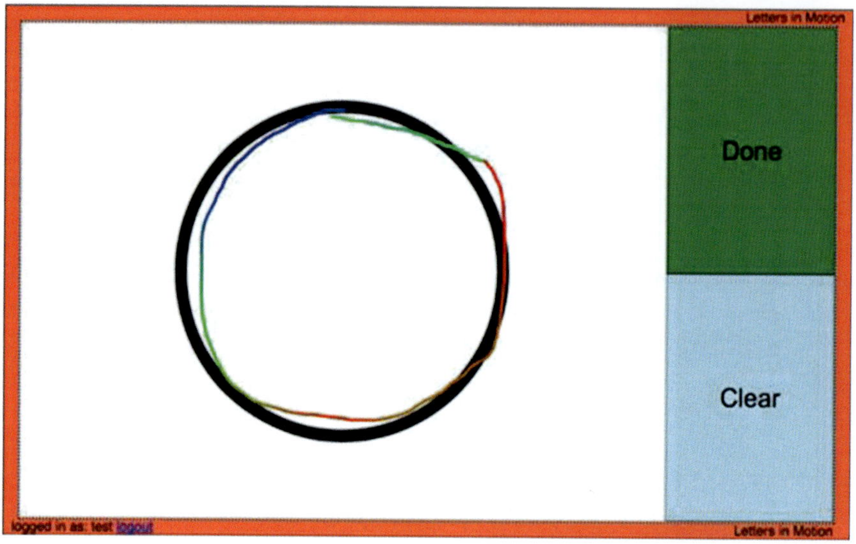

Fig. 4.14 With timing feedback, the inking of the student's stroke is presented in *green* if "on schedule," in *blue* if late, and *red* if early, in relation to the model

Supporting cursive instruction is slightly more challenging than handprinting, due to the more organic shapes of letterforms and the need for spatial continuity from letter to letter within each word. However, the methodology within the software is the same. A sample of modeling a cursive letter "u" together with a student's drawn "u" is given Fig. 4.15.

4.4.9 Gaming Aspects and Motivation

The manner of presentation to students of assessment information, independent of its volume and quality, has important consequences for student motivation. For example, showing a large volume of error messages to students may be disheartening to them, even if they are told that these don't really matter [7]. This was one reason that few of our graphical feedback schemes were incorporated into the latest versions of the HAWK lessons.

4.4.10 Self-Assessment

By simply presenting the modeled letterforms in juxtaposition with the student's work, we make it easy for the students to perform their own assessment of their work. Self-assessment is a natural enough process that we don't feel we have to teach it. Rather, our goal is simply to facilitate it by bringing together in time and space the student's work and the model.

Fig. 4.15 Model for a cursive u and a student's example

4.5 Experimental Findings

We have performed extensive trials of the HAWK lessons with grades 4 to 9 students in an after-school context. The experimental conditions and the detailed results including improvements in students' writing abilities are presented elsewhere, in [4, 10]. However, we mention some of the findings here in order to give a clearer context for the design studies we have described.

We compared student performance in two writing modes: stylus and touch. We found that performance did not vary, to any statistically significant degree, between these two conditions. This is probably because the practical differences between these two modes are small: both the capacitive styluses we used and the human finger have limited resolution, in spite of the iPad touch technology itself.

4.5.1 Stylus/Touch Versus Keyboarding

A second finding is anecdotal. Students reported that they preferred writing with the keyboard over using the stylus or finger touch. This is consistent with the findings of Read within the CobWeb interface [8]. When asked why, students reported that they liked the appearance of letters produced via the keyboard better than the looks of those they drew themselves. This begs the question of whether automatic replacement of recognized student-drawn letters by nice-looking letters from a font would make

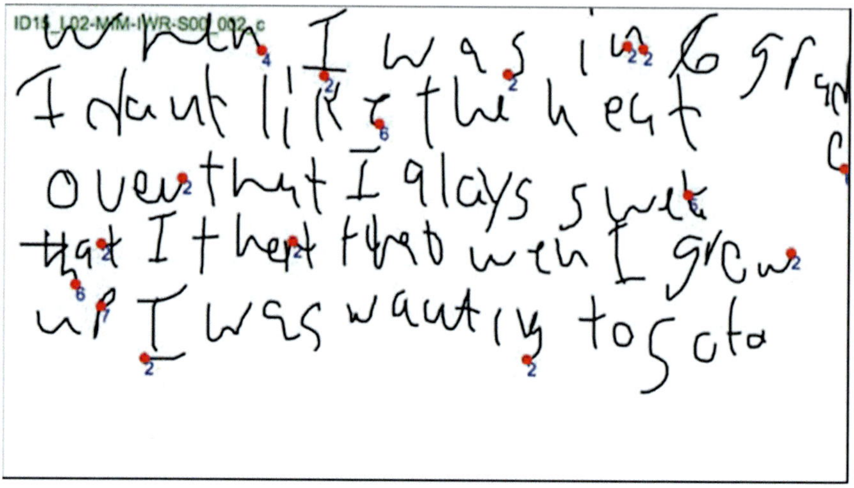

Fig. 4.16 Researcher's view provided by HAWK of pause length and location. A student's writing sample in the Minds in Motion module gives us more information about the process than the resulting text itself

the stylus or touch as desirable to the students as the keyboard. (We have not pursued this issue further.)

4.5.2 Analysis of Pauses

By capturing extensive data about the timing of student writing movements, we have the potential to learn about obstacles to students in the course of writing. Our instrumentation is less extensive than used by those studying the sensorimotor processes of writing [5], and yet we can offer new views to researchers who are looking for events, or lack thereof, in the writing process where problems occur. For example, Fig. 4.16 shows a view of one page of a student's composition which is automatically annotated with the loci, within the composition, where significant pauses took place during the student's process. The durations, in seconds, are also shown. Depending on location they may reflect thinking about forming the next letter, spelling the next word, or composing the rest of the sentence or the next sentence.

4.6 Conclusions

Stylus and touch-based interaction on tablets offer an effective set of affordances for writing instruction. The individualized tutoring provided by these systems is well-suited to the diversity of learning disabilities exhibited by special-needs learners.

Graphical feedback in writing is a rich research area with many possible approaches. However, the presentation of critical feedback must be balanced with students' tolerance for such criticism. Facilitation of self-assessment is an alternative approach. Further research is needed to carefully evaluate more of these schemes in terms of utility for assessment and for their appropriateness in student feedback.

Acknowledgments The authors gratefully acknowledge the support of this research under grant P50HD071764 from the Eunice Kennedy Shriver National Institute of Child Health and Human Development (NICHD) at the National Institutes of Health (NIH). We thank our co-workers at the University of Washington Learning Disabilities Research Center. Thanks also go to all the students who have used the software and to their parents who enabled their participation by bringing them to the university. We would also like to thank the reviewers for their encouragement and constructive suggestions.

References

1. Alstad Z, Sanders E, Abbott RD, Barnett AL, Henderson SE, Connelly V, Berninger VW (2015) Modes of alphabet letter production during middle childhood and adolescence: interrelationships with each other and other writing skills. J Writ Res 6(3):199
2. Berninger VW (2009) Highlights of programmatic, interdisciplinary research on writing. Learn Disabil Res Pract 24(2):69–80
3. Berninger VW, Winn WD, Stock P, Abbott RD, Eschen K, Lin SJC, Garcia N, Anderson-Youngstrom M, Murphy H, Lovitt D et al (2008) Tier 3 specialized writing instruction for students with dyslexia. Read Writ 21(1–2):95–129
4. Berninger VW, Nagy W, Tanimoto S, Thompson R, Abbott RD (2015) Computer instruction in handwriting, spelling, and composing for students with specific learning disabilities in grades 4–9. Comput Educ 81:154–168
5. Guinet E, Kandel S (2010) Ductus: a software package for the study of handwriting production. Behav Res Methods 42(1):326–332
6. Mann AM, Hinrichs U, Quigley A (2015) Digital pen technologys suitability to support handwriting learning. In: Hammond T, Valentine S, Adler A, Payton M (eds) The impact of pen and touch technology on education. Springer International Publishing, Switzerland, pp 7–22
7. Read JC (2008) Jabberwocky: children's digital ink story writing from nonsense to sense. In: Proceedings of the 3rd international conference on digital interactive media in entertainment and arts, DIMEA '08, ACM, New York, pp 85–90
8. Read JC, MacFarlane S, Casey C (2004) Cobweb-a handwriting recognition based writing environment for children. In: Proceedings of writing '04
9. Richards T, Berninger V, Stock P, Altemeier L, Trivedi P, Maravilla, K (2009) Feigned neurocognitive deficit: taxon or dimension? J Clin Exp Neuropsychol 29(8):1–17
10. Tanimoto S, Thompson R, Berninger V, Nagy W, Abbott R (2015) Computerized writing and reading instruction for students in grades 4–9 with specific learning disabilities affecting written language. J Comput Assist Learn 31(6):671–689

Chapter 5
Tablet-Based Technology to Support Students' Understanding of Division

Kimberle Koile and Andee Rubin

Abstract This article reports on the design, implementation, and testing of a new tablet-based tool designed to help upper elementary students develop a strong understanding of division. The tool provides an interactive visual model for the process of division and leverages students' understanding of the array as a model for multiplication. Classroom observations, preliminary analysis of student work, and feedback from both students and teachers in a 4th grade classroom, indicate that the tool has helped students increase their understanding of division and multiplication. The paper presents examples of student work that support this finding.

5.1 Problem Statement and Context

Many elementary school students struggle with division, and an inability to grasp and remember "long division" has been a tortuous part of many students' encounters with math in the upper elementary grades. This experience probably has persuaded many students that they are "bad at math." Division can be difficult, but it is also important. According to a 2012 study, "Analyses of large, nationally representative, longitudinal data sets from the United States and the United Kingdom revealed that elementary school students' knowledge of fractions and of division uniquely predicts those students' knowledge of algebra and overall mathematics achievement in high school, 5 or 6 years later, even after statistically controlling for other types of mathematical knowledge, general intellectual ability, working memory, and family income and education" [8]. While this study doesn't prove a cause and effect relationship between understanding division and later achievement in mathematics, helping students master division likely provides them with important support and the confidence to navigate more complex mathematical topics later.

K. Koile (✉)
MIT Center for Educational Computing Initiatives, Cambridge, MA, USA
e-mail: kkoile@mit.edu

A. Rubin
TERC, Cambridge, MA, USA
e-mail: andee_rubin@terc.edu

T. Hammond et al. (eds.), *Revolutionizing Education with Digital Ink*,
Human–Computer Interaction Series, DOI 10.1007/978-3-319-31193-7_5

An understanding of multiplication is an important prerequisite for division. Division, however, is conceptually more difficult for students than multiplication. Multiplication involves three main quantities: the size of a group, the number of groups, and the total number obtained by multiplying the group size by the number of groups. Division also involves a total number of objects, a group size, and number of groups, but in the process of working through a division problem, a student must also keep track of the number of groups already accounted for, the number of objects the groups represent, and the number of objects still to be grouped, all of which change as more groups are formed. Understanding division is further complicated by the fact that the operation is used to solve two very different categories of problems [9]. Problems called *quotative* have a grouping structure. In these problems, the total number of objects in consideration and the size of the groups into which they are to be partitioned are known; the number of groups that can be created from the objects is unknown. An example of a quotative problem is: Kiri has 28 donuts and wants to put 7 on each plate. How many plates can she fill? Problems called *partitive* have a sharing structure. In these problems, the total number of objects in consideration is known, as is the number of groups, but the size of the groups is unknown. An example of a partitive problem is: Jonah has 28 donuts to divide among 7 friends. How many donuts will each friend receive?

While people who have mastered division are not necessarily aware of these two different problem structures, students first encountering quotative and partitive division problems may see the two types of problems as unrelated and may approach them quite differently. In working on quotative problems, which specify total number of objects and group size, students have a tendency to create multiple groups of the appropriate size iteratively, counting how many grouped objects they have and adding groups until they reach the total [2]. So, at least at the start, students see quotative problems as involving repeated addition and comparing the sum of the number of grouped objects with the total number of objects. The student work in Fig. 5.1a, from a 4th grade class, illustrates this approach for a quotative problem.

Mastering partitive problems, which specify total number of objects and number of groups, requires students to understand that dealing out objects one at a time into groups results in an equal distribution of objects—a fact that is not obvious to many children. Once students realize this fact, they sometimes approach partitive problems by repeatedly subtracting one or more "rounds" of objects from the total until they have none left [2]. The student work in Fig. 5.1b, from the same 4th grade class, illustrates this approach to a partitive problem.

These two examples of student work illustrate both the kinds of thinking students do when they work on division problems and the pitfalls of their strategies. While the examples demonstrate successful attempts at solving division problems, there are many examples of students who embark on the same path but lose track along the way, especially when a strategy requires a long string of steps. In one such example for $72 \div 4$, shown in Fig. 5.1c, a student successively drew groups of four, keeping track of the accumulating total after each new group. He added correctly until he reached 24, at which point he drew a group of four but added eight to his total by mistake.

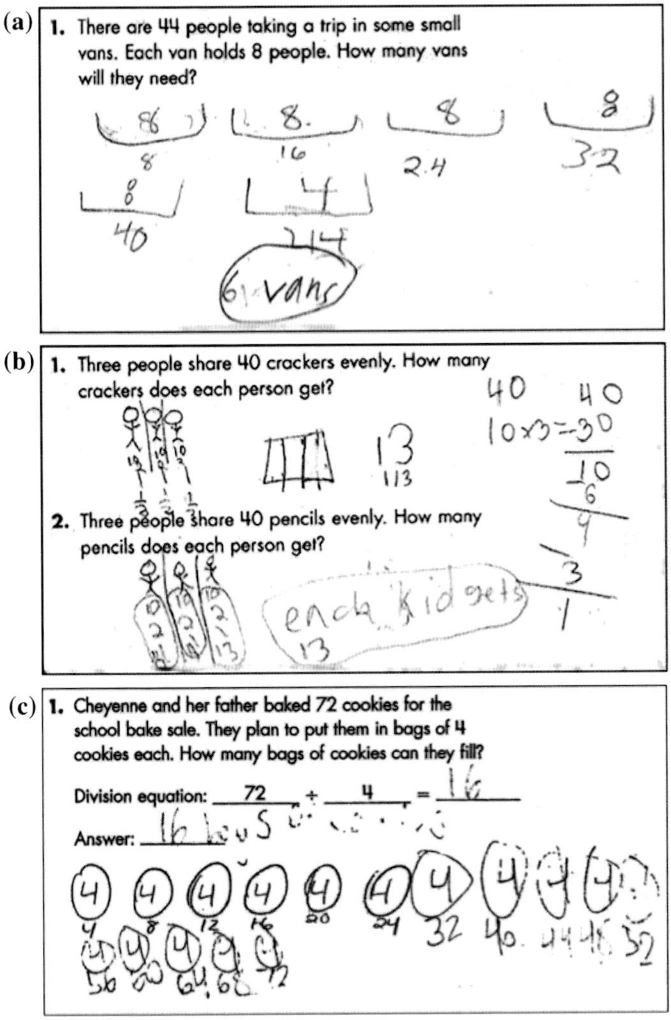

Fig. 5.1 **a** Example of student work for a quotative problem (size of group given); **b** Example of student work for a partitive problem (number of groups given); **c** Example of student losing track of counting in a division problem

Given both the difficulty and importance of division, helping students understand the conceptual basis of division is an important goal. Our work was guided by several perspectives on the learning of division: (1) Any approach to division, even the supposedly efficient long-division algorithm, has a bewildering set of numbers to keep track of. Whether the approach involves repeated addition or repeated subtraction, each time one more group is added or subtracted, several quantities change: the number of groups considered so far, the number of objects grouped so far, and the number of objects still to be grouped; (2) Understanding the relationship between multiplication and division is a crucial aspect of becoming proficient at division; and (3) Using arrays as a representation of multiplicative structures has the potential to help students see the relationship between multiplication and division and, eventually, to see the relationship between quotative and partitive division problems. This paper describes the tool we created to support students' understanding of division and our experiences using it with 4th grade students.

5.2 Related Work

Many of the educational software tools available for helping students learn division are "drill and practice" systems, which focus on developing mastery of multiplication and division facts rather than on understanding operations. Such systems, often with game-like formats, provide a series of structured exercises with immediate feedback and serve to review previously learned concepts rather than teaching new concepts. There are several tools, however, that focus on students' understanding of the operation of division, using visual models to reinforce the concept of grouping. One such example, Thinking Blocks (MathPlayground.com), supports students in creating bar models of division word problems. In these models, both dividend and divisor, i.e., group size, are represented as bars, and the task of dividing, at least for quotative problems, is figuring out how many divisor bars fit into the dividend bar. In the example shown in Fig. 5.2, a student is asked to fill in a model and find a solution for a quotative problem: Given the number of straws to create a kite and a total number of straws, find the number of kites that can be made. A student is provided with a bar model template and blocks representing the concepts of total (straws), group size (straws per kite), and unknown number of groups (kites, represented by the "?"), as shown in Fig. 5.2a. In a series of steps, the student adds both labels and numbers to the bar model, eventually arriving at Fig. 5.2b, where she can type in her answer.

The Rectangle Division tool from the National Library of Virtual Manipulatives (nlvm.usu.edu) is another tool that uses a visual model and the concept of groups to support students' understanding of division. Instead of the one-dimensional bar model used in Thinking Blocks, this tool uses an array model in which the dividend is represented as an array on a grid. The student can set both dividend and divisor with arrow keys to the right and a slider to the left of the grid, respectively. Changing the dividend or divisor causes the quotient and remainder, represented as blue and red shaded array cells, respectively, to change to reflect the new values. (See Fig. 5.3a) Students also can use the tool as shown in Fig. 5.3b, to request a division problem and create a visual representation to match it.

Dreambox (dreambox.com) also provides a tool that uses a visual grouping model for division. The Gumball Bag-O-Matic tool, shown in Fig. 5.4a, specifies a problem in terms of a total number of gumballs and a bag of a specified size; the students are to find the number of bags needed. This tool prompts students to practice a strategy for computing an answer: doing smaller "friendly" sub-problems. The visual model represents the dividend as a group of gumballs and the divisor as a bag of a certain

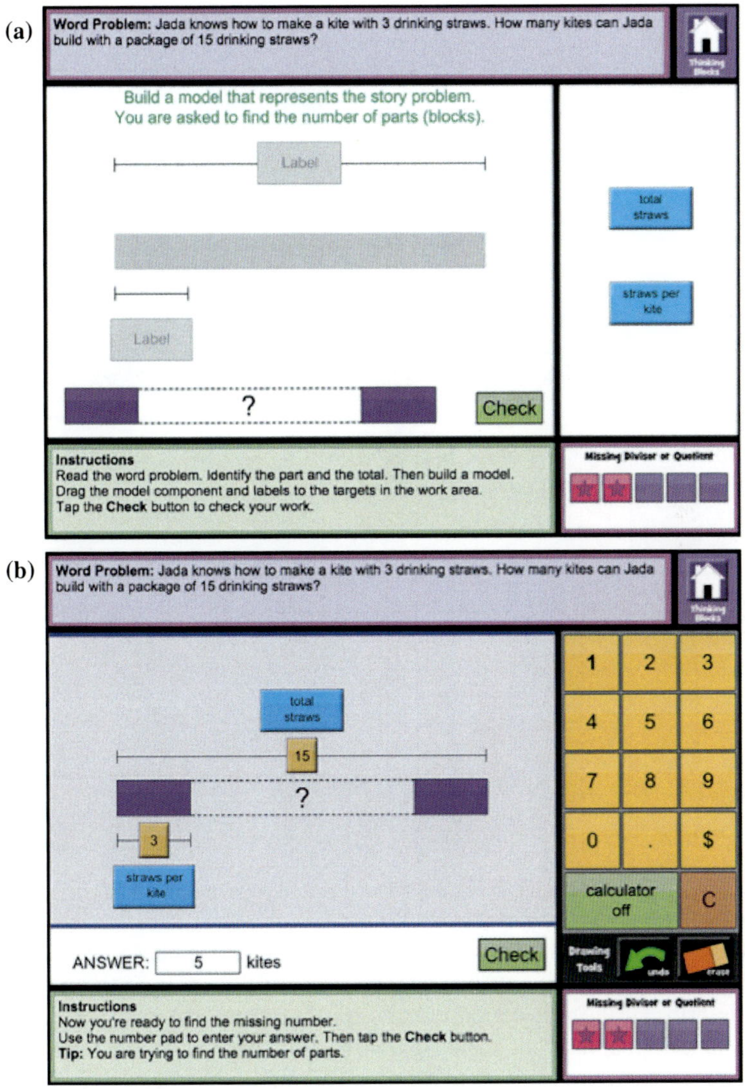

Fig. 5.2 **a** Quotative problem with bar model; **b** Student positions bars and numbers, then enters answer via number pad

size. Students work on the problem by specifying a number of bags to fill using an equation template. The tool keeps track of the intermediate states of the problem by displaying to the left of a divider the accumulating sum of grouped gumballs, to the right of the divider the number of ungrouped gumballs, and above the model the number of bags created so far. When no more bags can be added, the quotient is the

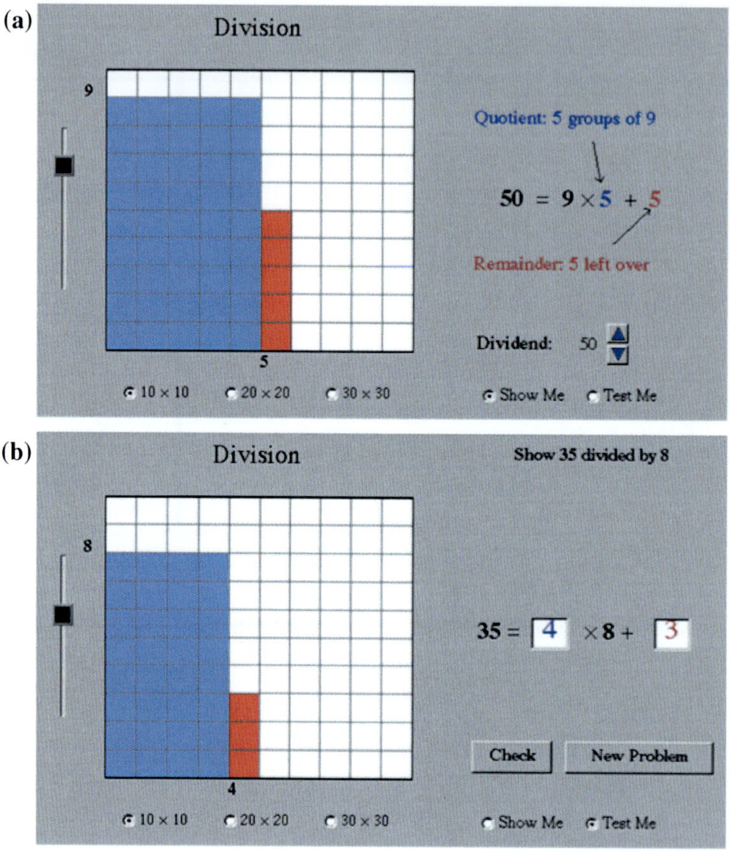

Fig. 5.3 **a** 50 ÷ 9 modeled with arrays; **b** Student is presented with a new problem

sum of the numbers at the top, and the remainder is the number to the right of the divider. (See Fig. 5.4b)

As described in the next section, our division tool shares features with each of these three examples, but also has some significant differences. Like the tools described above, our tool enables students to create visual models that reinforce the idea that division can be considered a process of figuring out the number of groups of a particular size that can be formed from a total. Our tool differs, however, in its consistent use of arrays for both dividend and intermediate sub-problems, as arrays explicitly support students in relating division to multiplication. Thus with our tool, students create sub-problems with arrays rather than with equations. Our tool enables students to create and modify their own models, resulting in a variety of student work that can serve as the basis for class discussion about alternate problem-solving strategies. Finally, because the tool is part of a tablet-based software system, students can annotate their models easily with a tablet pen in order to clarify and explain their work.

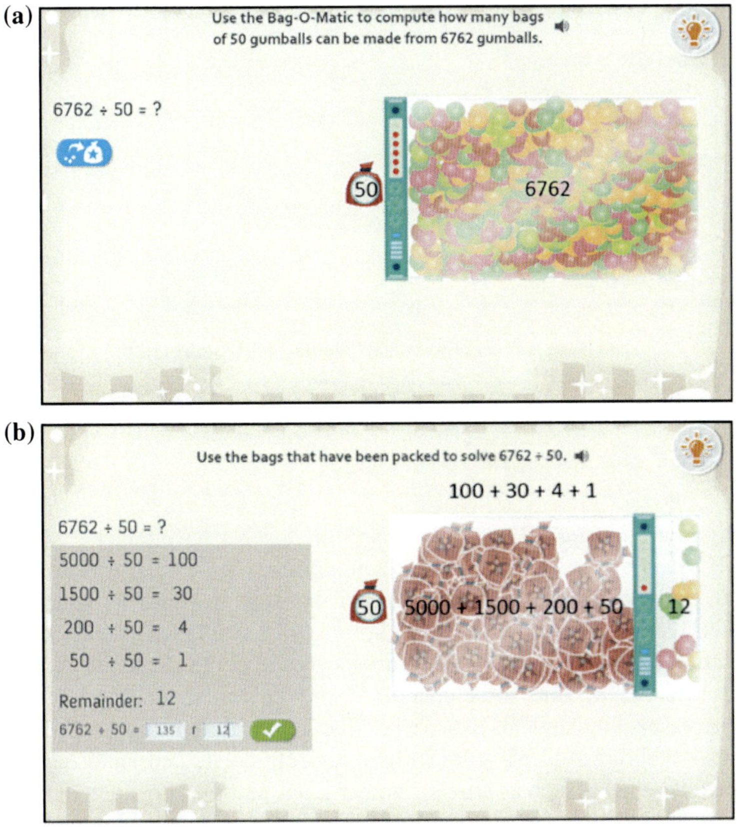

Fig. 5.4 **a** Student is presented with 6762 ÷ 50; **b** Quotient is sum above model, remainder is on right

5.3 Method Employed

The new tool reported in this paper was designed to help students develop a strong understanding of division. The tool enables students to visualize the repeated addition of quantities to reach a total and helps students keep track of the computation during this process. It is part of a tablet-based software system we have been developing called Classroom Learning Partner (CLP) [3–6]. CLP allows students to use a tablet pen to create answers to in-class problems and wirelessly send their answers to the teacher. Using CLP and a design-based research approach [1], we prototyped the new division tool, tested the tool in interviews with individual students and in a classroom setting, and used the results of testing to inform redesign.

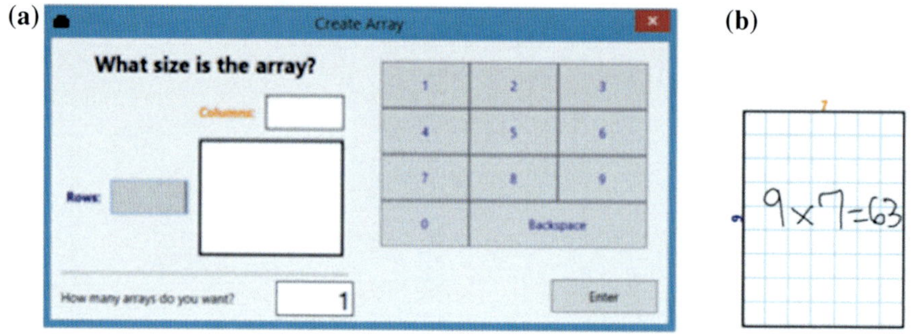

Fig. 5.5 **a** UI for specifying number of rows and columns; **b** 9x7 array created and annotated by a student

5.3.1 *CLP Background*

In a classroom using CLP, all students and the teacher have tablets,[1] and a tablet is connected to a projector. All tablets communicate via a local wireless network. CLP can be thought of as an electronic notebook, with pages on which students show their work. In the current CLP classrooms, that work involves the creation and modification of mathematical representations used in upper elementary school. CLP provides tools to facilitate these operations, and the tablet pen plays an important role: The pen enables students to use a familiar mode of interaction, namely writing, while also enabling students to quickly and easily create and annotate structured mathematical objects such as arrays, number lines, and the division tool reported in this paper. (See [7] for discussion of the importance of drawing and annotation in young students' learning of multiplication and division.)

The CLP tool most closely related to the division tool is the array tool, which is used to represent multiplicative relationships. Tapping on an array tool icon on CLPs command bar, a user is prompted to input numbers for rows and columns using a displayed number pad, shown in Fig. 5.5a.[2] An array of the specified size appears on the page. Shown in Fig. 5.5b, is a 9x7 array that a student has created and annotated.

5.3.2 *Division Template*

CLP's division tool provides an interactive visual model for the division process and leverages students' understanding of the array as a model for multiplication. A

[1]Students use Lenovo X201s; the teacher uses a Microsoft Surface Pro. CLP is written in C# and runs on Windows.

[2]Handwriting recognition software proved too inaccurate to support entry via handwritten numbers.

division problem is represented by what we call a division template, which can be thought of as an array with one unspecified dimension, which represents the quotient. The unspecified dimension is indicated by a wavy line at the right edge of the division template.[3] The specified dimension represents the divisor; the area enclosed by the division template represents the dividend. The template is particularly well-suited for quotative problems. For such problems, arrays represent groups of the specified size, and the area of an array represents the number of grouped objects. So a 9x1 array represents one group of nine objects, a 9x2 array represents two groups of nine objects, and so on. To solve a division problem using a template, a student creates a template by specifying the dividend and divisor, which are termed "product" and "factor" in order to make explicit connection to students' understanding of multiplication and arrays. The student then overlays arrays on the template until the template is "full", i.e., until the sum of the arrays' areas reaches the dividend or the unfilled area of the template is less than the divisor. When a template is full, the divisor is represented by the number of rows, the quotient is represented by the number of columns, and any remainder is represented by the unfilled area in the template.

To give visual feedback and to facilitate moving the template on the screen, arrays are "snapped" into the template so that they become a part of the template itself. A student may create and snap in a variety of small arrays or a single large array. To help students keep track of the changing state of the division problem, the template shows the original dividend, the snapped-in arrays' area so far, and the remaining area needed to reach the dividend. It also gives feedback by displaying the template boundary in red if a student attempts to snap in an array that is too large or has the wrong dimensions.

Figure 5.6 illustrates the use of a division template for a problem such as: Given 55 cookies and bags that hold 7 cookies, how many bags are needed? In this problem, the dividend of 55 cookies is represented as the total area of the template, the divisor of 7 cookies per bag is represented both as the number of rows in the template and as a 7x1 array, which represents the bag, and the quotient, i.e., the unknown number of bags, is represented by the number of columns needed to fill the division template. In Fig. 5.6a, the student has created a division template representing the problem. The template shows the dividend of 55 in the center of the template and the divisor of 7 along the left side of the template. Figure 5.6b shows the result of snapping in a 7x1 array and a 7x2 array: The arrays are inside the template, the accumulated array area is reported below the template as the equation $7 \times 3 = 21$, and the remaining area of 34 is reported in the "empty" space of the template. Figure 5.6c shows the full division template, with four snapped-in arrays: one 7x1 and three 7x2 arrays. The division template reports the original dividend of 55, an array area total shown at the bottom as the equation $7 \times 7 = 49$, and a remaining area of 6. From this representation the student can identify that there are 7 groups of 7 in 55, with 6 left over, so $55 \div 7$ is 7 remainder 6.

[3]Interviewed students thought that the wavy line was the clearest representation. Other designs included omitting the right edge entirely, dotting the right edge, or shading the edge so as to appear to fade into the background.

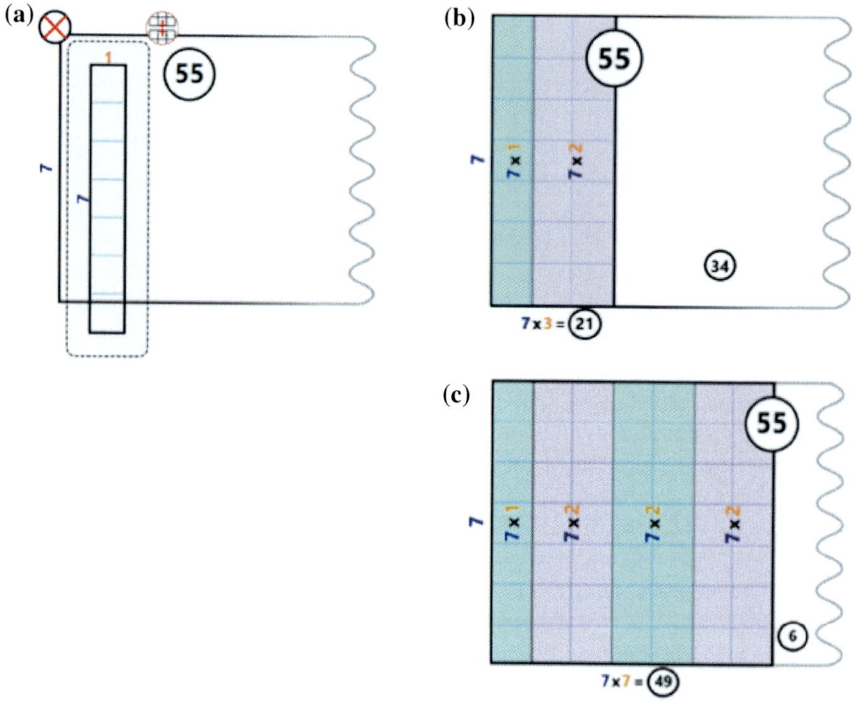

Fig. 5.6 Sequence of operations (**a**–**c**) in creating and filling a division template for 55 ÷ 7. **a** Template is created, then 7x1 array is created and will be dragged, then snapped in by tapping icon on the upper right corner of array; **b** 7x1 and 7x2 arrays snapped in, numbers updated automatically; **c** Full division template, answer is 7 remainder 6

The above example is a quotative division problem. The template also can be used for partitive problems: The group size is represented by the number of columns and the number of groups is represented by the number of rows. Adding an array corresponds to adding objects to each of the groups.

In the course of developing the division tool, we realized that the concept of division could be made even clearer if students had a visual representation for the objects still to be grouped. We developed a second version of the tool that employs "tiles"—small squares the size of an array's cells. The use of this version of the tool is shown in Fig. 5.7. The key idea is that the tiles reflect the current state of the division template: When the template is created, tiles are displayed as an additional representation for the dividend; as an array is created, the tiles corresponding to the array's area are automatically highlighted; then when an array is snapped into the template, the tiles automatically disappear as they are "added to" the template via the array.

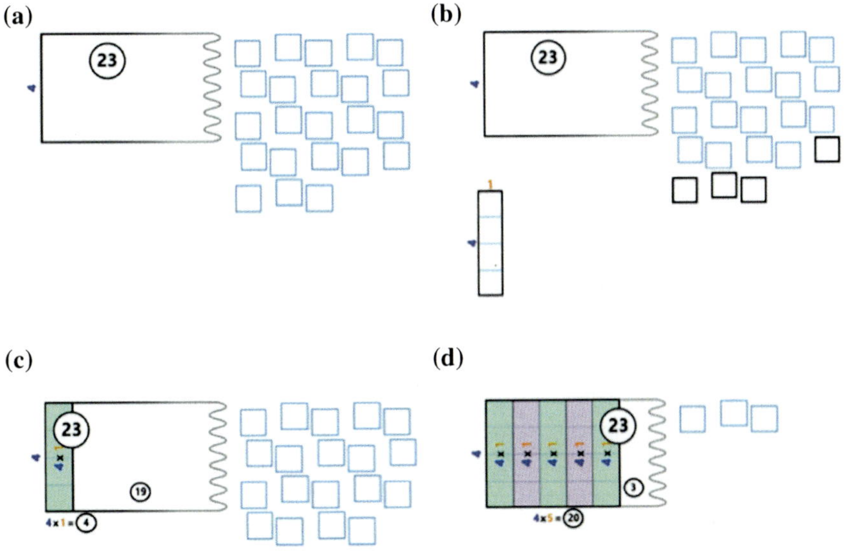

Fig. 5.7 Sequence of operations (**a–d**) in using a division template with tiles for 23 ÷ 4 **a** Division template created, template and 23 tiles displayed for dividend; **b** 4x1 array created, 4 corresponding tiles turn *black*; **c** 4x1 snapped in, corresponding tiles disappear; **d** Full template, tiles represent remainder

5.3.3 *Design Decisions*

One of the early design decisions was to have the division template support students by keeping track of the quantities involved in division, especially those that change as the student works through the problem. Three such quantities are always connected by an additive relationship: the total (dividend), the number already added to the template, and the number still left. The second and third numbers always add up to the first. The division template emphasizes the quantities, via circling, in order to help students notice and track the relationship among the quantities. The division template also helps students keep track of the arrays they have added: alternating colors for the arrays enable the individual arrays to be more easily seen, which makes it more obvious to the student that the array areas are being added to reach the total. The division template also uses color to distinguish the horizontal and vertical dimensions of the array: Anything referring to the vertical dimension is in blue, and anything referring to the horizontal dimension is in orange. This scheme means that all the blue numbers are the same—since all arrays that are snapped into the template have the same vertical dimension, i.e., number of rows. It also means that the orange numbers displayed inside the arrays always sum to the orange number shown in the equation below the template.

With any digital tool that supports students in developing computational fluency, there is always the question of how much computation to do for the student and how much to leave to the student. Our division template takes on much of the computational burden for the student, always updating the "number already added" and the "number still left." Doing this kind of bookkeeping for students runs the risk of making them dependent on the tool, but we decided that it was important for students to have this support in order for them to develop an overall model of division and confidence in their ability to navigate the process. A next step would be to gradually take away some of the support and transfer to the student more responsibility for keeping track of the computation.

We based the design of the division template on an array model for both multiplication and division for several reasons. Because students had used an array model for multiplication, carrying over this visual representation into the division template helped students to see the relationship between multiplication and division explicitly and to realize that knowledge of multiplication was relevant to division. Using arrays also sets the stage for students to eventually make the connection between quotative and partitive division contexts, as they can see that an array representing N groups of M is really the same structure as one representing M groups of N, only rotated [2, p. 54]. While we did not take advantage of this connection in our classroom work, we wanted to provide students with a model that would be able to support this understanding.

5.4 Results and Evaluation

We spent five weeks in a 4th grade classroom in Cambridge, MA, working with 19 students on a multiplication and division unit from TERC's Investigations curriculum, which we had adapted for use with our tablet-based software. Students did all of their math work on the tablets during this unit, allowing us to easily collect it, including re-playable interaction histories of their work on each problem. We took detailed field notes during class and interviewed several students at the end of the unit. During the last two weeks, the students used the division tool. Our ongoing analysis is qualitative in nature; our goal is to identify interesting patterns in the ways in which students use the division template in order to discover how the template may or may not support students' understanding of division.

Classroom observations, preliminary analysis of student work, and feedback from both students and teachers, indicate that the tool helped students, particularly those struggling with the concept of remainders, increase their understanding of division and multiplication. The visual representations enabled some students to grasp concepts that were difficult for them when they had only algorithmic methods to solve problems. The tool provided a specific starting point for students unsure of how to approach a problem, enabled students to create representations quickly without perseverating over details, and enabled struggling students to work more confidently and independently. The tool also enabled students to make visible the variety of strategies that could be used to solve problems, which supported valuable class discussions of alternate problem-solving strategies. Below are examples that illustrate these findings.

5.4.1 Understanding Division

The division tool's visual representation helped some students understand a difficult concept that was obscured when just using an algorithm. Seth was quite fluent in his ability to do long division using the traditional algorithm. Shown in Fig. 5.8a is his solution to 256 ÷ 16 via the traditional method. When we asked him in an interview also to do the problem using the division tool, he began with a 16x1 array, mimicking his "1" as the first digit of the solution (Fig. 5.8b). When he saw what happened, he was puzzled, because, as he said, "I thought this [referring to his long division problem] would be the same as the division tool, but it's not". The interviewer proceeded to show the student what would happen if he had added a 16x10 array (Fig. 5.8c) rather than a 16x1 array. For Seth, this step resulted in a major breakthrough in his understanding of place value in division, as he said, "I never thought of this [using red ink to circle the 1 and to add a 0 in his long division solution (Fig. 5.8d)]. I just thought of this as a 1, but it's really a 10." The student then added 16x13 and 16x2 arrays to fill the template. The final state of his work page is shown in Fig. 5.8e.

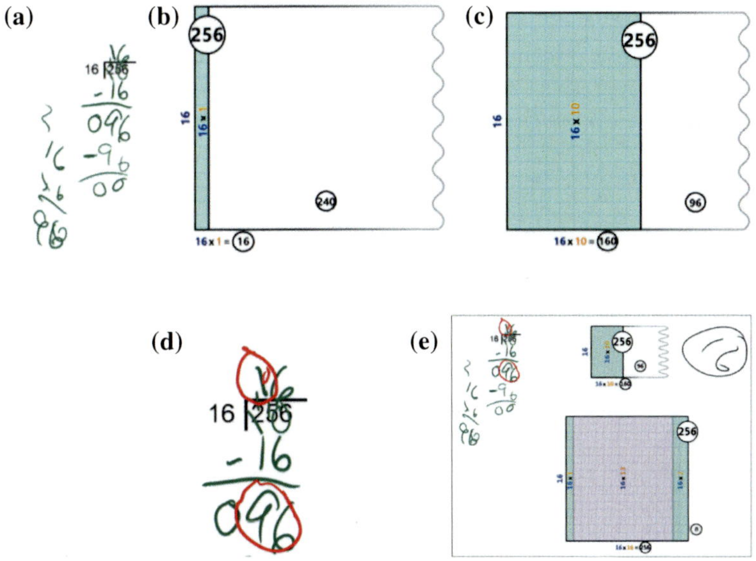

Fig. 5.8 **a** Student's algorithm use; **b** Student's partially filled template; **c** Interviewer's suggestion; **d** Student's annotation; **e** Final state of work page, with student's full template shown at the *bottom* (interviewer's template at top was resized)

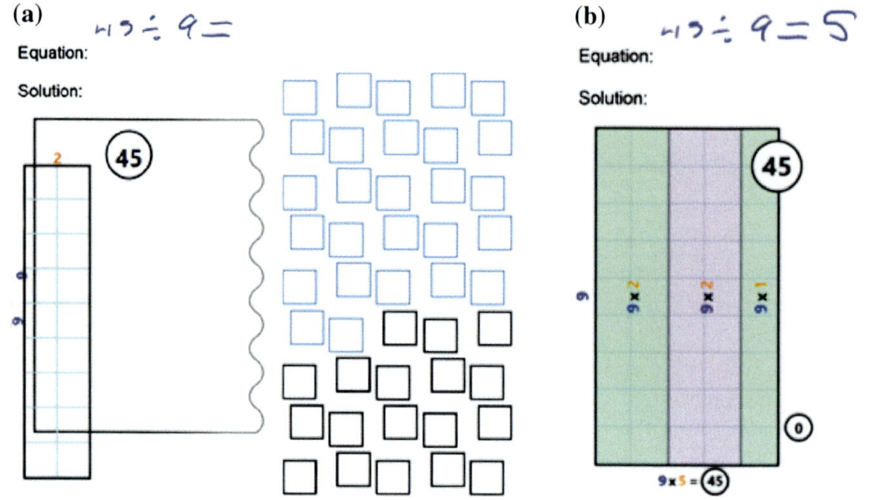

Fig. 5.9 A student uses tiles to help solve the division problem 45 ÷ 9. **a** Student creates a division template for 45 ÷ 9, creates 9x2 array; then 18 tiles for the array turn black; **b** Full division template showing student solved the problem by snapping in 9x2 and 9x1 arrays

The division template with tiles helped students better understand division, especially those struggling with the concept of remainders. Ivan did not have a clear understanding of division, particularly division with remainders, prior to using the division template. When introduced to the tiles version of the division template, he began using that version almost exclusively. He said that he liked the tiles because "tiles help you because it shows you what's left over. It helps you understand division." He was able to quickly create representations using a template and tiles. An example of his using the tiles is shown in Fig. 5.9. In subsequent problems, he was able to use the division template without tiles to create correct representations and find solutions.

5.4.2 *Using Structure and Organization*

The division tool gave students a starting point when working problems and helped them better organize their work. Ariel's math work on pencil and paper tended to be disorganized, and her solutions had many mistakes that appeared to be careless. When using the division tool, however, she created very organized representations; both she and her teacher remarked on the difference the tool made. An example of her work is shown in Fig. 5.10. Replaying the *interaction history*, i.e., the sequence of actions the student performed in creating representations, shows that she worked quickly and easily with no false starts. In addition, her annotation of "tada, as easy

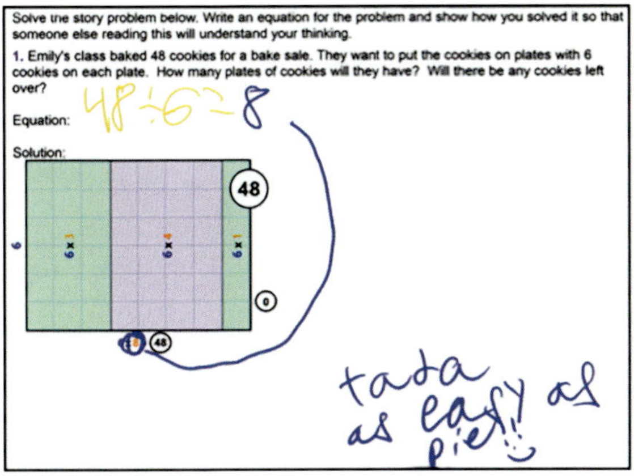

Fig. 5.10 Student example showing organized answer and confidence

as pie" shows a confidence that her teacher says was lacking from earlier lessons. For this student, as well as others, the teacher also noted that the tool slowed kids down and reduced careless errors.

5.4.3 *Working with Independence and Confidence*

The division tool also helped some students work more independently and confidently than when they solved math problems using pencil and paper. Kaitlin was below grade level in her math skills, and the teacher typically gave her problems with smaller numbers than the rest of the class got. Kaitlin also was anxious about math and had difficulty working independently. When using the tablets, and the division tool in particular, the teachers working with her noted that her anxiety was greatly reduced, she could work independently, and she no longer needed to be given smaller numbers. Prior to working with the division tool, Kaitlin had limited knowledge of division. While using the tool, she was able to start and complete division problems without assistance. She also contributed to class discussion, which the teacher reported was a rare occurrence. An example of her work with the division tool is shown in Fig. 5.11. Replay of the interaction history for this example shows that she completed the work without unnecessary actions.

5.4.4 *Creating a Variety of Representations*

The examples shown in Figs. 5.10 and 5.11 illustrate the tool's support for a variety of problem-solving strategies. The student work in Fig. 5.10 shows solving $48 \div 6$ with

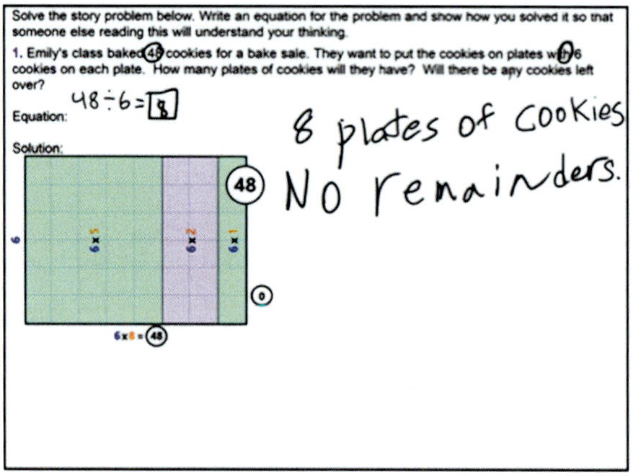

Fig. 5.11 Student example worked independently and with confidence

arrays of 6x3, 6x4, and 6x1; the work in Fig. 5.11 shows 6x5, 6x2, and 6x1. Other students chose 6x4 and 6x4; 6x2, 6x3, and 6x3; or 6x7 and 6x1. These variations in student work provide useful fodder for class discussions of different approaches to division, with an emphasis on efficiency ("How could you do this problem using fewer arrays?") and familiar number relationships ("What multiplication fact could you use to get started on this problem?").

5.5 Current and Future Work

We are continuing our data analysis, focusing on evidence of the affordances and effects of the division tool on students' understanding of division. In addition, we are continuing our work on developing and testing automatic analysis routines that will enable the software to interpret students representations [5]. Such interpretation enables students' thinking to be made visible to the teacher, who can more easily identify students who need help or choose student work for public display as a basis for class discussion. The analysis routines operate on both a representation and a students' interaction history, which captures the process of creating the representation. By analyzing the sequence of actions in creating each of the correct division templates shown in Fig. 5.12, for example, the analysis routines report that the student whose work is shown in Fig. 5.12a had no extraneous steps, which would indicate that the student understood how to use the tool to solve the problem. For the example in Fig. 5.12b, the analysis routines report that the student had a false start (creating a template then deleting it, then creating another one), created arrays that were too large to snap in, and tried many times to add an array when the remainder was smaller than the divisor, an action that, through observation and interview, can be identified as indicating a misunderstanding of remainders. We are studying our corpus of student

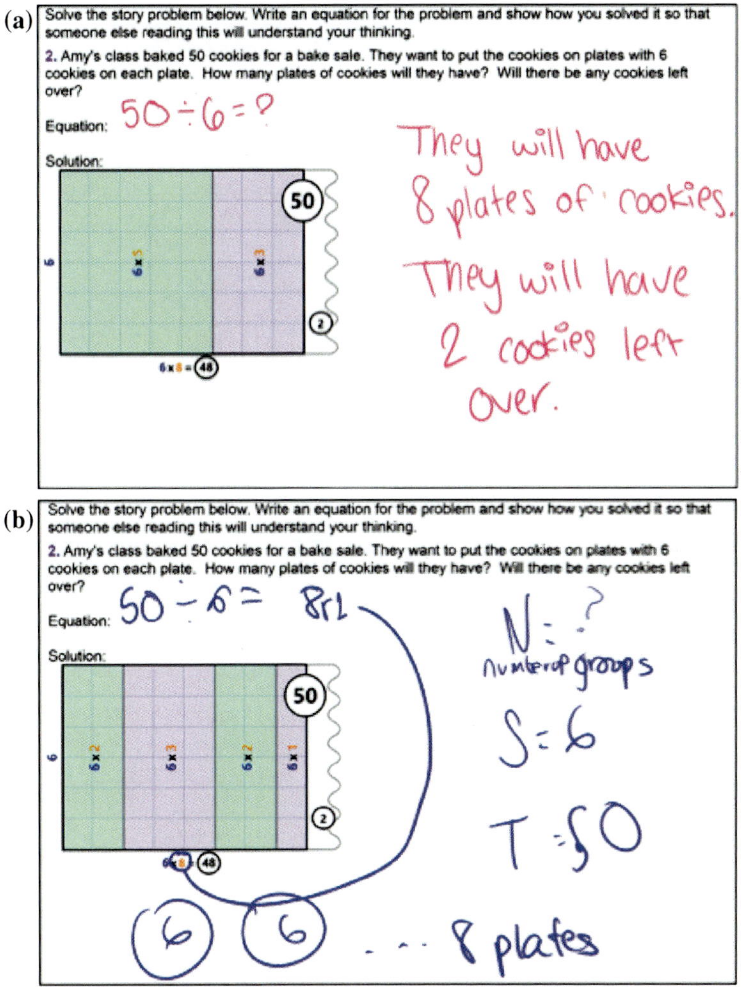

Fig. 5.12 **a** Analysis of interaction history indicates that the student had no trouble; **b** Analysis of interaction history indicates that the student had trouble with the concept of remainder

work in order to identify additional sequences of actions that will provide insight into what students do and do not understand about division.

We have prototyped a new division tool to be used with younger students who have not yet been introduced to arrays. The new tool is based on CLP's stamp representation [5, 7] and enables students to create a pictorial representation of partitive and quotative division problems and use either sharing or grouping strategies, respectively. It also keeps track of relevant numbers in the problem. A student starts by drawing an image to represent an object and another image to represent a group. (See the images in the boxes at the top of Fig. 5.13a, b.) She copies the object image,

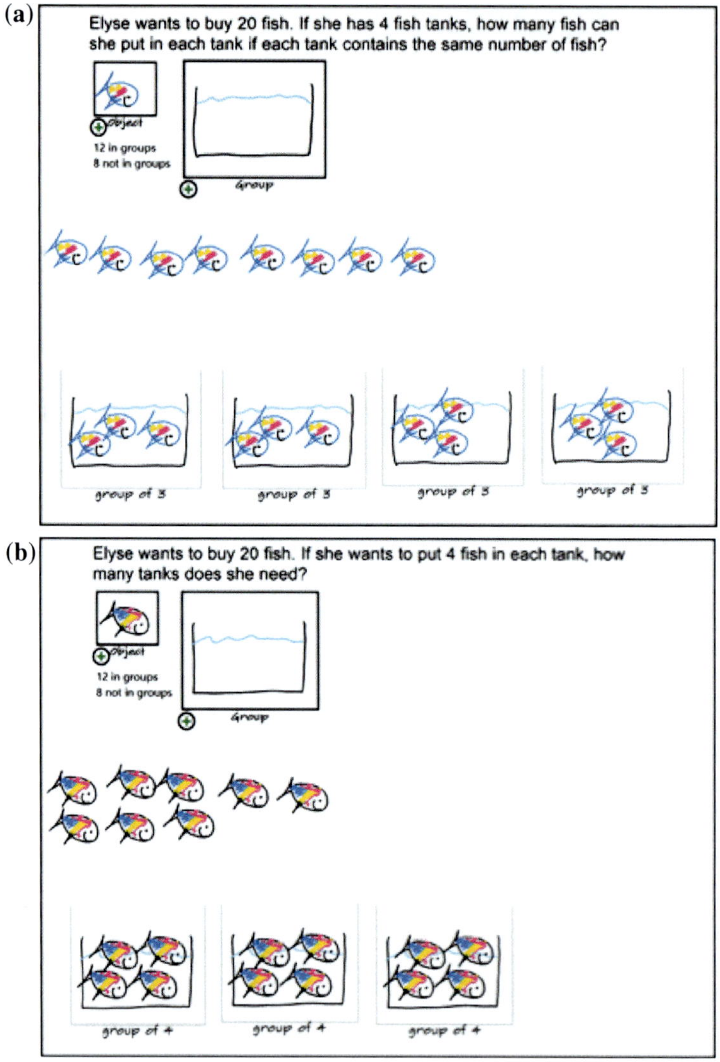

Fig. 5.13 **a** Dealing out: 20 objects and 4 groups created, 12 objects dealt into groups, 8 remain; **b** Grouping: 20 objects and 1 group created, 4 objects moved into the group, duplicating the group moves 8 objects into new groups

using a "+" operator, to make a "pile" containing the number of objects specified in the problem. If the number of groups is given, and the size of group is unknown, she uses a sharing strategy: She creates the given number of groups, using the "+" operator on the group image and drags all the objects onto the groups (see Fig. 5.13a). She is finished when all objects are in groups and each group contains the same number of objects. CLP keeps track of and reports the number of objects in each group below each group image. If the size of a group is given instead, she uses a grouping strategy: She creates one group object, drags the number of specified objects into the group object, then duplicates the group until all objects have been moved from the pile into groups (see Fig. 5.13b).

We plan to study how 2nd graders use this new stamp-based division tool and to continue studying how 3rd and 4th graders use the array-based tool. Such research will contribute significantly to our continued investigation of the role tablet-based technology can play in deepening students' conceptual understanding of division.

Acknowledgments This research is funded by the NSF INK-12: Teaching and Learning Using Interactive Ink Inscriptions project, DRL-1020152 (Koile), DRL-1019841 (Rubin); many thanks to program officers Michael Haney, Robert Gibbs, and Andres Henriquez. The PIs gratefully acknowledgment contributions from MITs CLP research group members Steve Chapman, Liz Simon, Casey McNamara, Matt Peairs, Claire DeRosa, and Eryn Maynard. The PIs also very much thank Lily Ko and Marlene Kliman at TERC, and David Reider at Education Design, Inc.

References

1. Collective DBRC (2003) Design-based research: an emerging paradigm for educational inquiry. Educ Res 32(1):5–8
2. Fosnot CT, Dolk M (2001) Young mathematicians at work: constructing multiplication and division. Heinemann, Portsmouth
3. Koile K, Chevalier K, Rbeiz M, Rogal A, Singer D, Sorensen J, Smith A, Tay KS, Wu K (2007) Supporting feedback and assessment of digital ink answers to in-class exercises. In: Proceedings of the national conference on artificial intelligence 2007, vol 2. AAAI Press; Menlo Park, CA, pp 1787–1794
4. Koile K, Reider D, Rubin A (2010) INK-12: a pen-based wireless classroom interaction system for K-12. The impact of tablet PCs and pen-based technology on education: evidence and outcomes. Purdue University Press, West Lafayette, pp 93–102
5. Koile K, Rubin A (2015) Machine interpretation of students' hand-drawn mathematical representations. In: Hammond T, Valentine S, Adler A, Payton M (eds) The impact of pen and touch technology on education. Springer International Publishing, Switzerland, pp 49–56
6. McIntosh A, Reys BJ, Reys RE (1992) A proposed framework for examining basic number sense. For the Learning of Mathematics 12(3):2–44
7. Rubin A, Storeygard J, Koile K (2015) Supporting special needs students in drawing mathematical representations. In: Hammond T, Valentine S, Adler A, Payton M (eds) The impact of pen and touch technology on education. Springer International Publishing, Switzerland, pp 57–66
8. Siegler RS, Duncan GJ, Davis-Kean PE, Duckworth K, Claessens A, Engel M, Susperreguy MI, Chen M (2012) Early predictors of high school mathematics achievement. Psychol Sci 23(7):691–697
9. Wickett M, Ohanian S, Burns M (2002) Lessons for introducing division: Grades 3–4. Math Solutions, Sausalito

Chapter 6
A Tablet-Based Math Tutor for Beginning Algebra

Guan Wang, Nathaniel Bowditch, Robert Zeleznik, Musik Kwon, and Joseph J. LaViola Jr.

Abstract This paper presents an interactive mathematical tutor application to assist middle school students with solving single-variable linear and quadratic equations and two-variable systems of linear equations. The system uses a gestural, pen-based interface to mimic and enhance the traditional step-by-step method of solving algebraic problems on paper. After the student handwrites each step, the system detects any mistakes, highlights incorrect terms or wrong expressions, and provides specific, localized messages to help the student understand their errors. Two qualitative user studies were conducted at a local school to gather general feedback from some students and their math teacher. Results indicate that most students found the application easy to learn and fun to use. Real-time mistake detection and highlighting of incorrect terms informed students of their errors and improved their ability to solve similar problems. Although many students found the mistake detection and highlighting helpful, our studies also suggested that some students needed more active help. We are currently conducting a Wizard of Oz study to rapidly investigate enhancements to the user experience, which may address this limitation.

G. Wang (✉) · N. Bowditch
Department of Computer Science, Brown University, Providence, RI 02912, USA
e-mail: wang@cs.brown.edu

N. Bowditch
Digital Results Group Inc., 125 Summer Street, Boston, MA 02110, USA
e-mail: nbowditch@cs.brown.edu; nhbowditch@gmail.com

R. Zeleznik
Brown University, Box 1910, Providence, RI 02912, USA
e-mail: bcz@cs.brown.edu

M. Kwon
Samsung Electronics, Co., Ltd., 129 Samsung-ro, Suwon-si, Gyeonggi-do 443-742, South Korea
e-mail: musik.kwon@gmail.com

J.J. LaViola Jr.
Dept. of EECS, University of Central Florida, 4000 Central Florida Blvd., Orlando, FL 32816, USA
e-mail: jjl@eecs.ucf.edu

T. Hammond et al. (eds.), *Revolutionizing Education with Digital Ink*, Human–Computer Interaction Series, DOI 10.1007/978-3-319-31193-7_6

6.1 Problem Statement and Context

6.1.1 Problem Statement

Traditionally in middle school mathematics, students first learn a new method or concept in class through their teacher. For algebra problems, methods of solving are taught to be executed step by step, with each step resulting in a new equation that is closer to the solution. Students then practice applying these methods by solving equations outside of the classroom, using pencil and paper. However, if a student makes a mistake while doing the assignment, it will go unnoticed until after the teacher has corrected and returned the assignment, and the student will have missed an opportunity to learn at the time of the mistake.

Though real-time error detection systems do exist for such problems, they do not support pen-and-touch handwriting for math, and usually only work for a limited set of problems tailored for the system [9]. That is to say, they only allow students to work on the problems stored in a database, which limits the number of practice problems. Additionally, existing step-by-step feedback systems often fail to accurately detect the wrong term when a student makes a mistake. Usually the extent of the feedback is a general indication of error, such as a message saying "You've made a mistake." Though this is useful, it is insufficient for many students who have not fully mastered the mathematical concepts. Furthermore, most existing systems support a limited number of solution methods, often accepting only a single solution path. Students should be encouraged to be proficient in many different solution methods [7, 10]. Finally, most existing intelligent tutoring systems (ITS) are time-consuming to design and build, requiring considerable manual effort to enter the specific information for each area of study.

In this paper, we present an interactive mathematical tutor application, Math Tutor, to help middle school students solve beginner-level algebra equations with an experience similar to traditional pen-and-paper methods using touch screen control. Math Tutor is an Android application designed to run on tablets and large touch-screen devices. It helps students solve equations by having them write out each step one at a time and checking their work using rule-based error detection. The application strives for an experience like that of writing on "intelligent" paper, although its internal rule-based nature means it is not an ITS. Students can directly handwrite mathematical expressions, scribble over mistakes to erase their input, make scratch-work in the margins of previous steps, and use familiar pinch-to-zoom and panning gestures to interact with the plots of the equations. The application is partly powered by a math recognizer developed by Samsung Electronics that interprets the students' handwriting as mathematical expressions. By doing the work on a tablet, students get the same self-guided practice as on paper, with the addition of automatic, in situ feedback. The current scope includes:

- linear single-variable equations
- quadratic single-variable equations
- two-variable systems of linear equations.

The system is generalized so that it works on any equation within this scope, and is not limited by a specific database of problems. Moreover, as long as a student's solution steps are valid, the system allows any method of reaching a solution. By analyzing each expression the student enters, the system can identify mistakes as they occur and identify the likely cause of the error. The system then provides user feedback in the form of highlighting "wrong" terms, and displaying a text message specific to the mistake and intended to explain why the input is wrong.

6.1.2 Related Work

There have been numerous attempts at creating interactive tutoring applications, with some works spanning back decades. In a 2011 study, Kurt Van Lehn demonstrated that automatic, computer-based tutoring systems, ITSs, were about as effective at teaching students as human tutoring [9]. The physics tutors used in the study are very similar to ours in that they work at finer granularities than answer-based systems [10]. Van Lehn's model inspired us to focus on step-by-step feedback for students and how to make it more specific and helpful.

Anderson, J.R. has led his team in CMU and his company, Carnegie Learning, to apply cognitive psychology to education, and developed a set of ITS projects. They provide cognitive tutors with a large scope of math and spend years to evaluate their effect [6]. Another project, a website (https://mathtutor.web.cmu.edu), covers a wide breadth of beginner-level algebra and arithmetic, and uses a variety of modules for different topics. Like our application, the modules are interactive and inform the student of mistakes. However, the interface for the module on solving algebra equations is primarily implemented through textboxes and other WIMP controls. Additionally, the error messages fail to highlight the mistake in the problem itself [1, 2]. Finally, the system draws on a database of problems, rather than working for any general problem. Students cannot, for example, use the system for help on problems from their textbooks.

There are also many other websites that can solve equations and algebra problems, such as Mathomatic, IXL, Khan Academy, Algebra.com, Wolfram Alpha and more [4, 5, 7, 8]. While many of these sites, such as Wolfram Alpha, provide solutions to any general equation, there is little to no direction how to reach these solutions. When they provide paths to a solution, they do not support following a student through the solution process and pointing out mistakes as they are made. Moreover, almost all of these products take only typing and clicking as input, and distance students from the familiar process of solving equations out in handwriting.

6.2 Gu2 Method Employed

6.2.1 User Experience

From a user experience standpoint, Math Tutor strives to feel similar to solving a problem with pen and paper [3]. In order for the system to catch mistakes, it requires that steps be entered one at a time. Our interface divides the screen into top and bottom sections. The top section holds the input from the previous step, and allows for scratch-work to be overdrawn. Scratch-work is ignored by the system, but can be useful to the student. The bottom section expects the next step; this can be one or two equations, depending on the type of the problem. As previously mentioned, the user writes an equation by hand using a stylus. The input is interpreted by a math recognizer and rendered in a typeset font at the top of this section so that the user can ensure the interpretation is correct. When the user is satisfied with the input, he can submit the step to be checked for mistakes. If a mistake is detected, the system will attempt to highlight what it believes to be incorrect, and provide the user with a message explaining the mistake. If the step is a correct final solution, the user has the option to view a graph of the original problem in a floating widget. Since this interface only allows two steps (the previous and current steps) to be viewed at a time, we include a sidebar listing the entire step history for review.

6.2.2 Implementation

It is important to note that while our application has behavior similar to ITSs, it cannot be classified as such, since it is powered by a set of algebraic rules rather than deep-model artificial intelligence. At each step in the problem we first calculate the solutions to the newly-entered expression. We then check whether or not the user's input has the same solutions as the original problem. If it doesn't, we must determine what mistake was made. To do this, we look at the previous step and perform a pattern matching analysis. Internally, our application maps a list of rules to certain patterns of equations. We divide the rules into different categories:

- Basic algebra rules: adding (to both sides of the equation), subtracting, multiplying, dividing, combining like terms, simplifying, factoring out coefficient, distributing
- Quadratic problems: quadratic formula, making square term, extracting roots, factorizing
- System of equations problems: combining equations, substituting …

With a combination of the rules, we can support more than thirty kinds of logical user actions. Thus, for any given equation, we can analyze what rules apply to it and create a set of new equations that could logically follow as the next step. Each equation in this set is annotated by the rules that were used to reach this equation. We then compare the user's input to each of the equations in this set and look for the most similar match. As a result we can form an accurate guess of what the user was trying to do when the mistake was made, as well as what specific term is incorrect. This information is used to highlight the problematic term and create an error message to inform the user of the mistake. If no close match is found, the mistake is too "out of bounds" for the system to recognize, and a general error message is displayed.

Because of its rule-based structure, our system is easy to design, build, and extend. Unlike most traditional ITS systems that require complementary pedagogical models for new content, our application can support a new scope of algebra by simply adding a solver for the new type of problems, new rules for valid next steps, and new actions and error messages. All the general mistakes that have been supported will work automatically for new scopes. Our model makes it possible to save large amount of work time for extension, which is important for such a tutoring system.

6.2.3 Use Case Scenario

When a student begins using the application, the first step is to enter the problem to be solved. The user is presented with three main sections, as previously described. The first step is special because there is no previous step, so the handwriting area is in the top section. We make this clear by graying out the bottom section. Additionally, the user can clear the contents of the handwriting area using the eraser button on the bottom right of the section, as seen in Fig. 6.1.

In this example, the user is attempting to solve a system of equations, as seen in Fig. 6.2. The application automatically detects it is solving a system when the first equation has two variables. After entering the equations, the background texture of the top section changes to solid white and the buttons disappear. A new handwriting section slides in on the bottom with the same "handwriting" background texture.

Fig. 6.1 The start of the application

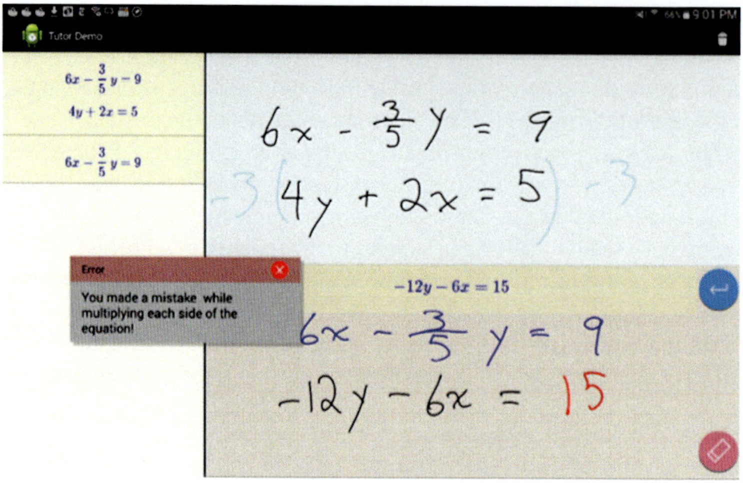

Fig. 6.2 A highlighted incorrect term and error message when a mistake is detected

Additionally, the user can review all the past steps on the left sidebar. In this example, the user is trying to combine the equations to isolate a variable. To do this, he wants to multiply both sides of the equation by "−3." To make this clear to himself, he marks it in the margins of the previous step. The application's internal rules anticipate this strategy, so when the user makes a mistake multiplying, it can highlight the incorrect term and provide a specific error message.

Thanks to the error message, the user can quickly identify and correct the error. The next step is to combine the equations to get rid of the "x." The user tries to combine the coefficients, but makes a mistake. Fortunately, the application also has a rule on how to combine equations to isolate a variable, so it anticipates a similar input and finds a close match to this mistake. It can once again highlight the incorrect term, the coefficient of the "y" term, in Fig. 6.3.

After the user has entered solutions for both "x" and "y," a button appears giving the user the option to graph the original problem, as seen in Fig. 6.4. In this example, the solution is at the intersection of the two lines represented by the starting equations. The graph is displayed in a small floating widget that can be moved around and manipulated to explore with pinch-to-zoom and pan gestures. Another large button appears at the bottom of the screen providing the option to start a new problem.

6.2.4 User Study

Two pilot studies were conducted at a local private school, The Wheeler School, in Providence, Rhode Island. Before these studies, we had a set of discussions with

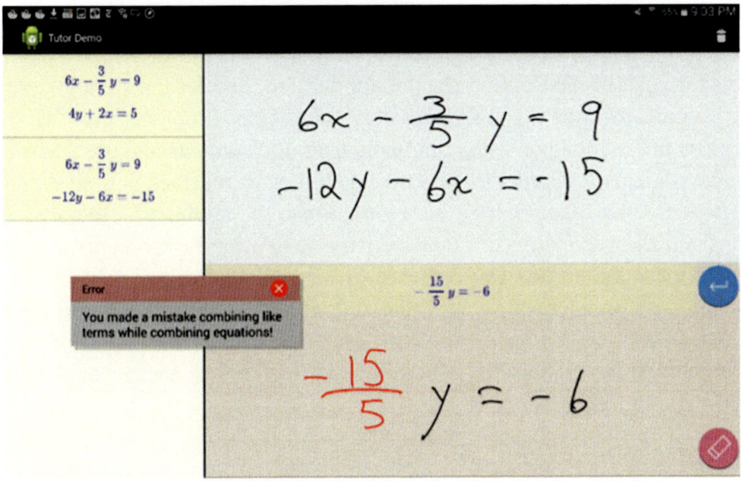

Fig. 6.3 Another error message from miscalculating while combining equations

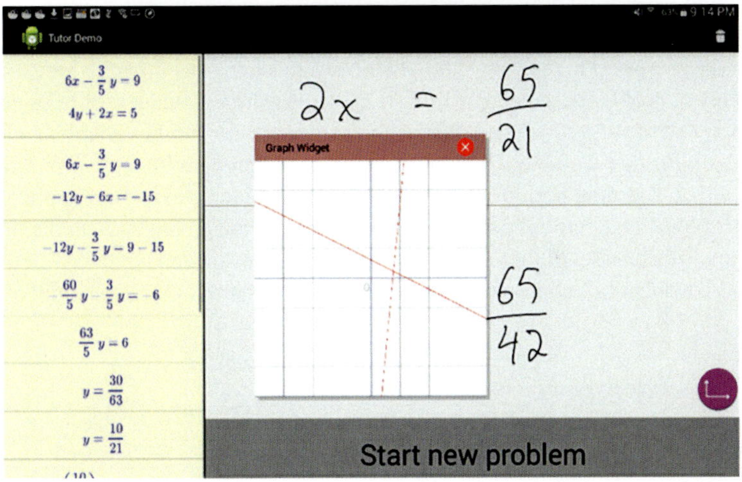

Fig. 6.4 The floating graph widget

the math teachers there, and collected useful feedback and suggestions regarding the Math Tutor user experience.

6.2.4.1 First Pilot Study

The first study was implemented to test the learning curve of our application, and to get a general idea of the overall user experience. Five 8th grade students participated in the study with their math teacher. We used four Galaxy Note 10.1 tablets to run our application. Videos of the students' performance with the application were taken. Initially, we gave no instruction for the application, and let the students play with it to see which parts of the interface were confusing. Problems that the students had were recorded together with comments from the students and the teacher. After giving the students a detailed instruction of the user interface and an explanation of the application's functionality, we let them use the application to solve a set of problems that we prepared. While they were trying to solve the problems, we observed their behavior and recorded any difficulties or issues that arose. Additionally, with the teacher's encouragement, we let the students use our application to review the problems of a test they had taken in class before our user study. In the end, we asked each student and the teacher for general feedback they had for our application and gathered their suggestions.

6.2.4.2 Second Study

The second user study aimed to test the learning of concepts and to gauge the usefulness of error suggestion messages. Two 7th grade students and three 8th grade students participated in the study with their math teacher. We prepared three different categories of problems, as seen in Table 6.1: single-variable linear problems necessitating the distribution of a term, quadratic problems with single variable, and linear problems with two variables. For each category, we prepared twelve problems. We began with a "learning period," where we asked the students to use our application to solve problems of a particular category. If a student made no mistakes in the first two problems, we considered that the student already knew the concept too well to learn from our application, and progressed to the next category. Once the student made

Table 6.1 Example problems

Single-variable linear equations w. distribution	Single-variable quadratic equations	Two-variable linear system of equations
$3(x - 2/5) = 7$	$2x^2 - 6x + 5 = 1$	$3x - 2y = 7$ $y + 2x = 1$
$2(3/4 - x) = 4$	$x^2 - 4x - 13 = 0$	$x - 2y = 2x + 2$ $y + 2x = 1$
$5(2x - 1/2) = 2$	$-3x^2 - 6x + 4 = 0$	$2y = x - 1$ $4x - y = 19$
$-2(x - 4/3) = 6$	$2x^2 - 3 = 0$	$2x - y = 6$ $5x - y = 8$
$4(x + 2/3) = 3$	$-(x - 2)^2 + 1 = 0$	$2x + y = 7$ $4x + 3y = 2$
$-3(x + 2/7) = 1$	$2x^2 - 8x = 42$	$4x + y = 19$ $3x - 4y = 8$

a mistake, he or she would continue doing more problems until solving two consecutive problems completely without error. If the student got to the sixth problem without achieving this (i.e., still making mistakes), we considered that the student had not obviously improved, and removed the student from the study. After solving two consecutive problems without error, the student moved into the "testing period" where he or she used pen and paper to do same number of problems completed in the learning period. We then compared their performances in the learning period and the testing period. In the end, we got some suggestions and feedback of how the students felt about our application.

6.3 Results and Evaluation

6.3.1 First Study

In general, following brief instruction from a researcher, students learned how to use the application after playing with it for only a few minutes. While using the application, one student quickly found mistakes that he had made in a test that he had taken earlier that day in class. The system helped him identify the reason for his mistake and correct it. All of the students gave positive feedback of the user experience, and said they would use the application for assignments if it was available.

The results were also helpful in finding how to improve the application. Before we provided instructions, some students were confused about how to use the application. One student tried to solve the whole problem in the margins of the first step. Others wrote the equation as an expression when one side was equal to zero. However, most problems we found during the study were related to the math recognizer. The immediate, on-the-fly recognition algorithm used context and thus became more accurate as more was written, but this often confused students in the midst of writing. Other times, characters were simply misinterpreted. Some common mis-recognitions were seven and one, two and alpha, four and y, and five and s. We hypothesize that this is caused by differences between U.S. and Korean writing of math since the recognizer is driven by training data collected in Korea. Unfortunately, we were not able to have changes made to the recognizer, as we did not have access to the necessary training data.

6.3.2 Second Study

The second study provided additional qualitative data. Since the system did not allow wrong solution steps, all the students finished their problems correctly with the application. Throughout the study, we observed the frequency of particular types of mistakes decreasing for each student. For example, one student initially made several mistakes with fractions, but after continued use of the application she succeeded in solving two consecutive problems without error. This may have resulted from students developing a better understanding of the concepts. It may also be a result of students being more attentive to a particular concept. We observed a clear trend in that students solved problems faster as the study progressed. This may indicate a growing familiarity with the concepts of the problems, and might also suggest increased experience with the application. At the end of the study, we asked students for general feedback. According to the students, the application helped them more quickly recognize mistakes that may have otherwise gone unnoticed and was enjoyable to use.

In this study, we did not require the students to finish the tasks in controlled environment. They could ask for the teacher's hints sometimes when they got stuck. As before, some students had trouble getting the math recognizer to correctly understand their input. All students made use of the highlighted handwriting when they made mistakes; often the highlighted mistake term was enough for them to recognize their error. However, we noticed that some students did not spend time reading the error messages, particularly in two cases: (1) Students who were confident with the concepts usually tended to ignore the error messages; they only cared about whether there was a mistake and which part of their handwriting was highlighted as incorrect. (2) Students who did not get enough help from the error messages; they often lacked the understanding of a basic concept, and needed the teacher to tell them where to begin or what to do next. Additionally, in rare cases, students gamed the system and used trial and error to search for the correct next step.

6.3.3 Conclusions

Although there are a wide variety of existing math tutors aimed at the middle school level, we believe that there is no system that allows for a flexible, investigative approach that closely mimics the established method of solving an equation on paper. We have provided a first version of such a system for solving beginner-level algebra problems with pen-and-touch control. Unlike other step-based intelligent tutors, our system allows students to solve any general problem within our initial (though admittedly narrow) mathematical scope using any method to reach a solution. Additionally, Math Tutor provides a familiar and yet novel user experience by sidestepping a traditional forms-based tutor interface in favor of an interface based on intuitive handwritten input. Mistakes found by our application are conveniently highlighted and explained to the student without any need for them to define what solution strategy they applied. Unlike some traditional ITS systems that require significant manual effort to design and build a new area of study, our model is straightforward and requires relatively little effort to extend. When presented to a small group of students in a pilot study, results demonstrated that the application provided an enjoyable experience and helped students be more careful in their work. Qualitative observations also suggested that students became more efficient and less prone to error as they used the application. However, there was also indication that our general approach did not help students who had not sufficiently mastered the basic concepts enough to know how to take a "next" step. Additionally, the system was limited by a student's ability to write clearly enough for the recognizer to understand their input. We believe the free-form nature of this application, like traditional pen-and-paper methods, creates a unique challenge for the research that it requires a deep understanding of the underlying concepts. We feel there is great promise in the continued work on this application informed by the results of our studies.

6.4 Future Work

Although the error messages were helpful to students who made careless mistakes, they were not helpful to students who did not understand some concept in the first place. This can lead to students being unsure of how to correct a mistake or what to do next at a given step. Many other tutors use some kind of hint mechanism, but these generally only appear as a block of text explaining what step to take next. Our study suggested that such messages are often ignored by students. We are doing a "Wizard of Oz" study to get feedback for user experiences that go beyond the original Math Tutor design.

In the study, Students will solve algebraic problems in similar pen-and-touch environment, except the system's visual feedback will be generated by an unseen researcher. We will study:

1. reverse-scaffolding model that provides different messages when the same types of mistakes occur repeatedly. If a student makes a mistake, he or she must demonstrate an understanding of the concept by solving a simpler example. As the student continues to make mistakes, the problems will continue to get simpler, until the student reaches a problem he or she is comfortable with. From there, standard scaffolding techniques will be used to rebuild understanding;
2. a description and example model that gives information from the text book (e.g., transformation rules), to students when needed;
3. a "What to do" model that sends hints when a student does not know how to proceed to the next step;
4. other models suggested by students and teachers.

Further work should also be done to expand the scope of math to include more complex problems. Students and teachers also suggested connecting with one another through a platform for assignments and tests so that teachers can review students' work and use our application to find gaps in their understanding, or receive help from the teacher.

Acknowledgments This work has been supported in part by funding from Samsung Electronics Co., Ltd. Professor Andries van Dam has provided guidance as supervisor. Ben Most, Alex Hills, Ruixiang Li, and Siyi Zhang have contributed to the implementation. The user study of this work was made possible at The Wheeler School with the help of Page Stites, Ianthe Hershberger, and the teachers in the Math Department.

References

1. Aleven V, McLaren BM, Sewall J (2009) Scaling up programming by demonstration for intelligent tutoring systems development: an open-access web site for middle school mathematics learning. IEEE Trans Learn Technol 2(2):64–78
2. Aleven V, Roll I, McLaren BM, Koedinger KR (2010) Automated, unobtrusive, action-by-action assessment of self-regulation during learning with an intelligent tutoring system. Educ Psychol 45(4):224–233
3. Carney DP, Forsberg A, LaViola Jr JJ, Zeleznik R, Osche E, Leblang J, Smith DR, Baldassari C (2014) Webfluidmath: evaluating a one-to-one (1:1) teaching tool for high school algebra. In: The eighth workshop on the impact of pen and touch technology on education. Presentation only
4. Heffernan NT, Heffernan CL (2014) The assistments ecosystem: building a platform that brings scientists and teachers together for minimally invasive research on human learning and teaching. Int J Artif Intell Educ 24(4):470–497
5. Joyner D (2006) Oscas: maxima. ACM Commun Comput Algebra 40(3–4):108–111
6. Ritter S, Anderson JR, Koedinger KR, Corbett A (2007) Cognitive tutor: applied research in mathematics education. Psychon Bull Rev 14(2):249–255
7. Salden RJ, Aleven V, Schwonke R, Renkl A (2010) The expertise reversal effect and worked examples in tutored problem solving. Instr Sci 38(3):289–307
8. Sangwin C (2012) The dragmath equation editor. MSOR Connect 12(2):5–8
9. VanLehn K (2011) The relative effectiveness of human tutoring, intelligent tutoring systems, and other tutoring systems. Educ Psychol 46(4):197–221
10. Woolf B, Aimeur E, Nkambou R, Lajoie S (2008) Intelligent tutoring systems: 9th international conference on intelligent tutoring systems, ITS 2008, Montreal, Canada, June 23–27, 2008, Proceedings, vol 5091. Springer

Chapter 7
Leveraging Trends in Student Interaction to Enhance the Effectiveness of Sketch-Based Educational Software

Seth Polsley, Jaideep Ray, Trevor Nelligan, Michael Helms, Julie Linsey, and Tracy Hammond

Abstract With the rapid adoption of software-based learning in classrooms, it is increasingly important to design more intelligent educational software, a goal of the emerging field of educational data mining. In this work, we analyze student activities from using a learning tool for engineers, Mechanix, in order to find trends that may be used to make the software a better tutor, combining its natural, sketch-based input with intelligent, experience-based feedback. We see a significant correlation between student performance and the amount of time they work on a problem before submitting; students who attempt to "game" the system by submitting their results too often perform worse than those who work longer ($p < 0.05$). We also found significance in the number of times a student attempted a problem before moving on, with a strong correlation between being willing to switch among problems and better performance ($p < 0.05$). Overall, we find that student trends like these could be paired with machine learning techniques to make more intelligent educational tools.

S. Polsley (✉) · J. Ray · T. Nelligan · T. Hammond
Sketch Recognition Lab, Computer Science & Engineering Department,
Texas A&M University, College Station, TX, USA
e-mail: spolsley@tamu.edu

J. Ray
e-mail: jaideep.ray@tamu.edu

T. Nelligan
e-mail: trevornelligan@tamu.edu

T. Hammond
e-mail: hammond@tamu.edu

M. Helms · J. Linsey
iDreem Lab at Georgia Institute of Technology, Atlanta, GA, USA
e-mail: mhelms3@gatech.edu

J. Linsey
e-mail: julie.linsey@me.gatech.edu

T. Hammond et al. (eds.), *Revolutionizing Education with Digital Ink*,
Human–Computer Interaction Series, DOI 10.1007/978-3-319-31193-7_7

7.1 Introduction

Analyzing the trends of student interaction in sketch-based educational software may be the key to building tools that understand students better. As online learning is being adopted by an increasing number of universities [13], designing software that students can understand is important in keeping students engaged. Sketch recognition in these teaching tools may help alleviate that concern by providing an experience similar to the pen-and-paper approaches that students are already comfortable using. However, beyond helping students understand and use educational software, there is an important opportunity that should not be overlooked—each student is individually interacting with the software at some point in the course. This one-on-one interaction provides the chance to do more than just administer and evaluate work, as many online learning tools are designed to do. By building the software with a better understanding of student behavior, it can be used as a more effective tutor, providing feedback on their progress, guidelines to help strengthen their problem-solving skills, and recommended courses of action when they are stuck. There is a wealth of student data available today from existing learning systems, and exploring that information for trends in student behavior and interaction can yield better approaches for developing educational software of all kinds.

There is a strong impetus behind creating better software learning tools. Managing large classes at the university level can be very difficult for departments seeking to reduce cost. This is especially true in STEM fields, where the material may be complicated and finding qualified teachers and graders is hard and expensive. In STEM courses, where drawing and sketching are necessary steps in many classes, sketch recognition can be a good alternative to standard true-false, fill-in-the-blank, or multiple choice software because of its capability to interpret student input throughout a complete problem. Mechanix, a sketch-based tutor for helping students learn about trusses and free body diagrams, was designed for engineering students for this reason [14, 21].

While sketch recognition may be a significant step in making software that students will comfortably use, there is still enormous potential for improving the software. Even when they do not realize it, students follow trends of behavior in completing assignments. Whether they start each problem and work on them simultaneously, go through each problem quickly and ask for help frequently, or don't even complete half of the assignment, their patterns of activity can be monitored in software in the same way a human tutor might. By applying some decision algorithms to this data, educational tools could more closely mimic the intelligence of a human helper and offer students a better experience by avoiding potential problems.

7.2 Previous Work

Online learning is not new, but it continues to grow significantly as the number of Internet users worldwide increases[1] [1]. Making software tools that interact naturally with students is crucial in order to accommodate the diverse array of individuals using them. As tablets and touchscreens have become more commonplace, input technologies like sketch recognition have begun to appear more widely in educational applications. Many such applications also include some form of automated feedback to users. For example, Sketch Worksheets is an educational tool in which instructors can program certain facts about drawings which may be used to generate feedback [12, 23, 24]. One system helps teach users to draw through a sketch interface by comparing how similar the input sketch is to the goal and sharing the evaluations with the students [18]. A similar idea has been applied specifically to drawing portraits; iCanDraw? guides students through drawing faces step-by-step with feedback along the way [10]. Mechanix also includes an evaluation system through which students can request updates on their progress [3].

Tracking student activity in online systems may be foremost associated with preventing cheating and has been studied extensively in that area [6, 17]. In recent years, the field of Educational Data Mining (EDM) has begun to emerge as an open approach to examining educational data from a multitude of perspectives [15, 16]. Among those perspectives is tracking student behavior in an attempt to characterize their engagement and correlate learning outcomes [8]. Champaign et al. recently used such an approach to correlate student improvement with the time spent on each task [9]. This work uses a similar basis, but sketch recognition provides an entirely new dynamic in that it creates a very personal connection with the student, as opposed to entering numbers on a keyboard or some similar means. Interpreting this data intelligently could be more useful than just as a source for basic feedback.

7.3 Overview of Mechanix

Mechanix is the source of student data that was analyzed. As mentioned before, it is a sketch-based grading and tutoring system, primarily designed for engineering statics courses [11, 19]. It allows instructors to upload assignments and tutorials, drawing trusses and diagrams by hand and defining equations, values, and units through the provided interface elements. Students may then complete assignments by hand drawing their solutions into the system [20, 22]. Mechanix provides real-time visual feedback through color-coding and personalized instructional feedback as requested. In the process, it aims to help them grasp the basic concepts behind the problem [4]. Figure 7.1 shows a screenshot of the student interface in Mechanix

[1]Miniwatts Marketing Group, Internet Growth Statistics, 2014, http://www.internetworldstats.com/emarketing.htm.

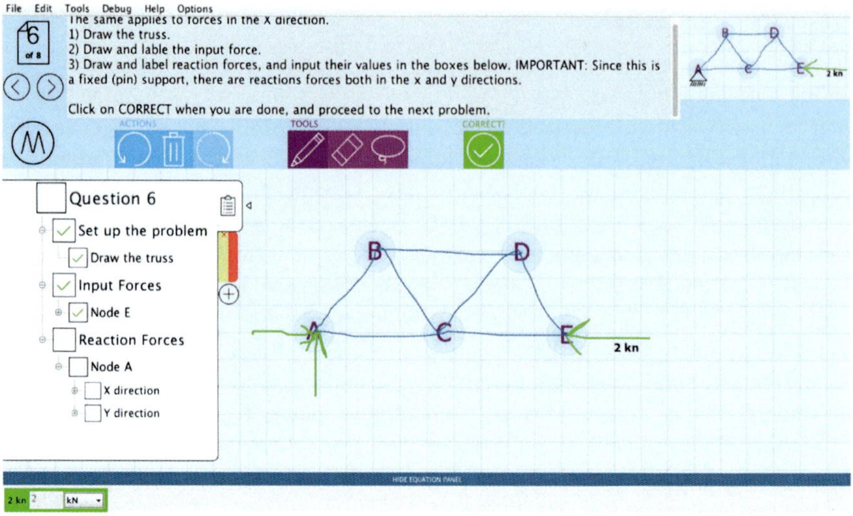

Fig. 7.1 A screenshot of the student interface in Mechanix, showing a truss with forces, labels, and color-coding

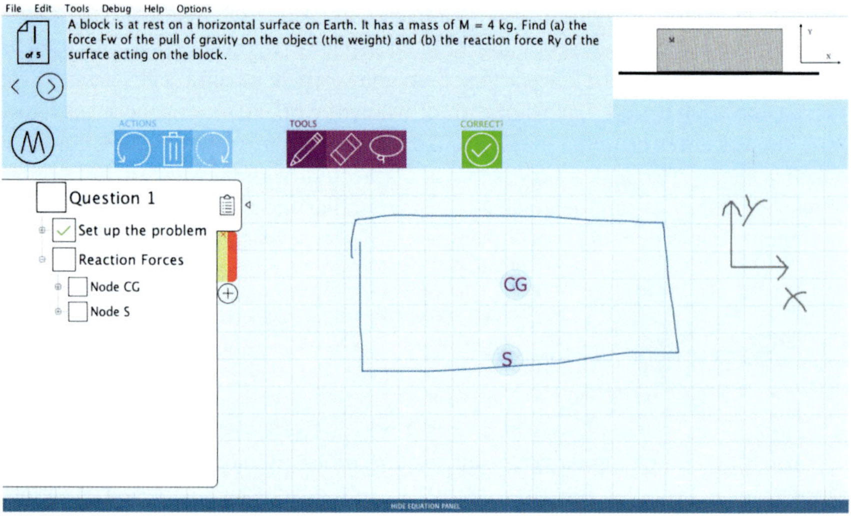

Fig. 7.2 Another screenshot of the Mechanix student interface showing recognition of free body diagrams and axes

while solving a truss-related problem, and Fig. 7.2 shows another screenshot of the interface while solving a free-body diagram problem.

By using a touch and pen interface, Mechanix keeps the real experience of pen and paper mode intact [5]. There is also a benefit to students when training tools closely resemble real world scenarios. Most of the available software used in teaching statics and engineering drawing have complicated interfaces leading to a steep learning curve. Mechanix is much more direct in its interaction, and the intuitive user interface takes much less time to learn.

7.4 Data Analysis

Mechanix was used as a supplemental teaching tool during the fall 2014 semester. Data was taken from 51 students who were enrolled in an introductory course at the Georgia Institute of Technology, learning the fundamentals of statics and mechanics that would become critical to their future engineering work. The students ranged in majors from mechanical engineering, aerospace engineering to biomedical engineering among others and were primarily in their freshman years. Two class assignments were given through Mechanix, as well as a tutorial that was offered for additional credit. Hundreds of megabytes of sketching data, primarily drawings of trusses, were gathered from these students, providing a great deal of potential for mining. While much can be learned from the sketches themselves, a component of sketch recognition with implications in artificial intelligence, computer security, and personal health, this data included much more information that could reveal the learning behavior of the students in the field of technology-based learning. Each sketch submitted by a student is saved with a time stamp and the feedback generated by the server for that submission, among other attributes. Mechanix's feedback system provides each student with personalized responses relevant to his or her work. Some of the suggestions the feedback may provide would be to identify missing nodes or forces and incorrect values to the students. Feedback is really helpful if used judiciously. The data collected suggests that a fraction of users request feedback at every step instead of attempting the problem on its merit. This often leads to a student dropping out in the middle of an exercise. Mechanix also informs students, when they are correct. A lot of interesting information can be gathered through the analysis of time and feedback alone.

It is important to note that in the sections that follow, a focus is placed on the students' homework completion rates. Such completion rates may seem like an arbitrary measure, but Atilola et al. have already demonstrated the effectiveness of Mechanix as a teaching tool [2]. Those results suggest that students will benefit more by continual use of the system for their Mechanix assignments rather than ceasing to use the software. As such, this work examines less how Mechanix can improve students' grades and more how their interaction with Mechanix may be improved to encourage them to use the system more. Completion rates are used because they are the best standalone measure of determining a student's sustained usage of the software.

7.4.1 Time Between Requests for Feedback

Because Mechanix is a feedback-based system, it is important to consider how students are using the feedback and whether or not it is benefiting them. One means of doing this is by examining the frequency of feedback requests against completion of problems for each student. By using the time stamp with each repeated submission of a problem, an average time between requests for feedback was generated for each student. Individual student behavior becomes apparent through this analysis, as we see that some students regularly ask for feedback at short intervals while others take more time thinking about the problem before checking. Patterns appear when considering the group of students. The results show that students with more time between feedback requests performed better on average than those that spent less time. This is not particularly surprising because students that spend more time on a problem without requesting help are more likely to think about the problem carefully to gain a good understanding of the concepts, which is reflected by a higher grade. Baker et al. demonstrated similar results in [7] in which students who were "gaming" the online learning system achieved lower learning rates than those who were not. Figure 7.3 shows the average time between feedback requests in minutes against the completion rates for the students. A trendline generated from regression analysis is overlaid.

From regression analysis, the linear prediction model fit to the data showed a statistically-significant pattern in the data ($p = 0.033 \mid$ Nonzero slope). As mentioned above, this model is easily understood when looking at students with little time between feedback requests; these students are not spending enough time on the problem before requesting feedback from the system. The more interesting result from this model is that we clearly see there is no benefit to students working longer

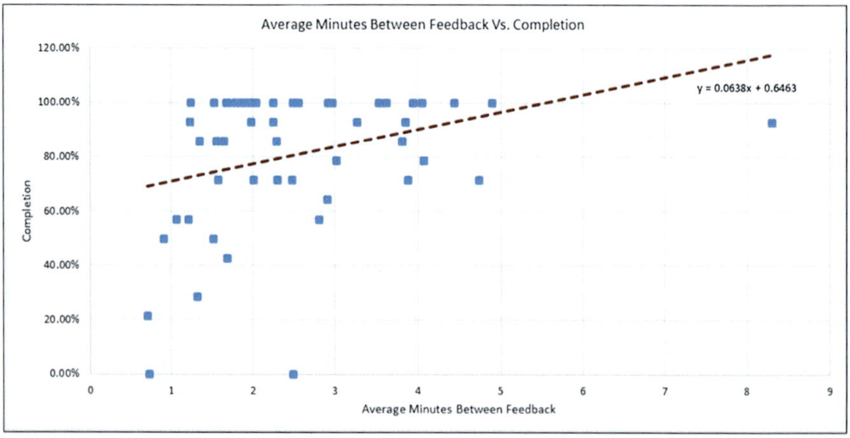

Fig. 7.3 Average time between submissions on a minute scale plotted versus the student completion rates

than 5 min on a problem. While working *longer than* 5 min did not seem to induce higher quitting rates, it obviously does not have any valuable return for the students. One way to apply this knowledge is to add recommendations to Mechanix. For example, by considering this metric across all the students of a given assignment, Mechanix could determine an *optimal time* for students to work a problem. If they seem to be taking too long, Mechanix could recommend they check the current status.

While it may not be very evident from the trendline, more detailed analysis of the data does show that students' completion rates increase significantly when they spend even two minutes on a problem as opposed to just one minute or less. In fact, many of the low completion rates are concentrated *below one minute*. The primary difficulty encountered by those in this category seemed to be an over-reliance on the feedback. A student might get stuck on a particular problem and check it repeatedly by testing different values or making slight alterations to their drawing but not take the time to solve the underlying issue. For instance, one such student (user58) received 14 errors (Fig. 7.4) related to missing or incorrectly drawn forces on a diagram within four minutes. Each error was very similar, and the student may have benefited most from redrawing the problem and considering more carefully what forces to draw. As it was, the student moved on from the problem and, after trying a couple more assignment questions later, eventually gave up without getting any problems correct.

This over-reliance on the auto-grading capabilities of the system can lead to frustration. To counter this frustration, it is certainly recommended that students spend more time focused on solving the problem than on the teaching tool's capabilities, but the data gathered from this experiment show that only a small amount of extra time might benefit students significantly. In this case, even thirty more seconds of thought before clicking the feedback button had could have a major impact on the student's

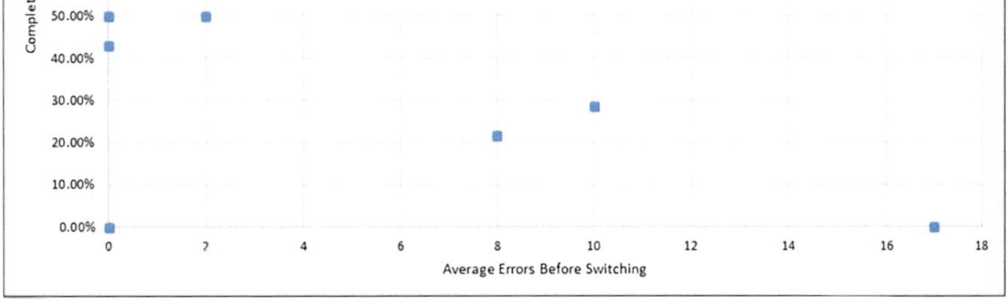

Fig. 7.4 Average number of submissions before switching without getting correct against the student completion rates

willingness to finish the assignment. Perhaps cooldowns on Mechanix's feedback could be paired with recommendations to service students more effectively. They could receive more appropriate recommendations based on their personal activity, whether to request feedback more or attempt to move on to other problems rather than get stuck. In essence we think that frequency of requests for feedback should be monitored and assistance on problems should be given accordingly. Such a feature would need to be implemented carefully so as to be a help and not a hindrance to students.

7.4.2 Number of Attempts Before Moving Forward

Students also encountered frustration in the form of not being able to solve a particular problem and giving up before moving forward. As it is important to spend time thinking about a problem rather than relying on feedback, it is likewise important to be able to move on when one is stuck. Some students do not practice this technique, but it is often recommended by teachers. By examining repeated submissions of the same problem before moving on without achieving a correct answer, an average number of errors to switching was generated for each student. When compared with the problem completion rate from before, it was found that the students who request large amounts of feedback before moving on are less likely to finish the assignment. These users seem to have difficulty recognizing when they are stuck and become too frustrated to move on after spending too many attempts on a single problem. For example, one student received 18 consecutive errors (Fig. 7.4) with the same message and gave up on completing the assignments before getting any questions outside of the tutorial correct. Such persistence does not seem helpful to the student at all.

Figure 7.4 shows the average errors to switching versus the average completion rates. Again, a linear trendline has been added using regression analysis. We can see a trend from this model which is interestingly the reverse of what we saw in the previous metric. Specifically, while spending increasingly more time on a single problem attempt before requesting feedback did not seem to harm students, however, spending more attempts on a single problem before switching does. Thus, multiple attempts lead to frustration more easily in students than single, long attempts. Unfortunately, though the trendline shows some interesting features, it is not statistically-significant for this metric with $p = 0.22$ (can not reject that slope is zero). This is mostly due to the fact that while students with more attempts before switching generally did more poorly, there were a number of students who never switched problems before completing them. These users added multiple zeros but may still have achieved reasonable grades on the assignments, indicating that the data may not be best approximated with a linear model.

To take a closer look at the impact of staying on a problem too long, the students were split into two groups: (1) those who completed everything and (2) those who quit without finishing. A t-test on these two groups did yield a statistically-significant separation ($p = 0.012$). Students with 100 % completion spent *3.6 attempts* on average before switching, while those who did not finish the assignments spent *6.7 attempts* on average. This approach more clearly proves the trend we discussed earlier that students are more prone to giving up after experiencing many repeated errors.

This result is particularly relevant to technology-based learning tools because they have the capability to help users recognize when they are stuck. For example, it may ultimately help students perform better to recommend that they move on to another problem after *five or six repeated errors*. Analysis of submission history data can help instructors detect specific concepts on which a number of students get stuck. Instructors can later create and upload more tutorials explaining these concepts. With real time analysis of submission data, one can implement automated tutors that identify higher-level concepts a student is struggling with and provide just-in-time instructional support.

7.4.3 Impact of Tutorials

In looking at general submission trends among all the students, another lesson may be learned that could be useful to other web-based learning tools or courses—the value of tutorials. Several students encountered difficulty in doing the assignments and so returned to the tutorial before completing the assignments. Because tutorials are so heavily relied upon, they should be thoughtfully crafted so that students can learn how to solve any type of problem they may encounter using the software tools. In this study, there was a noticeable jump in difficulty in the tutorial, plainly visible in the number of submissions for each question of the tutorial, which is shown in Fig. 7.5. By more closely examining the feedback students were receiving, it is apparent that some fundamental knowledge for using the software correctly was being forgotten. Since success of assignments depends upon skills to use the software and a good grasp of concepts, tutorials should be targeted towards both of them. Using simple questions early on to reinforce the most basic concepts may be one method to allow students to progress through problems more smoothly in the future.

Mechanix serves as a sketch based educational software for engineering statics course. One of the primary goals of this software is to keep students engaged in the course by helping them with automated tutoring and assignment grading. This aspect of Mechanix can be extended to Massive Online Open Courses as well. One of the main challenges of MOOCs is student persistence. Data shows that most MOOCs have completion rates of less than 13 %. Moreover auto graded MOOCs have a higher completion rates than peer graded ones.[2] To keep students invested and interested in an online course, short quizzes and tutorials that are automatically graded should be introduced between lectures. The data from Mechanix shows that students who complete the tutorials have a much higher chance of completing the assignments which shows that they have grasped the concepts better.

[2]Jordan, K. MOOC Completion Rates, 2013, http://www.katyjordan.com/MOOCproject.html.

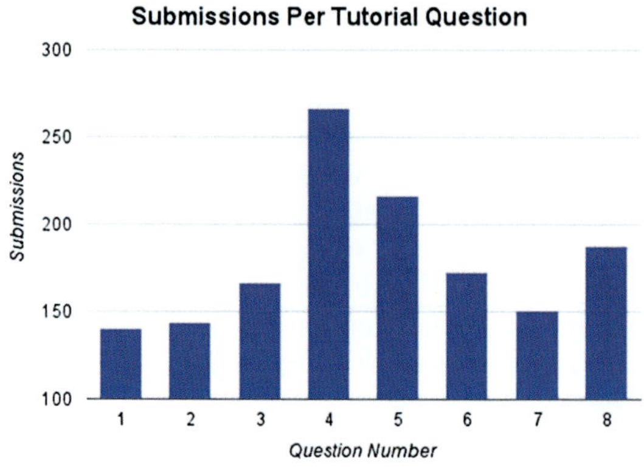

Fig. 7.5 Total number of submissions for each question in the tutorial

7.5 Future Work

The best way to improve Mechanix's interaction with students is to take cues from data, and there are some important results. Feedback is helpful in keeping students moving along, but it can be a hindrance. By incorporating cooldowns or more informative messages to assist students in thinking more carefully about a problem, a lot of potentially frustrating issues may be avoided. Students benefit from being flexible. Moving on to another problem after about four failed submissions gave students the most success in this study. Mechanix could use this result to provide recommendations in certain instances where students appear to be stuck. Tutorials are also extremely valuable. Not only should they be designed to teach students all the information they should need to know to use the software but also provide examples of each type of problem that may be encountered. Simple problems are a good way to reinforce software usage principles, but all types of different problems should appear so that students are prepared. We also wish to look more closely at these metrics in the future and compare them with data collected from more students. By gathering more data, it may be possible to fit a better model to the existing metrics or determine new ones that could be other avenues of software improvement.

7.6 Conclusion

There are vast amounts of data available from software-based educational tools, and trends in this data should be used to inform the development of next-generation education software. This software should be as straightforward for students as possible, through sketch recognition, and it should also make use of student behaviors to act as a tutor. The results found here, though primarily targeted at Mechanix, may be applicable to many different learning programs. Interaction based on an understanding of students could lead to systems that more closely resemble human teachers, allowing for less expensive but still very personal ways for students to learn.

Acknowledgments This research was funded by NSF EEC Grant No. 1129525. The authors would like to thank Dr. Matthew Green for using Mechanix in his classroom for testing; the members of the iDreem and Sketch Recognition Labs, particularly Stephanie Valentine and David Turner for their significant contributions to Mechanix; and the Computer Science & Engineering department at Texas A&M University.

References

1. Allen IE, Seaman J (2007) Online nation: five years of growth in online learning. ERIC
2. Atilola O, Field M, McTigue E, Hammond T, Linsey J (2011) Evaluation of a natural sketch interface for truss fbds and analysis. In: Frontiers in Education Conference (FIE), 2011, pp S2E-1–S2E-6. doi:10.1109/FIE.2011.6142959
3. Atilola O, Field M, McTigue E, Hammond T, Linsey J (2011) Mechanix: a sketch recognition truss tutoring system. In: ASME 2011 international design engineering technical conferences and computers and information in engineering conference. American Society of Mechanical Engineers, New York, pp 645–654
4. Atilola O, Vides F, Mctigue EM, Linsey JS, Hammond TA (2012) Automatic identification of student misconceptions and errors for truss analysis. In: 119th American society for engineering education annual conference and exposition (ASEE). American Society for Engineering Education, Washington, DC
5. Atilola O, Valentine S, Kim HH, Turner D, McTigue E, Hammond T, Linsey J (2014) Mechanix: a natural sketch interface tool for teaching truss analysis and free-body diagrams. Artif Intel Eng Des Anal Manuf 28(02):169–192
6. Baker RS, Corbett AT, Koedinger KR (2004) Detecting student misuse of intelligent tutoring systems. In: Intelligent tutoring systems. Springer, Heidelberg, pp 531–540
7. Baker RS, Corbett AT, Koedinger KR, Wagner AZ (2004) Off-task behavior in the cognitive tutor classroom: when students game the system. In: Proceedings of the SIGCHI conference on human factors in computing systems. ACM, pp 383–390
8. Baker RS, D'Mello SK, Rodrigo MMT, Graesser AC (2010) Better to be frustrated than bored: the incidence, persistence, and impact of learners cognitive-affective states during interactions with three different computer-based learning environments. Int J Hum-Comput Stud 68(4):223–241
9. Champaign J, Colvin KF, Liu A, Fredericks C, Seaton D, Pritchard DE (2014) Correlating skill and improvement in 2 moocs with a student's time on tasks. In: Proceedings of the first ACM conference on learning @ scale conference. ACM, pp 11–20
10. Dixon D, Prasad M, Hammond T (2010) Icandraw: using sketch recognition and corrective feedback to assist a user in drawing human faces. In: Proceedings of the SIGCHI conference on human factors in computing systems. ACM, pp 897–906
11. Field M, Valentine S, Linsey J, Hammond T (2011) Sketch recognition algorithms for comparing complex and unpredictable shapes. In: Proceedings of the twenty-second international joint conference on artificial intelligence, IJCAI '11, vol 3. AAAI Press, pp 2436–2441
12. Forbus K, Usher J, Chang M (2015) Sketch worksheets: a brief summary. In: Hammond AAT, Valentine S, Payton M (eds) The impact of pen and touch technology on education. Part III, Chapter 10. Springer, New York
13. Hiltz SR, Turoff M (2005) Education goes digital: the evolution of online learning and the revolution in higher education. Commun ACM 48(10):59–64

14. Nelligan T, Polsley S, Ray J, Helms M, Linsey J, Hammond T (2015) Mechanix: a sketch-based educational interface. In: Proceedings of the 2015 ACM international conference on intelligent user interface
15. Romero C, Ventura S (2010) Educational data mining: a review of the state of the art. IEEE Trans Syst, Man, Cybern, Part C: Appl Rev 40(6):601–618
16. Siemens G, d Baker RS (2012) Learning analytics and educational data mining: towards communication and collaboration. In: Proceedings of the 2nd international conference on learning analytics and knowledge. ACM, pp 252–254
17. Siyao L, Qianrang G (2011) The research on anti-cheating strategy of online examination system. In: 2011 2nd International conference on artificial intelligence, management science and electronic commerce (AIMSEC). IEEE, pp 1738–1741
18. Soga M, Matsuda N, Taki H (2008) A sketch learning support environment that gives area-dependent advice during drawing the sketch. Trans Jpn Soc Artif Intel 23:96–104
19. Valentine S, Field M, Hammond T, Smith A (2011) A shape comparison technique for use in sketch-based tutoring systems. In: Proceedings of the 2011 intelligent user interfaces workshop on sketch recognition, IUI, vol 11. Palo Alto
20. Valentine S, Vides F, Lucchese G, Turner D, Kim H-H, Li W, Linsey J, Hammond T (2012) Mechanix: a sketch-based tutoring and grading system for free-body diagrams. AI Mag 34(1):55
21. Valentine S, Vides F, Lucchese G, Turner D, Kim H-H, Li W, Linsey J, Hammond T (2012) Mechanix: a sketch-based tutoring system for statics courses. In: IAAI
22. Valentine S, Lara-Garduno R, Linsey J, Hammond T (2015) Mechanix: a sketch based tutoring system that automatically corrects hand-sketched statics homework. In: Hammond T, Valentine S, Adler A, Payton M (eds) The impact of pen and touch technology on education. Springer, New York
23. Wetzel J, Forbus K (2015) Increasing student confidence in engineering sketching via a software coach. In: Hammond AAT, Valentine S, Payton M (eds) The impact of pen and touch technology on education. Part III, Chapter 11. Springer International Publishing, Springer, New York
24. Yin P, Forbus K, Usher J, Sageman B, Jee B (2010) Sketch worksheets: a sketch-based educational software system. In: Proceedings of the 22nd annual conference on innovative applications of artificial intelligence. Atlanta, Georgia

Chapter 8
PerSketchTivity: An Intelligent Pen-Based Educational Application for Design Sketching Instruction

Blake Williford, Paul Taele, Trevor Nelligan, Wayne Li, Julie Linsey, and Tracy Hammond

Abstract Design sketching is an important and versatile skill for engineering students to master in order to translate their design thoughts effectively onto a visual medium, whether it is to proficiently produce hand-drawn sketches onto paper, seamlessly interact with intelligent sketch-based modeling interfaces, or reap the various educational benefits associated with drawing. Traditional instructional approaches for teaching design sketching are frequently constrained by the availability of experienced human instructors or the lack of supervised learning from self-practice, while relevant intelligent educational applications for sketch instruction have focused more on assessing users' art drawings or cognitive developmental progress. We introduce PerSketchTivity, an intelligent pen-based computing educational application that not only teaches engineering students how to hone and practice their design sketching skills through stylus-and-touchscreen interaction, but also aiding their motivation and self-regulated learning through real-time feedback. From the qualitative results of our usability tests of our application from eight university student participants

---

B. Williford (✉) · W. Li
Innovation and Design Collaborative,
Georgia Institute of Technology, Atlanta, GA, USA
e-mail: bwilliford@gmail.com

W. Li
e-mail: wayne.li@coa.gatech.edu

P. Taele · T. Nelligan · T. Hammond
Sketch Recognition Lab, Computer Science and Engineering Department,
Texas A&M University, College Station, TX, USA
e-mail: ptaele@cse.tamu.edu

T. Nelligan
e-mail: trevornelligan@yahoo.com

T. Hammond
e-mail: hammond@tamu.edu

J. Linsey
iDreem Lab, Georgia Institute of Technology, Atlanta, GA, USA
e-mail: julie.linsey@me.gatech.edu

T. Hammond et al. (eds.), *Revolutionizing Education with Digital Ink*,
Human–Computer Interaction Series, DOI 10.1007/978-3-319-31193-7_8

of varying skill levels and disciplines, we observed that participants well-rated the usability of the application while also providing valuable feedback to improve the application even further.

8.1 Problem Statement and Context

8.1.1 Benefits of Design Sketching

Engineering students must achieve expertise in a wide range of computing skills during their studies in order to properly prepare them for their future careers. However, design sketching continues to be a valuable skill that is applicable in a variety of use cases, since this skill enables engineers to translate their design thoughts effectively on a visual medium. These use cases can range from proficiently producing rough preliminary sketches and polished drafting designs using pen and paper, to seamlessly interacting with gesture-driven intelligent user interfaces and emerging sketch-based modeling applications with a stylus-and-touchscreen. Furthermore, engineering students can take advantage of the educational benefits associated with sketching in general, such as enhancing the communications of existing ideas [6] and inspiring a generation of new ones [5]. Mastery of design sketching can lead to benefits in creating diagrammatic representations that hold many advantages over textual representations alone, such as grouping information more usefully for improved problem-solving inference [8] and better representing ideas for conveying engineering ideas [1]. Combined with current engineering education, sketching therefore provides assistance in accessing knowledge that is based in the applied sciences through aesthetic and social inquiry.

8.1.2 Challenges of Traditional Design Sketching Instruction

While mastery of design sketching enables engineering students to exploit this skill for their coursework and subsequent real-world usage in post-university careers, the process of them achieving mastery provides its own challenges. From our interviews with two industrial design professors from a large research university and from university students who are learning how to sketch in order to apply this skill to their coursework, we were given insights into both the traditional sketching pedagogy and the difficulties that both students and instructors experienced. Among these difficulties for learners include low self-efficacy [2], discouragement from comparison with peers, and lack of motivation to practice and self-regulate their learning [11]. As for instructors, factors include difficulty in catering their teaching to each and every individual. Traditional approaches for teaching sketching principles primarily stem from either in-class instruction and dedicated workshops, which are constrained by the time and availability of experienced human instructors; or rote self-practice and sketching guidebooks, which lack supervised feedback for alleviating the possibility of incorrect learning and bad sketching habits [10].

8.1.3 Prior Work

With the challenges associated with traditional design sketching instruction, there is potential in engineering students taking advantage of the growing ubiquity and accessibility of pen-capable computing devices to utilize intelligent pen-driven educational applications, where such an application can guide the students' study of design sketching fundamentals through sketching practice and automated human instructor-emulated visualized feedback. We can see such examples for sketching in the domain of art (e.g., [3, 4]), where sketching interfaces guide students in drawing foundational concepts by providing step-by-step cues on drawing and automated real-time feedback on their drawing performance. Similar examples also exist for assessing young children's developmental progress through sketching (e.g., [7]) using playful interfaces that additionally guide children how to sketch basic shapes. However, there is a lack of work in developing appropriate educational applications that cater specifically to users with developed fine motor skills with little to no design sketching background for more technical domains such as engineering and design.

8.1.4 Proposed Solution

In this paper, we therefore introduce PerSketchTivity, our intelligent educational application for teaching design sketching to users through sketching practice and corresponding automated feedback on their sketched input, in order to address the various challenges that both students and instructors encounter during design sketching instruction. Our approach for automatic understanding of freehand sketch input relies on: (1) a variety of geometric, feature, temporal, contextual, multi-modal, and domain information that provides context about what shape is being drawn on the screen, (2) a way to describe the sketch information, and (3) the application of machine learning techniques that take advantage of, and learn from, the information provided. Additionally, insights from educational sketching books (e.g., [9]) help influence the design decisions of our interface's interactive lessons using existing successful practice for sketch instruction.

8.2 Method Employed

We implemented a web-based intelligent educational application that utilizes Paper. JS—an open source javascript vector graphics scripting framework—and which runs on top of HTML5 Canvas. Our application's interface is therefore platform-independent and appropriate for pen-driven input modalities. The accompanying hardware setup that we employed for our application consisted of a Wacom Cintiq touchscreen monitor that accepted accurate stylus input, but can easily be adapted to other hardware setups that accept stylus input such as mobile tablets and tabletop touchscreens.

In the latest version of our application, we designed an interface that consisted of several exercises—specifically those for teaching users how to draw straight lines, squares, and circles—while also accommodating future extensions for lessons on more advanced geometric primitives. We elaborate on our application's different exercises in this section.

8.2.1 Straight Line Exercise

Straight lines are the most fundamental technique of sketching, and the very first sketching technique designers and engineers are taught is typically straight lines, as they form a fundamental skill from which to construct all three-dimensional forms. Therefore, we introduce straight lines as our first interactive lesson within our application. Students are exposed to a "connect the dots" style of exercise, and typically practice repeatedly hundreds of times to master the technique. With traditional pedagogy, there is a focus on accuracy, speed, and line quality, so by leveraging existing sketch recognition approaches, we are able to provide real-time feedback in the form of color-coded bars (Fig. 8.1), as well as an evaluation that provides students with additional metrics regarding their accuracy and speed (Fig. 8.2).

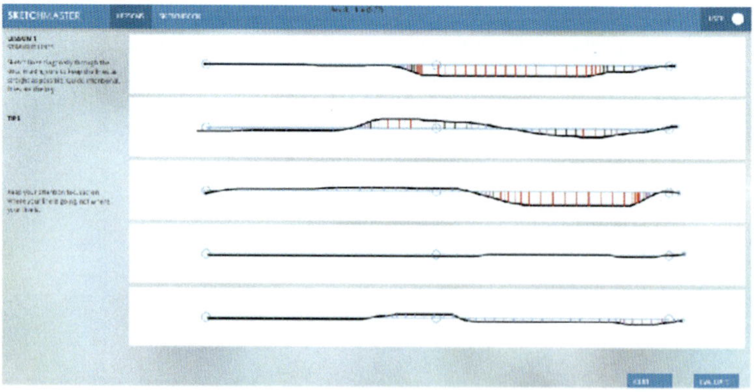

Fig. 8.1 Interface screenshot prompting the user to practice sketching straight lines at their own pace by connecting dots, and with accompanying feedback based on their sketching performance

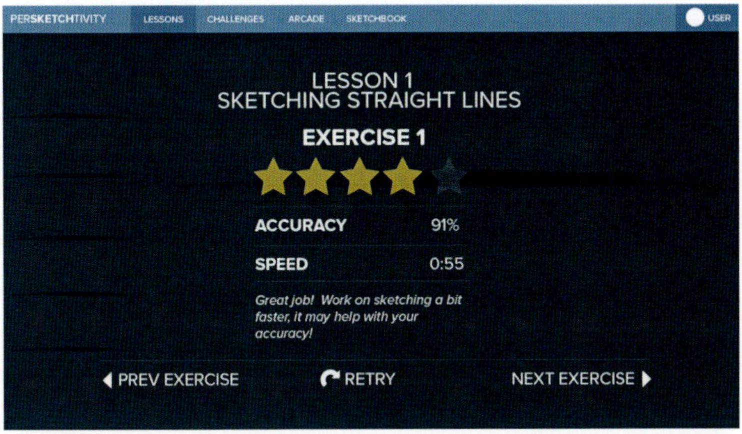

Fig. 8.2 Interface screenshot of automated feedback containing metrics regarding their accuracy and speed on sketched straight lines

8.2.2 *Square Exercise*

Comprised of straight lines perpendicular to their adjacent neighboring lines and parallel to lines on the other side, we introduce squares as the next basic shape for students to practice learning sketch technique on. Advancing from line exercises thus allows students to sketch multiple straight lines, in order to construct basic two-dimensional forms (Fig. 8.3). Multi-stroke detection allows students to sketch four lines for the squares.

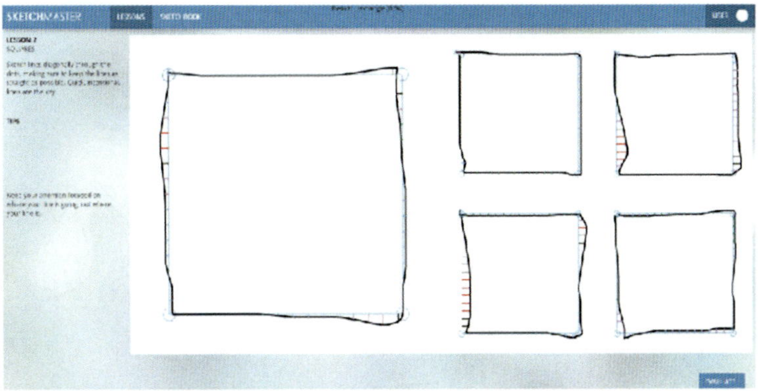

Fig. 8.3 Interface screenshot prompting the user to practice sketching *squares*, with accompanying feedback on their sketching performance

8.2.3 *Circle Exercise*

Using the knowledge of how to draw squares, our application subsequently allows students to practice sketching perfect circles inside reference squares (Fig. 8.4). Our application uses scaffolding in this way as a fundamental concept for students to experience during their sketching lesson, as more complex forms must similarly be "constructed" from basic forms.

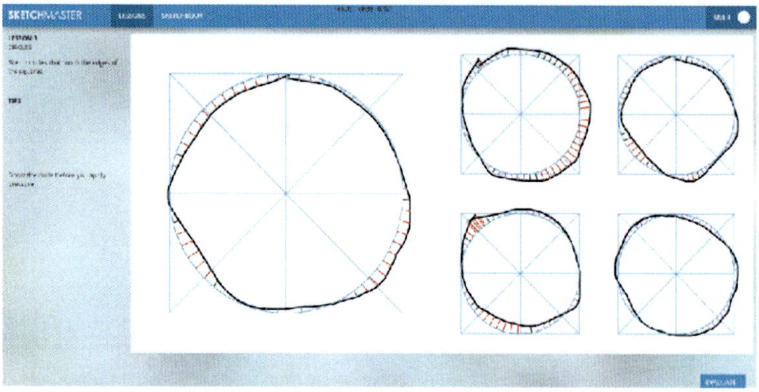

Fig. 8.4 Interface screenshot prompting the user to practice sketching *circles*, with accompanying feedback on their sketching performance

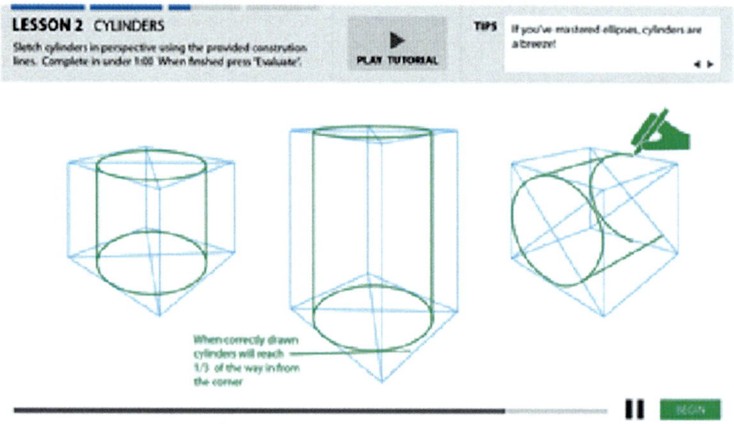

Fig. 8.5 Preliminary interface design for proposed future exercises that build and extend from the existing exercises

8.2.4 Future Exercises

With students completing their lesson practice on these prior sketching fundamentals for two-dimensional geometric primitives, we would like our application in the future to incorporate more advanced exercises that enables students to learn about perspectives and how to sketch three-dimensional geometric primitives such as cubes, cylinders, cones, and sphere (Fig. 8.5).

8.3 Results and Evaluation

8.3.1 Usability Study

In order to evaluate the performance of our current intelligent educational application for design sketching instruction, we recruited eight university students from a large research university for a usability study. They were from a variety of disciplinary backgrounds such as industrial design, mechanical engineering, computer science, and human-computer interaction. These students covered a spectrum of self-reported sketching experience from beginners with little to no sketching experience to intermediate-level students who still wanted to improve their ability.

For our usability study, we asked the participants to practice on four developed exercises, two of which utilized sketch recognition approaches. The focus of the exercises were on fundamental sketching components of lines and circles, each with two of their different exercise styles. One exercise style involved sketching many-at-a-time with an evaluation at the end, while the other exercise style involved sketching one-at-a time and evaluating between sketches. Since we designed our interface as a computer-assisted educational application, we therefore focused on learning outcomes and whether or not the pages and exercises were accomplishing the learning goals instead of traditional usability heuristics (e.g., task completion time, error rate). Our evaluation therefore placed greater emphasis on qualitative feedback, but also included collecting quantitative data using performance metrics to measure the effectiveness of pagination, exercises, and the user interface itself for determining their usability effectiveness.

8.3.2 Lesson Map Page Evaluation

One component that we included in our application was a lesson map page for showing the user what they will be learning, what they had already learned, and what can be navigated in the educational modules (Fig. 8.6). Using a self-assessed ten-point scale, our participants gave an average of 9.3 in terms of understanding what they will be learning, and an average of 8.0 for understanding what they had learned.

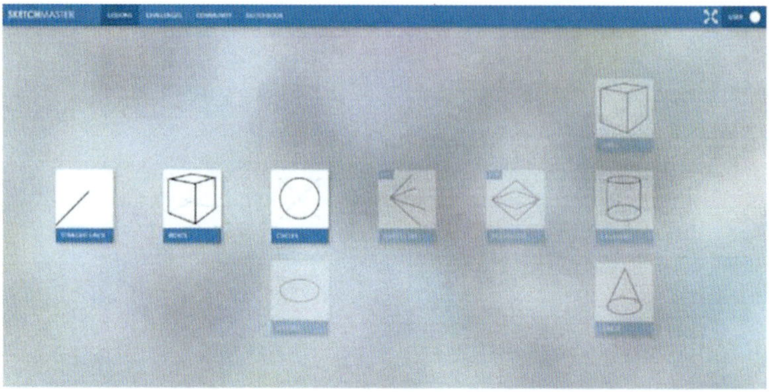

Fig. 8.6 Interface screenshot of lesson map page, which shows the user what they will be learning, what they already learned, and what can be navigated in the educational modules

In addition to the accompanying qualitative data, participants overall understood what they were going to learn from the lesson map page, but were less clear on what they had already learned or what they would learn next. Their feedback suggested having a more clear path between lessons and a visual indicator of their progress through each lesson.

8.3.3 Lesson Overview Page Evaluation

Another component included in our application was a lesson overview page for educating users on a specific skill or technique, as well as serving as a navigation for the exercises (Fig. 8.7). Using a ten-point scale, our participants gave an average of 9.4 in terms of understanding how to sketch the prompted shape using video, and an average of 8.9 for understanding how to sketch the prompted shape using pro tips infographics. In addition to the accompanying qualitative data, the lesson overview page received high performance metrics, but participants largely expressed having a desire for less scrolling and more clicking interaction from this page.

8.3.4 Shape Exercise Evaluation

The main component of the application was the different shape exercises, and participants were asked to progress through the different sketching lessons for the various prompted shapes. Overall, users on average rated the second iteration of the shape exercises at least 8.6 for initially understanding what to do in the exercise, at least 9.1 for their level of focus during the exercise, and at least 9.0 on their ability to

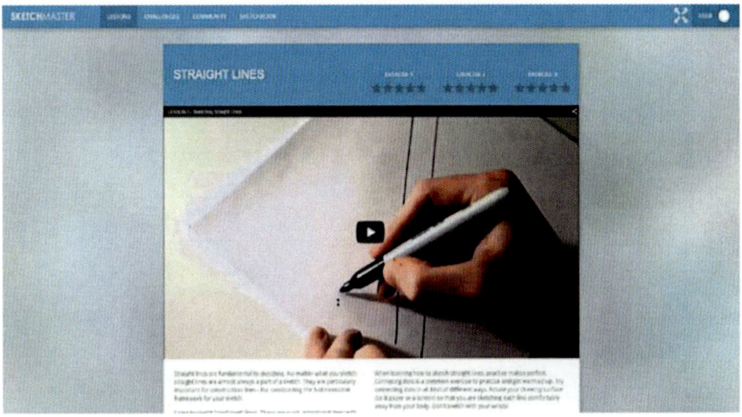

Fig. 8.7 Interface screenshot of lesson overview page, which educates the user on a specific skill or technique and serves as a navigation for exercises

sketch the prompted shapes more accurately. The accompanying qualitative data varied for each shape, but the general consensus was that the shape exercises were well-received while some had issues with the timing aspects of the application, such as the exercises being timed and timing oversensitivity of the prompted cues.

8.3.5 Interactive Coach Evaluation

A supplemental component of the application was the incorporation of an interactive coach to warm up users to the educational experience within the application. We proposed three candidate interactive coaches, and participants were most receptive to the candidate whom visually resembled historical artist Leonardo Da Vinci (Fig. 8.8).

8.3.6 Assessment Display Evaluation

One other component in the application was the assessment display, which was provided after completing a lesson (Fig. 8.9). Overall, participants reacted positively to and feeling accomplished with the automated assessment of their sketches, especially with real-time deviation lines and regardless of minor evaluation errors. One remark from participants was that they were open to assessment being displayed as either a five-star rating or as a full performance metrics overview, which we can implement in the future as a toggle. An additional remark was an option to view a history of their previous scores to self-determine their own improvements of their sketching ability over time.

Fig. 8.8 Visualization graph of candidate interactive coaches and the ratio of preference votes

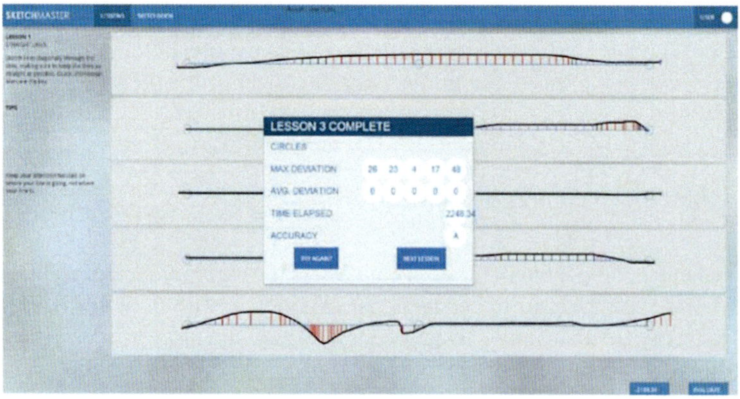

Fig. 8.9 Interface screenshot of assessment display

8.3.7 Overall Insights

From our evaluation, we observed the usability testing demonstrated the value of both exercise designs in terms of motivation, states of flow, and subjective opinions on their effectiveness as learning tools. We discovered that one effective approach would be to combine the positive aspects of both exercise styles into a single exercise style (Figs. 8.10 and 8.11).

A major flaw in our current interface design that we partially anticipated was that participants did not fully understand what to do before practicing a new exercise (Fig. 8.12). We believe that more care should be taken in guiding users through the

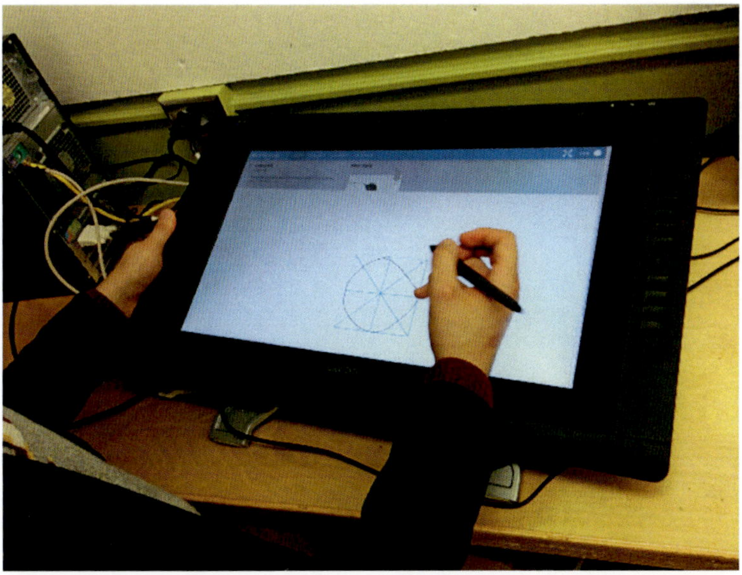

Fig. 8.10 A user during one-at-a-time exercises, where the participants expressed these types of exercises as "better practice" and were able to get in to more of a state of flow

Fig. 8.11 A user received real-time feedback from deviation lines generated from our sketch recognition approaches, which participants praised for their usefulness

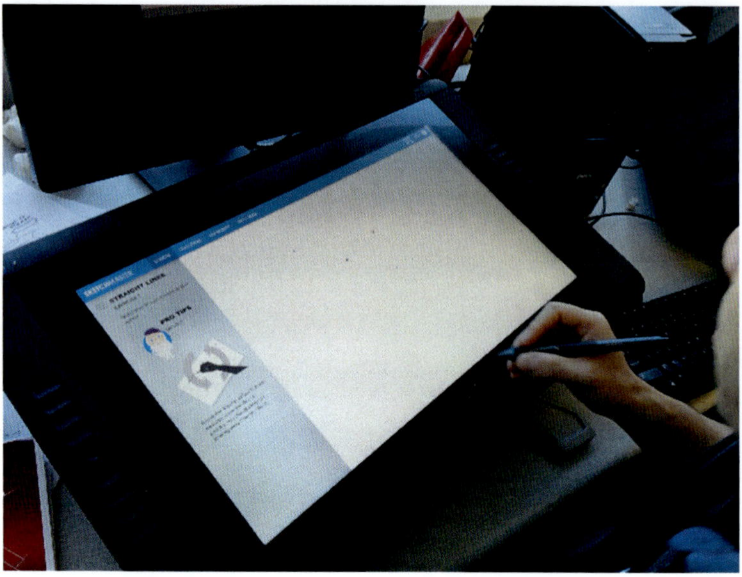

Fig. 8.12 An example of a user encountering confusion of what to do next after an exercise that is common with participants

experience and without surprising them. Furthermore, we observed that scrolling should generally be eliminated from the interface due to the way people interacted when using styluses.

8.4 Contributions

This paper introduces our preliminary prototype and evaluation of the PerSketchTivity system. Our results show that traditional paper-based methods for learning sketching can be translated to the digital medium. Further research will evaluate its effectiveness in raising motivation, self-efficacy, self-regulated learning, and spatial reasoning skills.

Acknowledgments Thanks to members of the Sketch Recognition Lab and the IDREEM Lab who helped with the ideas of the project and paper, in particular Seth Polsley from SRL and Bill Scott at Stanford deserve a special shout out. This project is funded in part by NSF Cyberlearning grants 1441331 and 1441291 (EXP: Collaborative Research: PerSketchTivity- Empowering and Inspiring Creative, Competent, Communicative, and Effective Engineers through Perspective Sketching).

References

1. Atilola O (2007) The effects of representation and analogy on engineering idea generation. Ph.D. thesis, Georgia Institute of Technology, Atlanta, Georgia, USA
2. Bandura A (1997) Self-efficacy: the exercise of self-control, 1st edn. Freeman, New York
3. Cummmings D, Vides F, Hammond T (2012) I don't believe my eyes!: geometric sketch recognition for a computer art tutorial. In: Proceedings of the international symposium on sketch-based interfaces and modeling. SBIM '12. Eurographics Association, Geneva, Switzerland, pp 97–106
4. Dixon D, Prasad M, Hammond T (2010) iCanDraw: using sketch recognition and corrective feedback to assist a user in drawing human faces. In: Proceedings of the SIGCHI conference on human factors in computing systems., CHI '10. ACM, New York, USA, pp 897–906
5. Franken R (2011) Human motivation, 1st edn. Cengage Learning, Boston
6. Gardner H (1983) Frames of mind: the theory of multiple intelligences, 1st edn. Basic Books, New York
7. Kim H, Taele P, Valentine S, McTigue E, Hammond T (2013) KimCHI: a sketch-based developmental skill classifier to enhance pen-driven educational interfaces for children. In: Proceedings of the international symposium on sketch-based interfaces and modeling pages, SBIM '13. ACM, New York, pp 33–42
8. Larkin J, Simon H (1987) Why a diagram is (sometimes) worth ten thousand words. Cogn Sci 11(1):65–100
9. Robertson S (2013) How to draw: drawing and sketching objects and environments from your imagination, 1st edn. Design Studio Press, Culver City
10. Taele P, Hammond T (2009) Hashigo: a next-generation sketch interactive system for japanese kanji. In: Proceedings of the twenty-first innovative applications artificial intelligence conference, IAAI '09. AAAI, Palo Alto, California, USA, pp 153–158
11. Zimmerman B (2008) Investigating self-regulation and motivation: historical background, methodological developments, and future prospects. Am Educ Res J 45(1):166–183

Chapter 9
An Intelligent Sketch-Based Educational Interface for Learning Complex Written East Asian Phonetic Symbols

Paul Taele and Tracy Hammond

Abstract Literacy in written phonetic symbols for East Asian languages is important but challenging for novice language students with only English language fluency, but pedagogical approaches such as rote writing practice and written technique have successfully assisted students towards written mastery. Researchers and developers are also adapting these approaches into intelligent educational apps for students to exploit interactive computing technologies for learning written East Asian language phonetic symbols, whether they are full-time students in K12 or higher education enrolled in conventional classrooms or non-traditional students studying the subject as a passionate interest. However, related pen and touch educational computing apps for sketching practice of East Asian language phonetic symbols provide limited assessment and flexibility of students' input and sketching style, while related recognition systems either focus more on expert users' writing styles or cannot provide assessment for more complex phonetic symbols. In this article, we describe our preliminary work on an intelligent sketch-based educational interface developed specifically for assessing students' sketched input of complex East Asian language phonetic symbols. The interface system relies on template matching from expert users' sketched training data and various heuristics for assessing the visual structure and technical correctness of students' more complex written phonetic symbols. From our evaluations of separate sketching data from both novice and expert writers, we were able to achieve reasonably robust performance for both visual structure and technical correctness of our workbook interface for complex written East Asian language phonetic symbols.

P. Taele (✉) · T. Hammond
Sketch Recognition Lab, Computer Science and Engineering Department,
Texas A&M University, College Station, TX, USA
e-mail: ptaele@cse.tamu.edu

T. Hammond
e-mail: hammond@tamu.edu

T. Hammond et al. (eds.), *Revolutionizing Education with Digital Ink*,
Human–Computer Interaction Series, DOI 10.1007/978-3-319-31193-7_9

9.1 Problem Statement and Context

The East Asian languages of Chinese, Japanese, and Korean (CJK) consist of several writing scripts that language students must master in order to attain reading and writing fluency in those languages. Some of those writing scripts consist of phonetic symbols that play varying important roles in the CJK languages, such as the hangul script that dominates written Korean, the hiragana and katakana scripts that is an essential aspect of written Japanese, and the zhuyin script that is an educational tool and computer input method popularly used in Taiwan for written Chinese. For novice language students whose primary writing fluency stems from languages such as English that utilize Latin alphabet letters, the phonetic symbols of these East Asian languages may prove challenging in comparison due to factors such as greater complexity, variety, and number of these symbols.

As a result, two successful pedagogical approaches that East Asian language instructors introduce to novice language students during exposure of the phonetic symbols are rote practice and written technique. The former involves repeatedly writing the symbols in order to develop muscle memory of writing and reading the symbols, while the latter consists of understanding patterns of the symbols through specific writing order and direction of the symbols' strokes.

These pedagogical approaches of rote practice and written technique are traditionally employed as in-class exercises with instructor feedback or as homework study with guided workbook instructions. With recent trends in mobile computing devices that offer self-study educational apps and recent advances in automated sketch and gesture recognition techniques that improve the types of feedback on written input, researchers and developers are motivated in developing intelligent educational applications including those for learning written East Asian language phonetic symbols. However, for relevant current intelligent educational applications and language computing tools that can benefit novice students in phonetic symbols, the major limitations of these resources either involve shallow assessment for a wide range of phonetic symbols or deep assessment for a narrow class of less complex phonetic symbols.

In this paper, we therefore propose an intelligent sketch-based workbook interface specifically for assisting novice students in practicing their learning of written East Asian language phonetic symbols. The major contribution of our work stems from the assessment provided by our digital workbook through both visual structure and written technique for more complex phonetic symbols. The former determines how visually similar a novice students' sketched input matches model sketched input from expert users, while the latter determines whether the student provided the correct count, order, and direction of the strokes.

9.1.1 *Prior Work*

While there are numerous works dedicated to related topics of educational applications and automated recognition of written East Asian language symbols, the most relevant works pertaining to the core contributions of our digital workbook stem from recent educational mobile apps, sketch recognition techniques, and intelligent educational applications.

9.1.1.1 Educational Mobile Apps

Computing devices such as smartphones and tablets enable novice students to take advantage of mobile computing resources to supplement their learning of phonetic symbols. Although a majority of these educational mobile apps rely solely on conventional flashcard-based content for only displaying phonetic symbols for visual review, a small segment of educational mobile apps have gone further in exploiting touch and pen modalities to accomplish writing practice. Examples of these applications exist for writing scripts such as Chinese zhuyin [9] and Japanese hiragana [2, 6]. While such educational mobile apps improve on the existing flashcard-based approach with actual incorporation of writing input or demonstrations, assessment is generally constrained to binary feedback of right or wrong while writing lacks variation and is restricted to one specific size and style.

9.1.1.2 Sketch Recognition Techniques

Similar to educational applications, there are also numerous works in machine learning and artificial intelligence techniques specific for automatically recognizing written East Asian languages such as phonetic symbols. Many of these techniques such as vision- and structure-based ones often focus on providing the best interpretation of what is written from expert users while also omitting relevant information such as proper writing and correct technique from novice users. As a result, techniques that focus on recognizing sketch diagrams have stronger applications for the analogous phonetic symbols. One direction includes first fragmenting the raw strokes of sketched input into segmeted corners using low-level recognizers (e.g., ShortStraw [19], IStraw [20]), then incorporating this corner information and additional heuristics for recognizing geometric primitives like lines and curves (e.g., PaleoSketch [7]), and finally recognizing collections of these strokes as an entire sketch (e.g., LADDER [4]).

While techniques from this direction perform well for sketch diagrams that have strong geometric properties such as simple line-based phonetic symbols, more complex multi-curved phonetic symbols may perform better for more applicable gesture recognizers such as from $-family recognizers [1]. Stroke-independent variants of existing gesture recognizers such as $P [17] and Hausdorff distance [13, 14] have further applicability with assessing the visual structure correctness of phonetic symbols since automated recognition is not tied to the order of how the strokes of the symbols were drawn.

9.1.1.3 Intelligent Educational Applications

Intelligent educational applications that automatically recognize sketch diagrams have been successfully explored in various domains, including but not limited to mechanical engineering (e.g., Mechanix [15, 16]), music (e.g., Maestoso [13]), drawing (e.g., iCanDraw [3]), and math (e.g., MathPad2 [5]). Similar prior work have been explored for intelligent workbook interfaces focused on other Asian languages [12] such as Hashigo [10] for introductory Japanese characters, LAMPS [11] for Chinese zhuyin symbols, and Urdu Qaeda [8] for Urdu alphabet letters. However, these latter prior work require that characters and symbols be first manually defined geometrically, which limits strong recognition performance to simpler symbols that can be strongly geometrically defined.

9.2 Method Employed

The contribution of our paper is an intelligent sketch-based workbook interface, in order to enable novice language students to practice their rote writing practice of complex East Asian phonetic symbols with valuable accompanying automated assessment for visual and technical correctness. Figure 9.1 shows a visualized demonstration of the interface's assessment system for an example phonetic symbol, where the system displays the closest training data match on the right, technique assessment on the top left, and a list of the closest matched training data on the bottom left. The remaining portion of this section will elaborate on the details of the visual and technique assessment, as well as an overview of the core intelligent workbook interface components.

9.2.1 Visual Assessment

The approach that we took for handling visual assessment of phonetic symbols in a pedagogical environment involves comparing novice students' sketched input with those from model input from expert users. As a result, we initially collected sets of sketched phonetic symbols from expert writers in Chinese, Japanese, and Korean. Using these model sketches, we train the visual assessor by first transforming these training data using resampling, scaling, and translating into templates similarly to [18, 19].

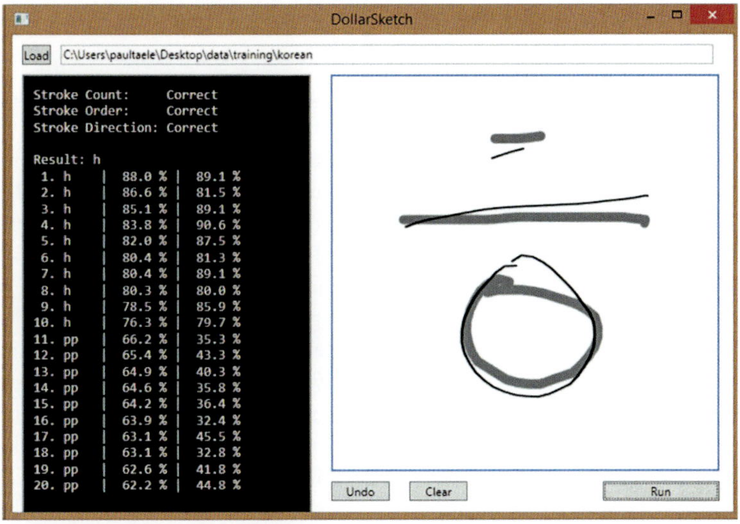

Fig. 9.1 Visual and technique assessment system for written East Asian language phonetic symbols

Once the templates are collected and transformed, we then use a Hausdorff distance-based template matching algorithm and score [14] to evaluate on the templates themselves using leave-one-out cross-validation to determine two different values in the set of phonetic symbols: the highest Hausdorff distance score [13], which calculates the distance between the two nearest points from the model and input strokes; and the associated coverage score, which calculates the ratio of how many points were selected in the model stroke that is nearest to the points in the input stroke. The latter coverage score is motivated by the existence of phonetic symbols that are visually similar but may differ by a difference of one additional stroke. Since Hausdorff distance does not differentiate between phonetic symbols exhibiting this kind of similarity, incorporating a coverage score as a feature further assists the visual assessor from differentiating such similar symbols.

Once the templates are matched with each other with leave-one-out cross-validation to remove self-classifications, we then record these highest distance and coverage scores as thresholds for comparison with novice students' sketched input, which are similarly transformed and template matched to the model training data. After the template matcher calculates the Hausdorff distance and coverage scores of the novice students' input sketch and is classified by the phonetic symbol of the model training data with the best distance score, these scores are then compared to the previously recorded thresholds. If both the distance and coverage scores are at most 5 % below the corresponding thresholds, then the sketched input retains its phonetic symbol classification. Otherwise, the symbol receives an empty classification. The motivation for variable thresholds instead of fixed thresholds is that we observed that distances between different phonetic symbols, especially symbols whose strokes do not overlap.

9.2.2 *Technique Assessment*

Following successful classification from the visual assessor, our system then proceeds to the technique assessor to determine if the sketched input has the correct stroke count, order, and direction. The technique assessor first trivially determines stroke count correctness by determining whether the input and model sketch share the same stroke count. For the other written technique properties, technique assessment from similar systems Hashigo [10] and LAMPS [11] rely on raw temporal information of the individual strokes to assess the written technique. However, transformed strokes from template match are omitted since they do not align exactly to resampled points.

The solution that we employ for our system first involves extracting the start and end times of each raw stroke, then evenly dividing the time for each point in the resampled stroke. Once the transformed input and model sketch contain these approximated times, the technique assessor then attempts to match each stroke from the input sketch to the model sketch by the smallest sum of distances between the corresponding corners of the strokes' associated bounding boxes. Once each of the strokes of the input and model sketches are paired together, we chronologically sort the stroke pairs by the model sketches' temporal information, and then assess correct stroke order by determining whether the chronological order of the input sketch is correct.

We similarly assess the stroke direction for the stroke pairs by first comparing the first point of an input stroke to the nearest and farthest endpoints of the corresponding model stroke. If the time of the nearer point of the model stroke is chronologically earlier than the farther point for all input strokes, then this implies that the entire input sketch has correct stroke direction. Otherwise, it does not.

9.2.3 *Workbook Interface*

Our digital workbook relies on the feedback from the visual and technique assessors in order to provide its intelligent sketch-based user interface. We first describe the digital workbook's overall layout, and then describe how the different displayed assessment types incorporate the assessors' feedback.

9.2.3.1 Overall Layout

When a novice user first opens the digital workbook, they are shown a window prompt displayed in front of a blank workbook (Fig. 9.2). The window prompt contains three different phonetic symbol sets for the user to practice from: the Chinese zhuyin script, the Japanese hiragana script, and the consonants from the Korean hangul script. These written scripts were chosen because they exhibit complex properties that do not perform well for similar systems that rely on geometric recognition techniques such as Hashigo and LAMPS.

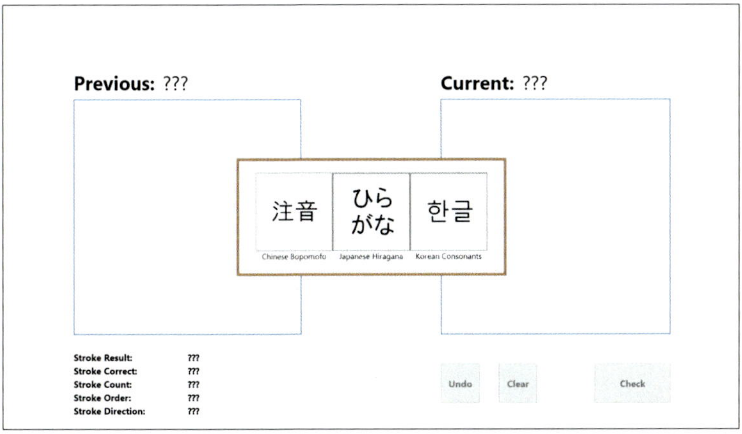

Fig. 9.2 Example of interface with prompted selections of phonetic symbol set lesson type in front of an initialized interface in the background

After the novice student makes a selection, they are exposed to two different windows on the left and right sides of the workbook. The left side is the viewing side, which contains automated visual and technique assessment of the previously prompted phonetic symbol; while the right side is the interaction side, which contains a drawing canvas to sketch the prompted phonetic symbol and accompanying buttons to delete or submit the input for assessment (Fig. 9.3).

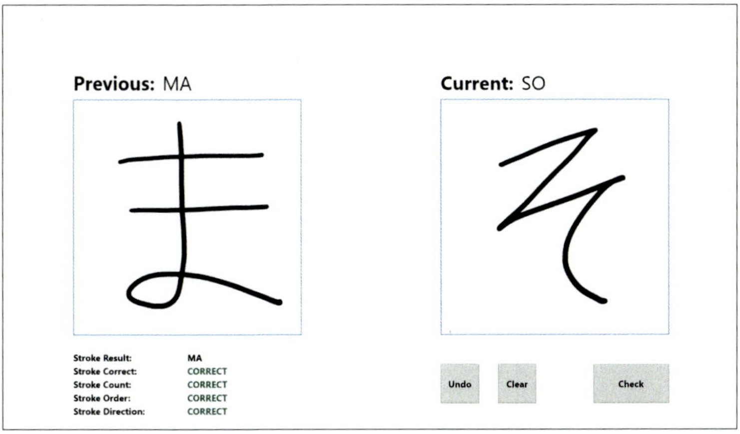

Fig. 9.3 Example of interface after feedback is given to previously prompted phonetic symbol and user is sketching answer for currently prompted phonetic symbol

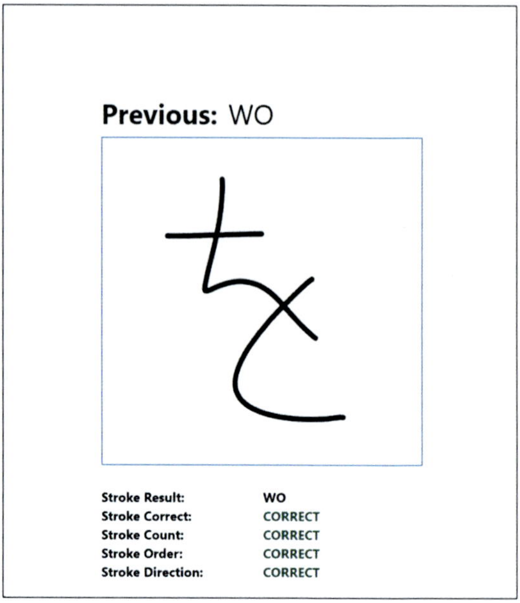

Fig. 9.4 Example assessment of correctly sketched phonetic symbol

9.2.3.2 Assessment Types

After the student submits their sketched input, the interface runs its strokes to the visual and technique assessors and processes the feedback into different assessment types. If the sketched input is both visually and technically correct, then the viewing portion of the digital workbook will provide assessment similar to that given in Fig. 9.4.

However, for cases when the sketched input is either visually or technically incorrect, other assessment types are instead given. For incorrect stroke order, the first incorrect stroke is highlighted and emphasized similar to Fig. 9.5a. For incorrect stroke direction, the first incorrect stroke is highlighted and the correct endpoint is shown similar to Fig. 9.5b. For incorrect phonetic symbol input, a model sketch of the originally prompted phonetic symbol is displayed over the sketched input similarly to Fig. 9.5c. Such a model sketch is also shown for visually improper phonetic symbol input, similarly to Fig. 9.5d.

9.3 Results and Evaluation

In order to provide a preliminary evaluation of the performance of the digital workbook's assessment, we follow a similar evaluation process previously used for both Hashigo [10] and LAMPS [11] that is described below.

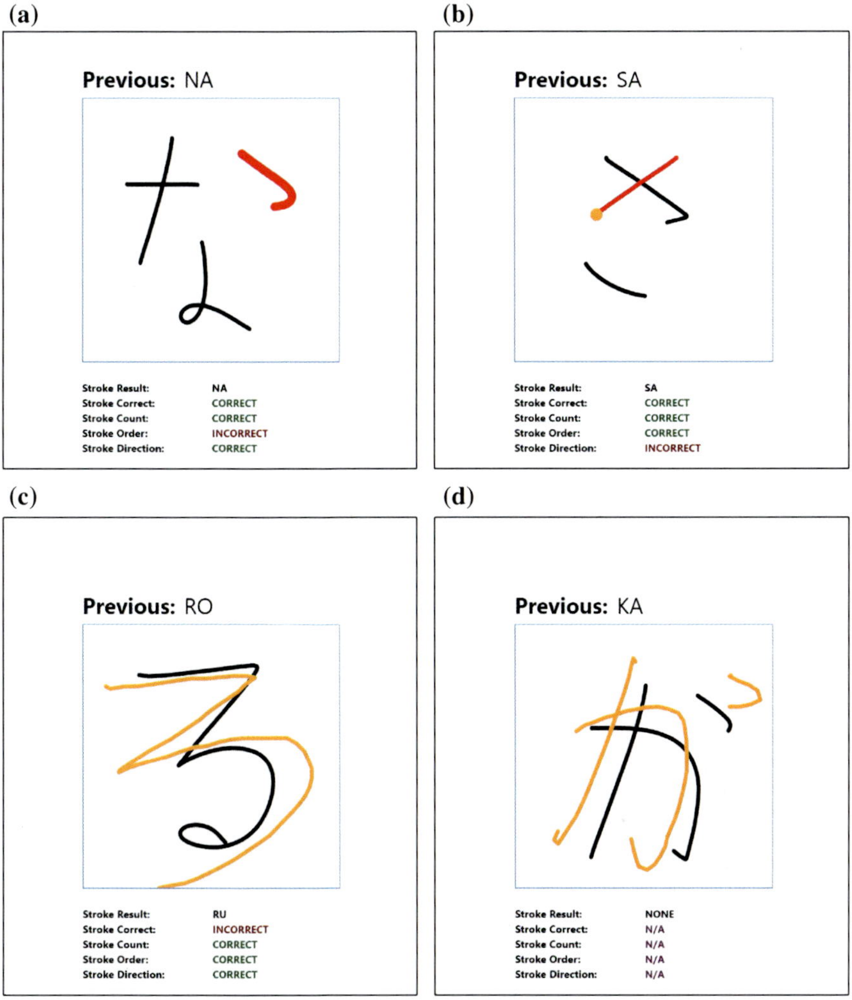

Fig. 9.5 Assessments for different user mistakes of sketched phonetic symbols. **a** incorrect stroke order, **b** incorrect stroke direction, **c** incorrect stroke, and **d** improper symbol

9.3.1 Data Collection

We recruited two expert users each for the three CJK phonetic symbols sets and requested that they provide ten samples for each symbol (Fig. 9.6). The participants were asked to either provide data from a stylus pen on a digital tablet or from their finger on a touchscreen. Each participant was verbally given the phonetic symbol to sketch, and submitted their sketches manually upon completion. The prompted phonetic symbols were selected at random until all symbols were exhausted.

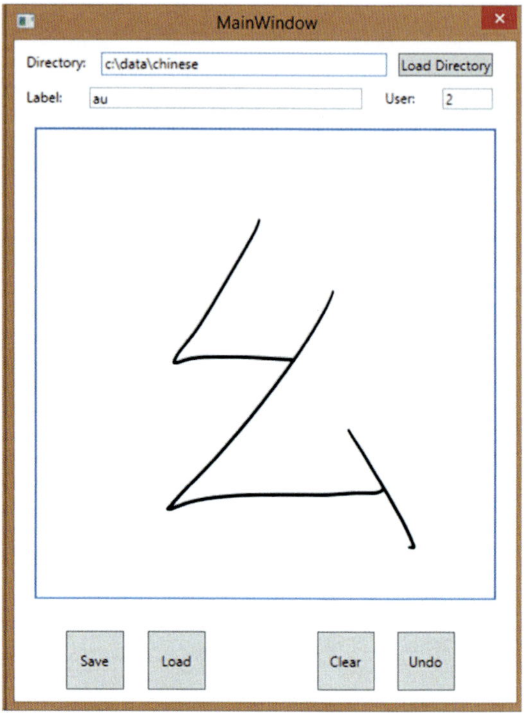

Fig. 9.6 Interface for collecting user-sketched phonetic symbol input

9.3.2 *Visual and Technique Assessment Evaluation*

After collecting the participants' sketching data, we then ran their sketched input through the visual assessor. Our visual assessment evaluation involved all-or-nothing recognition, where the predicted sketched input is only considered correct if it exactly matches the actual label, while the participants' data served entirely as test data for our trained visual assessor. From this evaluation setup, we received an overall average above 98 % for each of the phonetic symbol sets, where all misclassified symbols were limited to at most one instance from a phonetic symbol.

We then evaluated the technique assessor by requesting participants to use the digital workbook and go through one session of symbols, with the only direction that they purposely sketch the prompted symbol with at least one variation involving either incorrect stroke count, order, direction, or some combination of the three technique errors. From this evaluation, we visually observed that the digital workbook was able to detect incorrect written technique with 100 % accuracy.

9.4 Contributions

From our current research progress in developing an intelligent sketch-based educational interface for learning complex written East Asian phonetic symbols in languages such as Chinese, Japanese, and Korean, we have discovered that we can develop such an interface that accomplishes at least two different contributions. The first is reasonable robustness to handwritten input using a combination of template matching gesture recognition and geometric sketch recognition techniques, and the second is appropriate intuitiveness to student practice using a proposed interface that leverages stylus and touchscreen hardware for mimicking existing paper-based language workbooks. From the progress of our research work that currently focuses on writing practice, we see many exciting directions for expanding into specialized interfaces on not just the specific language scripts, but also in other types of writing instruction that further benefits students' self-practice and further complements instructors' existing curriculum.

Acknowledgments I would first like to give my great appreciation to the members of the Sketch Recognition Lab for sharing their many combined years of experience in shaping the direction of this research project. There have also been many influential East Asian language instructors in my life that allowed me to incorporate my language knowledge into intelligent sketch-based educational applications, especially to my Japanese language instructors Mr. George Adams and Ms. Kazue Kurokawa from Texas A&M University's Department of International Studies, and my Chinese language instructor Dr. Wen-Hua Teng from the University of Texas' Department of Asian Studies. Lastly, this project is funded in part by Microsoft (Microsoft Surface Hub Grant: Sketch and Gesture Recognition for Collaborative and Design Interfaces on the Surface Hub).

References

1. Anthony L, Wobbrock J (2012) $N-protractor: a fast and accurate multistroke recognizer. In: Proceedings of graphics interface 2012, GI '12, Canadian Information Processing Society, Mississauga, pp 117–120
2. Cornerstone Studio: Hiragana - read and write [application] (2015). Accessed 30 June 2015
3. Dixon D, Prasad M, Hammond T (2010) iCanDraw: using sketch recognition and corrective feedback to assist a user in drawing human faces. In: Proceedings of the SIGCHI conference on human factors in computing systems, CHI '10. ACM, New York, pp 897–906
4. Hammond T, Davis R (2003) LADDER: a language to describe drawing, display, and editing in sketch recognition. In: Proceedings of the 18th international joint conference on artificial intelligence, IJCAI '03. AAAI, Palo Alto, pp 461–467
5. LaViola J Jr (2007) Advances in mathematical sketching: moving toward the paradigm's full potential. IEEE Comput Graph Appl 27(1):38–48
6. Legendarya/Imaginactiva: Hiragana - learn Japanese [application] (2015). Accessed 14 Jan 2016
7. Paulson B, Hammond T (2008) Paleosketch: accurate primitive sketch recognition and beautification. In: Proceedings of the 13th international conference on intelligent user interfaces, IUI '08. ACM, New York, pp 1–10
8. Shahzad N, Paulson B, Hammond T (2009) Urdu qaeda: recognition system for isolated urdu characters. In: Proceedings of the workshop on sketch recognition at the 14th international conference of intelligent user interfaces, IUI-SR '09

9. Sigma Sky, LLC: Write bopomofo [application] (2015). Accessed 14 Jan 2016
10. Taele P, Hammond T (2009) Hashigo: a next-generation sketch interactive system for Japanese kanji. In: Proceedings of the twenty-first innovative applications artificial intelligence conference, IAAI '09. AAAI, Palo Alto, pp 153–158
11. Taele P, Hammond T (2010) Lamps: a sketch recognition-based teaching tool for mandarin phonetic symbols i. J Vis Lang Comput 21(2):109–120
12. Taele P, Hammond T (2015) Enhancing instruction of written east asian languages with sketch recognition-based "intelligent language workbook" interfaces. In: Hammond T, Valentine S, Adler A, Payton M (eds) The impact of pen and touch technology on education. Springer, Berlin, pp 119–126
13. Taele P, Barreto L, Hammond T (2015) Maestoso: an intelligent educational sketching tool for learning music theory. In: Proceedings of the twenty-seventh innovative applications of artificial intelligence conference, IAAI '15. AAAI, Palo Alto, pp 3999–4005
14. Valentine S, Field M, Hammond T, Smith A (2011) A shape comparison technique for use in sketch-based tutoring systems. In: Proceedings of the 2011 intelligent user interfaces workshop on sketch recognition, IUI SR '11
15. Valentine S, Vides F, Lucchese G, Turner D, Kim Hh, Li W, Linsey J, Hammond T (2012) Mechanix: A sketch-based tutoring system for statics courses. In: Proceedings of the twenty-fourth innovative applications of artificial intelligence conference, IAAI '12. AAAI, Palo Alto, pp 2253–2260
16. Valentine S, Lara-Garduno R, Linsey J, Hammond T (2015) Mechanix: a sketch based tutoring system that automatically corrects hand-sketched statics homework, The impact of pen and touch technology on education
17. Vatavu RD, Anthony L, Wobbrock JO (2012) Gestures as point clouds: a $p recognizer for user interface prototypes. In: Proceedings of the 14th ACM international conference on multimodal interaction. ACM, New York, pp 273–280
18. Wobbrock J, Wilson A, Li Y (2007) Gestures without libraries, toolkits or training: a $1 recognizer for user interface prototypes. In: Proceedings of the 20th annual ACM symposium on user interface software and technology, UIST '07. ACM, New York, pp 159–168
19. Wolin A, Eoff B, Hammond T (2008) Shortstraw: a simple and effective corner finder for polylines. In: Proceedings of the fifth eurographics conference on sketch-based interfaces and modeling, SBIM '08. Eurographics Association, Geneva, pp 33–40
20. Xiong Y, LaViola J Jr (2010) Technical section: a shortstraw-based algorithm for corner finding in sketch-based interfaces. Comput Graph 34(5):513–527

Chapter 10
A Stylus-Driven Intelligent Tutoring System for Music Education Instruction

Laura Barreto, Paul Taele, and Tracy Hammond

Abstract Inspiring musicians and non-musician hobbyists alike can enjoy various benefits from learning music theory beyond its importance in performing music itself. Such reasons include developing their mathematical abilities, improving their reading comprehension, expanding their memory capabilities, better appreciating music that they listen to, and so on. However, current resources that are available for teaching music theory to students present their own inherent disadvantages. Specifically, traditional music theory classroom centers assume that students already have existing musical knowledge, existing self-study paper-based materials lack immediate feedback, while emerging educational apps either lack stylus-based interaction or intelligent feedback appropriate for novice students. In this paper, we introduce a stylus-driven intelligent tutoring system for music education instruction that aims to combine the benefits while addressing the limitations of existing instructional resources for teaching music theory. Our proposed system provides an accessible educational application with an intelligent sketch user interface that is designed for novice students interested in learning music theory through a series of interactive music composition lessons and quizzes. Following the completion of a student's composed solution to a prompted music theory question, our system first leverages appropriate sketch and gesture recognition techniques to automatically understand the student's input, and then generates feedback and assessment of the student's input that emulates those from a music theory instructor. From our evaluations,

L. Barreto (✉) · P. Taele (✉) · T. Hammond
Sketch Recognition Lab, Computer Science & Engineering Department,
Texas A&M University, College Station, Texas, USA
e-mail: labarreto@vassar.edu

P. Taele
e-mail: ptaele@cse.tamu.edu

T. Hammond
e-mail: hammond@tamu.edu

L. Barreto
Computer Science Department, Vassar College, Poughkeepsie, New York, USA

T. Hammond et al. (eds.), *Revolutionizing Education with Digital Ink*,
Human–Computer Interaction Series, DOI 10.1007/978-3-319-31193-7_10

we demonstrate that not only did our system automatically understood students' composed solutions with reasonable accuracy, but also that novice students were able to successfully grasp introductory music theory concepts from a single session using our system.

10.1 Problem Statement and Context

10.1.1 Problem Statement

10.1.1.1 Benefits of Learning Music Theory

Much like how people have developed the practice of writing text so that it may be later read silently to themselves or aloud to others, people have similarly developed the practice of composing music so that it may be later performed aloud for themselves and for others. Moreover, understanding the syntax, semantics, and grammar of the notation used in music is incredibly crucial to aspiring musicians who wish to produce music that they may wish to play and perform. Therefore, a strong grasp of this particularly important aspect of music theory is directly beneficial to novice music students so that they actually know how to read music that they can later perform.

However, there are also less direct but similarly valuable benefits of learning music theory that can positively affect both aspiring musicians and music hobbyists alike. For the aspiring musicians, they can enjoy various practical benefits from mastering music theory that can enhance their overall musical skills. These benefits include the ability to compose and perform music more accurately, to better understand the art itself through the reading and listening of prior works, and to musically express their thoughts and ideas through musical notation more fully and expressively [17].

Non-professional music hobbyists can similarly enjoy the benefits of learning music theory for reasons that are indirectly related to the practice of performing music itself. For example, non-musicians with knowledge of music theory can enjoy practical benefits that relate to better fostering their critical thinking [28]. Music theory itself also presents an interesting real-world domain for non-musicians to more enthusiastically improve math analytical skills [29], especially for young children who are in the process of learning math. Furthermore, music hobbyists with at least some proficiency of music theory can even have a greater appreciation of the different types of music that they enjoy in their free time [18].

10.1.1.2 Conventional Pedagogical Practices

Conventional approaches for learning music theory in order for students of varying musical aspirations to reap its benefits have primarily stemmed from an assortment of existing pedagogical theories based on successful classroom practices. While more traditional approaches have included the tried-and-true practice of students learning from classroom instructors [23] and music theory textbooks [5], extensions of these traditional approaches have involved a combination of flipped classroom concepts and computer-assisted resources. These include practices in collaborative learning, such as face-to-face small group interactions [41] and computer-mediated learning [35]; as well as computer-assisted tutoring systems from early computing systems [8] to more recent technologies [40]. However, both traditional and emerging approaches still dominantly rely on the valuable support of actual human instructors or the existing practices found in the conventional classroom, which may not be the most viable solution for students who wish to pursue primarily in self-study, appreciate the expertise of human instructors outside the classroom, and so on.

10.1.1.3 Proposed Solution

With improving technological advances in both digital drawing and writing interfaces, mobile and touchscreen devices, and sketch and gesture recognition techniques, we propose a stylus-driven intelligent tutoring system (ITS) that both leverages these technological advances as well as the successful pedagogical practices of music theory classroom. Our latest interactive music theory educational application called Maestoso (Fig. 10.1) builds upon our stylus-driven ITS that combines the advantages of hands-on freehand writing of musical notation of prompted music theory concepts and also emulated intelligent feedback and assessment of human music theory instructors.

10.1.2 Context

The work in our system draws on the insights and lessons from a broad range of technological fields for creating a stylus-based ITS for music education instruction. These specifically include:

- existing music education applications, which can be driven by stylus and touch interactions;
- music notation software, which consist of either established mouse-and-keyboard input or emerging stylus-or-touch input;
- non-music education sketch-enabled intelligent tutoring systems, which include those that utilize sketch recognition techniques that are also relevant for intelligent user interfaces in music education;
- and finally handwritten music recognition techniques, which range from more vision-based optical music recognition algorithms to more heuristics-based sketch recognition algorithms.

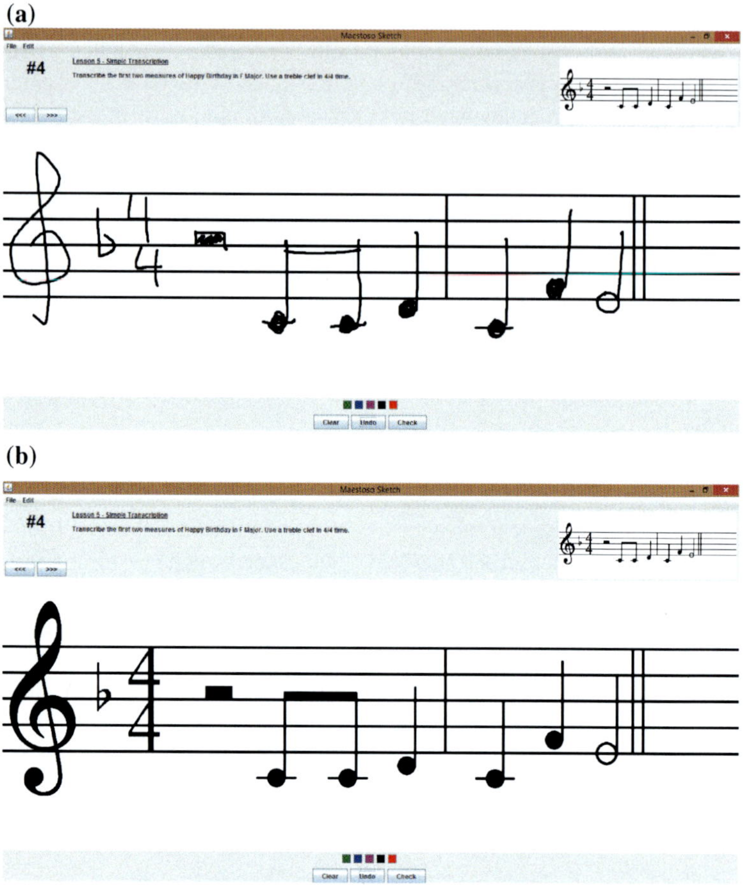

Fig. 10.1 A sample screenshot of the Maetoso educational application: **a** with the original raw strokes displayed, and **b** with the generated beautified strokes displayed

We first describe influential prior work to our system from these different fields before describing the specifics of our system.

10.1.2.1 Music Education Applications

Since our system is a music education application, more specifically an intelligent music tutoring system, one type of prior work includes those that have digitized self-study review-based practices such as Tenuto[1] and Theory Lessons,[2] which allow students to use mobile devices to visually review music education concepts. Another

[1] http://www.musictheory.net/products/tenuto.

[2] http://www.musictheory.net/products/lessons.

type of prior work has more directly targeted younger children that focus more on learning novelty over conventional classroom practices such as Paint Melody,[3] which presents a unique interactive experience combining drawing and sounds for creative free-form expression. Prior work that takes a different direction by tapping into the online strengths of the internet includes massively open online courses (MOOCs) such as the music theory lessons found in Coursera.[4] Lastly, prior work such as Foundations of Music [18] extend from traditional music education textbooks that not only provide a digital analog of content in paper-based textbooks, but also interactive review exercises based on content from these textbooks. However, these music education applications have limitations as they provide general binary feedback or no feedback at all. Such binary feedback only tests students on music theory concepts that they were instructed to review and does not engage students in directly writing out music with either touch or a stylus.

10.1.2.2 Music Composition Applications

Unlike music education applications, which dominantly assume that users are generally students with novice knowledge and experience with music theory, music composition applications instead dominantly assume that users are generally music industry professionals or at least aspiring musicians and composers who are well-versed in music theory. Two such well-established music notation tools specific to professional musicians include Finale[5] and Sibelius,[6] both of which provide rich features within their applications. For the former, users can compose music using input devices such as a mouse, microphone, scanner, or musical keyboard, while the latter also incorporates limited educational capabilities such as flashcards related to music concepts. Other similar applications make use of alternative emerging modalities of pen and touch, whether they are stylus-driven applications such as Music Notepad [11] and MusicReader [15], which are earlier works for penning or annotating onto music notation, respectively; or touch-driven mobile apps such as NotateMe[7] and StaffPad,[8] which allow users to directly write basic annotations onto written music. Other applications such as MusicFlow [27] and SoundBrush [3] also incorporate multi-touch capabilities for users to notate music, either using traditional approaches for the former or more novel ones for the latter. However, all of these tools largely assume that users already have at least strong familiarity of music theory for notating music, while also lacking features that effectively target practices for users studying music theory.

---

[3] http://apple.co/1mYsOnk.

[4] https://www.coursera.org/course/musictheory.

[5] http://www.finalemusic.com/.

[6] http://www.sibelius.com/.

[7] http://www.neuratron.com/notateme.html.

[8] http://bit.ly/19Mq6z5.

10.1.2.3 Sketch-Enabled Intelligent Tutoring Systems

Sketching, writing, and drawing interactions play pivotal roles in a diverse range of educational subjects outside of music theory as well, and stylus- and touch-driven ITS have similarly incorporated such interactions for assisting students in studying these subjects. A sampling of these ITS with educational applications include:

- Physicsbook [4] for physics, where students can draw physical systems and write out physics equations that can automatically generate animations of the corresponding physics-based phenomena;
- Mechanix [31, 32] for mechanical engineering, where students can sketch engineering trusses and test the correctness of forces applied on them;
- Hashigo [24] for Japanese, where students can write out Japanaese kanji symbols and receive feedback on the correctness on the symbol matching and their visual structure and writing technique;
- iCanDraw [9] and Eye Can See [6] for figure drawing, where students can receive step-by-step guidance and assessment of their drawing performance;
- LADDER and Tahuti for diagrammatic drawing, where students can draw diagrams for general domains for the former or specific domains such as UML drawing for the latter;
- MathPad2 [13] for mathematics, where students can write out mathematical equations and corresponding diagrams and subsequently receive feedback and visualizations of their input;
- BiologySketch [25] for biology, where students can write out prompts of biological diagrams and determine whether their input is correct;
- Maestoso [26] for music theory, where students can test their music theory knowledge by notating music of prompted music concepts.

This last system is the focus of this paper and is discussed in further detail in terms of implementation and evaluation.

10.1.2.4 Written Music Recognition Techniques

Recognizing how people express music has not only been well-explored, but remains active in the research community. This is true for music expressed acoustically [20], emotionally [38], and especially through both printed and handwriting [22]. Printed and handwriting efforts have relied on different solutions under the umbrella of optical music recognition (OMR), where representative OMR techniques include k-nearest neighbor-based OMRs for handwritten scores [21], writer identification and staff removal [10], hidden Markov-based OMR for notation input [14], as well as conventional OMRs and image processing techniques for automatically recognizing and playing back simple handwritten music notation [2, 39]. Existing OMR approaches such as these generally either focus on recognizing handwritten music on paper or on recognizing stylus input from advanced users. For more novice users who use styluses, music education-based ITS may be better suited to recognition techniques that are capable of automatically understanding and properly assessing their music writing behaviors such as the sketch and gesture recognition techniques proposed within our system.

10.2 Method Employed

For our proposed music education-based ITS, we developed the methodology of the automated recognition system and the implementation of the sketch user interface by first conducting an interaction design study to determine the range of interaction cues from potential users, then implementing an optimal collection of sketch and gesture recognition techniques that are appropriate for our proposed ITS, and lastly developing a corresponding stylus- and touch-capable sketch user interface that takes advantage of intelligent capabilities and self-study practices.

10.2.1 Interaction Design Study

In order to optimally develop a music educational application for teaching novice music students music notation, it is important that we suitably understand how users of such skill level actually notate music using the tried-and-true tools of paper and pen. In this regard, we first recruited a set of six participants through convenience sampling to take part in our interaction design study. The six different users were of ages between 21 and 32 years of age, two of whom were female. Additionally, all six users not only self-reported that they were non-musicians, but also reported having limited knowledge of general music theory.

For each of our six participants, we conducted our study by taking foundational music theory questions from established music educational textbooks such as [18]. Our selection of questions focused specifically on writing solutions to prompted questions displayed on paper, where users needed to identify correct individual components found in music notation such as notes, clefs, and staff. The participants were then tasked to write out their solutions with a pencil (Fig. 10.2). We used our video recording of participants' hands and their written answers on paper to match established observational drawing studies found in [30], so that we would be able to review the participants' interaction drawing cues. Whenever a participant informed the study conductor that they did not know how to draw a specific musical component, the study conductor would guide that participant by briefly showing them a visualization of the musical component in question as a reference. We chose to briefly show this visualization instead of making it easily available, so that our study did not influence the participants' drawing styles from those found in the reference solutions.

Fig. 10.2 A user with novice music theory knowledge writing music component responses

Following the completion of each of the six participants in the interaction design study, we analyzed the video recordings and discovered several valuable drawing interaction cues. The first observation that we derived from all the participants was that they drew their handwritten musical components very carefully and methodically. The second observation is that the participants drew individual musical components in multiple strokes. For example, if a participant were prompted to draw a musical note, they would draw the different sub-components of the note such as the head and the stem in separate strokes instead of as one merged stroke. From these observations, we applied these insights in order to help us design the recognition and interaction capabilities of our proposed system.

10.2.2 Music Recognition System

Designing a system for automatically recognizing handwritten music notation is challenging overall, and for handwritten music of novice users in particular, our prior interaction study design better clarified what kinds of strokes novice users are writing in their musical symbols and how they are doing so. However, another major challenge in automatically recognizing handwritten music notation is in utilizing recognition techniques that can optimally accommodate a diverse set of symbols in music notation that novice students need to know. Such music symbols can be geometrically complex, such that they cannot be easily defined with geometric definitions (e.g., certain clefs and certain rests); geometrically simple, such that they can be easily defined with geometric definitions (e.g., staffs and empty notes); or scribble-like, such as they can be filled in its entirety with a scribbled stroke (e.g., filled notes and rests).

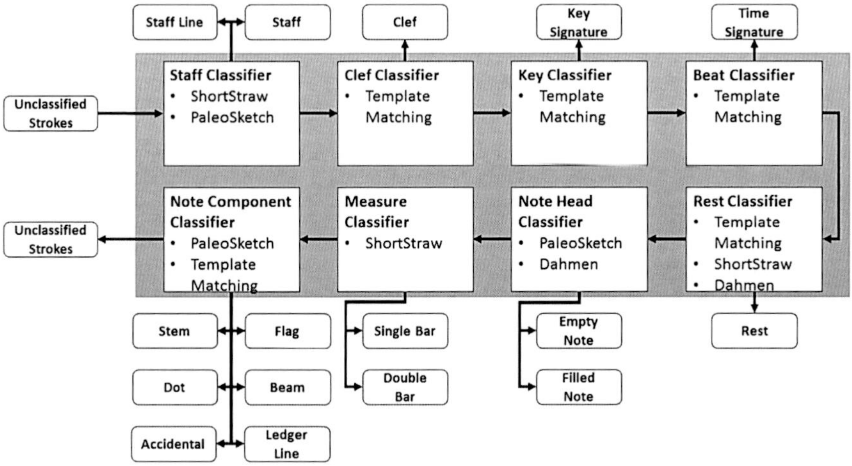

Fig. 10.3 Hierarchy of classifiers used in Maestoso, in order of execution

We therefore approached the recognition system of our music educational application using a hierarchy of sketch and gesture recognition techniques that specializes in optimally classifying specific musical components (Fig. 10.3). Furthermore, we chose to incorporate sketch and gesture recognition techniques over alternative OMR techniques, since OMR techniques cater more towards achieving the best interpretation of the input over supporting properly-written symbols [26]. The following content will go into more detail of the automated recognition techniques and the hierarchical components found in our music recognition system.

10.2.2.1 Template Matching

One area of our recognition system that we wish to highlight involves the gesture recognition technique of template matching, which involves visually classifying a written symbol to the label of an existing template. This approach works especially well for musical symbols such as clefs, accidentals, and shorter duration rests that are more difficult to geometrically classify using existing sketch recognition techniques. However, since geometrically complex symbols found in music notation are visually more complex than the types of symbols that are appropriate for existing template matching algorithms, we describe our specialized template matching algorithm that is adapted to musical symbols that novice students will be exposed to.

The first step in our specialized template matching algorithm involves uniformly transforming the set of points of the user's original handwritten symbol to simplify the classification when comparing the original symbol to candidate templates. For this case, we utilize the stroke transformation steps in the ShortStraw corner-finding algorithm [37], where we transform both the original symbol and each of the templates by first resampling them to 64 points, scaling them to 250 pixels, and then translating them to the origin in Cartesian coordinates. In our templates, each musical symbol that will be used in our educational application consists of twenty distinct candidate templates for comparison with handwritten input symbols.

After transforming both the input and template symbols, we performed general template matching algorithm steps similar to those found in prior touch gesture recognition techniques such as \$1 [36] and Protractor [16], which involve comparing the handwritten input symbol to the set of template symbols. In order to accommodate input symbols that are drawn with more than one stroke, we take similar cues from the multi-stroke template matching algorithm \$N-Protractor [1] in combining strokes. Finally, when it comes to comparing the user's input symbol to the best template symbol candidate, we followed the comparison methods in [12, 33, 34] by using Hausdorff distance, where distances are calculated as between the closest pair of points between the input symbol and each template symbol; instead of Eucliden distance found in [16, 36], where distances are calculated as one-to-one between the input symbol and each template symbol. The reason is that we empirically observed that Hausdorff-based template matching performed better recognition in comparison for the types of musical symbols that we introduce to novice students. We subsequently refined the similarity score calculation—previously used in touch gesture recognizers such as \$1—specifically for Hausdorff distance, in order to provide more well-defined similarity confidence values between the sketched strokes and the candidate template below. From this similarity score, the label of the template with the highest score is used to classify the input symbol.

$$score = 1 - \frac{\left|\frac{1-d}{\sqrt{s^2+s^2}}\right|}{10}$$

10.2.2.2 Staff Classification

The staff plays a pivotal role as the first type of symbol that people would draw when composing music from scratch. Consisting of five long horizontal lines that are adjacent to each other, the staff serves to help people position the remaining musical symbols. Since the staff consists of these horizontal lines, we build a classifier for the staff and its individual lines that specifically looks for five such lines that span the width of the drawing area. We can therefore rely on the insights of geometric sketch recognition algorithms such as the line tests used in PaleoSketch [19] and ShortStraw [37] for determining whether or not an input stroke is a staff line and whether or not a set of input strokes form a staff.

One of the two capabilities of the staff classifier is determining whether an individual input stroke forms a staff line. To do so, the classifier first calculates the entire path distance of the input stroke and compares that path distance to the width of the entire drawing area. If the ratio of the input stroke's path distance to the drawing area's entire width exceeds 0.75, then the classifier checks if the input stroke is a line. We rely on a line test that relies on two values: the path distance of the input stroke and the Euclidean distance between the endpoints of the input stroke. If the ratio of the smaller to the larger value exceeds 0.95, then we consider the input stroke to be a line. Finally, we perform a horizontal test to determine if the line is horizontal. This is accomplished by calculating the incline angle formed between the two endpoints of the Euclidean line formed between the input stroke's endpoints. If the incline angle is within 5 % of the ideal horizontal line angle, then we can finally classify the input stroke as a staff line.

The second capability of the staff classifier is actually determining whether a set of existing horizontal lines forms the staff itself. In order to do so, the classifier first checks to see if a set of five classified staff lines exists. When this set is confirmed as such, the staff classifier proceeds to group these lines as a staff before beautifying these lines. The beautification process consists of straightening the topmost and bottommost staff lines, and then evenly spacing and similarly straightening the remaining in-between three staff lines. Additional information is stored as metadata within this new staff sketch object, such as the vertical distance between adjacent staff lines, and the enumerations of the five staff lines. The vertical distance is referenced in our later classifiers to determine the relative size of the musical symbols, while the enumerations will be referenced to determine the correctness of the input compared to the model answers during assessment.

10.2.2.3 Clef, Key, and Beat Classification

Input strokes that do not pass the staff classifier are sent to subsequent classifiers, specifically classifiers such as the clef, key, and beat classifiers (in that order). These passive musical components serve a purpose in music notation as setting the properties of a range of active musical properties that are played (i.e., notes) or not played (i.e., rests). For novice students in particular, these passive musical components are usually expected to be written after the staff.

The first classifier in this category of music notation classifiers is the clef classifier, where we identify two essential clefs that novice music theory students must know: the treble clef and the bass clef. Classification for these two clefs first involves using template matching to identify whether they visually match existing templates of such clefs. When template matching confirms that the user's input is visually a musical clef, our classifier then checks to see if the clef is spatially appropriate such that it is not only relatively proportional to the musical staff, but that it is also located within the correct relative area of the music staff as well. The latter check takes into account the bounding area of the input relative to the location of the individual and entire lines of the music clef.

The next classifier in this category is the key classifier, where we identify the three essential keys that are the flat, sharp, and neutral. To identify the visual existence of the keys, we rely on template matching for each key. We then determine the location of the key on the musical staff—since its position is crucial in written music notation—by finding the center of the user input's bounding box and locating the musical staff line that is closest to that center. Unlike the clefs and beats, keys are optional and so the key classifier may be skipped entirely if all cases for keys fails either the template matching or relative spatial checks.

The last classifier in this category is the beat classifier, which identifies the beats of the written music notation, specifically with two numbers located one on top of the other adjacent to the clef. Classification in this case first involves identifying what the number is, then determining if it is located in the top or bottom half of the music staff as defined by the defined musical semantics of musical beats, and lastly determines if the musical beat is both semantically complete (i.e., contains two numbers) and spatially correct (i.e., the numbers are located adjacently and closely to the right of the clef and are horizontally adjacent to each other). To identify the individual numbers of the beat, we rely on template matching, while location of the numbers involves checking the bounding boxes of both the individual numbers relative to each other and to the musical staff. Since novice students are expected to know only a small set of possible musical beats, we limit the recognition of the top and bottom beats to single-digit numbers.

10.2.2.4 Rest, Note Head, and Measure Line Classification

The next category of classifiers specific to rests, note heads, and measures focuses on most of the musical notation that follows after the clef, key, and beat notations. The only remaining musical notation that is not covered in this category are the specific subcomponents of the notes, which are highly variable and are handled as a separate classifier category in the next subsection.

Rests in music notation can be visually grouped into two different types: those that contain complex curves and multiple shapes (e.g., quarter and eighth rests) and those that consist of simple filled or unfilled geometric shapes (e.g., quarter, half, and whole rests). For the former complex symbols, we rely dominantly on template matching similar to other template-matched musical notations. For the latter simple symbols, we similarly perform template matching for both filled and unfilled symbols on the outer rectangular outline due to simplicity of implementation while still performing well in recognition. However, if the latter is a filled shape, we also employ an additional scribble recognition technique from [7] which determines whether the shape is filled or not. Once we determine if the input is a rest, we then perform a last step that determines if the rest is located in the vertical center of the musical staff. If these constraints are fulfilled, the input is classified as a rest.

Unlike rests, note heads are less varied and consist of either filled or unfilled approximated circles. Therefore, for the note head classifier for both filled and unfilled note heads, we rely on PaleoSketch's circle test heuristic to classify note heads. If the note head is also filled, we similarly apply the scribble recognition test from the rest classifier. If the note head passes these constraints, it is classified as such. We then determine the placement of the note head based on whether its center is closer to the middle of two staff lines or on a staff line itself.

The last classifier in this category is the measure classifier: the simplest of the group and one of the simplest of all the classifiers in the recognition system. The measure classifier consists of a vertical line that spans from the top of the musical staff line to the bottom. For this test, we simply perform a vertical line test from PaleoSketch and determine if the top and bottom endpoints of the input are relatively close to the corresponding top and bottom regions of the musical staff. If these constraints are met, then the input is classified as a measure line.

10.2.2.5 Note Components Classification

The last category of classifying written musical notation is for the variable components that augment note heads. Since these components vary depending on the note's duration and are specific to only notes, this category is treated separately and last in the recognition system.

Specifically for each note component, we first determine if the component is within half a step of a specific area of a note head (e.g., stems, dots, ledger lines, accidentals) or stem (e.g., beams, flags). We then apply geometric shape tests from PaleoSketch to try to classify those note components. For example, for note components that can be at least approximated by a line such as stems, ledger lines, beams, and flags, we apply the line test heuristic from PaleoSketch to determine whether it is a visually valid note component. The classifier then adjusts accordingly for more specific classification on these note components such as their orientation and endpoint positioning relative to the note head or its other note components (e.g., stem).

For note components that are not directly connected to the note head or its connected note components but are relatively nearby, such as dots and accidentals, we first determine whether those note components are close enough by a distance threshold (within one note head distance) and whether they are vertically aligned with the note head itself, and then apply specific classification steps for those note components. For dots, we employ a dot test heuristic to determine if the stroke contains at most two points, which we apply template matching for accidentals.

10.2.3 Learning Interface System

We created a learning interface system with pen- and touch-capabilities so that students can directly draw their music notation in responses to prompted music theory questions. We supplemented our interface with the recognition system in order to provide students with targeted feedback and assessment similar to human instructors, so that they may receive such feedback at their own individual pace. The interface system was designed with separate interfaces that target both students and instructors.

10.2.3.1 Student Interface

The main window of the student interface (Fig. 10.4) consists of several different areas of interest to the student: the top lesson area, the middle drawing area, and the bottom interaction area. The main window also allows students to select one of two possible modes: practice mode that enables all features, and quiz mode that disables certain features such as hints.

The lesson area (at the top) consists of elements such as the question number, the question text, an accompanying text hint, an image solution, and buttons for navigating between the different questions while in practice mode. If the student instead selected quiz mode, then the text hint, image solution, and back navigation button are disabled.

The sketching area (in the middle) consists entirely of a drawing space for students to input their answers with either touch or stylus. By default, input from the user is automatically beautified to their corresponding recognized music components, but can also be disabled by the user manually from the menu bar if they prefer to view their original raw strokes instead.

At the bottom is an interaction area that contains a color palette consisting of selectable stylus ink color, as well as buttons for clearing and undoing strokes, and for checking their solution.

Once users click the last button for checking their solution, they will be shown a feedback window (Fig. 10.5) of their performance, as well as a report window (Fig. 10.6) after completing the lesson.

Users can check their responses to the question on the feedback window by viewing the following components: a sentence indicating whether the response is correct or not, the model solution image, a set of criteria checks (i.e., staff, clef, key signature, time signature, duration, measure) that are individually enabled depending on

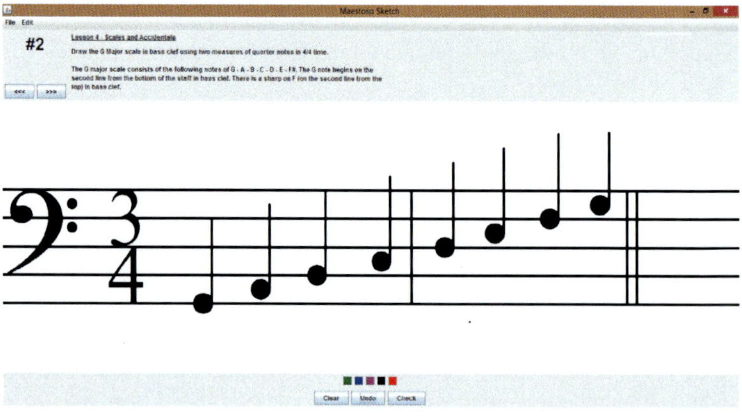

Fig. 10.4 Interface for practicing on prompted music theory questions. The quiz interface removes the text hints and graphic solution

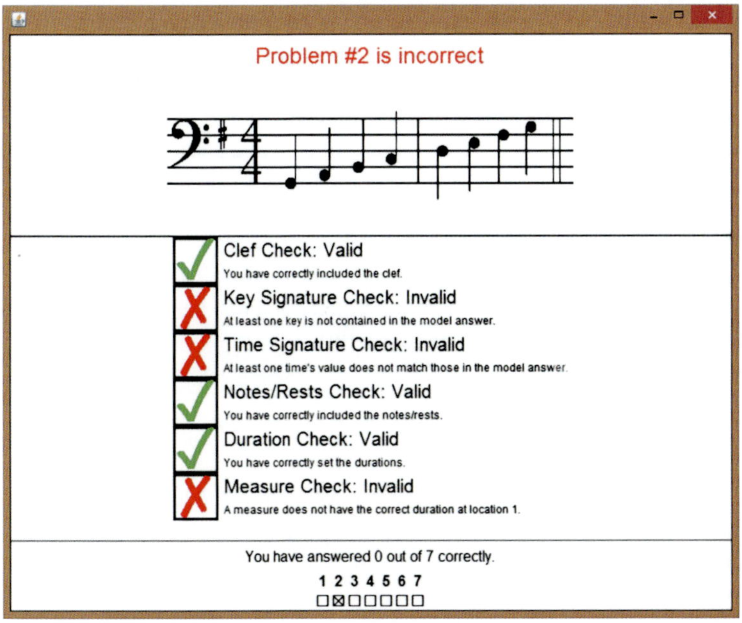

Fig. 10.5 Interface and its output window displaying personalized feedback to users of the individual question feedback

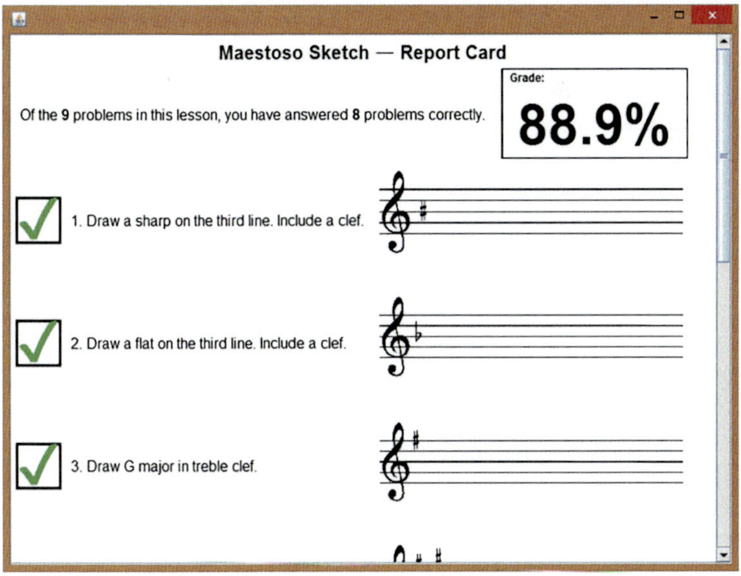

Fig. 10.6 Output window displaying personalized feedback to users of the entire quiz overall report

the given problem, and a progress of questions answered correctly, incorrectly, and in progress. Each criteria check not only lists the general criteria being checked, but also includes more specific detail related to that criteria. For example, if a user drew a note in the incorrect position or wrong duration, wrote the incorrect clef or key signature, or included the incorrect number of beats in a particular measure, then the criteria check's detailed feedback will specifically indicate it.

The report window appears after the last question is checked during quiz mode only. Not only does this window give users an overall score of the quiz and an update of the number of questions answered correctly, but it also displays a list of the questions that includes the question number and contents, the model solution image, and whether the user answered them correctly.

10.2.3.2 Instructor Interface

In addition to the core Maestoso application, we also included an accompanying lesson builder for instructors to develop lessons specific to their curriculum (Fig. 10.7). In order to assist in the development of our lesson builder, we consulted with four different music experts for their feedback on appropriate features: an engineering student with years of music study, a professional music instructor with a formal graduate degree in music studies, a part-time music instructor with over a decade of music training, and a music department graduate student from a major university.

Based on our discussions with these experts on the development of a automatic lesson generator, we included the following features: editable question numbers for easy rearranging of the questions, a text box for inputting questions, an additional text box for inputting hints, buttons for including answer and image files, and checkboxes for selectable criteria checks used in Maestoso. This last feature was strongly suggested from the music experts as it allowed them to provide greater flexibility on how they can design the questions. For example, an instructor can disable checks on clefs if either the bass clef or treblc is allowable, disable checks on key signature specifications if the solution allows for any key, or disable requiring particular notes if the instructor only requires that they total the correct duration each measure. The selection of these criteria checks thus determines which classifiers are enabled during the practice and quiz modes in Maestoso.

There are two reasons why it is important to note that as the instructor is designing the lesson, they may not have files readily available containing the model answer and solution image. The first reason is that we allow the instructor to first sketch the model answer after running the lesson once on the Maestoso interface, then save the answer as an XML file, and finally include it in the lesson builder. The second reason is that the instructor can have flexibility in what kind of graphic to include as the solution image (e.g., screeenshot, handwritten, animation).

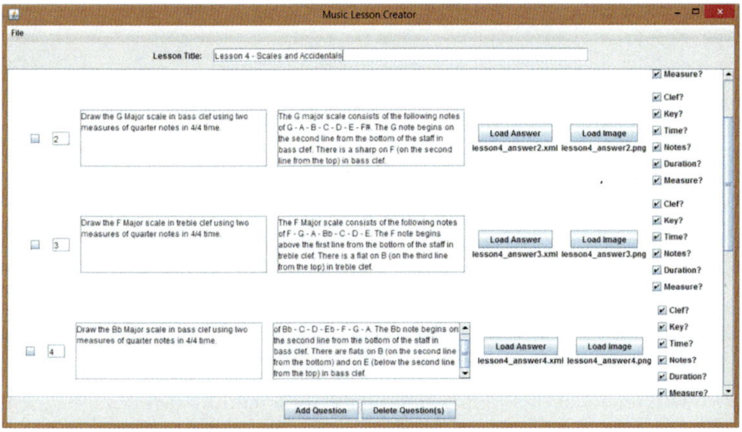

Fig. 10.7 Interface for instructors to create personalized music lessons

10.3 Results and Evaluation

In order to fully evaluate the performance of our work, we focus our evaluation in two stages: the recognition evaluation for measuring the performance of how well the recognition system handles users' written music notation, and the interaction evaluation for measuring the intuitiveness and usefulness of the interfaces.

10.3.1 Recognition Evaluation

For our first evaluation, we wanted to determine how well the music recognition system performed for novice users' written music input. In order to do that, we made use of the original group of novice users that provided sketches of musical components made on paper, and asked them to similarly provide written input on those musical components with a stylus. The setup uses a Wacom Bamboo tablet connected to a laptop, and the data set consisted of all the components that were used in the music recognition system, such as staffs, clefs, keys, beats, rests, notes of different variations, measure bars, and so on. We lastly asked the participants to sketch twenty instances of each component in consecutive order while we recorded their sketched input.

Following the completion of these tasks, we then analyzed the performance of the music recognition system by using all-or-nothing recognition [37] for determining a component as being either completely correct or not at all. What we discovered was that all the users were able to draw the musical components in the data set with average accuracy of over 95 %. Easier components, such as measure bars and staves, were recognized with almost perfect accuracy, while more complex components, such as clefs and more complex note variants, performed with greater than 90 % accuracy.

10.3.2 Interaction Evaluation

Our second evaluation consisted of having participants run through music lessons in practice mode, and subsequently strive to achieve the highest score in quiz mode after they felt comfortable with that lesson's set of questions. For this evaluation, we recruited a separate group of ten participants—ages 18–27, six females—whom self-reported that they had only passing knowledge of music theory but had at least some familiarity with using stylus- and touch-enabled computing devices. We then asked them to run through five different lessons of varying difficulty. These lessons were designed to be self-contained for introducing core beginner music theory concepts, and we consulted with our four music experts as well as different music theory textbooks and online music theory websites to define the specific questions of these lessons. These five lessons consisted of the following topics: (1) staffs and clefs, (2) key and time signatures, (3) basic notation, (4) scales and accidentals, and (5) simple transcription.

After instructing the participants to go through the five lessons in both practice and quiz modes, we allowed them to perform the study while we observed and timed their performance and became available if they encountered any issues. In general, the participants were able to complete all five lessons in one session that lasted from forty-five minutes for one user to two hours for another. From the study, we observed that all the users were able to complete the quizzes while making either zero mistakes most of the time and erring on a question on a few occasions. We also discovered that users who spent longer in their session scored slightly higher, and that everyone had varying difficulties once they reached the last lesson, since that lesson tested their memorization skills of transcribing measures of classic well-known songs.

10.4 Contributions

In this paper, we describe our contributions from developing an intelligent tutoring system for teaching novice users the foundational elements of written music theory through a combination of written music notation and accompanying feedback and assessment. The main contributions of our work include allowing users to practice their knowledge of written music theory with emulated assistance similar to human instructors, creating an interface that mimics the intuitiveness of existing traditional paper interfaces for music instruction, and developing a recognition system that is robust to written music notation from novice users.

Acknowledgments The authors thank members of the Sketch Recognition Lab and the WIPTTE community for their support and feedback throughout this project. L. Barreto is supported by the CRA-W Distributed Research Experience for Undergraduates Grant. This work is funded in part by the Microsoft Surface Hub Research Grant: Sketch and Gesture Recognition for Collaborative and Design Interfaces on the Surface Hub. We would also like to thank Texas A&M University and Vassar College for their support of this project.

References

1. Anthony L, Wobbrock J (2012) $N-protractor: a fast and accurate multistroke recognizer. In: Proceedings of graphics interface 2012, GI '12. Canadian information processing society, Mississauga, Ontario, Canada, pp 117–120
2. Baba T, Kikukawa Y, Yoshiike T, Suzuki T, Shoji R, Kushiyama K, Aoki M (2012) Gocen: a handwritten notational interface for musical performance and learning music. In: ACM SIGGRAPH 2012 emerging technologies SIGGRAPH '12. ACM, New York, USA, pp 9–9
3. Brooke E (2013) SoundBrush, an app that lets you draw music, turns the untrained into musicians [Online News Article]. Accessed 12 July 2013
4. Cheema S, LaViola J Jr (2012) PhysicsBook: a sketch-based interface for animating physics diagrams. In: Proceedings of the 2012 ACM international conference on intelligent user interfaces IUI '12. ACM, New York, USA, pp 51–60
5. Colletti C (2014) A comparative review of five music fundamentals textbooks. J Music Theory Pedag 28(1)
6. Cummmings D, Vides F, Hammond T (2012) I don't believe my eyes!: geometric sketch recognition for a computer art tutorial. In: Proceedings of the international symposium on sketch-based interfaces and modeling, SBIM'12. Eurographics Association, Geneva, Switzerland, pp 97–106
7. Dahmen K, Hammond T (2008) Distinguishing between sketched scribble look alikes. In: Proceedings of the 23rd national conference on artificial intelligence AAAI '08. AAAI, Palo Alto, California, USA, pp 1790–1791
8. Deihl N (1971) Computer-assisted instruction and instrumental music: implications for teaching and research. J Res Music Educ 19(3):299–306
9. Dixon D, Prasad M, Hammond T (2010) iCanDraw: using sketch recognition and corrective feedback to assist a user in drawing human faces. In: Proceedings of the SIGCHI conference on human factors in computing systems CHI '10. ACM, New York, USA, pp 897–906
10. Fornés A, Dutta A, Gordo A, Llads J (2012) CVC-MUSCIMA: a ground truth of handwritten music score images for writer identification and staff removal. Int J Doc Anal Recognit 15(3):243–251
11. Forsberg A, Dieterich M, Zeleznik R (1998) The music notepad. In: Proceedings of the 11th annual ACM symposium on user interface software and technology UIST '98. ACM, New York, USA, pp 203–210
12. Kara L, Stahovich T (2005) An image-based, trainable symbol recognizer for hand-drawn sketches. Comput Gr 29(4):501–517
13. LaViola J Jr (2007) Advances in mathematical sketching: moving toward the paradigm's full potential. IEEE Comput Gr Appl 27(1):38–48
14. Lee K, Phon-Amnuaisuk S, Ting CY (2010) Handwritten music notation recognition using HMM—a non-gestural approach. In: 2010 international conference on information retrieval & knowledge management CIKM '10. ICMS, Australasia, Melbourne, Victoria, Australia, pp 255–259
15. Leoné M, van Dijk B, van Beijnum BJ (2008) Design and trial evaluation of the user interface for musicReader. In: Proceedings of the 12th international conference on entertainment and media in the ubiquitous era, MindTrek '08. ACM, New York, USA, pp 95–99

16. Li Y (2010) Protractor: a fast and accurate gesture recognizer. In: Proceedings of the SIGCHI conference on human factors in computing systems CHI '10. ACM, New York, USA, pp 2169–2172
17. Miller M (2005) The complete idiot's guide to music theory, 1st edn. Alpha Books, New York
18. Nelson R, Christensen C (2014) Foundations of music, enhanced, 1st edn. Cengage Learning, Stamford
19. Paulson B, Hammond T (2008) Paleosketch: accurate primitive sketch recognition and beautification. In: Proceedings of the 13th international conference on intelligent user interfaces IUI '08. ACM, New York, USA, pp 1–10
20. Ramirez R, Hazan A, Mariner J, Maestre E (2006) A sequential covering evolutionary algorithm for expressive music performance. In: Proceedings of the 18th conference on innovative applications of artificial intelligence IAAI '06. AAAI, Palo Alto, California, USA, pp 1830–1835
21. Rebelo A, Tkaczuk J, Sousa R, Cardoso J (2011) Metric learning for music symbol recognition. In: 2011 10th international conference on machine learning and applications and workshops ICMLA '11. IEEE, New York, USA, pp 106–111
22. Rebelo A, Fujinaga I, Paszkiewicz F, Marcal A, Guedes C, Cardoso J (2012) Optical music recognition: state-of-the-art and open issues. Int J Multimed Inf Retr 1(3):173–190
23. Rogers M (2004) Teaching approaches in music theory: an overview of pedagogical philosophies, 2nd edn. Southern Illinois University Press, Carbondale
24. Taele P, Hammond T (2009) Hashigo: a next-generation sketch interactive system for japanese kanji. In: Proceedings of the twenty-first innovative applications artificial intelligence conference IAAI '09. AAAI, Palo Alto, California, USA, pp 153–158
25. Taele P, Peschel J, Hammond T (2009) A sketch interactive approach to computer-assisted biology instruction. In: 2009 intelligent user interfaces workshop on sketch recognition IUISR'09
26. Taele P, Barreto L, Hammond T (2015) Maestoso: an intelligent educational sketching tool for learning music theory. In: Proceedings of the twenty-seventh innovative applications of artificial intelligence conference IAAI '15. AAAI, Palo Alto, California, USA, pp 3999–4005
27. Tan S, Hu Z, Koh A, Felicia A, Zhao S (2010) Musicflow: an interactive music composition system. In: Proceedings of SPIE visual communications and image processing 2010, SPIE
28. The telegraph: The telegraph: Music helps children learn maths (2012) [Online Artcile]. 22 March 2012. Accessed 30 June 2015
29. Topolu O (2014) Critical thinking and music education. Procedia—Soc Behav Sci 116:2252–2256
30. van Sommers P (2009) Drawing and cognition: descriptive and experimental studies of graphic production processes, 1st edn. Cambridge University Press, Cambridge
31. Valentine SMF, Hammond T, Smith A (2011) A shape comparison technique for use in sketch-based tutoring systems. In: Proceedings of the 2011 intelligent user interfaces workshop on sketch recognition IUI SR '11
32. Valentine S, Vides F, Lucchese G, Turner D, Kim Hh, Li W, Linsey J, Hammond T (2012) Mechanix: a sketch-based tutoring system for statics courses. In: Proceedings of the twenty-fourth innovative applications of artificial intelligence conference IAAI '12. AAAI, Palo Alto, California, USA, pp 2253–2260
33. Valentine S, Lara-Garduno R, Linsey J, Hammond T (2015) Mechanix: a sketch based tutoring system that automatically corrects hand-sketched statics homework. In: Hammond T, Valentine S, Adler A (eds) The impact of pen and touch technology on education. Springer International Publishing, Heidelberg
34. Vatavu RD, Anthony L, Wobbrock J (2012) Gestures as point clouds: a $p recognizer for user interface prototypes. In: Proceedings of the ACM international conference on multimodal interfaces ICMI '12. ACM, New York, USA, pp 273–280
35. Warschauer M (1997) Computer-mediated collaborative learning: theory and practice. Mod Lang J Spec Issue: Interact Collab Coop: Learn Lang Prep Lang Teach 81(4):470–481
36. Wobbrock J, Wilson A, Li Y (2007) Gestures without libraries, toolkits or training: a $1 recognizer for user interface prototypes. In: Proceedings of the 20th annual ACM symposium on user interface software and technology UIST '07. ACM, New York, USA, pp 159–168

37. Wolin A, Eoff B, Hammond T (2008) Shortstraw: a simple and effective corner finder for polylines. In: Proceedings of the fifth eurographics conference on sketch-based interfaces and modeling SBIM '08. Eurographics Association, Geneva, Switzerland, pp 33–40
38. Wu B, Zhong E, Horner A, Yang Q (2014) Music emotion recognition by multi-label multi-layer multi-instance multi-view learning. In: Proceedings of the ACM international conference on multimedia MM '14. ACM, New York, USA, pp 117–126
39. Yamamoto Y, Uchiyama H, Kakehi Y (2011) onNote: playing printed music scores as a musical instrument. In: Proceedings of the 24th annual ACM symposium on user interface software and technology UIST '11. ACM, New York, USA, pp 413–422
40. Yeary M (2014) Computer-assisted instruction and remedial music fundamentals. J Music Theory Pedag 28(1)
41. Zbikowski L, Long C (1994) Cooperative learning in the music theory classroom. J Music Theory Pedag 8(1):135–157

Chapter 11
SmartStrokes: Digitizing Paper-Based Neuropsychological Tests

Raniero Lara-Garduno, Nancy Leslie, and Tracy Hammond

Abstract Clinical neuropsychologists develop comprehensive behavioral profiles on their patients primarily by using paper-and-pencil test stimuli. Despite these tests being significantly cheaper and faster than complex procedures such as MRI scans, multiple drawbacks remain. Constructing these behavioral profiles can take upwards of six hours to fully complete, and the analysis of the sketches from these pencil-and-paper tests is still largely subjective and qualitative. We developed SmartStrokes, a testing suite that implements digital versions of common clinical neuropsychology pencil-and-paper tests, with the purpose of helping to automate and analyze patient sketches using the principles of sketch recognition.

11.1 Introduction and Background Information

Strokes continue to be prevalent in public health, with the last year seeing nearly 800,000 strokes and 100,000 deaths from strokes in the United States [6]. Victims of strokes and similar cognitive disabilities suffer from difficulties with speech, movement, critical thinking, short and long term memory, conveying and understanding emotion, and difficulties in performing many physical day-to-day tasks to remain independent. Diagnosis and early detection in disorders that deteriorate these functions such as Alzheimer's disease can prove difficult, since noticeable cognitive deficiencies may not manifest for several years. Medical experts use several testing methods in order to accurately measure and gauge the severity of cognitive

R. Lara-Garduno (✉) · T. Hammond
Sketch Recognition Lab, Computer Science & Engineering Department,
Texas A&M University, College Station, TX, USA
e-mail: raniero@tamu.edu

T. Hammond
e-mail: hammond@tamu.edu

N. Leslie
Texas Brain and Spine Institute & Health Science Center,
Texas A&M University, Bryan, TX, USA
e-mail: nleslie.phd@gmail.com

T. Hammond et al. (eds.), *Revolutionizing Education with Digital Ink*,
Human–Computer Interaction Series, DOI 10.1007/978-3-319-31193-7_11

deficiencies in patients suffering from severe concussions, Alzheimer's disease, and stroke patients, among others [5].

The most established method of diagnosing these issues cheaply and efficiently is via standardized tests administered on paper. These tests often task users with a cognitively challenging exercise that requires higher than resting-level mental function in order to complete effectively. Medical professionals meet with their patients and ask them to complete several of these tests, observing their behavior while patients complete them. These behaviors include: the patient's ability to comprehend and act on instructions, their sitting position, manner of holding the pen, maintaining eye contact during instructions, behavior upon committing a mistake, willingness to complete the examination, etc. Clinical neuropsychologists then use these evaluations to diagnose and, if applicable, determine the extent of cognitive deficiencies and type of therapy. They also use this information to make important decisions such as whether the patient is able to perform tasks involving heavy machinery or driving a vehicle during their daily lives.

11.1.1 Existing Neuropsychology Examinations

Three commonly used neuropsychological tests include the Trail-Making test that measures search speed and executive functioning [14], the Clock Drawing test measuring memory, concentration, and mental clarity,[1] and the Rey-Osterrieth Complex Figure test measuring visuospatial abilities and working memory [15]. Clinical neuropsychologists use a combination of these and other tests to build a comprehensive behavioral profile on the patient. The clinician measures test time completion via a stopwatch, and these tests can sometimes be recorded via audio or video for later review. These and several other tests have been established in the field of neuropsychology as effective probes into the cognitive functions of patients [11, 17, 18].

The Trail-Making test is an evaluation in which the worksheet is a single sheet of paper that contains several labeled dots of incrementing value, and the patient is asked to connect the dots in the correct order according to the labels. Neuropsychologists use these two tests frequently in forensic evaluations for its reliability and relative ease of administration [10]. The test is frequently administered as a pair, where the patient completes a Trail-Making test of the "A" variation and then a test of the "B" variation immediately afterward. In the "A" variation, the dots are ordered in incremental numerical order, that is "1" to "2" to "3", until the dot "25" has been reached. The "B" variation alternates the dots between incremental letters and numbers, requiring the patient to keep track of both "lists" at the same time. The correct order of dots in this variation is "1" to "A" to "2" to "B" to "3" to "C", etc. Variation "B" is typically more rigorous for the patient and requires considerably more effort to complete. Figure 11.1 depicts an example of how these would be

[1]Clock Drawing Test, Iowa Geriatric Education Center, 2014, https://www.healthcare.uiowa.edu/igec/tools/cognitive/clockDrawing.pdf.

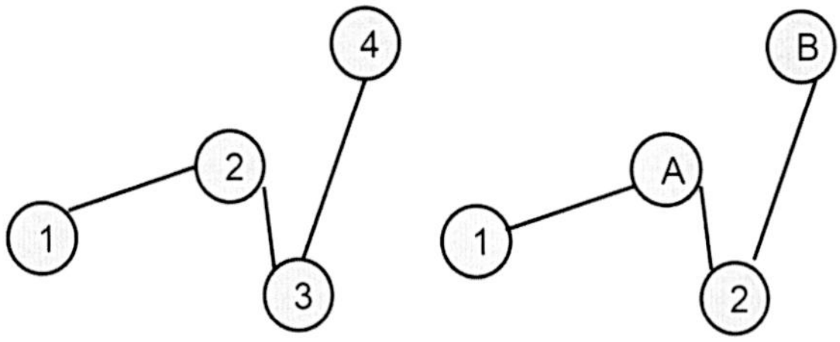

Fig. 11.1 The *dots* on the Trails-A variation follow the order shown on the *left*; those of the Trails-B variation are shown on the *right*

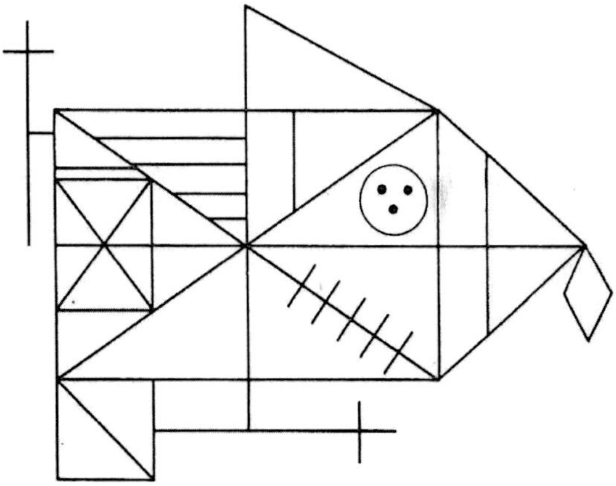

Fig. 11.2 The complex figure that the patient is expected to copy, memorize, and recall in a Rey-Osterrieth Complex Figure test

shown and connected on a test. The tests are administered using a universal testing procedure to maintain consistent evaluations among clinicians and patients [2].

The Clock Drawing test consists of the clinician handing the patient a piece of paper with a large round circle printed on it, and the clinician asks him or her to draw an analog clock with the hour and minute hands in a specific location to depict a predetermined time. The desired locations for the minute and hour hands are instructed by time, such as "please draw the hands to show 10 min past 9" rather than simply saying "please place the hour hand in 9 and minute hand in 2." This encourages the patient to evaluate the representation of time in an analog clock instead of simply following directions.

The Rey-Osterrieth Complex Figure test is a three-part test that involves recall of a complex abstract figure shown on a piece of paper [16]. Each part of this test is called a "condition" as per the established test instructions: Copy, Immediate Recall, and Delayed Recall. In the Copy condition, the clinician presents the patient with a figure depicting a standardized complex figure, shown in Fig. 11.2, consisting of various abstract geometric figures drawn in different areas of the paper, all connected via shared shape edges, lines, or intersecting points. In this condition, the patient is not timed for completion, but rather his or her progress is carefully observed by the clinician, who can take notes as necessary. Some variations of the Copy condition involve periodically using different colored pencils for sketching to record the order in which the sketch is drawn, but the most recent Complex Figure Test instructions discourage this practice as patients might use the differently colored pencils as a mnemonic device. In the second condition, Immediate Recall, the patient is asked to redraw the figure from memory, without the aid of the pre-drawn complex figure for reference. In this condition, the clinician might use a timer. The final condition, Delayed Recall, involves the clinician asking the patient to once again redraw the abstract figure from memory after a long delay (typically after 20–30 min). The clinician does not inform the patient of this third condition, ensuring that the patient will not know of this third part of the test beforehand, aiding in testing the patient's incidental memory as fully as possible.

There exist multiple variations on each of these tests, and small differences may exist between clinicians. For our application, we aim to recreate the rules of each test as we have described above.

11.1.2 Motivation

Despite the fact that administering paper-and-pencil tests is effective and relatively low in cost, there exist multiple drawbacks and limitations. Comprehensive behavioral profiles can take several hours at a time to complete, and the subjective evaluation as well as the testing style of different neuropsychologists can differ significantly. Furthermore, the sketch-based nature of these paper tests makes recording this information in its entirety difficult to digitize, and long-term statistical tracking and numerical precision is unfeasible. They can also be used as an enhancement for more advanced applications of these tests. For instance, recognition trials, such as the Meyers and Meyers Recognition Trial for the Rey-Osterrieth Complex figure Test, is used to detect instances of "suspect effort" in which a patient feigns cognitive disabilities to use to their advantage [13]. Modern sketch recognition techniques can be an invaluable tool in detecting said suspect efforts.

Most importantly, we believe that the physical sketches that the patients produce in and of themselves contain a vast amount of rich information. Tests used on healthy populations yeild subtleties in performance that have been shown to be significant, and we believe that analyzing information-rich sketch data can help emphasize said subtleties [20]. Should we collect this data digitally and perform established sketch recognition techniques on them, we believe that we can extract novel information about patients with fine granularity that is not possible through evaluating traditional paper-and-pencil tests.

11.2 Related Work

Trail-Making tests, the focus of this paper, have been previously used to determine tangentially related information about the populations they test. Davis et al. has analyzed Clock Drawing tests using sketch recognition and supports both sketch analysis and real-time drawing replay to allow clinicians to review the sketches [3]. Kim et al. implemented the Clock Drawing test as well as the Trail-Making test in a preliminary tablet computer application, although the system relies on older tablet and pen technology [8]. Their work has also extended in making sketch recognition optimizations specifically for the Clock Drawing test [7]. Cavaco et al. gathered normative data through the Trail-Making test from the Portuguese population. Their findings included a negative correlation between the participants' completion time and age/education. They also noted that age and education were not significantly different between men and women [15]. This suggests the potential of Trail-Making tests in determining new information about a user, as this test was not originally developed for the sole purpose of finding such a correlation. Other related work to this study includes digitizing pencil and paper tasks to specifically determine cognitive function in mental disabilities, such as the work of Aly et al. [1]. Using digital pen tests, Aly analyzed pen activity to detect tremors in users with a reported case of Parkinson's disease. Rey-Osterrieth tests have been used in other cutting-edge research, such as the work of Li et al., which used this classic memory test and applied it to a haptic system to record user input in 3 dimensions [12]. Using sketch recognition for neuropsychological sketch-based tests is motivated in efforts such as Eoff and Hammond, allowing a system to accurately attribute pen strokes to a user without relying on sketch context, instead using solely pen pressure and tilt data [4]. Because sketches from neuropsychological tests are a direct result of a user's cognitive functions, we believe there is a strong link in attributing this sketch data to a user's cognitive abilities. This prior work legitimizes the interest in digitizing these paper tests to provide a wider range of data and precision. It also shows the unreached potential of sketch recognition in this application.

11.3 SmartStrokes

SmartStrokes is a digital neuropsychology test platform that records pen input for the purpose of sketch recognition analysis. The platform was developed on the Windows 8 Modern App platform, designed to be used on a Microsoft Surface Pro 2 tablet. A version of this application can be seen in Fig. 11.3. Forward compatibility of the Modern App platform enables us also to work with the Surface Pro 3 and future iterations of the hardware, as well as the Windows 10 operating system. We chose these devices due to their accuracy in simulating the pen-and-paper writing experience given their number of integrated pen writing technologies built into the hardware and firmware. Additionally, the amount of information that the Surface devices are able to record such as pen pressure data and hover data yield multiple dimensions of information on the same sketch data. It provides richer amounts of information without having to alter the way the test is taken or administered.

SmartStrokes is primarily developed for use by a clinical neuropsychologist. The application operates under an account system that focuses on the clinician, with their user name being linked to the various patients he or she has. Once the clinician logs

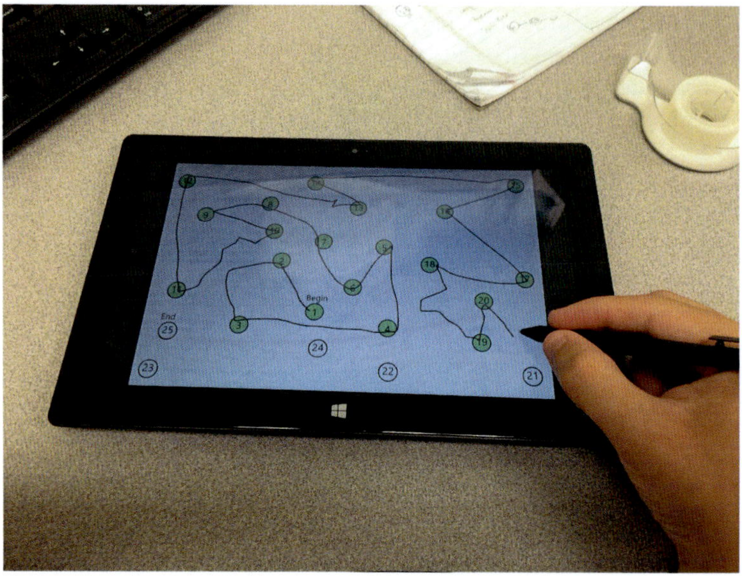

Fig. 11.3 A patient completing the Trail-Making test in the SmartStrokes application

in, SmartStrokes displays all of the patients associated with that clinician and the choice to register a new one.

Our current studies involve performing sketch recognition analysis on the Trail-Making test, although our future goals include performing the same analysis on the remaining tests. We intend to compare our Trail-Making test data with existing data from pen-and-paper studies to analyze differences between the paper tests and their digital counterparts [19]. Clinical trials on this software will begin once we have completed automated test analysis.

11.3.1 Patient Registration

Doctor-Patient confidentiality is an important principle that we do our best to uphold with SmartStrokes. Under the direction of our clinical neuropsychologist team member, we follow the standard format of patient ID that helps the clinician remember which identification number belongs to which patient, while also being impersonal enough to preserve the anonymity of his or her patient. The format is: the first letter of the patient's first name, followed by a two-number representation of the current month, a two-number representation of the current year, and ending with the first lettter of the patient's last name. For example, a patient name John Doe seeing the clinician for the first time on a March 17 will have a patient ID of J0317D. This allows the clinician to easily link the patient with an anonymous ID without requiring an extensive code system.

11.3.2 Test Administration

Once the patient has been selected, the clinician can then select the test to administer in a menu as shown in Fig. 11.4. Once the patient has been selected, the clinician can then select the test to administer. We have integrated two variations of the Trail-Making test, the Clock Drawing test, and the Rey-Osterrieth Complex Figure test on this platform. The clinician has the ability to have the patient take the test as many times as the clinician wishes, enabling him or her to record the patient's progress over a short or long period of time. The clinician would select one of these tests and review the test instructions that will appear on the screen with the patient. The patient will then press the "Begin" button on the screen when he or she is ready and complete the test.

For the Trail-Making tests, there is no functionality to cancel or pause the test, since at that point the patient is in control of the device, and through some preliminary studies we have found that patients subconsciously pressed a "Cancel" button when it was on the screen whenever they made a mistake. In the paper-and-pencil tests the rules stipulate that all patients preserve their mistakes and complete the test in one try, and as such our application functionality is implemented to mimic those testing conditions as closely as possible. The Clock Drawing and Rey-Osterrieth Complex figure Tests in SmartStrokes do have a "Finish" button to indicate that the patient has finished the test, similar to how a patient with a paper-and-pencil version of the test would have to indicate that he or she is finished. However, there are no "Cancel" buttons for the same reason as in the Trail-Making tests.

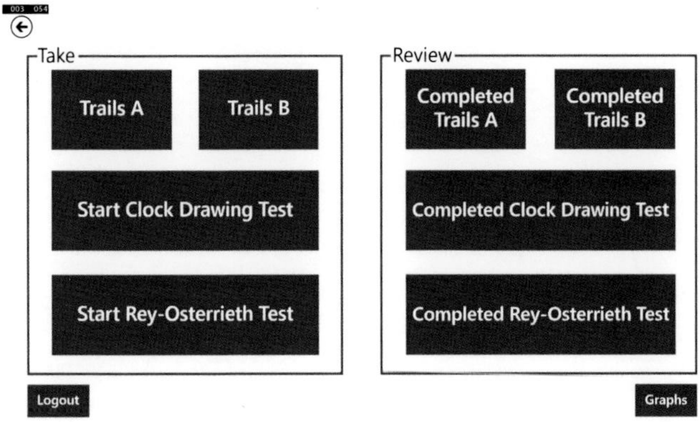

Fig. 11.4 The main menu of the SmartStrokes testing suite after a clinician has logged in and chosen a patient

11.3.3 Past Test Records

In addition to performing sketch recognition on digitized patient sketches, another advantage to using a digitized application for these paper-and-pencil tests is providing many different forms of data visualization for clinicians that may be difficult or unfeasible to perform for every patient on paper. The "Replay" features of SmartStrokes are tailored for the individual test types and use the advantages of digitized sketch data to provide more relevant information to the clinician.

11.3.3.1 Trail-Making Test Records

The Trail-Making tests record displays are the same for both the A and B variations of the test. When a clinician chooses to view a patient's past Trail-Making test, the patient's sketch for that particular test is displayed for the clinician, along with the total completion time toward the top of the screen. In this mode, the patient's sketch is color coded, with the color of the sketch changing for every set amount of time, with the interval based on the total test completion time. For example, a patient's sketch color may change in the clinician's records that corresponds to five seconds passing when the patient was taking the test. This way, the clinician is provided with a "heat map" of sorts, such that if the color of the sketch changes several times in one particular part of the test, the clinician can easily identify that the patient took a long time in that particular region. An example of this interface can be seen in Fig. 11.5. We can contrast this to a clinician viewing a patient's completed paper test from his or her file; the clinician has no way of knowing how much time a patient spent in any particular region of the test without a video recording of the patient's performance. Finally, SmartStrokes can show the clinician a table comprised of every

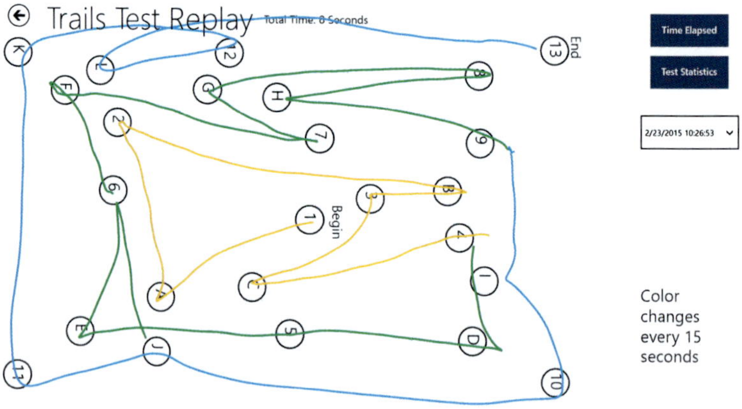

Fig. 11.5 The Trail-Making test as shown in the SmartStrokes application

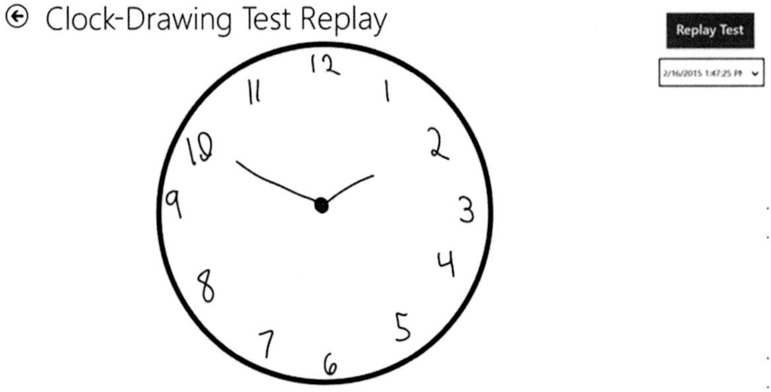

Fig. 11.6 The Clock Drawing test as shown in the SmartStrokes application

mistake that the patient committed during the test, along with how long the patient took to correctly move from one dot to the next.

11.3.3.2 Clock Drawing Test Records

The Clock Drawing records display their information differently in that they provide a real-time replay of the patient sketch. The replay is automatically started when the clinician selects the patient's test and ends only when the replay completes. The replay is performed at a slightly slower rate than real-time in order for the clinician to be able to notice nuances in the patient's sketch creation patterns. Additionally, all erasures are preserved in the sketch. Although erased lines fully disappear when completing the test, when the clinician is viewing the replay all of these erased lines instead appear as light-gray. This allows the clinician to see where and when mistakes were made and to compare the initial attempts of the patient along with the final submission of the sketches. An image of the replay interface can be seen in Fig. 11.6.

11.3.3.3 Rey-Osterrieth Complex Figure Test Records

The Rey-Osterrieth replay involves comparing two different sketches due to the nature of the test itself. The clinician is asked to pick two different test completions of the Rey-Osterrieth test, and once the "Replay" button is pressed, both sketches are played adjacent to each other. The actual replay works similarly to that of the Clock Drawing test replays, in that the sketches are played at a slightly slower time, and they only stop when the respective sketches are fully drawn. The clinician is able to not only pick the sketches within one particular set of Rey-Osterrieth tests, but also compare between different testing sessions. Figure 11.7 depicts this part of the interface.

Completion times of all patients can also be visualized in a built-in normative data view that compiles completion times of all patients. This feature can be seen in Fig. 11.8. Norms are separated by test type (with Trail-Making test variations A and B separated into their own respective categories) and results can be further filtered based on patient age range, gender, and education level. Norm comparison is an important aspect of these neuropsychological tests, and implementing them for automatic organization and visualization is just one of the multiple advantages of a fully digitized neuropsychological testing suite.

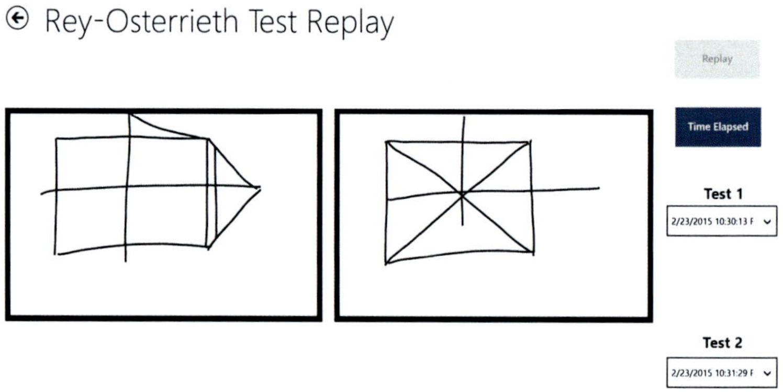

Fig. 11.7 Two consecutive Rey-Osterrieth Complex Figure tests being replayed in real time next to each other. The clinician is able to compare two different tests from either the same patient or different ones

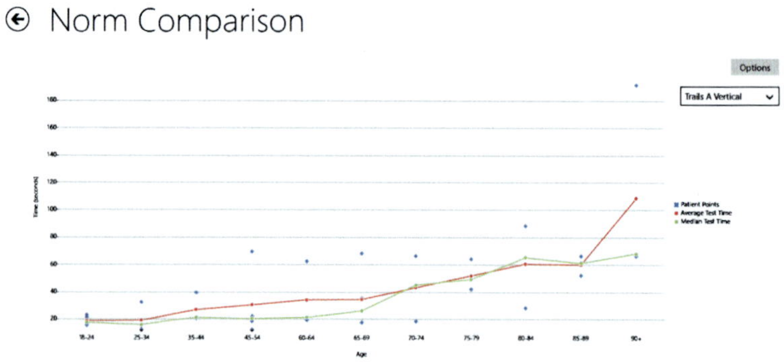

Fig. 11.8 A sample graph depicting a display of every patient's completion times for Trail-Making test A (the data is a sample)

11.4 You-Try-It Demonstration

Our You-Try-It demonstration at the 2015 Workshop on the Impact of Pen and Touch Technology on Education involved a guided walk-through outlining the different features of the SmartStrokes platform. In addition, participants simulated a patient's test-taking experience by completing each of the two Trail-Making test variations, the Clock Drawing test, and the Rey-Osterrieth Complex Figure test. Each of these tests took only a few minutes to complete and helped to provide insight into the components and importance of neuropsychological tests, as well as gain an understanding of the sketch data and how it can be used to find new information about patients that would not be possible with a typical pen-and-paper format. Participants in this demonstration expressed interest in the field of study and believed that the use of technology in this domain has the potential to make a large impact in the field of clinical neuropsychology.

11.5 Overview and Impact

At its core, the motivation behind SmartStrokes is to provide clinical neuropsychologists with information-rich data on their patients by administering a digital version of existing pen-and-paper cognitive tests. This means that doctors will have access to new data with little to no additional testing procedures, effort, or time requirements on their part. As we have outlined in the previous section, the fact that these sketches are recorded digitally, with thousands of individually timestamped points that make up each sketch, allows us to visualize the same records in new ways that were previously unfeasible using the paper-and-pencil format.

With enough user data we can also develop a model of both healthy and cognitive deficient patients to help automate some of the testing process strictly by analyzing the sketch data. This provides clinicians useful pre-diagnosis information as well as helps patients living in remote regions of the world to perform these tests outside of a clinic and send the results digitally to their doctor.

In addition to aiding practicing clinicians, SmartStrokes can also be used to aid clinical neuropsychology students by providing them with existing patient sketches and sketch replay data and asking them to identify areas of concern, such as significant tremors, several mistakes in one region, and prolonged hesitation. SmartStrokes can then provide them with a fully analyzed version of this test and compare the student's answers, identifying any areas of concern that the student may have missed.

11.6 Future Work

We have conducted preliminary studies on healthy users using the two variations on the Trail-Making test that have allowed us to predict user age based on broad age categories [9]. We performed this work using common sketch recognition techniques that allowed us to identify sketch areas and features important in determining the age of the user. This promising data leads us to conduct more studies on a larger scale to solidify the validity of the recent findings, as well as helping to develop a more thorough model of what the sketch data of a healthy patient looks like in order to help identify symptoms of cognitive issues.

Additionally, we intend to add more neuropsychological tests into the testing suite in order to generate more sketch data that can be used to classify illnesses. We ultimately intend to conduct user studies similar to those that we have completed for the Trail-Making tests to develop a more comprehensive prediction model as we integrate the results from all of these digitized tests.

11.7 Conclusion

In the field of neuropsychology, paper-and-pencil cognitive tests remain a reliable and low-cost tool for clinicians to diagnose patients. We believe that digitizing these tests and performing common sketch recognition techniques can yield a vast amount of automated information that can help clinicians in developing comprehensive behavioral profiles more quickly than would otherwise be possible. In addition, digitized testing suites can serve as databases of information that could store every test, related video, and accompanying information on paper-based test results, all in one application for the convenience of the clinician. We are hopeful that we will find interesting and novel data in the field of neuropsychology as we progress in this project.

Acknowledgments We would like to thank the Texas A&M Health Science Center for the invaluable feedback and guidance in the development of this project. We also thank several team members of Texas A&M's Sketch Recognition Lab, especially Folami Alamudun, Paul Taele, and all the members who continue to provide feedback and useful sketch data as they aid in completing user studies. Additionally, we would like to thank Nick Melnyk, Laramie Goode, Andy Hurley, Thomas Klingshirn, and Josh Rispoli for their significant contributions during the project's inception in concept and implementation.

References

1. Aly N, Playfer J, Smith S, Halliday D (2007) A novel computer-based technique for the assessment of tremor in parkinson's disease. Age Ageing 36(4):395–399
2. Bowie CR, Harvey PD (2006) Administration and interpretation of the trail making test. Nat Protoc 1:2277–2281

3. Cunningham H, Penney D, Davis R, Tanner J, Nguyen P, Schwab N, Malaty I, Okun MS, Bowers D, Libon DJ, Price CC (2012) Clock drawing in pd: what makes the clock drawing test tick? J Int Neuropsychol Soc, p 222
4. Eoff BD, Hammond T (2009) Who dotted that 'i'?: context free user differentiation through pressure and tilt pen data. In: Proceedings of graphics interface 2009, GI'09. Canadian information processing society, Toronto, Ont, Canada pp 149–156
5. Hodges JR (2007) Cognitive Assessment for Clinicians, 2nd edn. Oxford University Press, Oxford
6. Hoyert DL, Xu J et al (2012) Deaths: preliminary data for 2011. Natl Vital Stat Rep 61(6):1–52
7. Kim H, Cho YS, Do EYL (2010) Context-bounded refinement filter algorithm: improving recognizer accuracy of handwriting in clock drawing test
8. Kim H, Cho YS, Do EYL (2011) Using pen-based computing in technology for health. Human-computer interaction, Users and applications, Lecture notes in computer science, vol 6764. Springer, Berlin, pp 192–201
9. Lara-Garduno R, Melnyk N, Taele P, Hammond T (2015) Evaluating automated cognitive testing for stroke patient diagnosis and recovery. In: ACM Richard Tapia celebration of diversity in computing, ACM, Poster presentation
10. Lees-Haley PR, Smith HH, Williams CW, Dunn JT (1996) Forensic neuropsychological test usage: an empirical survey. Arch Clin Neuropsychol 11(1):45–51
11. Lezak MD (1995) Neuropsychological assessment, 3rd edn. Oxford University Press, Oxford
12. Li Y, Kaber DB, Tupler L, Lee YS (2011) Haptic-based virtual environment design and modeling of motor skill assessment for brain injury patientsrehabilitation. Comput Aided Des Appl 8(2):149–162
13. Lu PH, Boone KB, Cozolino L, Mitchell C (2003) Effectiveness of the Rey-Osterrieth complex figure test and the meyers and meyers recognition trial in the detection of suspect effort. Clin Neuropsychol 17(3):426–440
14. Reitan RM (1992) Trail making test: manual for administration and scoring. Reitan neuropsychology laboratory
15. Rosselli M, Ardila A (1991) Effects of age, education, and gender on the Rey-Osterrieth complex figure. Clin Neuropsychol 5(4):370–376
16. Shorr JS, Delis DC, Massman PJ (1992) Memory for the Rey-Osterrieth figure: perceptual clustering, encoding, and storage. Neuropsychology 6(1):43–50
17. Shulman KI, Feinstein A (2003) Quick cognitive screening for clinicians: mini-mental, Clock-drawing and other brief tests, 1st edn. CRC Press, Boca Raton
18. Strauss E, Sherman EM, Spreen O (2006) A compendium of neuropsychological tests, 3rd edn. Oxford University Press Inc., Oxford
19. Tombaugh TN (2004) Trail making test a and b: normative data stratified by age and education. Arch Clin Neuropsychol 19(2):203–214
20. Wahlin TBR, Bckman L, ke Wahlin A, Winblad B (1996) Trail making test performance in a community-based sample of healthy very old adults: effects of age on completion time, but not on accuracy. Arch Gerontol Geriatr 22(1): 87–102

Part IV
The Empowering Effects of Active Media-Making

Chapter 12
The Digital Sash: A Sketch-Based Badge System in a Social Network for Children

Stephanie Valentine, Angelica Leyva-McMurtry, Katya Borgos-Rodriguez, and Tracy Hammond

Abstract In this chapter, we present a sketch-based reward system for promoting the practice of digital citizenship skills within our custom social network for children aged 7 to 12 years. This badge system prompts budding social networkers to complete fun, creative sketching activities and short writing tasks. Because we have deployed our custom social network (KidGab) within our local Girl Scouts Council, our badge system takes the form of a digital Girl Scout sash. In this work, we discuss the badges that prompted the most participation from our users and provide example responses for each. Finally, we consider methods in which our system and results might be generalized to suit non-scouting populations of children such as classrooms, clubs, and sports teams.

12.1 Motivation and Context

Cyberbullying, defined as "[w]illful and repeated harm inflicted through the use of computers, cell phones, and other electronic devices" [6], is a digital phenomenon affecting as many as 35 % of today's youth [8]. In a 2010 survey, Microsoft found that 40 % of parents said their child was involved in a cyberbullying incident and that 76 % of educators rank cyberbullying as a "severe" issue [13].

S. Valentine (✉) · A. Leyva-McMurtry · K. Borgos-Rodriguez · T. Hammond
Sketch Recognition Lab, Computer Science & Engineering Department,
Texas A&M University, College Station, TX, USA
e-mail: valentine@tamu.edu

T. Hammond
e-mail: hammond@tamu.edu

A. Leyva-McMurtry
Mills College, Oakland, CA, USA
e-mail: angelica.lm94@gmail.com

K. Borgos-Rodriguez
University of Puerto Rico at Mayaguez, Mayaguez, PR, USA
e-mail: katya.borgos@upr.edu

T. Hammond et al. (eds.), *Revolutionizing Education with Digital Ink*,
Human–Computer Interaction Series, DOI 10.1007/978-3-319-31193-7_12

After experiencing cyberbullying ourselves and witnessing the tragic effects of cyberbullying in the lives of young people close to us, we knew we wanted to direct our research focus toward this massive societal problem. An extensive literature search (e.g. [1, 5–7, 9, 10, 14, 15, 17]) into existing cyberbullying research revealed a choice: we can work to recognize and identify cyberbullying as it happens, or we can work to prevent cyberbullying from happening at all. We chose to attempt the latter, building a social network for children ages 7–12 years that serves as an active training ground for establishing and practicing healthy digital friendships.

Our sketch-based social network, named KidGab and explained in more detail in Sect. 12.2, is a departure from most research applications for children in that it requires participants to engage with the system in their free time and by their own volition. Active participation is necessary to achieve the practice and experiences necessary to learn safe and healthy social networking habits. To achieve our goal of longitudinal participation, participants must remain engaged with the system for an extended period of time (8+ weeks). Given these difficulties, we needed to design our social network to be as exciting and appealing as possible, in order to sustain longitudinal participation.

In this chapter, we discuss one of our many strategies for sustaining participation: our sketch-based badge system. A badge system provides users with the ability to earn rewards for completing small tasks within a site or system (in our case, those tasks are creative sketches and/or short writing prompts). Badge systems provide many benefits: badges communicate community values and expected behaviors to new users [2], scaffolded goal setting is highly motivating (rewards just outside a user's reach) [11], badges allow and encourage users to obtain community reputation (enhanced by the belief that other users will look on one more favorably for participating) [3], and finally badges promote the feeling of similarity between a user and the other community members because of the shared experience [2]. However, extrinsic motivation in the form of digital rewards can be seen as manipulative [4], so children should never feel obligated to participate in badge earning activities. Autonomy on digital systems for children can increase intrinsic motivation [16], thus providing a balance in the source of motivation to participate.

The remainder of this paper will introduce our social network, KidGab; explain the implementation of our badge system; discuss preliminary results from our deployments; provide examples of how one might generalize our system for other domains; and finally, we summarize our contribution to the community of pen and touch technology in education.

12.2 KidGab

We developed KidGab to bring together existing networks of children such as scouting troops, classrooms, and sport teams. By remaining closed to the general public, children can stay safe from ill-intentioned Internet users. An example profile page on KidGab can be seen in Fig. 12.1a.

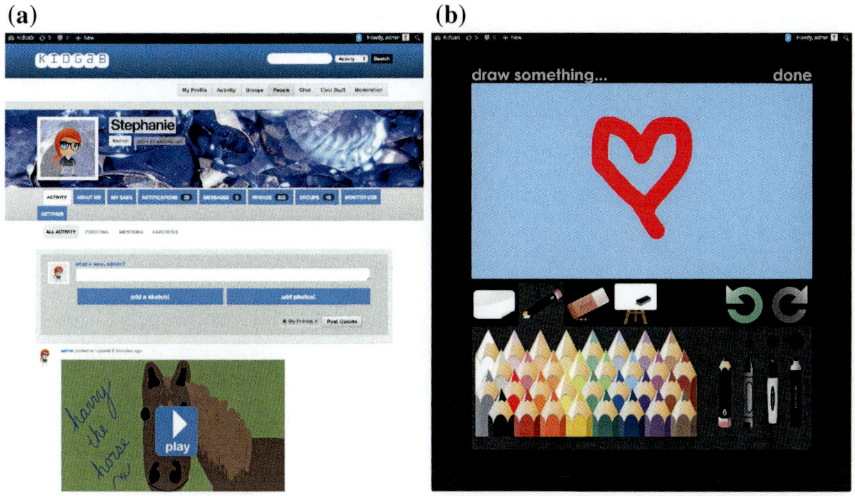

Fig. 12.1 Screenshots from KidGab's interface. **a** A profile page in KidGab. **b** KidGab's sketch interface

Authority figures within these networks such as parents, teachers, coaches, and group leaders are encouraged to join the site. Parent accounts are linked to child accounts, allowing parents to monitor their children's online activities. If a parent has not logged in to KidGab for seven days, their child's account becomes blocked until the parent logs in again. Parents cannot befriend other children and the child is not allowed to de-friend their parent.

Distinct from traditional social networks, KidGab is sketch-based. KidGab allows children to send sketches to one another either in lieu of or in addition to textual communications. A screenshot of our sketching interface can be seen in Fig. 12.1b. Sketches are not stored as static images; they are stored as videos for action-by-action playback of the sketch construction. For example, the recipient can view each stroke being added, undo/redo actions, the background color changing, etc. This sketching facilitates simple animations, multi-scene sketches, etc., which is a richer temporal experience than static sketches alone. The sketch videos can be a useful curricular tool, as they can capture step-by-step procedures quite well (e.g. how to solve math problems, growth cycles, multi-scene creative writing).

In place of a profile picture, KidGab uses custom cartoon avatars. Through the avatars, children can change their appearance as they please, providing freedom of expression and customization. The user can choose their avatar's skin color, hair color and style, their eye color and shape, their clothing (sporty or dressy), optional facial features (freckles and mustaches), and other accessories (hat, glasses, or a bow).

After styling their avatars, users can take one of our fun personality quizzes. KidGab has a variety of quizzes in diverse areas of interest (sports, fashion, animals, anime, books, etc.). These quizzes have appealed greatly to the users in our deployments. The children in the age group currently using KidGab (7–12 years) are constantly molding and shaping their identities. Personality quizzes are very popular amongst this age of children and it is up to the child to decide how they are to interpret the results. We post a new quiz once every two to three days. On quiz result pages, the user has the ability to share their results with their friends.

12.3 Our Domain

For the deployment of KidGab, we are working closely with the Girl Scouts of Central Texas. The Girl Scouts organization consists of close-knit communities of girls, which is an ideal base on which KidGab can grow. Presently, we introduce cohorts of 10–20 girls to KidGab through our Digital Friendship Workshops.[1]

One advantage of working with Girl Scouts for our preliminary deployments as opposed to a classroom environment is that participation in the site is optional. By introducing KidGab to a classroom, school, or school system (which we are open to, but have not yet attempted), using the site would be mandatory. Our results with the Girl Scouts, therefore, closer represent what works to motivate children to participate in digital and educational activities 'in the wild'.

12.4 Our Badge System: The Digital Sash

Many digital applications (most notably video games) contain a rewards system, whereby completing specific tasks, the user earns a small reward. Having a reward system encourages users to continue to engage with the application in order to earn more awards or achievements. Girl Scouts and other scouting organizations have a similar, but physical system, where members have a vest or a sash and can earn fabric patches by completing specific fun activities. Patch activities are usually intended to teach a valuable skill such as money management, woodworking, expressive writing, etc. In order to simulate a similar environment for our Girl Scout users, we have created KidGab's Digital Sash, where the girls can earn digital badges by completing creative drawing tasks and sharing opinions.

12.4.1 User: Earning Badge

Earning badges in KidGab is quite easy. Consider this scenario: A girl logs in to KidGab and (after checking out her friends' recent posts) navigates to the page that displays her Digital Sash (Fig. 12.2a). She scans her sash and sees a new grayscale

[1]The curriculum of our Digital Friendship Workshops is not the main focus of this manuscript, but more information can be found at http://www.digitalfriendship.org.

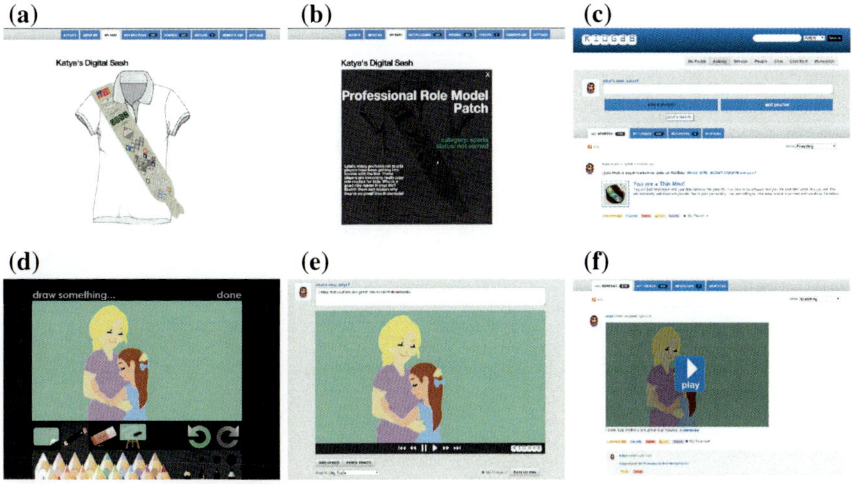

Fig. 12.2 A step-by-step illustration of the steps to earning a badge. This particular example earns the Professional Role Model Badge. Other badges require similar steps but regard different themes. **a** The Digital Sash. **b** Viewing a badge. **c** Starting a sketch. **d** Finishing the sketch. **e** Adding some text. **f** Posting and earning

badge she hadn't seen before. The girl knows that badges she's already earned appear in color and the grayscale badges are yet to be completed, so she knows this is badge is something new she can earn. She clicks on the badge (Fig. 12.2b) and reads the description: "Lately, many professional sports players have been getting into trouble with the law. These players are becoming really poor role models for kids. Who is a good role model in your life? Sketch them and explain why they're so great! Use #rolemodel". The girl decides she wants to earn this patch. She navigates to her activity feed and begins a new sketch (Fig. 12.2c). She sketches an image of herself and her mother, with their arms around each other's shoulders, showing the love and bond between them (Fig. 12.2d). After finishing her sketch, she types "I think that mothers are great role models #rolemodel" making sure to include #rolemodel, because that is part of the requirement for earning the badge (Fig. 12.2e). The girl posts her sketch and instantly sees a comment below her post, saying she earned the Professional Role Model Patch (Fig. 12.2f). She clicks the link in the comment, which navigates the girl back to her Digital Sash. The Professional Role Model patch is now in color!

12.4.2 Administrator: Badge Creation

Creating badges on KidGab is equally easy. An admin can create a new badge in the Badges Manager section of KidGab's administrator menu. In defining a new badge, the admin must provide the new badge's name, the hashtag required to earn it, and a

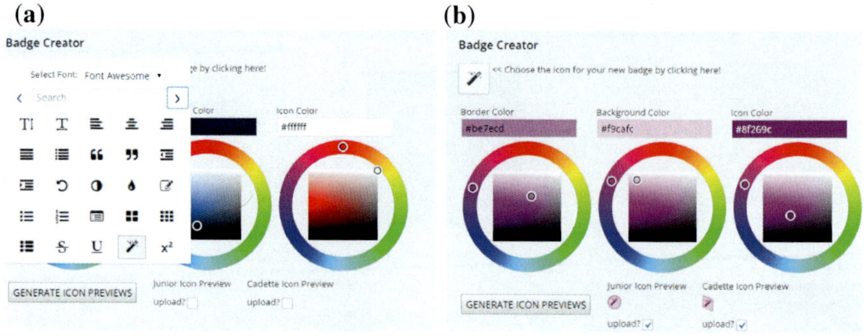

Fig. 12.3 KidGab can automatically generate the artwork for Badges based on an administrator's choice of icon and colors. Generated badges are small and appear in the lower portion of **b**. **a** Choose an icon. **b** Generate previews

description of the earning requirements, so users can understand what they must do to earn the badge. The final step in creating a badge is to select the artwork that will serve as the face of the badge. The admin can choose whether to upload a badge image she manually created or whether to use KidGab's custom-built badge-creator tool. The badge creator tool allows the administrator to choose between a variety of vector icons to become the decorative and descriptive centerpiece of the badge (Fig. 12.3a). After choosing an icon, the administrator can choose the border color, background color, and the icon color of the badge. With a click of a button, KidGab generates SVG images using the icon and colors selected (Fig. 12.3b), thus providing great time savings compared with designing, creating, saving, and uploading the images manually. The admin can tweak the design of the badge until satisfied, and can "Save Badge" when the artwork and descriptions are complete.

12.4.3 Administrator: Badge Curricula

For each cohort of children joining KidGab (all children who have joined KidGab have done so through one of our Digital Friendship Workshops), we design a custom curriculum of badges to suit their unique interests, upcoming holidays, etc. On average, we release about one badge per cohort per day. In the days immediately following the workshop, we release more than one badge per day, and we progressively slow the release rate to about one every other day. Badge curricula usually span about 6 weeks. Badge releases are automatically announced by KidGab in the form of status updates by the "KidGab Admin". A released badge will also appear in grayscale on a girl's sash, indicating that it is ready to be earned.

Randomness and variety within the badge curriculum is important. We found that focusing on one theme (e.g. March Madness or Weather Patterns, etc.) generally reduced interest in the earning of badges. Now, we try to alternate between serious, silly, fashion-related, sporty, and creative badges in order to reach girls with a wide range of interests. Varying the requirements for earning badges is also important, so in our curricula we attempt to strike a balance between text-based and sketch-based badges.

12.5 Deployment Results

At the time of preparing this manuscript, 157 Girl Scouts have joined KidGab. The Girl Scouts have created a total of 895 posts and 373 of those posts included sketches. The girls have earned a total of 508 badges (some of which are awarded for simple account setup tasks like changing passwords and creating avatars).

The most popular post-to-earn badges are American Girl (with 77 earners) (we include the earning of this badge in our workshops), Texas Girl (with 18 earners), Dream Diary (with 14 earners), A Sister to Every Girl Scout (with 11 earners), and SuperPowerful with (10 earners). All but the Sister to Every Girl Scout badge require sketches, but often girls chose to add sketches anyway. We provide descriptions and a selection of girl responses for all five of these badges in Fig. 12.4.

One badge that was not among the most popular, but surprised us in terms of the thoughtfulness of the responses is the Water Is Important badge. This badge is one of our "serious" badges and encourages the girls to think with a global perspective. Instructions for earning this badge are: "Did you know that there are people around the world that don't have access to fresh water everyday? Write how you feel about that, use #waterisimportant." One girl wrote:

> I hate how some places don't have access to water. I learned in my geography class this year that most 3rd-world countries aren't able to have water because the "government" there won't let go to the poorer cities: It's like they play favorites and they give the water to the better cities rather than the poorer ones. I hate it. #waterisimportant

Another girl wrote:

> I think everybody should appreciate the water they have cause some people don't have any water so we should all preserve water so we can have water hopefully someday everbody in the world will have water #waterisimportant

Seven girls have earned the Water Is Important badge, which is significant, since it is usually released in weeks three or four of the badge curricula (earlier-released badges usually receive many more responses). We think this reveals that children are capable and willing to communicate serious and even political opinions on KidGab, providing them with valuable experience in practicing digital citizenship skills.

Badge Name & Description	Example Girl Response	Example Girl Response
American Girl Earn the American Girl Patch by posting a sketch of an object that you think is uniquely American. Use hashtag #americangirl!	 #americangirl	 #americangirl
Texas Girl Earn the Texas Girl Patch by posting a sketch that reflects how you feel about living in Texas. Use the hashtag #texasgirl!	 #texasgirl	 #Texasgirl How I feel about Texas:
Dream Diary Earn the Dream Diary Patch by sharing a dream you have had with your friends on KidGab! Sketch out what happened and be sure to tell the story in words too! Use hashtag #dreamer!	 I had this dream of me and my family when I was like in the third grade #dreamer	 By far the best dream I had was CANDY LAND! It was so cool. Everything was made up of your favorite type of candy you name it had it. #dreamer
A Sister to Every Girl Scout KidGab was built in order to provide Girl Scouts a place to talk, joke, laugh, and make friendships stronger online. How do you think you can use KidGab to be a sister to every Girl Scout? Use #sister to share your idea and earn the Sister to Every Girl Scout patch!	#sister Kid gab helps me be a sister to everybody because it gives me the chance to meet new people and have a great time with them online! Its great to know that I have my fellow sisters that are there for me!	 #sister
SuperPowerful As girls, we get to be whatever we want to be! If you could have any superhero power, what kind of superpower would you want? Explain in words and sketch it out to earn your SuperPowerful Patch! Be sure to use #superpower!!	 I can fly and shoot lasers out of my eyes #superpower	 my superpower would be invzabilite #superpower

Fig. 12.4 Descriptions and example responses (drawn by KidGab Girl Scouts) for the five most popular badges. The A Sister to Every Girl Scout Patch does not require a sketch, but some girls choose to add a sketch anyway

12.6 Generalizability

Our Digital Sash has faced criticism for being too specific to the Girl Scouts domain and too difficult to generalize to other populations. We see great potential for our results to generalize to a wide range of domains, and we illustrate a few alternative badge system metaphors below.

Our first metaphor is the marble jar. A marble jar metaphor (a mock-up example of which can be seen in Fig. 12.5a) would be ideal for a school or classroom environment. This is a digital representation of a physical reward system used in elementary classrooms. When a class behaves exceptionally well or accomplishes preset goals, the teacher adds marbles to a clear glass jar. If the class behaves poorly, the teacher removes marbles from the jar. When the jar fills, the class earns a treat, like a special holiday party or extra recess. This metaphor can easily extend to a digital badge system. As a user completes the digital activities and the marble jar fills, he can see his progress toward earning some other great reward (as determined by the teacher, coach, etc.). Advantages of the Marble Jar are the perceptually quantifiable progress

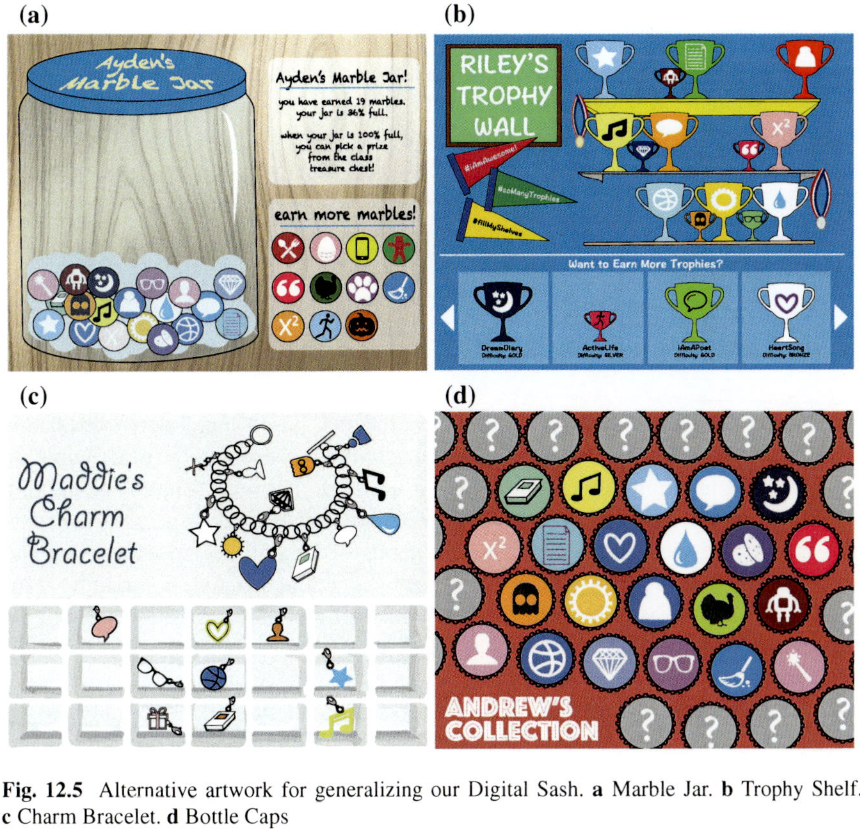

Fig. 12.5 Alternative artwork for generalizing our Digital Sash. **a** Marble Jar. **b** Trophy Shelf. **c** Charm Bracelet. **d** Bottle Caps

level and the ease of comprehending which activities have been completed (those inside the jar) and which have not (those outside the jar).

Another approach might take the form of a trophy shelf (a mock-up example of which can be seen in Fig. 12.5b). In the same way that participants are rewarded trophies for excelling in sports competitions, children could be awarded trophies for completing activities and being active on the site. As in competitions, trophies would be given a rank according to the difficulty to obtain them. These ranks could be bronze, silver and gold. Once obtained, the trophies would be placed on the respective shelf within the user's trophy wall, as seen in Fig. 12.5b. This Trophy Shelf approach to a badge system is gender-neutral; both boys and girls are likely to enjoy collecting trophies and the satisfaction of owning a significant amount of them.

A slightly more gender-specific badge metaphor is the concept of charm bracelets (a mock-up example of which can be seen in Fig. 12.5c). Many young girls enjoy collecting charms that identify items or activities they love. Each completed activity would provide a new charm for her digital bracelet. While this approach is specific to an audience of girls, it would be a fun and age-appropriate rewards system for girls within our target age-group (7–12 years).

Collecting bottle caps is a hobby that has been practiced for many years. More than a hobby, it has become an art. Inspired by bottle cap walls, we propose a system (an example of which can be seen in Fig. 12.5d) that will award KidGab users bottle caps for their participation in the website and allow them to have personal bottle cap walls. Once obtained, the bottle caps may be arranged within the wall to their liking, thus allowing users to be creative with their spaces. This itself allows for another appealing activity; being able to share bottle cap walls and observing other users' creations. Such customizations have been shown to improve intrinsic motivation and participation rates for children's software applications [12, 16].

12.7 Conclusion

The focus of this paper is a description of our sketch-based social network's badge system, the Digital Sash. We use the badge activities to sustain active participation and to impart learning and creativity in our users' digital lives. The badge-earning activities present users the opportunity to practice posting introspective, creative, and appropriate messages, so they retain habits of healthy digital expression and netiquette skills. Presently, KidGab is in use by an extracurricular community (Girl Scouts), but could easily be used as a powerful tool within a classroom community. KidGab and it's sketch-based badges could be a fun place to complete bellwork (quiet activities to be completed in the minutes just before and after the morning bell), exam review (the sketch playback functions can support temporally-solved math problems or even flashcard-like actions), and infinitely more curricular uses. Our contribution to the community of pen and touch technology in education is a process for encouraging sketch-based learning and technological participation by a child's own choice within the context of a fun and social environment.

Acknowledgments The authors thank the Sketch Recognition Lab, the Girl Scouts of Central Texas (particularly Emily Magnotta), Jung In Koh, Cassandra Odoula, and Andrew Giese for their support throughout this project. S. Valentine is supported in part by an NSF Graduate Research Fellowship. A. McMurtry and K. Borgos are supported by CRA-W Distributed Research Experience for Undergraduates Grants.

References

1. Ackers MJ (2012) Cyberbullying: through the eyes of children and young people. Educ Psychol Pract 28(2):141–157
2. Antin J, Churchill EF (2011) Badges in social media: a social psychological perspective. In: CHI 2011 gamification workshop proceedings. Vancouver, BC, Canada
3. Berger J, Cohen BP, Zelditch M Jr (1972) Status characteristics and social interaction. Am Sociol Rev 37(3):241–255
4. Deci EL, Koestner R, Ryan RM (1999) A meta-analytic review of experiments examining the effects of extrinsic rewards on intrinsic motivation. Psychol Bull 125(6):627–668
5. Dinakar K, Jones B, Havasi C, Lieberman H, Picard R (2012) Timeout: commonsense reasoning for detection, prevention, and mitigation of cyberbullying. ACM Transactions on Intelligent Interactive Systems (ACM TiiS) 18:1–18:30
6. Hinduja S, Patchin JW (2008) Bullying beyond the schoolyard: preventing and responding to cyberbullying. Corwin Press Incorporated, Thousand Oaks
7. Hinduja S, Patchin JW (2012) School climate 2.0: preventing cyberbullying and sexting one classroom at a time. SAGE Publications, Thousand Oaks
8. Huang Yy, Chou C (2010) An analysis of multiple factors of cyberbullying among junior high school students in Taiwan. Comput Human Behav 26(6):1581–1590
9. Kumazaki A, Suzuki K, Katsura R, Sakamoto A, Kashibuchi M (2011) The effects of netiquette and ICT skills on school-bullying and cyber-bullying: the two-wave panel study of japanese elementary, secondary, and high school students. Procedia - Soc Behav Sci 29:735–741
10. Li Q (2008) A cross-cultural comparison of adolescents' experience related to cyberbullying. Educ Res 50(3):223–234
11. Ling K, Beenen G, Ludford P, Wang X, Chang K, Li X, Cosley D, Frankowski D, Terveen L, Rashid AM, Resnick P, Kraut R (2005) Using social psychology to motivate contributions to online communities. J Comput-Mediat Commun 10(4):212–221
12. Malone TW (1980) What makes things fun to learn? Heuristics for designing instructional computer games. In: Proceedings of the 3rd ACM SIGSMALL symposium - SIGSMALL '80. ACM Press, New York, pp 162–169
13. Microsoft research: Microsoft online safety research (2010)
14. Oliveros M, Amemiya I, Condorimay Y, Oliveros R, Barrientos A, Rivas B (2012) Ciberbullying - nueva tecnologa electrnica al servicio del acoso escolar en alumnos de dos distritos de lima, per. Anales de la Facultad de Medicina 73(1):13–8
15. Popović-Ćitić B, Djurić S, Cvetković V (2011) The prevalence of cyberbullying among adolescents: a case study of middle schools in Serbia. School Psychol Int 32(4):412–424
16. Ryan RM, Rigby CS, Przybylski A (2006) The motivational pull of video games: a self-determination theory approach. Motiv Emot 30(4):344–360
17. Winn MR (2012) Promote digital citizenship through school-based social networking. Learn Lead Mag 39(4):10–13

Chapter 13
A Cyberensemble of Inversion, Immersion, Shared Knowledge Areas, Query, and Digital Media-Making in STEM Classrooms

Eric Hamilton, George Foe-Aman, Lynette Foe-Aman, and Israel Ramirez-Gamez

Abstract This paper reports on the theoretical underpinnings, design, and initial findings of a research project funded by the US National Science Foundation's Cyberlearning Program. At the epicenter of the project is the use of digital ink both in collaborative "what you see is what I see" workspaces to reshape the nature of flipped classrooms, and in creating interactive digital media, especially videos, used as lessons for the flipped arrangements. In addition to pen-based computing, flipped classrooms, collaborative workspaces, and digital media making, the project deploys help-giving software agents. The purpose of creating the ensemble is to understand the interaction between enabling technologies that can contribute to highly immersive and high-performance learning settings. The classroom ecosystem this ensemble produces appears to foster significant development across multiple accepted categories of social and emotional growth in service of academic learning. For that reason, the focus on learner engagement has expanded to include these growth areas.

13.1 Introduction

This research focuses on ways to draw students into deep, sustained interaction with and manipulation of mathematical ideas. It does so in classroom contexts designed to permit the student to shift seamlessly between social interactions and deep personal concentration. It is premised on the belief that immersive engagement with chal-

E. Hamilton (✉)
Pepperdine University, Malibu, CA 90263, USA
e-mail: eric.hamilton@pepperdine.edu

G. Foe-Aman · L. Foe-Aman
Cabrillo High School, Long Beach, CA, USA
e-mail: gfoeaman@lbusd.org

L. Foe-Aman
e-mail: lfoeaman@lbusd.org

I. Ramirez-Gamez
Spring Valley High School, Las Vegas, NV, USA
e-mail: jramirez-gamez@interact.ccsd.net

T. Hammond et al. (eds.), *Revolutionizing Education with Digital Ink*,
Human–Computer Interaction Series, DOI 10.1007/978-3-319-31193-7_13

lenging mathematics is the most promising pathway to satisfying, joyful and successful mathematical growth and development of complex reasoning skills. It is also premised on the conviction that in the absence of tools and approaches that have been unavailable in so-called "traditional" lecture based classrooms, classroom environments characterized by such engrossing and social-rich experiences with mathematics are virtually impossible or difficult to sustain. This research, with activities taking place in California, Nevada, and multiple Sub-Saharan sites, seeks to build understanding of how to operationalize personally absorbing mathematical experiences on a routine basis.

13.2 Why Pen-Based Computing: To See and to Make Visible

Two enablements that pen-based computing provides are critical to the research appearing below. The research draws on an eclectic theory of "personalized learning communities" [22] that prioritizes what we refer to as *interactional bandwidth* of a learning environment—its capacity to permit the communication and exchange of rich, visible subject matter content between individuals, teacher and students alike, in a classroom setting. In previous work, we have characterized the interactional bandwidth of traditional classrooms as very low and stilted [22]. Perhaps the most salient aspect of a bandwidth profile is the degree to which it promotes "sightlines" whereby students and teachers can both (a) see one another's mathematical conceptualizations and, (b) by implication, the degree to which each person in the learning community can make their own ideas visible.

Pen-based computing makes it possible to represent conceptual structures through natural, non-keyboard mediated written mathematical symbol systems, and to make those structures visible. It does so in this research by providing a teacher the means to view in thumbnail and full-size versions the mathematical writing of any and all students.

13.3 Classroom Flipping in This Research

The project relies on the process of "classroom flipping," an increasingly prominent strategy that opens up time and space in the classroom for the interactions that this research studies. Following the brief recap of flipping below, the paper introduces the notion of a "cyberensemble" of tools and approaches designed to play off of one another with the intent of augmenting the capacity of each tool to optimize learner experience. Part of the purpose of the research is to test these intended design and optimization relationships.

Perhaps the most familiar teaching pattern of formal K16 classroom environments involves a sequence whereby a teacher presents material in class and that material becomes the basis for assignments that students subsequently complete outside of class. The variations within this broad pattern are almost limitless, but the pattern itself is robust and durable. One of the most interesting and potentially promising developments in education over the past decade involves reversing this pattern. Often referred to as classroom flipping, this educational approach has a growing number of adherents. The original proposal for funding to the US National Science Foundation (NSF) that led to this research noted that the agency had not yet appeared to investigate flipping or to capitalize on its momentum [19], though since then NSF has supported research in this area. US high school science teachers Jonathan Bergmann and Aaron Sams are credited as the first to popularize this approach [43]. Salman Khan, developer of the well-known video site https://www.khanacademy.org/, has also been associated with the ascendancy of classroom flipping [51]. Flipping involves students viewing, from home or elsewhere outside of school, the teacher's presentation or lecture prior to class, and then using class time to work with the teacher on activities that reflect that material. The teacher's presentation takes place outside of class; the "homework" takes place in class, where the teacher is available to help the student. Although the term "inversion" to represent lectures outside of class and interaction within class was apparently first coined in 2000 in connection with college teaching [34], the K12 classroom flipping phenomenon has garnered a rapidly growing community of practitioners. The primary logic for flipping is that, while challenging and time-consuming to carry out, **it can make class time available for more sustained interaction between students and teacher, greater engagement of the student with subject matter, and increased learning**. Classroom flipping is held by many as a powerful concept for widely held aspirations to open class time and shift the dynamics of classroom activities and assignments, placing emphasis on both engagement and the interaction between teacher and students to promote learning. It has attracted a wide followership, primarily based on such perceived increases in student engagement and motivation [51]. This research makes no claims about classroom flipping, but employs the device of flipping because it vacates from classroom periods the time necessary to give full lecture introductions, and structures more time for the teacher and students to interact directly, doing so around student engagement in homework-like activities. The research seeks to optimize and examine this interaction time.

The research treats as an exemplar of the concept of blending multiple potentially synergistic technologies one particular ensemble of six approaches and tools (see Fig. 13.1). The ensemble is anchored in pen-based computing, combined with "what you see is what I see" collaborative software permitting teachers and students to see and interact with each other's digital ink-based work (Fig. 13.2). It also includes video creation, editing and mixing tools, with screen capture software. Coming later in the study, the cyberensemble will include natural language dialog software to promote question-asking and digital resource access through desktop or mobile interfaces. The final element of the ensemble involves low-cost mobile video playback devices to assure equitable opportunity to participate in the flipped classroom strategy.

The vision animating this cyberlearning "ensemble" or innovation

- Routine, multidimensional immersion in learning challenging content, that is, "flow in learning".

Six cyberlearning technologies and approaches that each contribute uniquely to one adaptable ensemble

1. Use of pen-based computing to enable learners and teachers to make ideas more visible and to be able to see mathematical ideas more clearly
2. "Collaborative workspaces" that enable teachers and students to view each other's work in real time, both individually and in a group setting;
3. Video production for creativity, teaching and learning;
4. Agent-based dialog and query systems;
5. Classroom inversion or flipping; and
6. Low-cost mobile devices for media playback

Prominent research questions:

- How does this cyberensemble foster deeply absorbing and effective experience in learning?
- How can schools successfully plan, realize and improve this type of educational ecosystem?
- What insights does the ensemble furnish about important dynamics associated with learning, such as learner engagement, immersion, flow, question-asking, self-explanation, creativity, help-giving and seeking, iterative formation of STEM ideas, and self-regulation.
- What design principles should guide other ensemble designs?

Three core areas of research underpinning (how kids think about math affects how they think mathematically)

- Learner engagement, immersion, flow and creativity;
- Natural language dialog practices of question asking and self-explanation in subject matter contexts;
- The "DNR" principle of duality, necessity, and repeated reasoning, emerging from math education research.

Diverse upper school partners

- Located in Nevada and California, each with over 80% Latino populations. Multiple sites for limited exposure in Ghana and Namibia. The study involves mathematics courses identified by each school's design team.

Useful media that captures important aspects of the research

- http://bit.ly/media-making-ghana-2014 shows teachers and students working together to create instructional media, with an example of a short GeoGebra video by two Ghanaian students and interview with them.
- http://bit.ly/cyberlearning-sharktank-teachersandstudentscreate-2015 is a short video that depicts a combination of screen sharing and media-making, followed by three short interviews in Los Angeles and Ghana.

Fig. 13.1 Summary of cyberensemble research elements

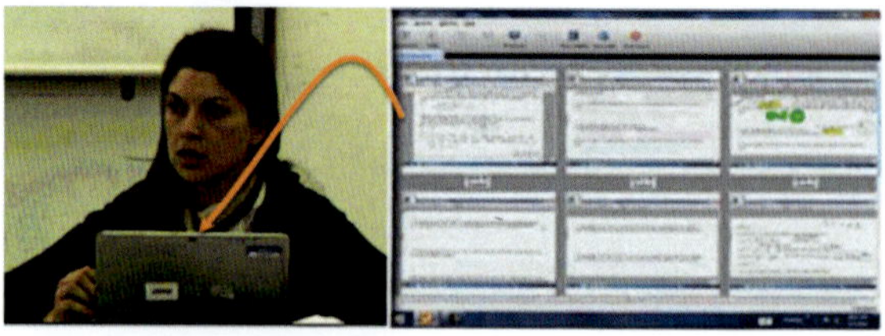

Fig. 13.2 The teacher view of student work on project papers. Students use digital ink in working through classroom activity sets (USA)

As a design study [35, 48], the project investigates, through multiple iterations and adjustments, whether ways of designing a set of six features into a classroom ecosystem can routinely result in transformed school experience, beginning with mathematics. Each of the six strategies and technologies is well-defined, stable, and important in its own right; collectively they appear to fit together like the tumblers of a lock falling into place. Each, in our preliminary work, appears to expand the affordances for learning of the others, and each relies on the affordances of the others. Situating them in juxtaposition with each other, we hope, will yield truly compelling advances in pathways to deep and sustained learning. Our expectation is that cyberlearning tools (such as this ensemble) may not only lead to more routine attainment of goals widely held for education, but also alter and enrich what we mean by learning.

Research Questions. This R&D project has multiple points of origin, but the most salient may be that it studies, through the lens of deep engagement, the relationship between the cyberensemble and learning in educational settings. How does the cyberensemble foster deeply absorbing and effective experience in learning? How can schools successfully plan, realize and improve this type of educational ecosystem? Fig. 13.1 lists these as the two primary research questions of the study. They can be understood as asking whether and how the ensemble will function in a design study with a research team, and then whether and how teacher and school teams can carry out their own versions of the ensemble beyond the boundaries of this project.

13.4 Project Background

The design and implementation considerations for the envisioned ensemble are sizable. Practical aspects of in situ research in the high stakes assessment environments of urban high schools are daunting in their own right, but are only one part of the planning process that an exploratory effort of this nature must address. The requirements of high stakes testing in the US mirror national curriculum and testing requirements in the Sub-Saharan countries where the research also takes place.

13.5 Theoretical Foundations

Three prominent, cross-cutting theoretical themes discussed below have guided this initial design: learner engagement, question-asking and self-explaining, and the mathematical cognition theory of dualism, necessity, and repetition.

Learner engagement. Four of the ensemble elements have produced distinct findings relative to learner engagement; each in some fashion relies on feedback systems and platform design to maintain a balance between an activity's challenge level and a student's ability. **That is, as cyberenabled tools and strategies, each has proven productive in helping classroom ecosystems maintain the equilibrium**

between difficulty and ability in school learning. The separate discussions about the components highlight these findings. The emphasis on challenge at the outer edge of but not exceeding ability aligns closely with the familiar Vygotskian theory of proximal development zones [54]. It also aligns closely with flow theory on activity sets "between boredom and anxiety," [10] to use the title of an early and foundational volume by theorist Mihali Csikzenthmihali. With the exception of cognitive tutoring tools that seek to manage lesson episodes relatively comprehensively without the aid of a teacher, cybertools cannot maintain the delicate equilibrium between difficulty and ability in learning environment design. They can, however, make thinking sufficiently visible and feedback loops sufficiently rapid and well-calibrated to allow teachers and students to function within this zone. They can provide the essential sightlines or means for teachers and students to express mathematical or scientific ideas effectively in ways that allow them to "see" each other's thinking through cyber-enablements. For the teacher, cybertools expand the pedagogical skills sets teachers need to size up student thinking and adjust the equilibrium between task difficulty and student ability [38, 44].

The relationship between engagement and learning has proven difficult to specify theoretically [44, 45]. A number of researchers investigating the effects of educational interventions will connect learner engagement with outcomes that show evidence of increased learning [39]. The data sets appearing in Table 2 will assist the research team in drawing well-grounded connections between engagement and learning. Our interest in engagement extends to a construct referenced above, namely flow states. Since the mid-1970s, the term "flow," adopted by Csikszentmihalyi [10], has been used to characterize and analyze optimal performance in human experience. While flow remains a multiply-defined term with at least sixteen separate operational definitions [41], the majority of these definitions are generally variants of Csikszentmihalyi's [10] original flow description:

In the flow state action follows upon action according to an internal logic that seems to need no conscious intervention by the actor. He experiences it as a unified flowing from one moment to the next, in which he is in control of his actions, and in which there is little distinction between self and environment, between stimulus and response, or between past, present, and future (p. 36).

The flow state [11–13] is characterized by intense engagement in the activity at hand accompanied by enjoyment and a sense of control over the activity. In popular terminology, especially in sports, flow states are referred to as "being in the zone" of high performance. Persons in the flow state are responsive to intrinsic motivators and participate in the activity for its own sake. The individual glides almost without consciously thinking from one step to the next, experiences a state of complete immersion, and loses track of time [11]. We consider these conditions to be desirable—and attainable—attributes of STEM learning environments. That is, the design of formal or informal environments that routinely result in intense focus, engagement, enjoyment, a sense of control, and intrinsic motivation, is a worthy and humane aspiration for cyberlearning research. We conjecture that the more fully learners are engaged in an activity, up to and including what can be considered a flow state, the more likely they are to internalize the structure of what they are learning and to become inventive about how that content's structure connects with other knowledge.

The link between flow and imagination is part of the premise behind Csikszentmihalyi's 1996 summative volume, *Creativity: Flow and the Psychology of Discovery and Invention* [11]. It is an understatement to assert that learners do not typically experience living and learning "in the zone" in traditional school and homework experiences [16, 50]. This project continues a thread of research that seeks to understand and implement conditions conducive to routinely high levels of learner engagement. Our past research has documented antecedent features that can be designed into learning environments to improve the likelihood of high engagement and flow states [18]. This project is motivated by a quest to find conditions for inducing flow states.

Question-asking and Self-explaining. A second area of guiding research coincidentally originates in work on cognitive tutoring. It involves the leveraging role of spoken and written language that has emerged from that research. In particular, self-explanation and question-asking behavior each has proven to obligate a broad series of cognitive and affective mechanisms that clarify and stabilize conceptual structures, and/or expose them to externalized scrutiny. Spoken language to explain or clarify conceptual structures that are typically expressed in notation (such as mathematics or science) is a proven and generally underutilized resource in classroom settings. Landmark work by Chi and others [8, 9] documenting the value of self-explanation in tutorial environments prepared the groundwork for a broader body of work focusing on the benefits for cognitive and metacognitive growth of self-explanation practice [1, 33, 55]. The cyberensemble emphasizes or requires self-explanation practice recurrently through video creation by students, peer assistance in class sessions, and dialog exchanges over the collaborative workspaces. A related competence involves question-asking behavior. Early research in cognitive tutors, including by Graesser [14] and Chi [46], has also proven foundational in this area, documenting problem-solving growth through the practice of posing questions about problem scenarios. The ensemble creates an expectation that students will routinely pose structurally nuanced questions, especially through the increased availability of the teacher, the collaborative workspaces that invite anonymous question-asking; and the spoken language query system that brings a digital resource based on short dialogs with an avatar.

DNR. A third critical foundation for this project originates in mathematics education research. Principles formalized by Harel, Lesh and others [29, 36] are economically summarized with the acronym DNR. DNR theory involves dualism, or the distinctly metacognitive notion that what students understand about mathematics and how they think about mathematics are interdependent; necessity, or the notion that effective mathematical growth requires an authentically motivating context or sense of need; and repeated reasoning, or the notion that mathematical growth requires repeated examination and manipulation of structural relationships between ideas in different contexts. This project does not focus extensively on the metacognitive interplay between how a learner thinks about mathematics and how a learner thinks mathematically. That critical interdependency behind mathematical growth, however, will occur in the classrooms we will study. The two other principles are a more immediate consideration. The process of creating videos is challenge- or task- oriented and thus intrinsically need-based. Building this and other social dynamics into the freed-up class time in which students work with peers and teacher on mathematics assignments adds an intrinsically socio-motivational element to mathematical problem-solving that does not exist when students do mathematics homework in isolation [3]. The repeated reasoning principle comes into play as students become adept at creating media to help peers learn. The practice of building a coherent short video, and the editing and remixing a production entails, requires a playing, replaying, and analysis of a representation in order to make the ideas coherent to the viewer. The videos, as developed for this ensemble, also stress or emphasize examining ideas from repeated vantages.

These three broad areas of research (engagement, question-asking and self-explanation, and the DNR principle) take a significant role guiding this ensemble's design. The project is also guided by work in various other fields, most prominently self-regulation [42, 49], efforts to integrate creativity and the arts into mathematics and science education [40], and efforts to define research-based principles for learning environment design [47, 53].

13.6 Elena's Experience: A Cyberensemble Scenario

It may be useful to outline the kind of experience that a hypothetical student ("Elena") might find in this ensemble ecosystem, beginning with her arrival home at the end of the school day. For the purpose of illustration we will assume that Elena has neither reliable access to the Internet from home nor a smart phone that permits high-resolution video playback. Thus, she is using one of the school's mp4 players, a $40 device with a 6-inch screen and a solid state memory populated with the math courses' full bank of videos.

Elena's teacher ("Ms. Jones") has asked the class to view two four-minute videos. One is notational and assumes that the student has experience with factorial notation. It reintroduces the notation and illustrates simple but important manipulations involving rational expressions with factorials, which happen to be especially well-suited for representation by video. The video includes a small number of "Pause and you try" breakpoints where Elena can pause the playback and try a simple problem before resuming the playback to check for understanding. The second video defines and contrasts permutations and combinations, again with uncomplicated examples that Elena can attempt.

The distinction between combinations and permutations is one of the most difficult for high school students to recognize. Ms. Jones developed this video in collaboration with students who had mastered the distinction. Following a lesson study format, other teachers and students at the school helped to refine it further, and teachers and students from other schools gave it positive feedback when it was posted on the

Internet. Ms. Jones feels that this particular explanation and set of examples will serve her students more effectively than a possibly unpredictable class presentation might.

Elena spends 20 min viewing the videos on the mp4 player and trying the short exercises they include. She finds that she prefers viewing interactive videos at home over struggling alone with frustrating homework assignments. She is accustomed to videos that outline concepts with helpful visualizations and simple warm-up exercises to prepare her for doing problems in class, where she will have help. Both how she views math in general and how she thinks mathematically have changed.

The next day proves challenging. Along with the other students, she checks in as having completed the video assignment and begins the in-class work. The assignment includes simple combination and permutation problems, along with more complex problems that require interpretation and may involve both. Some questions ask her to consider the possibility of a subset of replaceable objects in a set of other objects not replaceable, a topic not yet covered in any introductory videos that she has viewed and that she has to think about. In this class, students have the option of working in pairs or alone, using a tablet device with a stylus. Ms. Jones can see everyone's work as they go about the problems and underlying computations. Everything about this experience hinges on the students being able to write their computations and express their ideas with digital ink. The scenario simply cannot happen without this representational mediation. Elena goes about a number of overlapping problems, finding herself "in a groove," at least through the first few. She is pinged by her friend across the room who jots down a question to her about division with factorials. Elena drew a diagram over their collaborative workspace explaining how the confusing symbols seemed to cancel out. Her friend thanked her and Elena returned to her own problems and questions that were arising.

One of her first questions is simple. She's forgotten the value of zero factorial (0!) though she knows she saw it. She notices that Ms. Jones is scanning the bird's eye view display at her station and simply jots down a quick question. Her teacher sees the question and answers it right away. Elena's next problem seems to involve both elements and she does not know what to use. By now Ms. Jones is engaged with another group of students. Elena retrieves Marni, the animated avatar, on her tablet device, and asks, "what is the difference between a permutation and a combination?" She already knows that this general question will not get at the heart of her confusion. Marni responds by explaining that the difference relates to the order in which items are arranged and asks her to express her question differently if this is not what she is trying to understand. Elena realizes she is actually wondering whether a permutation can have a combination in it, or vice versa. So she asks, "Is it possible to find combinations that involve permutations?"

Marni responds by re-stating the problem in a clearer form and listing the descriptions of four videos that contrast the counting methods, including two that specifically promise to show a worked example of problems that combine the counting methods. Elena accesses the first one and finds that, although it does not fully duplicate the problem she is working, it gives a helpful example of counting combinations. Elena realizes that in her previous math courses, she likely would have given up far sooner in the process or would have become distracted or anxious, angry that her teacher didn't explain things well in class or that the homework assignment was unrealistic. She snaps out of this reverie when she notices the tablet display in front of her shows comments that Ms. Jones has written to her from thirty feet away, congratulating her on completing the current problem, circling a minor error on a previous problem, and asking her if she has any questions. It's her turn to work with the teacher on some interesting mathematics.

13.7 Ensemble Design

The scenario above is meant to furnish a holistic view of one student's idealized experience of the ensemble this cyberensemble seeks to test. This section separates out and explains the ensemble components as they function in isolation and together. As noted earlier, classroom flipping, often referred to as some variation of "homework in class, lessons at home," can free class time for more interaction between teachers and students [5, 51]. The two individuals mentioned earlier as credited with formalizing and popularizing the approach, Aaron Sams and Jon Bergmann, argue that the most important question teachers seeking to experiment with flipping should pose is how they will spend class time [5]. The starting points are assignments traditionally considered homework. Teachers report that they can walk around the classroom and help students on a more individualized basis and promote greater activity around learning [2, 6].

The "collaborative workspace" component of this ensemble is designed to improve the interactivity between students and teachers in this class time. The prior section discusses the role of "sightlines" in helping teachers maintain rapid feedback loops. With the aid of the collaboration software such as that in Fig. 13.2, the teacher can focus on a student's workspace, make annotations, and suggest changes, etc., either directly on the workspace or orally. Students can pose questions privately and out of view of classmates, in line with research demonstrating significant positive benefits from forms of anonymity in collaborative classroom environments [4]. Their work takes place in full view of the teacher, who has immediate visual access—a sightline—into the students' work. Students at high school and college levels repeatedly and by wide margin express appreciation and a sense of enjoyment in using the collaborative screen or shared knowledge area approach to science and mathematics class time [7, 21, 27].

Figure 13.2 depicts the interface of SmartSync software from Smart Technologies; a similar tool is available from DyKnow, Inc., and specialized software for this type of affordance has been developed under IES support [20]. Early versions of this type of pen-based software were developed by this project's PI prior to the advent of tablet computers, with early pen-input devices [15, 26]. The commercial software is stable, but it is not widely used with pen-based computers. The combination of pen-based computing with the "what you see is what I see" affordances of a collaborative workspace impacts student engagement levels. Using experience sampling methodologies (ESM), studies at the US Air Force Academy documented statistically significant engagement increases in classroom learning activities when students used a combination of a collaboration screen system and pen-based computers [7, 31], in comparison with parallel sections not employing the approach. Interviews and observations confirmed what experienced teachers might predict: students were more likely to stay on task when their space was observable by a teacher; students who might be reluctant to pose questions publicly were more likely to do so privately; teachers appreciated the ability to see the work of any student on-demand and respond to questions; and, perhaps most importantly, the collaboration screen approach afforded rapid feedback between teacher and student and the continual calibration and recalibration of tasks and support. The pen or digital ink interface makes the collaborative workspace valuable any time that students are engaged in activities that use the freehand writing or sketching predominant in mathematics and science classrooms. Flipping gives extended class time for the highly engaging and interactive affordances of the collaborative workspaces. Coupled with the digital pen and ink interface, these collaborative workspaces prove a powerful tool to teachers in planning and carrying out their in-class activities. **Furnishing a teacher with accurate sightlines into student cognition and affording the teacher an opportunity to interact, on demand, with any student digitally through a shared space may prove to be among the most effective facilitators possible for direct student–teacher-subject–matter interaction**.

Recent developments in video production and editing for classroom instruction have made notable inroads to STEM education. User-generated content and presentation (e.g., YouTube) are ascendant in the social media revolution of the past ten years, and are undeniably impacting education. Three developments are important for this project. In terms of educational practice, repositories such as https://www.youtube.com/ and https://www.khanacademy.org/ [51] have furnished a large body of organized content both to teachers and students, and are frequently associated with classroom flipping [37]. These repositories are an important resource, but it is the second and third developments that are of greater interest. First, the use of videos in **teacher professional development** research, in both the US and our African partners in Kenya, Ghana, and Namibia, has gained traction in promoting highly detailed and nuanced understandings of mathematical content and cognition. In some contexts, this is referred to as "noticing"—observing on an almost frame-by-frame basis mathematical misconceptions or understandings. In the work leading to this research through the NSF's National Science Digital Library Program (NSDL), we have adopted the expression "microgenetic analysis" to refer to the fine-grained analyses teachers engage in through video production [17, 23]. The NSDL-supported work focuses on changes that take place as teachers become creative agents and, rather than simply conveying curriculum, they generate content. In addition, they gain opportunities to reflect on the link between their evolving expertise in media production and issues of content and cognition. The most prevalent experience over 200 teachers have reported in NSF-funded "teacherscreate" professional development is a deep and satisfying sense of engagement and losing track of time in preparing instructional videos [28]. One wrote, "*Oh my gosh! This is like the treasure box that I have been looking for! Not even that, it's better than what I've* *imagined it would be*." Student–teacher collaboration teams have struck at some of the most elusive goals teachers have to understand their students and for students to understand them. Student teacher collaboration in producing instructional media for classroom use was featured at the 2012 National Cyberlearning Research Summit in Washington [52] and in different venues associated with mathematics and science education in developing countries [24, 25]. When asked what she felt when she discovered she would be working with her teacher in designing videos for classmates, one Kenyan high school girl featured at the Summit simply said "*I felt like someone was finally recognizing my intelligence*." Another student, from Los Angeles and also featured at the Summit spoke of his experience, saying that "*my relationship with my teacher has changed…(making videos together) brings us closer now to talking about a subject that I enjoy and she enjoys and we could work together because we could both give each other advice…because I can give her advice and tell her like all the students won't like this, and she could also tell me the same thing. And we can both…work hands-on from there. And, it's really great, just working with a teacher, to know that wow, like I am working with my teacher to improve this class and this subject*." The student began his academic year as a student with a low-proficient rating. As he became a collaborating media author, his standardized mathematics scores rose to the highest in his class. He reflected, "*…as I did more videos, more I guess ways of doing math got stuck in my head, so my scores went up to advanced proficient, like to the highest in the class*."

This, of course, is anecdotal; data that this project will collect will furnish a broader picture of success that students attain in their high-stakes testing environments. It is not unrealistic however, to expect that a practice of student participation in media authorship will result in significant gains for those students. This project thus builds on prior NSF-funded efforts and embeds teacher and student–teacher collaboration team media authoring in the cyber ensemble. This represents a departure from the common practice in classroom flipping of using externally produced videos such as those from https://www.khanacademy.org/, or others media for out-of-school lessons. Learning science research communities have not yet sorted out all of the complex and evolving issues associated with locally versus centralized media generation. The cyberensemble in this project places a high priority on a learning ecosystem that draws a significant fraction of its distributed content from those in the school community. The notion of the "local context" has proven to be a powerful one for many reasons. It leverages a broad sweep of tacit local knowledge and teacher creativity, professionalism and imagination [23]. This project instead represents a sharp operational and philosophical departure from the approach of using centrally-produced media. Our team applauds, for example, the availability of videos from sources like https://www.khanacademy.org/, but our interest is less in having students follow videos created by outside individuals than it is in having teachers and student peers acquire and exercise the technical fluencies and evolving technological pedagogical content knowledge (TPCK) [30, 32] that permit them to create their own videos effectively.

13.8 Teacher–Student Planning Around Media-Making

One of the most interesting phenomena in informal learning and society more generally is the so-called maker movement. The maker movement takes many forms, and is not important in itself for our purposes as much as the dynamics underlying the movement, including the energy and enthusiasm behind imaginative do-it-yourself projects that take advantage of emerging technologies such as 3D printers. This ensemble project capitalizes on those same dynamics, but within the context of formal school settings.

We have sought to understand more deeply the specific components of engagement in the more planfully orchestrated process of teacher student collaboration for instructional planning and co-design of new videos. What happens when a teacher and a small team of students meet to map out lessons and plan video curation and video creation to fit a classroom inversion or flipping model? We observe—and teachers and students both report—losing track of time, a sense of well-being, and full absorption in their media-making. Because of results so far, our aim is to test the possibility that well-designed educational ecosystems can alter myriad classroom dynamics along social, behavioral, and academic dimensions. The Collaborative for Social and Emotional Learning Core Competencies (http://www.casel.org/) identifies five competency categories of self-awareness, social awareness, self- management, relationship skills, and responsible decision-making as crucial ingredients to social and emotional learning. It turns out that components of the overall cyberensemble promote or nourish growth in each of these categories. Whether the full ensemble can drive an effective educational ecosystem and can be scaled is the research question under investigation, but component by component, the results are promising. For the purposes of this paper, some types of typical survey responses may prove useful. Three are noted here. The first is that the process of students co-planning lessons with teachers has the **effect of altering student perceptions of their teachers, and elevating their social awareness**.

- *As a student, what surprised me the most from this experience was that I got to see the point of view from my teacher on how they teach us, the students.*
- *One surprising thing was seeing how much work is put into lesson planning.*
- *I learned the value of team work and what it's like to be on the teacher's shoes.*

This, in turn, has enabled the students **to function differently with their teachers, altering their relationship skills**.

- *I feel like I am a part of something bigger and I am able to help the teachers out. Instead of just learning from the teachers, it is cool that the teachers can learn from us as well.*
- *The most surprising thing is that us students and teachers are learning from each other; it's not just the teacher taking control.*
- *Although everyone does things differently, students can easily understand and compare to one another, but with teachers it is more difficult. Teachers also have their own way of learning things. Their way doesn't seem so easy to us students,*

but these videos can help them see the way we think and be able to improve their ways of teaching

Unsurprisingly, and also in the category of **building social awareness, students must look through the eyes of their peers** when creating videos for them.

- *I have learned that you need to be really specific and detailed with what you are trying to teach to other students, which are eventually going to learn this, because if you don't explain well they won't understand and be confused as I was at some point in time.*
- *Thinking through what must be taught and what students must learn.*

Finally, students have identified collaboration with teachers as a source of confidence building and accomplishment through effort:

- *The most unusual thing that has happened with planning and preparing is that it brings out the most in us.*
- *From this experience, I understand things like midsegments better than before I did when I was just learning in class. But really, in general, I've more confidence about me doing this by myself than with others.*
- *I have gained a better work ethic. This experience has given me the confidence to take on calculus.*
- *I have learned that the teachers also benefit from the students help from time to time.I feel more confident in my math skills. I also feel more comfortable working with teachers.*

We expect that further results will allow more defined conclusions in the areas above, and will allow analysis of student perceptions of mathematics and science and of self-efficacy in mathematics and science.

13.9 Why Standards-Based Content as a Focus of a Transformation Research in Education?

Teacher action research plans necessarily will involve and map to specific state and common core standards in the curriculum they teach. This raises an important issue associated with this research. Nearly every video in the repository that teachers and student-tutors are steadily building and accumulating at creationsforlearning.net and other repositories of their choice is explicitly keyed to a California state or Common Core State Standards in Mathematics (CCSSM) [32] standard. It is up to the media-makers how to use these materials (or whether to place them at that site or other repositories). While acknowledging the argument that over-adherence to standards and the high-stakes accountability often associated with standards might limit teacher flexibility and autonomy, we also acknowledge two other facts. The first is that curriculum accountability standards are a reality that teachers and students face daily, and the widespread adoption of CCSSM assures that a standards-based approach to curriculum will continue to be a defining paradigm well into the future. **There is likely no path to scaled cyberlearning transformation in the current educational infrastructure that does not go through state standards, or through the emerging Common Core standards**. A second is that there remains infinite room for creatively matching any mathematical ideas and structure to learner cognition in this paradigm [17].

Acknowledgments Additional contributors to this research include Hiroo Kato, Pepperdine University (hiroo.kato@pepperdine.edu) and Joseph Carilus Ogwel, Kenyan Ministry of Education (ogwel26@gmail.com). The authors acknowledge the generous financial support of the US National Science Foundation, Pepperdine University, and the Kenyan Ministry of Education, the African Institute for Mathematical Sciences in Ghana, the University of Namibia, and the Namibian Ministry of Education. The work reported here reflects the views of the authors alone.

References

1. Aleven VA, Koedinger KR (2002) An effective metacognitive strategy: learning by doing and explaining with a computer-based cognitive tutor. Cognit Sci 26(2):147–179
2. Alvarez B (2012) Flipping the classroom: homework in class, lessons at home. Educ Dig: Essent Read Condens Quick Re 77(8):18–21
3. Amelink CT, Meszaros PS (2011) A comparison of educational factors promoting or discouraging the intent to remain in engineering by gender. Eur J Eng Educ 36(1):47–62
4. Bazeley P (2007) Qualitative data analysis with NVivo. SAGE, London
5. Bergmann J, Sams A (2012) Before you flip, consider this: Leaders of the flipped classroom movement say each teacher will have a different experience, but securing school leadership support, time, and IT resources will be important to every effort. Phi Delta Kappan 94(2):25
6. Brown B (2012) Flipping the classroom (abstract only). In: Proceedings of the 43rd ACM technical symposium on computer science education. SIGCSE '12. ACM, New York, USA, pp 681–681
7. Chen HL, Lattuca LR, Hamilton ER (2008) Conceptualizing engagement: contributions of faculty to student engagement in engineering. J Eng Educ 97(3):339–353
8. Chi MT, Bassok M, Lewis MW, Reimann P, Glaser R (1989) Self-explanations: how students study and use examples in learning to solve problems. Cognit Sci 13(2):145–182
9. Chi MT, Leeuw N, Chiu MH, LaVancher C (1994) Eliciting self-explanations improves understanding. Cognit Sci 18(3):439–477
10. Csikszentmihalyi M (1975) Beyond boredom and anxiety. Jossey-Bass, San Francisco
11. Csikszentmihalyi M (1996) Creativity: flow and the psychology of discovery and invention. Harper Collins, New York
12. Csikszentmihalyi M (2000) Finding flow: the psychology of engagement with everyday life. Basic Books, New York
13. Csikszentmihalyi M, Csikszentmihalyi IS (1988) Optimal experience: psychological studies of flow in consciousness. Cambridge University Press, Cambridge
14. Graesser AC, Person NK (1994) Question asking during tutoring. Am Educ Res J 31(1):104–137
15. Hamilton E (1992) Remote sharing of electronic paper in international conference on technology in education (ICTE). Massachusetts Institute of Technology
16. Hamilton E (2007) Emerging metaphors and constructs from pedagogical agent networks. Educ Technol 47(1):62. (Special Issue, A. Baylor editor)
17. Hamilton E (2010) PREDICATE project: targeted research on teacher creativity at the intersection of content. Student Cognition, and Digital Media: Award DUE104478, National Science Foundation

18. Hamilton E (ed) (2011) NSF: cyberlearning: transforming education (cyberlearning), program solicitation, pp 11–587. Accessed 14 Jan 2016
19. Hamilton E (2013) A cyber-ensemble of inversion, immersion, collaborative workspaces, query and media-making in mathematics classrooms. National Science Foundation Award IIS-1321162
20. Hamilton E, Harding N (2008) IES grant: agent and library augmented shared knowledge areas (ALASKA). Institute for Education Sciences Award 305A080667
21. Hamilton E, Hurford A (2007) Combining collaborative workspaces with tablet computing: research in learner engagement and conditions of flow. In: Frontiers in education conference-global engineering: knowledge without borders, opportunities without passports, 2007. FIE'07. 37th Annual. IEEE, pp T3C–3
22. Hamilton E, Jago M (2001) Toward a theory of personalized learning communities. In: Rieman P, Jacobson M (eds) Designs for learning environments of the future. Springer, New York, pp 263–281
23. Hamilton E, Harding N, Berque D, Reed R (2010) Tablet computing, creativity and teachers as applied microgenetic analysts: a paradigm shift in math teacher professional development. Impact of pen-based technology on education, pp 47–56
24. Hamilton E et al (2012) Advancing mathematics and science education in low-ICT nations through mobile and creative computing cycles. In: Mobiles for education alliance international symposium: partnering for scale and impact, international m4Ed4Dev symposium
25. Hamilton E et al (2012) Advancing mathematics and science education in low-ICT nations through mobile and creative computing cycles. In: Social mobile video and panoramic video workshop. Stanford University
26. Hamilton ER (1993) Computer assisted instructional delivery system and method. US Patent 5,176,520
27. Hamilton ER (1999) Computer assisted instructional delivery system. United Kingdom Patent 479408
28. Hamilton ER (2013) Finding creativity and flow in a high-stakes assessment context. Ir Educ Stud 32(1):109–117
29. Harel G (2007) The DNR system as a conceptual framework for curriculum development and instruction. In: Lesh R, Hamilton E, Kaput J (eds) Foundations for the future in mathematics education, pp 263–280
30. Harris J, Mishra P, Koehler M (2009) Teachers technological pedagogical content knowledge and learning activity types: curriculum-based technology integration reframed. J Res Technol Educ 41(4):393–416
31. Hurford A, Hamilton E (2007) Pen-based collaborative workspaces to promote learner engagement and flow. In: Hirashima T, Hoppe U, Young SSC (eds) Supporting learning flow through integrative technologies. IOS Press, Amsterdam
32. Koehler MJ, Mishra P (2005) What happens when teachers design educational technology? the development of technological pedagogical content knowledge. J Educ Comput Res 32(2):131–152
33. Koschmann T, LeBaron C (2002) Learner articulation as interactional achievement: studying the conversation of gesture. Cognit Instr 20(2):249–282
34. Lage MJ, Platt GJ, Treglia M (2000) Inverting the classroom: a gateway to creating an inclusive learning environment. J Econ Educ 31(1):30–43
35. Lesh R (2006) Modeling students modeling abilities: the teaching and learning of complex systems in education. J Learn Sci 15(1):45–52
36. Lesh R, Harel G (2003) Problem solving, modeling, and local conceptual development. Math Think Learn 5(2–3):157–189
37. MacIsaac D et al (2011) the flipped classroom and Khan Academy video-lecture-based educational reform discussed by the Economist magazine, MSNBC, Salman Khan, and Frank Noschese. Phys Teach 49(8):526–526
38. Mahn H, John-Steiner V (2002) The gift of confidence: a Vygotskian view of emotions. Learning for Life in the 21st Century, pp 46–58

39. Miller RB, Greene BA, Montalvo GP, Ravindran B, Nichols JD (1996) Engagement in academic work: the role of learning goals, future consequences, pleasing others, and perceived ability. Contemp Educ Psychol 21(4):388–422
40. Mishra P, Henriksen D (2012) Rethinking technology & creativity in the 21st century: on being in-disciplined. TechTrends 56(6):18–21
41. Novak TP, Hoffman DL (1997) Measuring the flow experience among web users. Interval Research Corporation 31
42. Paris SG, Paris AH (2001) Classroom applications of research on self-regulated learning. Educ Psychol 36(2):89–101
43. Patrick H, Ryan AM, Kaplan A (2007) Early adolescents' perceptions of the classroom social environment, motivational beliefs, and engagement. J Educ Psychol 99(1):83
44. Pekrun R, Linnenbrink-Garcia L (2012) Academic emotions and student engagement. Handbook of research on student engagement. Springer, New York, pp 259–282
45. Robinson C (2012) Student engagement: what does this mean in practice in the context of higher education institutions? J Appl Res High Educ 4(2):94–108
46. Roscoe RD, Chi MT (2007) Understanding tutor learning: knowledge-building and knowledge-telling in peer tutors explanations and questions. Rev Educ Res 77(4):534–574
47. Rose DH, Strangman N (2007) Universal design for learning: meeting the challenge of individual learning differences through a neurocognitive perspective. Univ Access Inf Soc 5(4):381–391
48. Sabelli N, Bell P (2006) The learning sciences and the need for close couplings between researchl paradigms. Educ Technol: Mag Manag Change Educ 3:45–53
49. Selart M, Nordström T, Kuvaas B, Takemura K (2008) Effects of reward on self-regulation, intrinsic motivation and creativity. Scand J Educ Res 52(5):439–458
50. Shernoff DJ, Csikszentmihalyi M, Shneider B, Shernoff ES (2003) Student engagement in high school classrooms from the perspective of flow theory. Sch Psychol Q 18(2):158–176
51. Sparks SD (2011) Schools "flip" for lesson model promoted by Khan Academy. Educ Week 31(5):1–14
52. SRI International (2012) The cyberlearning summit, in collaboration with the William and Melinda Gates Foundation and the National Geographic Society (2012). National Science Foundation: Washington, DC
53. University of Memphis Department of Psychology: 25 learning principles to guide pedagogy and the design of learning environments (2008). Accessed 14 Jan 2016
54. Vygotsky LS (1978) Mind in society: the development of higher mental process. Harvard University Press, Cambridge
55. Wong RM, Lawson MJ, Keeves J (2002) The effects of self-explanation training on students' problem solving in high-school mathematics. Learn Instr 12(2):233–262

Chapter 14
A System Dynamics Approach to Process Evaluation of Pen-Based Digital Media-Making Projects

Moses Okumu, Hiroo Kato, and Nishesh Chalise

Abstract This chapter explains a systematic way of conducting process evaluation of pen-based digital media-making projects using system dynamics modeling. The study aimed to understand student and teacher experiences and changes in behavior while engaged in the digital media-making process. Data was collected at a pen-based digital media-making summer program held at Pepperdine University's Los Angeles and Ventura County campuses. After transcribing and coding raw data using grounded theory, the authors generated causal loop maps. The study indicated that the production of videos depends on both the students' and teachers' engagement in the digital media-making process. Active engagement of teachers and students improved the quality of the learning environment. The use of system dynamics allowed us to see the flaws and unique aspects within the digital making process.

14.1 Introduction

The term "process evaluation" in this paper means understanding and monitoring how change occurs when students and teachers engage in pen-based digital media-making. The main goal in this context is to understand the implementation of pen-based programs towards students' educational outcomes. In this scenario, process evaluation will allow us to capture the experiences of the students as they interact with the new innovation. Also, we will understand why the innovation positively or

M. Okumu (✉)
School of Social Work, University of Texas, Arlington, TX, USA
e-mail: tkmose@gmail.com

H. Kato
Graduate School of Education and Psychology, Pepperdine University, Los Angeles, CA, USA
e-mail: hirookato@gmail.com

N. Chalise
School of Social Work, Augsburg College, Minneapolis, MN, USA
e-mail: nishesh.chalise@gmail.com

T. Hammond et al. (eds.), *Revolutionizing Education with Digital Ink*, Human–Computer Interaction Series, DOI 10.1007/978-3-319-31193-7_14

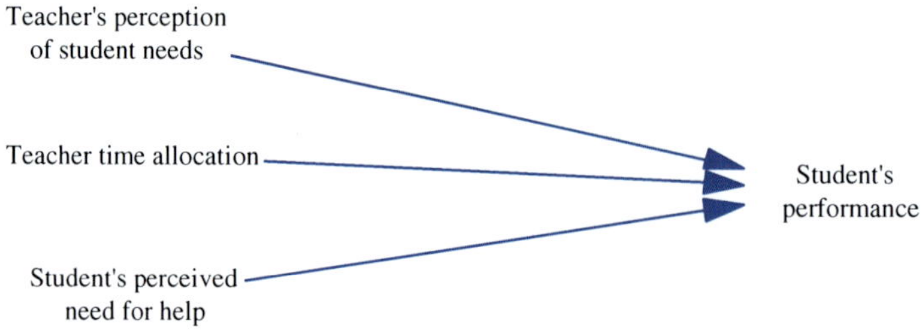

Fig. 14.1 Causal chain perspective [11, 20]

negatively influences students' educational outcomes. As a result, findings from the study may facilitate program improvements.

Traditionally, process evaluation has been conducted by analyzing texts or measuring the effect size of the intervention [21]. Most program evaluators use logic models, which examine a causal chain relation [18]. In most cases, there is a dependent variable which evaluators are most interested in studying. Although this method might be effective, the variables interactions are usually linear rather than dynamic [6]. The use of causal chain models does not allow evaluators to capture participants' experiences or change in their behavior over time [6].

For example, Fig. 14.1 represents a causal chain perspective that shows three factors (teacher's perception of student needs, teacher time allocation, and student's perceived need for help) that impact a student's performance. It can be argued that these three factors give rise to interventions that change a student's performance; however, it does not take into account how a change in a student's performance in turn impacts the three factors. If a student's performance improves, a teacher may decide to lessen time allocated helping this student. If a student's performance improves, the student's perceived need for help may diminish, thereby improving self-confidence, and may further improve performance. The point is that these factors, or variables, can be construed as having dynamic relationships, where a causal chain is not sufficient in explaining how changes occur over time. Mostly, there is no way to capture the transformation processes that turn interventions into outcomes. What is needed is an evaluation that considers the details of what occurs in the process—the rationale that proposes that an intervention will produce the desired results. Moreover, efforts to change a system must consider how components of a system work together to locate the root cause of the problem. Allowing for an in-depth learning and explicit analysis of the program through analysis of the components of the system. This analysis should lead to the improvement of the theoretical model of a project.

14.1.1 Why Use System Dynamics for Process Evaluation?

System dynamics is a method that uses both qualitative and quantitative models to understand how a particular phenomenon changes over time. It attempts to understand the system behavior by looking at how the parts of the system are interconnected

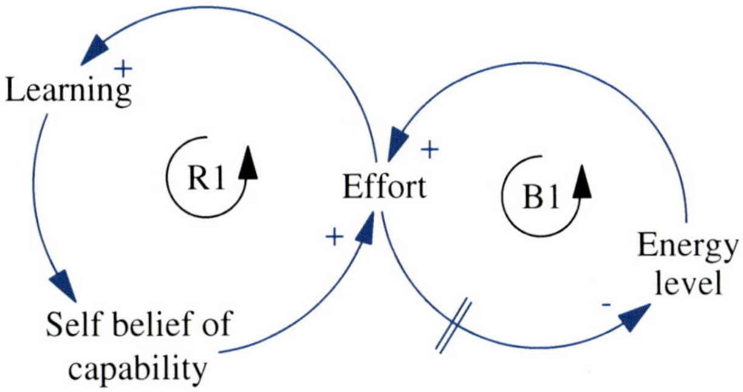

Fig. 14.2 Causal loop diagram ([26], pg. 364)

through feedback processes. In other words, the primary goal in system dynamics is to understand how the underlying feedback processes result in the system behavior.

A feedback perspective, in this context, entails that student engagement not only leads to development of digital materials, but also to working to create the digital materials in turn affects student engagement. One of the goals of this paper is to show that capturing such feedback processes is essential in understanding how development of digital instructional materials can lead to improved learning. Here, there are no dependent variables, and every variable plays a role.

Feedback processes are represented in the form of a Causal Loop Diagram (CLD), which consists of variables connected by arrows as they form feedback loops. There are two types of feedback loops: reinforcing and balancing. Reinforcing feedback loops pushes the variables in the same direction. If a variable in the reinforcing feedback loop is increasing, it will keep increasing or vice versa. Balancing loops push variables in the opposite direction. If a variable in the balancing feedback loop is increasing, it will decrease in the next iteration.

Figure 14.2, shows a simple example of reinforcing and balancing loop. The plus +/− sign on the arrows indicate the direction of relationship between the two variables. Plus sign means that the variables move in the same direction and the negative sign indicates that the variables have inverse relationship. In the figure, the reinforcing loop (R) suggests that as learning increases, self-belief of capacity increases further increasing the effort. The balancing loop (B) suggests that as energy level increases, effort decreases.

14.2 Background

To ensure that all students are provided with an opportunity to understand challenging Science, Technology, Engineering and Math (STEM) content, digital library repositories need to be furnished with instructional media that involved students in the entire production process. Recent studies indicate that students learn better when actively engaged in processes that promote cognition and knowledge retention [9, 19, 22]. For example, when students are introduced to digital media-making, they quickly learn the process and embrace new roles as producers of educational materials for their peers [9, 16]. These educational materials can include short videos of worked examples of day-to-day curriculum, which other students can use to advance individual learning [9].

Furthermore, providing students with opportunities to create knowledge allows them to critically think about all problems from both a consumer and producer's perspective [1, 5, 16]. For example, in a study conducted by O'Neil et al. [17], students were involved in playing a mathematical game that had self-explanation prompts at every level of the game. The questions, instructions, and feedback provided were aligned to student's advancement within the game. After every game, students were required to self-reflect on what motivated their decision-making process throughout the game. The study found that learner outcomes were related to the self-reflective process [17]. Research suggests that effective self-reflection transforms students into active learners [2, 9, 17].

These methods depart from didactic teaching, as teachers partner with students to create user-friendly learning media materials [4, 6, 9]. In previous years, most students have defined the study of STEM as boring and none "sexy" [13]. With students being mentored as tutors, exciting and engaging materials are being produced that capture and sustain the attention of student-users [9]. The produced media is in the form of tutorial observation aides [7] and brief worked out videos that stimulate self-learning [9].

While using a combination of multimedia tools, students take on the roles of peer tutors. Tutoring refers to the process when a more knowledgeable student offers to facilitate the learning process of another student [23]. This relationship results in concept mastery, problem solving skills and knowledge building [1]. More recently, one on one peer interactions have been substituted with short videos produced by fellow peers, allowing for self-directed learning [3, 9]. While in peer-to-tutor situations with one-on-one meetings between the tutors and tutees the learner asks their peers all questions with less regard for self-direction and monitoring [22, 24].

This paper set out to understand how students' and teachers' experiences change when they are involved in digital making projects.

14.3 Case Study

This process evaluation is situated within the larger research context of teacher creativity and digital repository development led by Dr. Eric Hamilton at Pepperdine University. This field of research is working toward establishing a better science for understanding learner engagement. This evaluation draws from research that involved teachers and students developing media repositories for K12 mathematics education called student mathematics learning through self-explanation, peer tutoring and digital media production. Broadly speaking, the goal of this research was to understand how student-tutors and teachers change and exercise creativity through participating in digital media production.

The developmental action research was conducted at Pepperdine University's Los Angeles and Ventura County campuses. In this project, student-tutors and teachers were involved in iterative processes of creating, adapting, testing and sharing content. The project engaged two twelve-student cohorts. Students who were in tenth to twelfth grade and enrolled in Algebra II were invited to participate in Mathematics Media Makers clubs. Over the course of three years, seventy students were involved in the research activities.

During a ten-day media-making institute, the teachers and students were introduced to the use of Pen and Touch technology in the creation of digital materials. The teachers were exposed to existing repositories, trained in the project's foundational video creation software (Camtasia) and the technical requirements for media creation. The students worked in student teams and also alongside teachers to create localized media that met the local California State Standards.[1] While making videos, student-tutors and teachers would determine what variables while explaining mathematical problems using Wacom tablets.

The project had students engage in a stepwise process of understanding how mathematical problems are solved by use of worked out examples from real-time needs of classrooms. As they made the videos, students and teachers were required to self-reflect as they collectively edited their videos and later subjected to interviews. In order to ensure "mathematical integrity, pedagogical usability, and presentation quality" of made videos, they were subjected to a review by teachers, mathematics experts and peers through Japanese Lesson Study [9].

14.3.1 Phases of Video Making

The creation of digital instructional materials occurred in multiple phases. The teams of students and teachers first developed lessons storyboard based on windows journals where they shared their personal experiences. These storyboards were converted into short videos. These videos were edited and voice was added. Finally, the students and teachers applied lesson study to these videos creating videos of worked out examples.

This process is depicted as a stock-flow diagram in Fig. 14.5 above. Stock is a type of variable that accumulates over time and flow is rate variable that increases or drains the stock. For example, the variable videos created are a stock (represented with a rectangular box) and the variable creating videos is a flow (represented with double line arrows and a valve). In other words, the stock flow diagram represents the production process of digital materials. Every stage of the process required student and teacher engagement. Similarly, every stage contributed to student learning. The final stock, worked out example videos in repository represents all the instructional digital material that have been developed are ready for use in future lessons.

---

[1] http://creationsforlearning.net.

14.4 Method Employed

14.4.1 Data Collection

Although initially provided with a set form of interview questions, as the program progressed, team members deliberately employed a strategy of unstructured interviews and personal reflections, which tailored interviews to students' and teachers' individual interests. Through these strategies, the study interviewers were able to address emerging themes over the course of the study. The study recorded and transcribed more than 150 individual interviews, videos and self-reflections over three years.

14.4.2 Data Analysis

The study draws on grounded theory developed in sociology to facilitate theory development [8]. Analysis of data drew from successful system dynamics modelers who used grounded theory to conceptualize the models [14, 15]. Using fully completed interviews and personal reflections from students and teachers, ten transcripts were analyzed. Raw data was imported into HyperRESEARCH[2] software in preparation for coding [10]. During the coding process, grounded theory's three types of coding were used to separate and organize concepts from the raw data [25]. First, initial coding was used to identify ideas and meanings from raw data before attaching a label [25]. Responses were broken into words, short sentences, and phrases in order to identify similarities and differences from the raw data. Second, axial coding was conducted to identify and categorize relationships among the codes. Third, selective coding led to generating of a theory. As a result of the coding process, concepts were identified and the raw data organized with corresponding labels.

In order to start building a system dynamics model, the first step was to identify the problem, set system boundary and key variables [14]. To identify the problem, the coded raw data was revisited and analyzed for a common thread of the problem, taking into account the context of the study. To limit the boundary of the research, we considered the experiences of students and teachers during digital media-making process (Table 14.1).

The digital media-making process helped in the development of causal flow maps. Variables used for the modeling process were derived from the coded data. A causal relationship was identified among system variables. Additionally, information about an observed or expected behavior of a variable, or the direction or strength of a causal relationship was also determined [14].

After identifying variables, they were connected to word and arrow diagrams, creating a composite diagram and after merged into a single causal flow map. This

[2]http://researchware.com.

Table 14.1 Identifying variables and their causal relationships [14]

I love using any form of digital media that will enhance a lesson and keep the students motivated. I would like to learn more about creating video that will motivate the students. Using digital media is interesting and motivating to the students. After creating my second video, I am noticing how much more careful I am when planning the sequence of events I want to show. I am much more cognizant that other people will be watching this and therefore much more careful.				
Cause Variable	Development of Instructional short videos	Development of Instructional short videos	Development of Instructional short videos	Development of Instructional short videos
Effect Variable	Identifying learning needs	Visualization of lessons	Proficiency in making videos	Time taken to develop instructional short videos
Relationship type	Positive	Positive	Positive	Positive

led to the development of causal diagrams that are consistent with system dynamics modeling. With a connected CLD, implicit structures were identified. For example, "a causal relationship A-C may be decomposed and coded as A-B-C if the context implies the existence of the intermediate variable" ([14], pg. 322). Depending on the direction of the relationship, the variables were either assigned a positive or negative sign.

14.5 Results and Evaluation

The processes that connect student learning and development of digital instructional material is represented as a CLD in Fig. 14.3. The production process shown in Fig. 14.5 has been aggregated as development of instructional short videos for simplification. There are five reinforcing loops and one balancing loop in the model (Fig. 14.3). The first three reinforcing loops (R1, R2, R3) shows the feedback processes where engagement of students and teachers leads to production of digital instructional short videos. The instructional videos create a quality learning environment which helps student learning and retention. As students realize that they are learning more and enjoying the process they are more engaged in the process with their teachers. The development of short videos improves quality learning environments in three different ways (Fig. 14.4).

First, the model helps identify student's learning needs (R1). Through the process both teachers and students get a better grasp of what students already know where the gaps are. Therefore, the learning and teaching is more focused (Table 14.2).

Second, working on the videos, teachers discover that they can be more innovative and creative with their teaching materials (R2). The teachers and students add arti-

Fig. 14.3 Students and teachers creating media

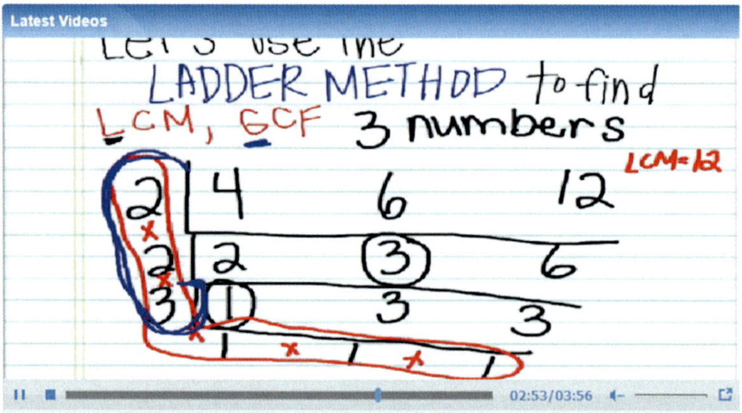

Fig. 14.4 Example of created video

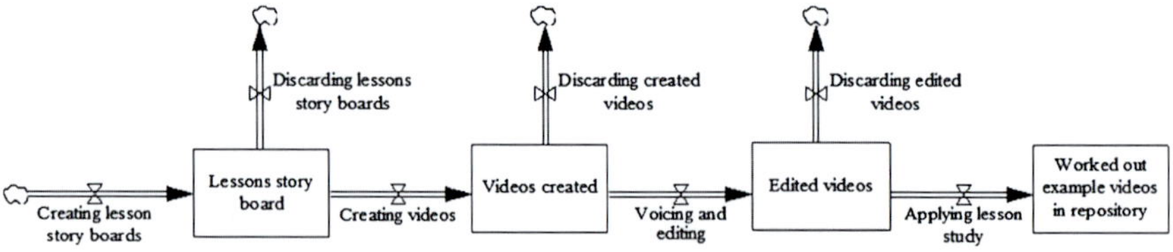

Fig. 14.5 Stock flow diagram showing the production process of digital instruction short videos

facts that make lessons more fun and engaging for students. This process is usually completed during editing and lesson study sessions. The teachers and students add call outs, quizzes and music to stimulate the learning environment (Figs. 14.6, 14.7 and 14.8).

Table 14.2 Generalization of the structure representation [12]

Mechanism	Label	Teacher/student responses
Identify learning needs	R1	"Producing media for instruction does alter my sense of personal creativity slightly by forcing me to focus on not just what would be effective if I was the student but on what I think the students will enjoy"
Discovering creative, innovative ways of teaching and learning	R2	"When making videos, it is not about how creative you can get but what you can do with the creativity you have"
Ease of explanation of concepts for teachers	R3	"You can show image examples as well as videos to further explain the concept because every student learns in a different way and the more the merrier"
Time taken while developing videos	B1	"It does not take me fourteen minutes to go over one example in class. That is how long it took me to do my first unedited video"
Proficiency in video making	R4	"I find that I have become more comfortable"
Quality of instructional short videos	R5	"Teachers can make modifications to their video content throughout the year as they see a need develop among their students"

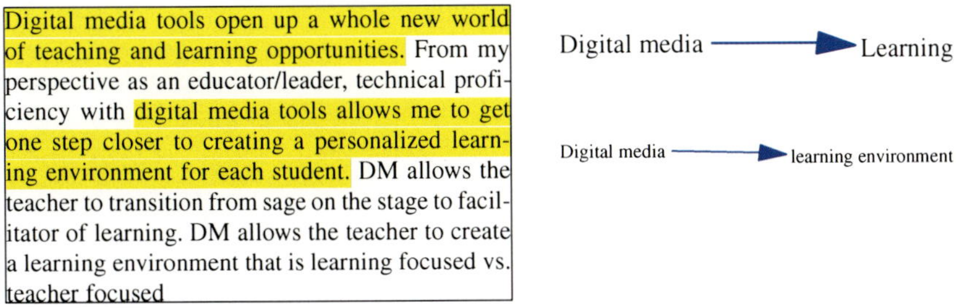

Fig. 14.6 Discovering themes from the data [14]

Third, the visual nature of the short videos makes it easier for teachers to explain the concepts (R3). Developing instructional short videos improves quality of environment but it requires extra time commitment from both teachers and students. As the development of such material increases more time has to be devoted to developing these materials. However, as students and teachers start developing more materials they become more proficient at it. Gaining proficiency can take some time, which is denoted by a hash mark on the arrow connecting development of instructional videos and proficiency in making videos. Being proficient reduces the time taken to develop these short videos allowing more time for students and teachers to focus on learning and the substantive parts of the process (R4).

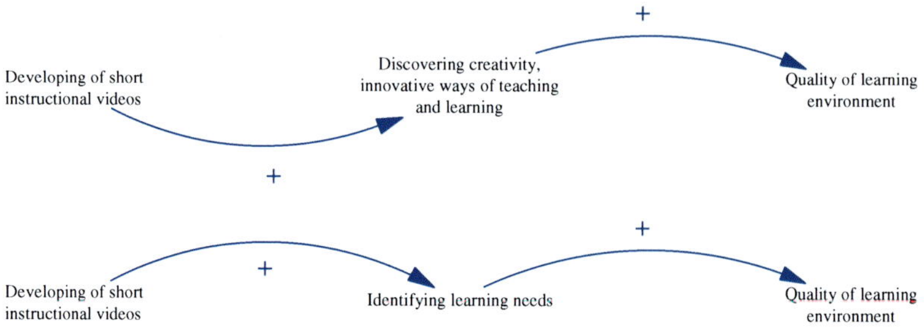

Fig. 14.7 Transforming text into word and arrow diagrams [14]

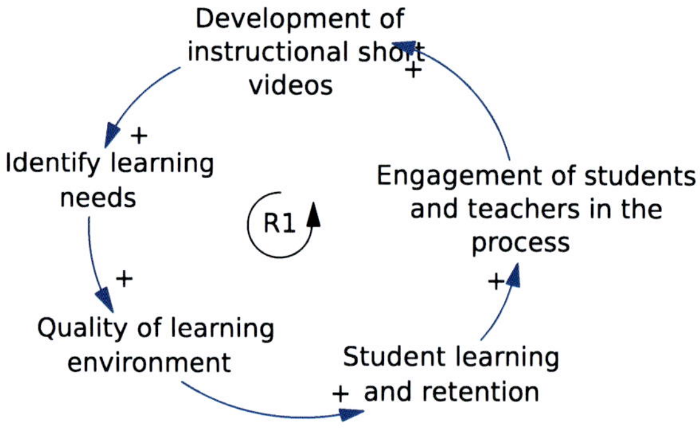

Fig. 14.8 Shows how development of instructional instructions helps identify student's learning needs

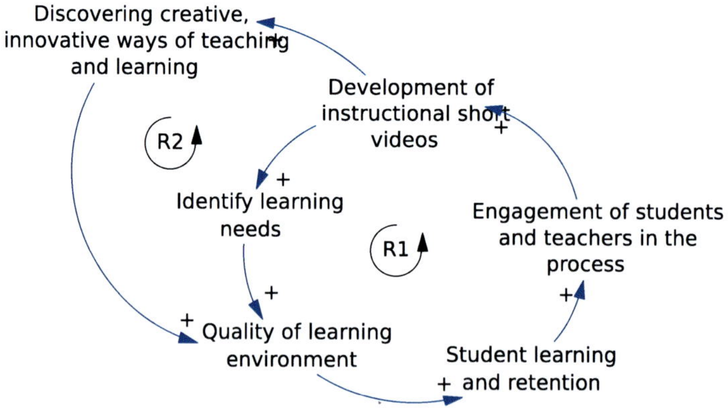

Fig. 14.9 Shows how making media leads to innovation in material development

Finally, as proficiency increases the quality of videos also increase which makes it easier for teachers to explain the concepts and improves the quality of learning environment (R5). When more time is invested, it reduces student and teacher engagement in the process, which limits the development of the instructional materials (B1) (Figs. 14.9, 14.10 and 14.11).

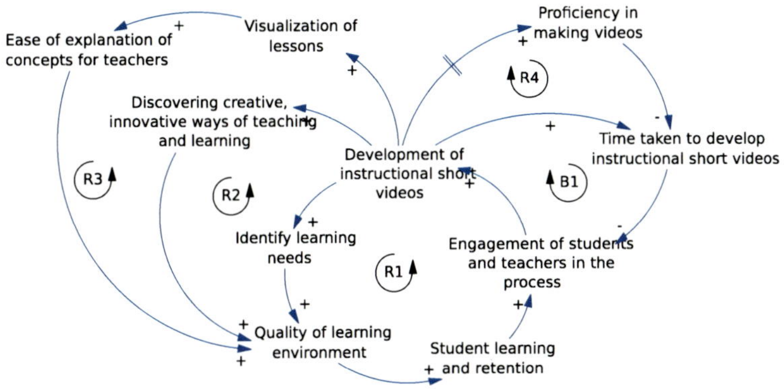

Fig. 14.10 Visualization helps explanation and how proficiency reduced time in media-making

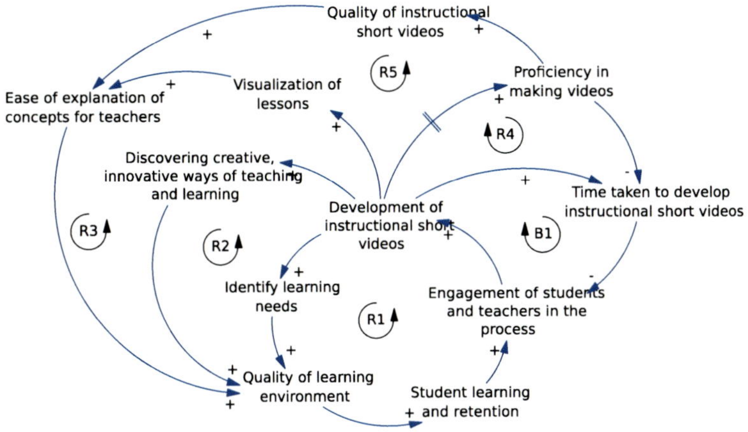

Fig. 14.11 Causal loop diagram showing the process related to engagement of students and teachers, development of instructional short videos, and quality of learning environment

14.6 Conclusion

The goal of this paper was to introduce a novel method that can provide a new perspective in our understanding of how developing pen-based digital instructional material relates to student learning. By use of pen-based technology, students and teachers are provided with opportunities to be creative. The visualization of the lessons provides students with an opportunity to connect with the concepts being taught.

The visual nature of causal loop diagrams makes the processes more explicit. Consequently, it becomes easier to find flaws, critique, and see how the processes would be different in different contexts. For example, within the school context, less time commitment might hinder the quality of videos produced. However, as the teachers and students find time outside school, and become proficient in digital media-making, the higher the quality of the videos produced. Program improvements in this case move toward developing initiatives that will allow teachers and students to spend quality time outside school making videos.

One of the limitations of this paper is that the data used was not geared toward developing a causal loop diagram. Further studies should explore how system dynamics can inform innovation implementation and improvements within education. Conducting a study using group model-building with participants of a pen-based computing project would help in the understanding of the program.

Acknowledgments The authors acknowledge the generous support of the United States National Science Foundation, as well as the schools that participated in media-making projects.

References

1. Chi MT (2000) Self-explaining expository texts: the dual processes of generating inferences and repairing mental models. Adv Instr Psychol 5:161–238
2. Cook-Sather A (2006) Change based on what students say: preparing teachers for a paradoxical model of leadership. Int J Lead Educ 9(4):345–358
3. Crippen KJ, Earl BL (2007) The impact of web-based worked examples and self-explanation on performance, problem solving, and self-efficacy. Comput Educ 49(3):809–821
4. Cuban L, Kirkpatrick H, Peck C (2001) High access and low use of technologies in high school classrooms: explaining an apparent paradox. Am Educ Res J 38(4):813–834
5. Davis EA (2003) Prompting middle school science students for productive reflection: generic and directed prompts. J Learn Sci 12(1):91–142
6. Dyehouse M, Bennett D, Harbor J, Childress A, Dark M (2009) A comparison of linear and systems thinking approaches for program evaluation illustrated using the Indiana interdisciplinary GK-12. Eval Program Plan 32(3):187–196
7. Gholson B, Craig SD (2006) Promoting constructive activities that support vicarious learning during computer-based instruction. Educ Psychol Rev 18(2):119–139
8. Glaser B, Strauss A (1967) The discovery grounded theory: strategies for qualitative inquiry. Aldin, Chicago
9. Hamilton ER (2013) Finding creativity and flow in a high-stakes assessment context. Ir Educ Stud 32(1):109–117
10. Hesse-Biber S, Dupuis P, Kinder TS (1991) Hyperresearch: a computer program for the analysis of qualitative data with an emphasis on hypothesis testing and multimedia analysis. Qual Sociol 14(4):289–306
11. Hirsch GB, Levine R, Miller RL (2007) Using system dynamics modeling to understand the impact of social change initiatives. Am J Community Psychol 39(3–4):239–253
12. Hovmand PS, Gillespie DF (2010) Implementation of evidence-based practice and organizational performance. J Behav Health Serv Res 37(1):79–94
13. Jawaharlal M (2011) Why is STEM boring? [Blog Post]. Accessed 4 Jan 2016
14. Kim H, Andersen DF (2012) Building confidence in causal maps generated from purposive text data: mapping transcripts of the federal reserve. Syst Dyn Rev 28(4):311–328
15. Kopainsky B, Luna-Reyes LF (2008) Closing the loop: promoting synergies with other theory building approaches to improve system dynamics practice. Syst Res Behav Sci 25(4):471–486
16. Lewis C, Causey L (2015) Critical engagement through digital media production. New directions in teaching english: reimagining teaching, teacher education, and research. Rowman & Littlefield, Lanham, p 123

17. O'Neil HF, Chung GK, Kerr D, Vendlinski TP, Buschang RE, Mayer RE (2014) Adding self-explanation prompts to an educational computer game. Comput Hum Behav 30:23–28
18. Prinsen G, Nijhof S (2015) Between logframes and theory of change: reviewing debates and a practical experience. Dev Prac 25(2). doi:10.1080/09614524.2015.1003532
19. Qureshi MA, Stormyhr E (2012) Group dynamics and peer-tutoring a pedagogical tool for learning in higher education. Int Educ Stud 5(2):118. doi:10.5539/ies.v5n2p118
20. Roberts N (1976) The structure of student-teacher interaction in the elementary classroom. In: Levin G, Roberts EB (eds) The dynamics of human service delivery. Ballinger Publishing Company, Cambridge, pp 93–103
21. Rogers PJ, Weiss CH (2007) Theory-based evaluation: reflections ten years on: theory-based evaluation: past, present, and future. New Dir Eval 2007(114):63–81
22. Roscoe RD (2014) Self-monitoring and knowledge-building in learning by teaching. Instr Sci 42(3):327–351
23. Roscoe RD, Chi MT (2007) Understanding tutor learning: knowledge-building and knowledge-telling in peer tutors explanations and questions. Rev Educ Res 77(4):534–574
24. Roscoe RD, Chi MT (2008) Tutor learning: the role of explaining and responding to questions. Instr Sci 36(4):321–350
25. Strauss A, Corbin J (1998) Basics of qualitative research: techniques and procedures for developing grounded theory. SAGE, Thousand Oaks
26. Wood R, Bandura A (1989) Social cognitive theory of organizational management. Acad Manag Rev 14(3):361–384

Chapter 15
A Model and Research Agenda for Teacher and Student Collaboration Using Pen-Based Tablets in Digital Media Making in Sub-Saharan Africa

Eric Hamilton, Loide Kapenda, Zachary Mbasu, Helena Miranda, Elizabeth Ngololo, Joseph Carilus Ogwel, Sandra Sarmonpal, and David Stern

Abstract This paper reports exploratory work that investigates inter-generational collaboration between students and teachers in a digitized version of the maker movement. The work is supported by the US National Science Foundation, the US State Department's Fulbright Research Program, and partnering education ministries and NGOs. The core feature of digital media-making entails the use of pen-based tablet computers to create videos for teaching science and mathematics concepts in alignment with state and national curriculum. Results were visible along

E. Hamilton (✉)
Graduate School of Educational Psychology, Pepperdine University, Malibu, CA, USA
e-mail: eric.hamilton@pepperdine.edu

L. Kapenda · E. Ngololo
Namibian Ministry of Education, Windhoek, Namibia
e-mail: loidekapenda@yahoo.com

E. Ngololo
e-mail: engololo@unam.na

Z. Mbasu
African Maths Initiative, Nairobi, Kenya
e-mail: zmbasu@gmail.com

H. Miranda
University of Namibia, Ongwediva, Namibia
e-mail: hmiranda@unama.na

J.C. Ogwel
Kenyan Ministry of Education, Karen, Kenya
e-mail: ogwel26@gmail.com

S. Sarmonpal
Pepperdine University, Malibu, CA, USA
e-mail: ssarmonpal@pepperdine.edu

D. Stern
African Maths Initiative, Nairobi, Kenya
e-mail: volloholic@hotmail.com

T. Hammond et al. (eds.), *Revolutionizing Education with Digital Ink*, Human–Computer Interaction Series, DOI 10.1007/978-3-319-31193-7_15

several dimensions: (1) Learners exhibited a high affective valence and enthusiasm for media-making with their teachers; (2) Important relational shifts occurred and were reported by both teachers and students; and (3) Students and teachers alike engaged in cognitive re-imagining and re-imaging of one another's roles and of subject matter.

15.1 Introduction

This paper report summarizes efforts to test and implement pen and touch based computing in a variety of Sub-Saharan school contexts. It introduces the four-year history of this work as a quasi-design and quasi-action research project and describes a number of breakthroughs that lead to cultural and procedural advances at each step of the process. Finally, we propose a viable path for future research.

The opportunity for this work originated in a series of workshops focusing on innovative practices in engineering education supported by Microsoft, but grew to encompass research in the use of pen-based tablet devices paralleling research that the US National Science Foundation began to support in 2010 [2–4]. This work explores ways to draw students into deep, sustained interaction with mathematical and scientific ideas using the natural handwriting and symbol systems that those fields typically require both from professionals and from school-aged learners.

Before discussing the research itself, some context may be useful. Most westerners have little to no knowledge of the difficulties placed on educational practitioners in low-income countries. These include class sizes that routinely exceed fifty and sometimes exceeding one hundred students with inadequate time to meaningfully engage learners; outdated curriculum with abstract content; physically rigid, uncomfortable and hot classrooms; curriculum materials almost always produced in languages other than the primary languages of the students using those materials; and teacher preparation that falls significantly below standards enjoyed elsewhere in more developed countries. Students rarely benefit significantly from technology use, or else use technologies delivered in the form of "helicopter drops" by government agencies, NGOs, and other sources of computer labs, labs whose value devolves to using computers for teaching word processing and spreadsheets, and are not subject to routine upgrades and maintenance. Internet access is extremely limited. The only pedagogy that has been routinely and reliably implemented in such settings involves traditional lecture formats that tend to alienate students everywhere, especially when not supplemented by other approaches. There is no shortage of efforts, both large and small, to promote more effective schools. The reach of these initiatives, though, usually extends into only a small fraction of schools or else fall short along multiple dimensions. One of the most effective overall efforts involves UNESCO's Strengthening Mathematics and Science Education (SMASE) initiative [13], but this one is inherently limited by lack of focus or attention on the use of technology in schools.

While westerners experience the teaching profession to be intensely demanding, these additional challenges faced by teachers in low-income countries make it especially difficult for teaching and learning to occur. Of particular concern is the absence of curricular materials that reflect students' primary languages. In US classrooms, the language used in classrooms reflects the primary language of the majority of students and students who are English language learners often receive specialized support. Sub-Saharan students and their teachers are mandated to use either English or French. Consequently, the language of instruction is usually the second language for both students and teachers. This becomes a compounding challenge where students are the inevitable losers because instruction is mediated through languages that are somewhat unfamiliar to both students and their teachers. As noted below, it is increasingly clear that learning ecosystems that constrain or prohibit students' use of their primary language inevitably leave important and complex cognition behind [7]. Digital media-making by teachers and students in this context has the potential to both fill curriculum needs and present new models for teaching and learning that are effective for large class sizes.

15.2 Research Description

During two workshops in the summer of 2010 and early 2011, we introduced pen-based mathematics video-making to both mathematics teachers and students in Kenya and Uganda. These workshops were co-funded by the National Science Foundation, Pepperdine University, the Kenyan Ministry of Education, and the Study Gateway NGO based in Kampala, Uganda. Additional workshops in Kenya, Uganda, Ghana, and Namibia have been conducted since that time [8]. We collected semi-structured and non-structured interview data and survey responses under the auspices of Pepperdine's IRB approval and informed consent from teachers and students involved in the research.

Some of the most compelling data from these workshops are contained in video recordings of research interviews. Table 15.1 summarizes seven clips from interviews that depict actual pen-based media-making and then reflections by teachers and students on the nature of their experiences. Some overarching themes in the responses of both teachers and students address the role of pen-based media making in nurturing personal creativity, building precision into mathematical and scientific expression, fostering deep and immersive engagement, promoting collaboration between students and teachers, and introducing new possibilities for more effective instructional approaches.

The video clips furnish evidence that teachers and students are ready to seek and implement effective alternatives to 'chalk and talk' and other conventional approaches to teaching and learning that are characteristic of instructional practices in Sub-Saharan Africa. These alternative approaches rely on the affordances of technology to promote collaboration and elicit subject matter immersion. While there is a seemingly universally shared aspiration to implement technology in ways that improve classroom instruction, the associated costs and infrastructure requirements present obstacles that are especially daunting in low income nations such as those in Sub-Saharan Africa.

Table 15.1 Seven media clips depicting multiple aspects of pen-based media-making in Sub-Saharan countries

Powerful dynamics of teachers and students collaborating to create instructional videos. Students and teachers working together strengthened relationships; infusing in them a sense of mutual respect and trust. Students feel validated in their own learning and teachers overcome fears associated with adopting new technologies. http://youtu.be/qK9FQFCMaOM
Building relevance and enjoyment into learning by video making. Students report that using videos to learn is a welcome relief from the traditional lecture-based classroom with engaging, relevant content. http://youtu.be/841UIXaueqk
Authentic and routine experience of flow. Both teachers and students found themselves completely immersed in video creation and collaboration, routinely experience psychological flow states. http://youtu.be/WEVEAZ7LEEA
Creativity and imagination become crucial. The process of creating video, which combines verbal, visual, and written literacy skills provides a context for teachers and students to creatively think through topics. http://youtu.be/NrJZmMimH7s
New Possibilities for Lesson Planning and Differentiation. Teachers felt that videos gave them an opportunity to differentiate instruction. http://youtu.be/MGuFwlubViA
An experiment in collaboration with the African Institute for Mathematics Sciences (AIMS-Ghana). Four schools near Accra hold teacher-student workshops that depict active collaboration between students and teachers. http://bit.ly/media-making-ghana-2014
Early 2015 teacher reflections. These teachers in the far north regions of Namibia describe the nature of their experience in constructing scientific and mathematical explanations use pen-based devices. http://bit.ly/namibia-m4-2015

15.3 Historical Considerations

The post-WWII era introduced large swaths of mass prosperity for the first time in history. However, those not yet experiencing such prosperity constitute a much larger fraction of the world's population than those who do benefit. The aspirational efforts by outsiders to help elevate living standards and knowledge formation, for any motivation, are counterproductive if not grounded in dispositions that acknowledge the insiders as first among partners. Hiroshima University scholar Nobuhide Sawamura's article entitled "Local Spirit, Global Knowledge: A Japanese approach to knowledge development in international cooperation" [12] perfectly captures in its first four words what should be the zeitgeist of collaboration.

Deft solutions must find ways to channel energy and ambition for change into approaches that work around human and fiscal resource limitations. Those solutions must be structurally astute, and scalable. Westerners working in this space, such as for the purposes of research, commerce, or aid will find no shortage of good will and forward thinking among their colleagues, and no small amount of heroism among the teachers and educational communities that face the difficulties mentioned above. Solutions must be strategically clever enough to map to the particulars of these multiple challenges. However, most importantly, solutions must be owned and managed by those facing the challenges everyday while engaging the substantive participation of those furnishing technical and financial assistance.

It is in this context and with such principles that we believe collaborative instructional media-making may occupy an exceptionally promising role in helping to meet ideals for universal and effective, highly engaging education.

15.4 Path Forward: Implementation at Scale and Parallel Research

Among the advantages of such approaches to locally developed and owned materials is that teachers and students can produce contextually relevant curricular materials at lower cost and greater effectiveness than conventionally produced materials. To even greater benefit, it turns out that the very process of creating those materials engenders new, respectful, and socially powerful interaction between students and teachers. Media-making also presents a powerful model for professional development because it benignly coerces teachers to review, rehearse, edit, mix and remix content, through the lens of how students structure their own knowledge conceptualizations. Media-making in the context of this research immerses teachers in both content and pedagogy, while upgrading their technological fluency. There are multiple long-term synergies at play: lower cost, more availability of relevant content, perceptive professional development activities, and more engaging and successful social dynamics in schools.

These potentials within the policy and practice realm require resource considerations similar to those for pursuing the research agenda appearing in the next section. There is no question that engaging teachers and students in collaborative instructional media-making is immersive, highly engaging, and pro-social in its effect on teacher and student relationships. That finding is of limited value with-out ways of embedding the approach into policy structures, other school and government agency initiatives, local school and teacher preferences, and resource constraints.

In our efforts involving multiple stakeholder types, we have concluded that the most systemically promising approaches rest in concurrent and coordinated efforts between education ministries, mathematics and science specialists, teacher preparation programs, and most importantly, teachers and students whose energy and imagination fuel the process. That there are other crucial stakeholders that must be engaged is a given, but at the core, these communities must own the locus of control and direction. We are exploring the possibility of media-making to spark a large and potentially disruptive positive change in Sub-Saharan classrooms by first creating sufficient capacity for teachers and students to produce imaginative and engaging artifacts for learning, whether videos, electronic books, games, apps, and other digital objects. The potential for self-regulated learning, for culturally authentic content, for linguistically accessible content, for cognitively and affectively powerful tools of learning by teaching, and for reshaping the economics for provisioning schools, is

Fig. 15.1 Teachers and students engaged in collaborative media making in mathematics using pen-based computing in Ghana

difficult to overstate. This vision is one that ultimately seeks to infuse classrooms with the joy and human satisfaction that accompanies knowledge discovery, formation, and sharing.

The process is stepwise, but it is one whose first principles include the notion that creating shared representations of knowledge—the end goal of our media making efforts—is a sine qua non dimension to recovering present and future learning opportunities by wresting control from those who are not in or of the culture and context of the learner. This does not mean to exclude outside engagement, involvement, and partnership. Rather, it acknowledges that the great national liberation movements of the postwar era in Africa have too often been thwarted by the interference of individuals and groups who take on the same oppressive and malignant aspects of governance that had initially motivated those movements. The long process from changing colonial structures to preserving a culture to building a unique and successful national identity will ultimately fall short without high performance educational approaches that are primarily led and served by community members and are connected to the global knowledge society. Those solutions are not possible without new and effective ways to more fully activate the creative imaginations and potentiality within the minds of the next generation (Fig. 15.1).

How does such an assertion fit within the proceedings of a research volume on digital ink? Digital ink enables the technological representation of mathematical and scientific cognition. It does so uniquely and in readily observable ways that foster different conceptions of classroom learning and content ownership and, thus, challenges traditional conceptions of how education can unfold in any country, but with particular significance for developing countries. While the path is stepwise, the vision for using digital ink and media-making technology to make positive disruptive changes in education has a long and consequential horizon.

15.5 Parallel Research Agenda

Such coordination of multiple communities in fostering, testing, and scaling change requires an interdependent parallel research agenda that would rely heavily on important recent learning science research. The dynamics of self-explanation [1, 10] and peer tutoring [5, 11] for youngsters are powerful for building deep understandings of disciplinary content, English usage, and expression. Media that combines science ideas with language acquisition and skills has been repeatedly and unsurprisingly—proven to provide synergistic benefit both to development of scientific reasoning and to successful language development. The project also capitalizes on aspects of empowerment and agency, but which considered buzzwords in US educational circles are nevertheless profoundly meaningful here. When learners and teachers see themselves as media-makers or producers, not just text-book users or consumers, their dispositions change in highly charged and positive ways. At the same time, they bring to bear true localized culture and language dimensions that simply are not possible to import with any of the official English-language textbooks now in use. Important research in the US, most recently by Jones et al. [7], documents the importance of preserving first language discourse in childhood and adolescent development; her work demonstrates decline in complex reasoning indicators when bilingual youngsters are disallowed use of any first language options. The videos by teachers will, when appropriate, entail both English and local languages. And, it turns out, this will benefit teachers as much as learners. While English is the official language in Namibia (the nation where most of this research currently takes place), the aversion that most Namibians carry for speaking in English rather than in first language illustrates the importance of permitting organic use of language switching. Each video this effort produces can, through the affordances of peer-assistance and review demonstrate accurate applications of the English language. Additionally, both educational and neuroscientific research shows that important cognition is left behind when language options are limited. In sum, there is ample evidence to support our belief that producing and using multilingual media is a key activity on the path to developing sophisticated English fluency in the Sub-Saharan context.

Our research agenda also entails peer-review through a digital emulation of Japanese style lesson study, perhaps the most widely assimilated foreign approach assimilated in African educational systems in the past 15 years (see http://bit.ly/namibia-m4-2015 for an example). In this example, peer-review focuses on the fitting usage of the English language and its expressions. This peer-review process and the subsequent revision by the author serves as a mechanism for quality control. It is well-known that interactive digital media has a profoundly alluring effect on learners [9], and it turns out this is the case for teachers also. We call media-making a "superfood" for learning [6], because it nourishes so many cognitive, affective and social dynamics, and skills in a way that simultaneously stokes and relies on imagination and creativity. It is satisfying work that results in a rewarding new dynamic between learners and their teachers. Finally, we see this effort as potentially opening nourishing entrepreneurial skill sets and technical fluencies, by which older learners, students, and teachers develop the capacity to create media both in other domains and in school-based media. This expansive topic cannot be fully treated here but is an important aspect of future research.

Acknowledgments The authors acknowledge the generous support of the US National Science Foundation, the US State Department Fulbright Program, the Kenyan Ministry of Education, the African Institute for Mathematical Sciences in Ghana, the University of Namibia, Pepperdine University and the Namibian Ministry of Education. The work reported here reflects the views of the authors alone.

References

1. Chi MT, Leeuw N, Chiu MH, LaVancher C (1994) Eliciting self-explanations improves understanding. Cognit Sci 18(3):439–477
2. Hamilton E (2010) Targeted research on teacher creativity at the intersection of content, student cognition, and digital media. In: Award DUE104478, National Science Foundation
3. Hamilton E (2011) Student mathematics learning through self-explanation, peer tutoring and digital media production. In: Award DRL-1119654, US National Science Foundation
4. Hamilton E (2013) A cyber-ensemble of inversion, immersion, collaborative workspaces, query and media-making in mathematics classrooms. In: Award IIS-1321162, National Science Foundation
5. Hamilton E, Chaves G, Chaves W, Harding N (2011) Creativity of teachers and peer-student-tutors through video media at the intersection of content and cognition. In: Proceedings of the international conference on computer supported collaboration (CSCL2011), Hong Kong
6. Hamilton E, Garff T, Holt A, Kato H, Samuels J, Sarmonpal S, Teague H, Welch K (2015) Media-making as a superfood for learning in and out of classrooms: identity shifts for learners and teachers. In: Ruokamo H (ed) Media education conference (MEC 2015), in the light of the midnight sun. Salla, Finland
7. Jones S, Cotterill R, Dewdney N, Muir K, Joinson A (2014) Finding zelig in text: a measure for normalising linguistic accommodation. In: 25th international conference on computational linguistics
8. MacKinnon A (2013) Dr Eric Hamilton the sublime, engrossing experience of video. Perspectives on ICT and education in Africa, E-Learning Africa News Portal
9. Pavlik JV (2013) Media in the digital age. Columbia University Press
10. Nathan MJ et al (1994) Learning through self-explanation of mathematics examples: effects of cognitive load [Technical Report], Accessed 14 Jan 2016
11. Roscoe RD, Chi MT (2007) Understanding tutor learning: knowledge-building and knowledge-telling in peer tutors explanations and questions. Rev Educ Res 77(4):534–574
12. Sawamura N (2002) Local Spirit, global knowledge: a Japanese approach to knowledge development in international cooperation. Comp J Comp Int Edu 32(3):339–348
13. UNESCO: Strengthening mathematics and science education (SMASE): enhancing the effectiveness of in-service teacher training (2015)

Chapter 16
Student Producers: OneNote, Camtasia Studio, and the Authentic Project

Audrey Lampe Ploesser

Abstract This past academic year saw the implementation of digital ink in OneNote notebooks into the 10th grade Modern World History: 1800-Present classroom. The main sophomore project involved creating historically and culturally accurate educational videos for the Boeing Company. Upon conclusion of the project, Boeing would have multiple educational videos about Middle Eastern countries to share with their employees and their families in preparation for their relocation. All students saw the benefits of using digital ink in their daily homework assignments, however the fruits of this new technology were not fully displayed until the completion of their large scale research project (Global Interactions: Boeing) at the end of the school year. This project motivated students to engage in a historical conversation with a reputable company and see a clear connection between history and the real world. OneNote allowed for a unique approach to peer collaboration as well as teacher feedback throughout this project. Students had the ability to draw concept maps, brainstorm, and connect major ideas with the simple use of their stylus. The students were freer to play around with the components of their visual timeline, knowing that they could edit and perfect as they went forward. Collaborating teachers saw major improvements in problem solving skills, peer feedback, and overall investment when using this pen and video technology. The authentic nature of the Global Interactions project combined with the use of digital ink allowed for an in-depth understanding and investment in the social studies curriculum and final video. The Whitfield community as well as The Boeing Company partners were immensely impressed with the end product and methods used. This project reflected the potential use of digital ink in the Whitfield classroom and inspired modern technological additions to previously outdated projects.

A.L. Ploesser (✉)
Whitfield School, Saint Louis, MO, USA
e-mail: audrey.ploesser@whitfieldschool.org

T. Hammond et al. (eds.), *Revolutionizing Education with Digital Ink*,
Human–Computer Interaction Series, DOI 10.1007/978-3-319-31193-7_16

16.1 Problem Statement and Context

The teachers and students at Whitfield School work in a 1:1 tablet computer environment. Students are given the basic training for how to use their stylus and tablet and appear well-versed in how to use their computers. However confident they feel using technology, many high school students tend to stick to the techniques and programs they know well [2, 3]. Entering sophomore year, many students have gone through the historical research process and about three quarters of them have completed a basic video project. During the fourth quarter of sophomore year, the students begin to learn about the Middle East and the diverse political, social, cultural, and religious aspects of those particular countries. In many schools, this vast area of the world is often misunderstood and glossed over in the classroom for fear of controversy and inaccurate information. Students rarely fully understand the complicated issues of the Middle East. The Global Interaction: Boeing video project was designed as a way to combat this general misunderstanding of the Middle East. However, it would only be successful if students were able to explore controversial topics in a collaborative learning environment with the motivation to be as creative as possible. During the designing phase of this project, two major problems appeared immediately:

1. How do you promote creativity and brainstorming between group members on an unfamiliar historical research project?
2. How do you increase student investment and honest collaboration in the research process (questioning, searching, analyzing)?

A member of the technology department offered to be a consultant on this project. We quickly realized one of the first obvious solutions to problem #1 was the creation of productive student groups. Creating groups that allowed for trust, collaboration, and creativity was crucial if we were going to be able to use digital ink as we wanted. We carefully collected feedback from the students about which of their peers they trusted and felt the most comfortable working with. Once we organized the class sections into groups (2–3 students maximum), we were able to create custom shared OneNote notebooks between all group members as well as the teacher. These notebooks were first introduced as a main tool for the collecting and sharing of ideas. Each student had their own tab within the notebook, but they also shared a brainstorming tab, script tab, storyboard tab, and sources tab (see Fig. 16.1). Students were encouraged to dream big with this project and allow all ideas to flow freely so as to not limit their creativity.

Once we created and set up shared notebooks for each group, students started to brainstorm and research their particular Middle Eastern topic. Some students hesitated when asked to write down their ideas as they assumed perfection was

Fig. 16.1 OneNote notebook layout

required from the beginning. With the use of pen technology, we were able to show students how creating fabulous educational videos and creative brainstorming go hand-in-hand. We encouraged students to be honest when critiquing their group members and to implement the many methods shown when doing so. They could elaborate on an idea in a new pen color, highlight and annotate, or even edit while still allowing the other group members to see the original idea. Because this project had an authentic audience and purpose, we were also able to reference The Boeing Company and their expectations of the end video product in order to encourage mature and constructive collaboration. Further along in the process, we even shared our notebooks with multiple Boeing executives for their feedback. Our goal was to have the Boeing executives provide pen feedback directly on the students' storyboards and scripts. Unfortunately, due to security restrictions within The Boeing Company network, this direct pen feedback was limited. We were able to have one employee send us written feedback for many students via email. Once students received this feedback, they were then instructed to write that into their notebooks so they could reference it in the future.

Eventually the storyboards were edited and finalized which lead to a great starting point for the video. Students were taught how to use Camtasia Studio software for their videos, although they were given the freedom to use whatever video editing program they wanted. Many of them chose to use Camtasia Studio as that was something they were comfortable with and very "user friendly". We feel confident that if it were not for the use of digital ink in the creative storyboarding process, the final videos would not have evolved as they did. Students could connect with each other by drawing and editing on each other's visuals and it made a huge difference in the creative process as a whole. Once they felt certain they had created the best flow of images and story line for their video, the transition of ideas from screen to video was a lot more manageable.

Using digital ink during this process proved to be crucial to solve our main problems (listed above). Students connected more to the content and visual component of this project when they were able to write directly on the screen. They could quickly give honest feedback to one another on a daily basis, which made each group think more deeply about their topic. Students felt comfortable pushing each other to look at the storyboard in a new way and then were able to actually show what they intended to produce using pen technology.

16.2 Methods Employed

Many steps had to be taken in order for our students to reach the end goal of an educational video for a Boeing employee and their family. Throughout the entirety of the process, students were highly encouraged to use digital ink to document their research, brainstorming, note taking, and storyboarding. Students spent time using online library databases to find reliable and relevant readings regarding many aspects of daily life in their chosen country including food, religion, family, marriage, education, government, etc. (see Fig. 16.2).

From this point, students identified the key ideas they wanted to focus on for their video. Some student groups used digital ink methods such as concept maps (see Fig. 16.3) while some groups created lists of main ideas and then wrote out what the overall consensus was for the group (see Fig. 16.4).

Once groups were satisfied with their research, students then collected or created visuals that would eventually be shown in the video. Students were expected to create a storyboard, or visual outline of what they wanted to communicate and show in their video. This part of the process was the most rewarding from an educator's standpoint. All students felt inspired and motivated to critique and elaborate on each other's storyboards. Some students wanted first to get a general overview of their

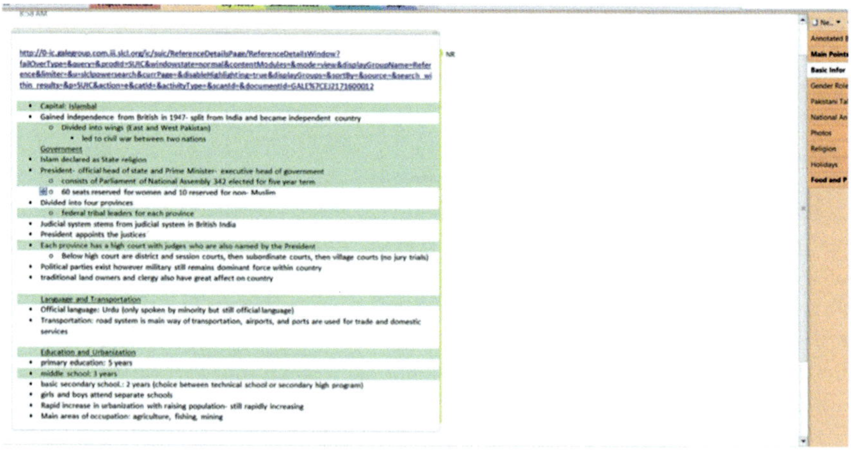

Fig. 16.2 This student's notes are clearly categorized on the *right* side. She has the ability to explore her group members' notes as well by clicking on their tab across the *top*

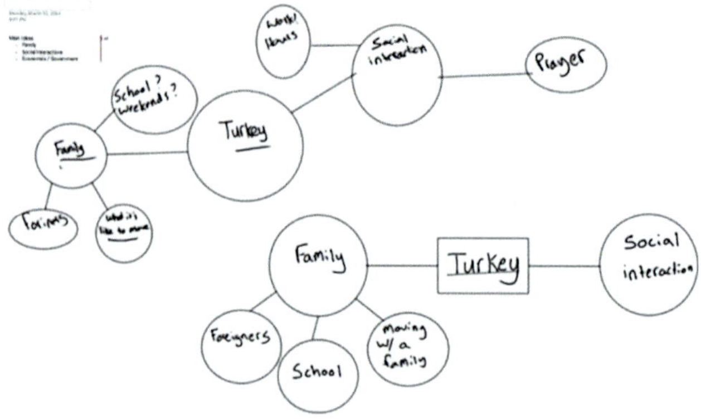

Fig. 16.3 This group's preliminary brainstorming of possible main ideas in a concept map

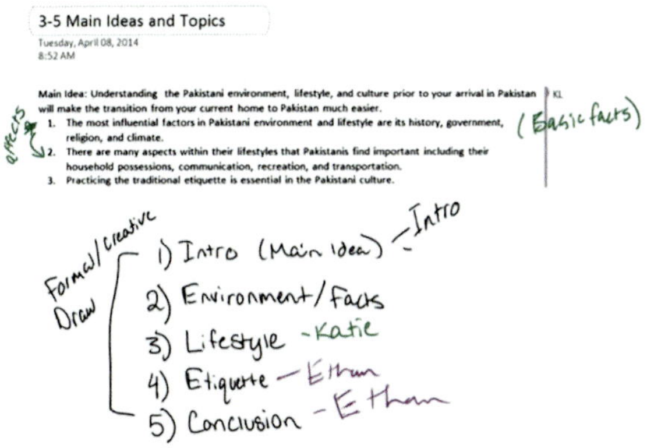

Fig. 16.4 One group's main ideas are listed *above*. They have separated their ideas according to each individual's role in the project

Fig. 16.5 Storyboard overview with no visuals

ideas before they even considered visuals or text (see Fig. 16.5). Another group was further ahead in the process and included visuals, time stamps, and possible text in their storyboard (see Fig. 16.6). One can also see this group's storyboard includes suggestions and edits from other peers; something that was easily added when using digital ink. Students were not only able to critique group members flow of ideas, but peers from other class sections were also able to see fellow classmate's storyboards and make suggestions.

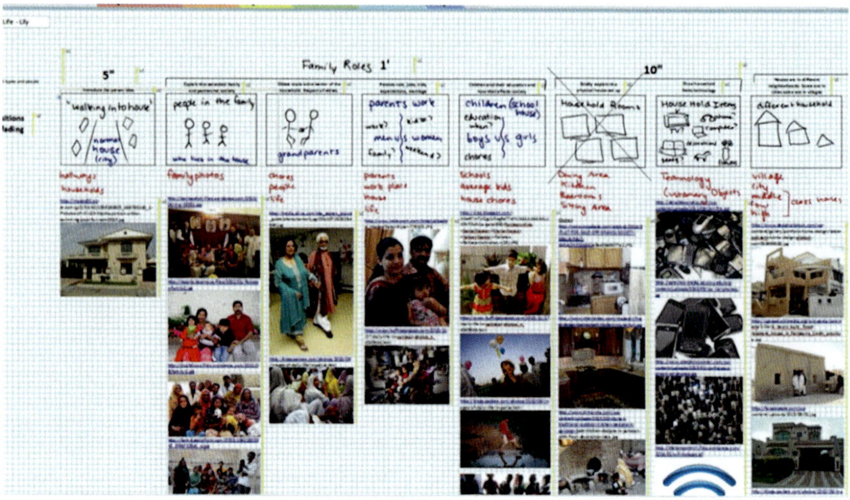

Fig. 16.6 Storyboard with visuals and edits by other peers

Teachers were able to easily track student progress within each shared notebook and therefore teacher feedback was frequent and timely (see Fig. 16.7). When students fell behind on the research and creative video process, it was immediately apparent when looking into each notebook. We were then able to give suggestions on techniques that would make the end product more real, accurate or professional looking.

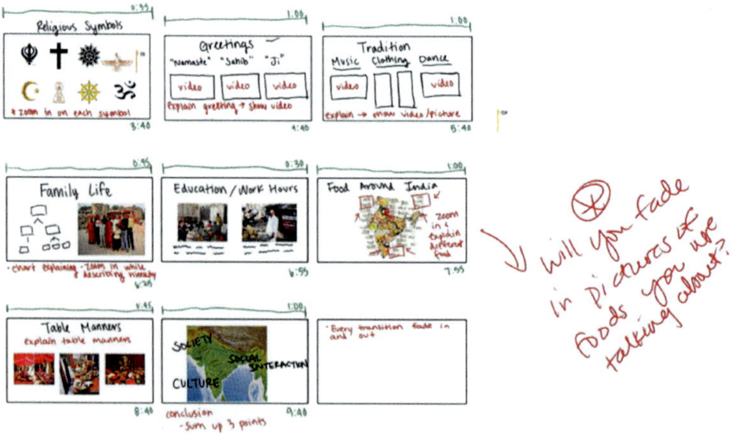

Fig. 16.7 Storyboard with visuals and edits by other peers

Students worked hard to create their storyboards and then, when approved by the teacher, they were able to start taking their storyboards and bringing them to life through the use of Camtasia Studio software. It was amazing to see their creative minds taking a complicated historical topic, such as Middle Eastern culture, politics, and religion, and turning it into an informative and professional video. Throughout the process of turning their storyboard into video, we worked with the Boeing employees and our students to make them as authentic as possible. We were able to use digital ink to give clear feedback to many groups at one time. Figure 16.8 shows how easy it was to give feedback to student groups about areas of their videos that needed improvement and areas that were well done. The highlighting and symbols also seen in Fig. 16.8 mean specific things to the teachers and students. Using the pen was also a large help when trying to decipher which student videos would go to the final rounds

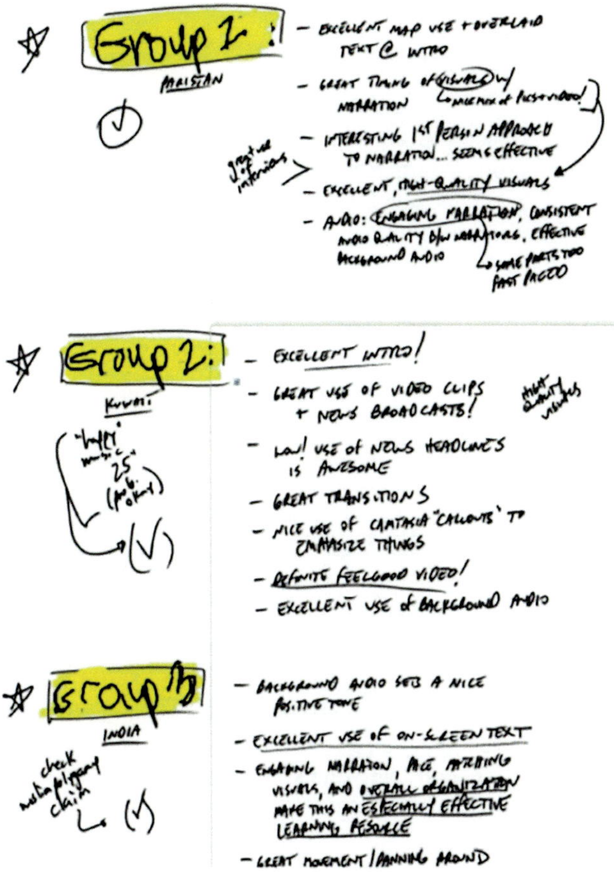

Fig. 16.8 Digital ink technology allowed for quick teacher and peer feedback on the final videos. Students had immediate access to this feedback once their notebooks synced

of the video contest. Each teacher was able to watch a video while simultaneously sketching their thoughts on their individual notebook. When we finished watching all the videos, we could read each other's feedback and then continue to comment or highlight each other's wording to clarify. We were able to weed out videos that did not include enough visually stimulating content or were simply lacking accuracy and professionalism.

Overall, the methods implemented throughout the Global Interactions: Boeing video project was made possible by an intelligent use of digital ink and other technologies. Students were pushed to be creative and think outside the box on a hard and complex historical, social, and cultural topic. They were able to use digital ink to explore new topics, brainstorm ideas, and learn to give constructive and clear feedback. As shown above, the steps to this process were made possible due to the pen technology employed.

16.3 Results and Evaluation

The impact of this project was immense from all angles including: students, parents, Whitfield community, Whitfield educators, and The Boeing Company. Students reported after the project concluded that there were fewer issues related to the creation of the video than in past projects. Upon further review of these statements, we found that while students did have issues throughout the entirety of the project, they felt more at ease going into the video creating component. Students were able to reflect on the use of digital ink, stating that the guidelines and resources at their disposal were crucial in making a large scale project like this feel less intimidating. Feedback was given often through the use of digital ink by peers, teachers, and indirectly by Boeing employees. Once the notebooks synced, the most recent feedback was shown clearly in all groups' notebooks.

While the research process was split up into multiple steps for the students, there could have been time for cross-group peer review. Students were constantly encouraged to peer review other members in their group, but we did not save as much time for students to give feedback to other classmates throughout the process. It would also be ideal for more Boeing members to give their immediate feedback throughout the process. We mainly focused on their feedback when we were starting to convert the storyboard into the actual video, but it would be helpful to have their input on the content and areas of focus earlier in the process. On the flip side, the drawback of having too much Boeing input too early would be that students' creativity may be squashed if they are constantly thinking about what a well-respected Boeing employee may say about their ideas.

Once final videos were completed, each group showed their 8–10 min video to their class section (5 in the sophomore class). They were able to get more feedback from their peers on their final video. In the future, we could have students give feedback directly in their OneNote notebook. At the time, this option was not considered and therefore many students gave concrete feedback on a paper form and handed them directly to the group presenting. Out of 72 students in the sophomore class, 35 total videos were created. We were then able to share the pros and cons of each video and reduce 35 good videos to the top 11 outstanding videos. It was at this point where we enlisted fellow faculty members to give input on the top 11 videos. Each faculty member was given criteria for a great educational video. They were instructed to not only examine the content of each video, but also the visual and artistic appeal. These teachers also used digital ink to give feedback on each video and rank them from 11 videos to their personal top 5. Once the results came in from the teachers, we realized that there would be 6 finalist videos to be presented to the Boeing panel for review. Each member on the Boeing panel had experience traveling and working in the Middle East. After almost two months of preparation, these students were finally seeing the payoff of all of their hard work. It was amazing to see them truly engaged in an authentic project and genuinely wanting feedback because they knew that their work was for something real.

Students with the top 6 videos and their families were invited to a showing at the beginning of May. Students dressed up in their most professional attire and parents came to support them as they presented their hard work. Two members of the Boeing panel came as well and gave their honest feedback at the end of each video. We were amazed to see how each student group truly looked to find ways they could improve their work in the future. At the end of the night, the top video was announced. While some students were disappointed that they did not get labeled as the #1 video, every student left that evening with a smile on their face. You could see the pride beaming through their eyes as well as their parents. Without the use of the technology and the creative collaboration explained above, we may not have made it to a point where these student videos were worthy of being shown to Boeing.

16.4 Future Work

In the future, there are many aspects of this project that could be tweaked or elaborated upon. It would be fun to see how other teachers in different subject areas may be able to collaborate on this project. Generally, when an educator combines different classes together to inspire innovation and creativity, they have a recipe for engagement and success. The pen technology was extremely useful throughout the entirety of the process, but it would be helpful to find a way to make sure notebooks sync outside of the school server. In an ideal situation, students could write constructive notes on each other's research paper while they were away from school. It would also help to be able to share a notebook with a particular company, such as Boeing, without the fear of security breaches.

16.5 Conclusion

First of all, from an educator's perspective, the use of digital ink throughout the entirety of this project was absolutely necessary [1]. The ability for individual creativity, group collaboration, and teacher feedback was crucial to making outstanding educational videos. Second of all, when you work to make a project authentic and real, the need for useful and reliable technologies becomes even more imperative. We needed to have access to each student's research on a daily basis as well as feel confident that their videos would be made in the highest quality possible. We needed the ability to give timely feedback so students were acutely aware of any misinformation. Not only did we need to write throughout this process, but students and teachers needed to be able to express themselves through drawings, arrows, and highlighting as ways to connect main ideas. Lastly, the value of collaboration cannot be overstated during a project such as this. Students needed to feel comfortable brainstorming their ideas so they could create something new and different and something that catches the eye of the Boeing panel. When students do this and feel comfortable taking a risk, the end product is so much more rewarding. Digital ink allowed for this to happen on a daily basis with Whitfield students throughout this project.

Acknowledgments I extend my great appreciation to Mark Payton and Matt DiGiulio who worked hard to see the vision of this project carried out. They were instrumental in making this project and its analysis a success. I also thank all the volunteers and all publications support and staff, who wrote and provided helpful comments on previous versions of this document.

References

1. Armstrong C, Llorin J (2015) Using shared microsoft onenote binders to create a school environment for sharing, continual formative assessment, and information organization. In: Hammond T, Valentine S, Adler A, Payton M (eds) The impact of pen and touch technology on education. Springer, Heidelberg, pp 241–247
2. Hammond JP (2015) The impact of tablets on school leadership. In: Hammond T, Valentine S, Adler A, Payton M (eds) The impact of pen and touch technology on education. Springer, Heidelberg, pp 331–337
3. Romney A (2015) Tablet computers in the university classroom of 2012: opportunities and challenges. In: Hammond T, Valentine S, Adler A, Payton M (eds) The impact of pen and touch technology on education. Springer, Heidelberg, pp 277–282

Chapter 17
An Aqua Squiggle and Giggles: Pre-Teens as Researchers Influencing Little Lives Through Inking and Touch Devices

Michelle Zimmerman

Abstract Using technology for the good of society is a skill that needs to be modeled, instructed, and practiced as young students prepare for the future. The primary objective of this action research was to locate the emergence of skill development through an intersection of human connection and touch screen laptop use in a cross-age mentoring model with middle school and preschool students in an urban independent school representing 27 ethnic groups. To increase understanding of new forms of learning within a non-traditional grouping of sixth- and seventh-graders in a 1:1 laptop environment, I drew on their perspective and creativity as they utilized production and internet tools to facilitate their own data collection as they researched and tracked learning of the little buddy they mentored in literacy projects. The data showed students in this grouping becoming active pursuers of relational bonding with preschoolers and simultaneously developing a mindset parallel with that of adult teacher-researchers. Touch and inking unexpectedly became the tool that helped facilitate interpersonal conversational skills and social emotional development with English Language Learning in one case study.

17.1 Motion and Direction

> Like a baby shaking a rattle, we seem to be utterly content with action, provided it is sufficiently vigorous and noisy. In the last analysis a very large part of American educational thought, inquiry, and experimentation is much ado about nothing. And, if we are permitted to push the analogy of the rattle a bit further, our consecration to motion is encouraged and supported in order to keep us out of mischief.
>
> —George Counts, 1932 [7], (p. 4)

M. Zimmerman (✉)
Educational Design and Technology, Concordia University Wisconsin,
Mequon, WI, USA
e-mail: michelle.zimmerman@cuw.edu; m.zimmerman@agcschool.org

M. Zimmerman
Renton Preparatory Christian School, 200 Mill Avenue South, Suite 110,
Renton, WA, USA

T. Hammond et al. (eds.), *Revolutionizing Education with Digital Ink*,
Human–Computer Interaction Series, DOI 10.1007/978-3-319-31193-7_17

...the issue is about the people and not technology...

—Mark Gibbs, 2010 [13]

At the core of education is humanity. Technology is a tool [5] and therefore, an extension of humanity. It accelerates, expands, and magnifies the way we do things ([13], p. 34). In October 2010, just three months before the events in Egypt, Mark Gibbs, a columnist for Network World noted how people "dismiss Facebook and Twitter as trivial phenomena, yet that's exactly what's redefining the social landscape." Technology is changing the way we once knew the world. Simultaneously, there is "growing skepticism about classroom technology," along with concern regarding "unthinking trend followers," with evidence to support those claims ([27], p. xiii). Despite some concerns, it is no longer a question of "if" technology will become an integral part of our society, but, rather, "how."

Although there appears to be an increasing interest in shifting the way we look at education, one only needs to look back to 1932 and see that the cry for change has been reverberating since Counts called for meaningful impact on education. It is not enough to experience change for the sake of change. Action without direction will miss the end goal. The 9th Workshop on the Impact of Pen and Touch Technology (WIPTTE) provided an opportunity to collaborate and investigate essential questions including digital pens and touch devices, to look at the past and thoughtfully assess where we have been and where to incite future directions of research, including the transfer of learning. WIPTTE demonstrated how they value student voice in the future of technology in education by providing experiences for students through a high school design challenge and attending Keynotes and workshops to prepare them to use technology for the public good. As an outflow of this experience, three of my high school students who attended WIPTTE were so inspired to innovate for the public good, they independently worked on the Surface Hub for Research proposal without my knowledge, and presented me with a proposal to work with them to make the proposal and research a reality for the upcoming 2015–2016 academic year. The proposal included educators working on their Master's degree all the way down through Pre-Kindergarten students taking part in cross-age mentoring.

This study is part of a larger work that I began in 2007 investigating constructivism [43, 44], what paradigm shifts in a formal educational environment can look like in practice. I am concurrently a practitioner and a researcher. I have taught all the grades from preschool through 10th grade. I have been on the Professional Education Advisory Board for the College of Education at University of Washington for three years, and am currently Adjunct in the Educational Design and Technology program at Concordia University Wisconsin, where I am guiding in-service teachers through a Virtual Enhanced Online Master in Science program. This enables a parallel culture for educators to learn, design, and teach in an apprenticeship model, as they are obtaining credit for continuing graduate education. Educators benefit from apprentice models and training in teacher-research as do students trained as teacher-researchers when working with little buddies. In 2007, I started by studying an established cross-age mentoring paradigm existing within the small school in the Pacific Northwest in which I teach, where third-grade students mentored preschoolers. The program expanded and the school opened an additional site for secondary students. In the redesigned program based on my research, students in traditional middle and high school age levels prepare to enter college as high school juniors. The two years of college are paid for by the state of Washington as part of the Running Start program. With a Direct Transfer Agreement, students are able to enter a University with the first two years of college completed, simultaneously earning and associate degree and a high school diploma.

This shift in the way learning occurs requires training for educators who are not accustomed to teaching in close collaboration with other educators and designing blended, experiential learning models with authentic applications to help the transfer of learning. Therefore, the Virtual Enhanced Online Master's program became an essential necessity for the continued development of this program. The genesis of all of this began with cross-age mentoring research in 2007, leading to applying the model in other contexts. In 2009, touch devices with inking and webcams were introduced into the established model. This is where the story begins.

17.2 The Story Begins

At the beginning of the 2009 school year, my role as teacher and researcher was to lead the first group of students in the 1:1 laptop integration program at the school. The school was working toward breaking the divide of age-graded classrooms ([8], p. 8, [34]), and my class was a restructured sixth- and seventh-grade multi-age cohort. As an aside, I had the same cohort during the 2010–2011 school year and an additional age level was added for a combined sixth-, seventh-, and eighth-grade class cohort.

From what I learned during those years and obtaining my Ph.D. in Learning Sciences and Human Development, I put the theory and research to work in practice through design-based research with cycles of implementation, research, and redesign. Along the way, students have added to my work, become research-practitioners and co-presented with me at many conferences locally and across the United States, further deepening my understanding of non-traditional education.

At the time, we used HP TouchSmart Tx2 tablet computers at school. We used HP MediaSmart Webcam software for the project as well as two free programs downloaded from the internet: ArtRage and Windows Movie Maker. See Fig. 17.1.

In the past 5 years, technology has advanced and the HP tablets we had are no longer produced. The Surface Pro 3 has capabilities I only imagined then. However, this study shows a genesis of our use of touch and inking devices to connect humanity in the context of early literacy and teaching English Language Learners. The impact of the learning design has remained consistent across age groups, content, types of devices, and through distance collaboration across students in the small urban school in the Pacific Northwest, and an inner city public high school on the East Coast.

Although we are going into our ninth year of action research and technology integration at the school during the 2015–2016 academic year, and we have expanded to a two year blended high school model that prepares students for early entry into

Fig. 17.1 Aqua squiggles and telling a story to a big buddy mentor in 2010

college, this chapter is focused on a slice of the study from the 2009–2010 school year. It serves as a reflection on work that established the foundations of where we were during the 2014–2015 academic year and the ninth WIPTTE. The core still remains about humanity, and therefore, the underlying design is first about human interaction. It did not start with the device or tool. This type of approach allows for longevity of the concepts as devices change. Utilizing technology with the school's previously established apprenticeship model [35] and cross-age mentoring model introduced a dais for a project-based learning environment and provided a new twist to continue my grounded theory [4, 14] investigations of cross-age mentoring that commenced with third-graders mentoring preschoolers. I begin by outlining the process that led to the question development for this current study.

17.2.1 Previous Findings: Assertions Refine Research Questioning

This research is a form of action research, where "we may envision children as collaborative change agents in the settings and contexts of their lives" ([24], p. 61). I agree with Pitri [32] that my students "learn through interaction and communication," and that my role as practitioner is not merely to help them learn, but to be a researcher "whose inquiry is planned to have direct effect on [my] own beliefs and practices and on the children" (p. 42). Through attempting to answer my own questions about my students' experiences as experts instructing in an apprenticeship pairing, I more clearly learned what it meant for "teacher–researchers ... to observe closely and learn about their students in new ways" ([28], p. 53).

My previous study of cross-age mentoring where third-graders mentored preschoolers, allowed me to developed several assertions in beginning to understand the nature of cross-age mentoring interactions. The assertions I developed through that first study helped guide the structural choices in my middle school classroom starting in the 2009–2010 school year and consequently, my questioning for the current study. Knowing the assertions from my first study provide context for this study:

Assertion 1: Expert children generated multiple complex strategies for teaching their "buddies" that showed elements of guided learning and reciprocal teaching in facilitating instruction.

Assertion 2: The combination of teaching and learning within the context of the reciprocal teaching paradigm and apprenticeship model, along with engaging in group discussion and writing, shifts experts beyond the teaching role to that of a teacher–researcher who works with their apprentices.

Assertion 3: When experts are socially connected to their apprentices, authentic motivation increases to maintain the connection and to continue teaching their apprentices.

In the process of mentors guiding the learning of less experienced learners, I implemented a variation on the interactive procedure of reciprocal teaching to train the mentors and model for them how they can interact with their little buddies [29, 36, 45], and embedded it within an apprenticeship model [35] where a more experienced learner then guided the learning of someone less experienced. The mentors were the more experienced learners we called the "experts"[1] and they were referred to by the preschoolers as "the big kids" or "my big buddy" and the less experienced learners were called "apprentices" or "little buddies." One "big kid," in a sudden burst of insight in the middle of a chaotic moment during a mentoring session, exclaimed, "Oh! I get it! You teach the big kids, the big kids teach the little kids, and the little kids teach the grown-ups!" (Alessandra, a third-grade student). That is the goal. We learn from our students and share that learning with other adults.

[1] I am not entirely convinced of a single best descriptor for the process: "mentor" and "mentee" or "expert" and "apprentice." There exists a critique for describing children as experts because they are technically not expert in whatever area they are helping guide learning as they too, are still learning. But saying more experienced learners and "less experienced learners" is cumbersome. I have been critiqued for referring to them as "teacher-researchers" and "apprentices" as the older students are neither officially credentialed "teachers" nor "researchers" in the way we know adults to hold such titles. The term teacher-researcher more aptly describes what they are doing in this process and indicates something more is at work beyond the colloquial connotation of "mentor," especially when considering children are "mentors." I admit momentary definitional defeat and present a challenge to researchers and practitioners to continue the quest with me for descriptors that are, possibly a more agreeable fit.

When a shift of teaching power occurred, the third-grade students from the original study that informed this later application of touch devices, transitioned from primarily learners under my instruction to their role as expert teachers in an apprenticeship pairing. This shift of teaching power eased my ability to more fully transition from primary teacher of a skill through modeled and explicit instruction to my identity as participant–observer–researcher in my students' teaching and learning process. I was able to continue facilitating the learning process and make myself available for specific instruction if the expert third-grade students required additional scaffolded assistance in their new role as teachers to their apprentices. This foundation was essential knowledge for implementing the learning design later with middle school students using touch devices with preschool students, and further, during the 2015 academic year with high school students developing research questions for the Surface Hub for Research proposal.

The data from the results in that initial study were surprising on several levels, but it is beyond the scope of this chapter to discuss all of these results in detail. One surprise, however, was that the whole process allowed mentors to go beyond merely mentoring someone less experienced. Utilizing the combination of instructional techniques at the onset ostensibly helped to train the mentors to develop qualities of adult teacher-researchers. They began by questioning their own instructional methods based on observations they recorded in handwritten journals (prior to 1:1 or touch devices), set goals, created and tested hypotheses, and then analyzed, interpreted and altered their teaching to produce better results in their apprentices.

I was surprised by the depth of thought expressed by the third-graders in my initial study beginning in 2007 witnessing their collaborative speech and writing. During that first study that informed later studies, I wanted third grade students to hand write journals but we did not have the ability for all third grade journals to be inked. Journals were spiral-bound written in pencil. I transcribed the data. Reading the depth of thought, atypical compared to their other classroom writing, led me to question why this phenomenon appeared to be occurring. Searching for literature on the child as theorist or scientist pointed me to Bigozzi et al. [2] work on how children become scientists and their ability to explain why things happen. These ideas, along with Vygotsky's work [43, 44] led me to look for evidence and counterexamples in the data suggesting that children who became teachers displayed similar characteristics to teacher–researchers when determining how best to guide their apprentices through learning a skill [32].

I then decided to look at how such an environment allows for the emergence and development of a series of skills and behaviors in both the mentors and mentees that may not be otherwise observed in more traditionally structured age-graded instructional environments [11].

17.2.1.1 Research Questions

As in my previous work, I remained interested in understanding the experiences of the mentor and mentee. I also wanted to gain a greater understanding of the skills that emerged and develops through placing more "responsibility on the students to find information, to coordinate actions and people, to reach goals, and to monitor understanding" ([30], p. 94).

This study examined the following Research Question (RQ) and Sub Questions (SQ):

RQ: How does the use of touch devices in a 1:1 laptop environment facilitate or develop social relationships among cross-age mentors and apprentices?
SQ1: How do the middle school students in this classroom use technology as a tool in the mentoring process with their preschool buddies?
SQ2: What skills do the mentors learn?
SQ3: How does the implementation of technology support developing skills that move students from simply acting as a mentor to the process of acting as a teacher-researcher?
SQ4: How do teacher-researchers demonstrate and talk about their learning with the help of production and internet tools?

Drawing on the work of Strauss [42], I used characteristic examples of data to illustrate substantive grounded theory derived from my data. My purpose for utilizing grounded theory was twofold: (1) to focus on how substantive theory developed as a process with the assumption that it would continue to develop and others would build upon this work, and (2) that it would be applicable to instructional environments.

In a three-year study on the New Mexico Laptop Learning Initiative (NMLLI), Rutledge, Duran, and Carroll-Miranda state that "multimedia tools allow students to express more complex ideas in more sophisticated ways," and that "under the right conditions, opportunities created by technology enhance the learning experience (Keane, Gersick, Kim, and Honey, 2003, p. 27)" ([37], p. 341). Rutledge, Duran, and Carroll-Miranda, observed that we need to prepare students for "global competitiveness" ([37], p. 341).

But we cannot expect any of this to happen by placing a laptop with a webcam in front of a student. Students need to be taught how to utilize technology tools. It is only then that the tools can become an extension of learning goals. To succeed as architects of learning in this new landscape requires an identification of purpose for education, historical and current, the goals we as educators wish to accomplish, and the ability to apply uses for technology in practice.

We need to be more than mere facilitators of learning; rather, we need to become architects of their learning [3] and to provide them with a solid foundation in citizenship in the real world [21, 41] that will translate into citizenship in the digital world. Digital citizenship needs to be taught, and modeled and our youth need opportunities to engage in productive ways of relating to and creating with technology in conjunction with other human interaction. Humanity is at the core. The added benefits allow technology to be a vehicle for innovative literacy and inquiry projects. Children as young as preschool can gain positive experience with technology in a way that can support literacy [40] and social development in the context of human interaction and guidance [44] from their "big kid" buddies. Throughout history, there is evidence of social goals as part of education systems. With an end goal in mind, training can more easily be designed to match. Different cultures and times value different types of social interaction. In one system of education, behavior parallel to what we would call bullying today, translating into cyberbullying would have been an acceptable, and necessary form of training for the Spartans [31]. We need to clearly define end goals for the children we educate and ensure all aspects of the training are included in learning design, not just content.

There is little research on the intersection of socially mediated [45] learning using a cross-age mentoring model in a 1:1 laptop formal-education setting. There exists an unpublished thesis titled, the relational nature of mentoring gifted children using desktop videoconferencing in Australia, using grounded theory methods over a 2-year period, where adults were paired with children [23]. Another study looks at adults tutoring middle and high school students in literacy in person and via webcams [17]. Yang et al. [46] conducted a study in Taiwan with second-grade children learning English using a webcam for video-capture in a physically interactive learning environment. Enright [9] points out that "students of the New Mainstream who now fill America's classrooms not only challenge traditional teaching practices that assume a uniform set of backgrounds and skills from our students but also open up new possibilities by bringing into the classroom a wealth of unexpected talents, perspectives, and unique experiences" (p. 113). There exists work done on current knowledge gaps and recommendations for future research when integrating technology into K-12 teaching and learning [16]. Inan, and Lowther [19] looked at factors impacting instructional use of laptops in the K-12 classroom. Jacobsen and Lock [20] looked at technology and teacher education with a perspective of mentoring for student futures, as opposed to the past.

Interestingly enough, it was exactly that wealth of talents, perspectives, and unique experiences in my students that led to the use of webcams as part of this literacy project. I had no prior knowledge about webcam uses in the classroom at the time, but have since found the work of Sawyer et al. [39] and Harris [15]. In my classroom, the concept and added dimension of the webcam arose at an intersection of my own questions, theoretical perspectives, and creativity of my students. It emerged through their own research exploration of how to use their laptop as a tool for documenting their teaching and apprentice learning in the mentoring process. This occurred through mentors deciding to record teaching social swing dance with their webcams to analyze back in the classroom. Second, some mentors used the webcam as a way to initially connect with their little buddy while waiting to start dance practice, especially when their buddy did not initially respond verbally. The webcam brought mutual laughter to both mentor and apprentice through distorted image filters, special effects, and focused attention utilizing the stylus to draw on the tablet PC. It is essential to improving educational practice that we provide learners with "both experience-produced knowledge and research-produced knowledge" ([8], p. 4).

We, as teachers and researchers should strive to obtain both types of knowledge. I am resolved to depict the story of this study through both lenses of research-produced knowledge and the knowledge derived from experience. Therefore, I have chosen to present a wide-angle lens from which to view the structure of the general experience of the project in the hope that it may ignite thought and generate new possibilities of practical application in the classroom. Following this, I will present assertions through exemplars.

I have identified several learning categories, through triadic procedures [42] that may materialize in both the mentor and mentees as part of providing learners with experience-produced, and research-produced knowledge:

1. Literacy: reading and writing
2. Scientific inquiry
3. Social and emotional
4. Digital citizenship
5. Technology literacy

Within individual categories, there are slightly different manifestations for each in the mentor and mentee on appropriate developmental and academic levels of understanding. For example, reading and writing literacy for preschoolers is very introductory and basic and yet has the room to rise to the challenge mentors provide through scaffolding. The mentors reading and writing literacy develops through higher order questioning, reading aloud with expression, documenting their thoughts and reflections through journaling, and researching [14, 40].

Although there are multiple dimensions to this project, I have chosen to present a glimpse of the findings through the literacy lens primarily focused on the experience of the mentor because my guiding question asked how the use of computers in a 1:1 laptop environment facilitated or developed social relationships among cross-age mentors and apprentices.

17.3 The Project

One multi-level grouping of 19 sixth- and seventh-grade male and female students and one preschool classroom of 20 male and female students in a private school were studied during the 2009–2010 school year. The school is located in an urban setting of a major city in the Pacific Northwest. The surrounding community is racially and ethnically diverse and the school's population of enrolled students reflects the surrounding community. White children are a minority in the school. Out of the nineteen middle school students, nine received financial aid for part or full tuition due to low income reporting from PSAS forms.[2] Names have been changed.

[2]Private School Aid Service, www.psas.org.

17.3.1 Materials, Data Sources, and Analysis

During the first week of school, each of 19 middle school students in a cohort were issued the same model (NV174UA) HP TouchSmart Tx2 tablet computer for use at school. We used HP MediaSmart Webcam software for this project as well as two free programs downloaded from the internet: ArtRage and Windows MovieMaker. As recorded images were a large part of this study, Moran and Tegano [25] helped to situate the use of digital image data within teacher inquiry. Digital images have been suggested by Oken-Wright [26] as a tool to assist teachers and researchers in recording personal choices when their attention was focused during observations so that those observations could be analyzed later. Data sources included: digital photography [25], video, journals, student artifacts, and field notes. Artifacts included a student-created DVD documentary and digital art [18]. Students emailed me journal entries, images, and webcam videos or transferred them to my computer via USB drive.

Using triadic procedures, the data collection, analysis, and memoing were ongoing and simultaneous [42]. I used open coding, axial, and selective coding [42]. When watching webcam videos, I transcribed what was said and wrote down specific behaviors. At times, viewing segments a couple seconds in length multiple times. Strauss describes a similar process for "frequently coding minutely" during initial open coding procedures ([42], p. 31). This allowed for important understandings to emerge in a grounded theory process along the way [4, 14]. Strauss see "theory as a process; that is, theory as an ever-developing entity, not as a perfected productbut it is written with the assumption that it is still developing. Theory as process, we believe, renders quite well the reality of social interaction and its structural context" ([42], p. 32).

17.3.2 Method

This research is a type of action research considered participatory action research [24]. Students are involved in the research and are also change agents in the school. The mentoring partnership began in September and continued through the last day of school at the end of May. Mentoring typically occurred one or two times each week. The duration of each mentoring session ranged between fifteen and forty-five minute sessions, depending on the activity. We did not meet some weeks due to time constraints, field trips, or vacations. Mentors were generally paired with an apprentice of the same gender. Cross-gender and cross-age pairings occurred in one brother/sister pair and two students who were cousins.

The initial goal of the project was an expansion of previously established cross-age mentoring, allowing for both experience-produced knowledge and research-produced knowledge. The students decided to use webcams to record their progress in teaching dance to their buddies. They originally brought the webcams to the gym to record their teaching and their buddy's progress. The rationale was to facilitate memory retrieval for later journaling, analysis and strategy development, leading to more effective dance teaching.

Mentors started showing their buddies how their webcams worked. Some recorded their buddies and showed the screen effects. Screen effects, especially face distortions, turned out to be effective "ice breakers" for first meetings with buddies. One student had the idea to use her webcam to record her buddy as she drew on the screen with the stylus. That gave me the idea to have the kids draw a picture and tell a story about it. Students thought aloud [6]. This was in no way a new literacy technique, and can be done with paper and crayons. In this case, using the webcam, mentors captured the preschooler's facial expressions and using a process of drawing and letter formation over the captured faces, opened up dialog between the buddies and mentors. See Fig. 17.2. Though my students' primary purpose in using the webcam was to record data, innovative techniques like this allowed for greater effective data collection.

There is a wealth of information within the students' webcam recordings to learn more about middle and preschool students thought process, intentionality, social interaction, and non-verbal communication. I was surprised to see the visible leaps in communication ability for some English language learners over time. As the use of webcams contributing to data transpired out of my students' creativity, I recently re-discovered Erickson's [10] essay on video as data to help me better understand the various ways of approaching webcam data collected by mentors. I learned from Erickson that "the videotape itself is not data. It is a resource for data construction,

Fig. 17.2 A mentor on the left guiding early literacy and story-telling with a stylus while recording with the webcam. Dialog and facial expressions get recorded for later analysis

an information source containing potential data out of which actual data must be defined and searched for" ([10], p. 178). Erickson notes neo-Vygotskyan learning theory, a nice match with what I was already investigating, "which proposes that social interaction (including the use of language and other cultural tools) is the fundamental medium within which learning takes place…[and] when individuals are videotaped over time and their changing participation in group interaction is identified, this constitutes microgenetic evidence for learning" ([10], p. 181).

What started as teaching dance buddies a concrete physical motor skill of swing dancing, branched into reading buddies, and then expanded through collaboration with students, talking with a colleague, and a friend. Each provided a valuable thought, questioning, or additions I pulled together into a literacy project that culminated in sixth- and seventh-grade students producing a 'documentary' of their experiences using Windows MovieMaker.

The student-created culminating documentary was comprised of digital artifacts mentors collected as researchers through interactions with their buddies. Artifacts were in the forms of webcam video, screen shot still images Fig. 17.3 or digital camera images, and written evidence they recorded in their electronic journals. Journals included their thoughts, observations, reflections, hypotheses, predictions, failures, challenges and successes, goals and outcomes, as well as documenting behavior observations in their buddies. The preschoolers dictated creative writing stories to mentors based on art their buddies drew on the tablet computer using either ArtRage or HP MediaSmart Webcam software. The stories were also recorded in their journals.

I trained my students how to collect, organize, and look for patterns in data, and how to use that information to understand more about their little buddies. When a friend heard about the reading buddies and project, she asked if I ever considered having the mentors select books from the library to bring back for their buddies. I decided to add an additional component to give my students a chance to practice their research skills for a purpose. I asked the mentors to use the data they had been collecting to find patterns about their buddies' likes and dislikes, moods and reading

Fig. 17.3 One of Stacy's data artifacts collected by Camilla from co-created storytelling

habits and then them come up with predictions and identify types of books their buddies might like. They also tried to predict how their buddy would respond.

My students produced a small-scale research proposal and rational for their genre choices of book selection for their little buddy. I then taught them how to use the local online library catalog to search and select books before our off campus field trip to the local public library. This also provided a balance between utilizing online sources and experience with print sources. Mentors decided how they wanted to present the books to their buddies and devised methods to test their hypotheses and what types of behaviors might indicate whether or not their buddies liked the books. I was not anticipating the level of surprise and excitement their little buddies expressed on the day their mentors brought the library books. It was the type of reaction I would have expected if they receive a wrapped gift. Their little buddies quickly understood that the books were specially chosen for them resulting in a sense of relatedness.

The documentary DVD created by the middle schoolers served as only one type of assessment for tracking the progress of my students and the skills they acquired along the way [18]. We watched "Mad Hot Ballroom" [1] in class and talked about how it related to their work as dance mentors, techniques used by the instructors, and the construction of documentaries. The students' documentaries provided an authentic method of communicating their own personal experience to an audience outside the school, and a memory keepsake for their little buddy and family. This is an example of an experience-produced knowledge and research-produced knowledge assessment.

The mentors assumed a greater responsibility for directing not only their own learning, but took necessary steps to help direct the learning of a less experienced preschool student. In some cases, that meant they needed to further refine some of their own skills before they could help a buddy. It also helped mentors identify what they knew and what they did not know as soon as they started trying to explain a concept.

My students began to realize the importance of focusing attention. They started noticing patterns that when their buddy was not focusing or listening, they would not learn as quickly as when they were focused and listening. This concept seemed to produce the most observable behavioral change in student-mentors regarding focus in their own classroom. They experienced what it was like from the teacher's perspective and saw the results of focusing and listening in their data as researchers. It also became a great classroom management technique. When my students lost focus during the teaching of other subjects, I would say: "Remember how your buddy learns better when they focus?" "Oh yeah," was an immediate response.

Perspective taking is a valuable skill not just as a teacher or researcher, but in life outside of the school walls. The concept can be brought into various scenarios, including bullying in the real world or the digital world. Some of the boys with the most behavior problems in school have been the most vocal about their interest in webcam usage and the cross-age partnerships. There has been a positive change in their real life social interaction with their peers, as well as behaviors in classes unrelated to the mentoring. The goal is to translate that real world change into digital citizenship [12], a skill that needs to be taught and modeled. Our youth need opportunities to engage in productive ways of relating to, and creating with technology in conjunction with other human interaction.

17.3.2.1 Learning by Example

The use of computers in a 1:1 laptop environment can facilitate or develop social relationships among cross-age mentors and apprentices, along with other skills. I used two mentoring pairs as examples to describe what this looked like in my classroom. The first pair includes two girls Camilla, the mentor, and Stacy, the apprentice. I chose to tell their story due to observable applications for English language learning as well as a clear example of the interaction process between mentor and apprentice. I chose to present the second example with boys for a gender contrast, and a contrast in mentor personalities. Jeff, the mentor, and Greg, the apprentice, are of particular interest to me because Greg's presence as apprentice in the mentoring process had a profound influence on his mentor's own social and emotional development. This was evidence of a little buddy creating transformative impact in the older mentor student. I also selected Camilla and Jeff because neither of them were high academic achievers in class. Neither of them volunteered to speak in class during discussions or to answer questions. An additional contrast: one began as friendly, cheerful and social, and the other began quite the opposite, including bullying peers.

17.3.3 Finding More: "Pink Apples"—Camilla and Stacy

Camilla is a sixth grade girl. Her family is from the Philippines. She is rarely seen without a smile on her face and she is well-liked by her peers in class. After observing her in the classroom, she gives little indication, however, of being passionate about completing homework or engaging in class discussions. She often seems disinterested or aloof rather than engaged. Stacy is a four year old preschooler whose family speaks only Vietnamese at home. Enrolled in a three-hour, two-day a week program the previous year, she only spoke a few words in English, although she appeared to understand more than she could speak. Stacy usually responded to her teacher's questions or comments with a blank expression and no verbal response. I purposefully paired these students because of Camilla's outgoing and cheerful disposition and Stacy's quietness.

During their first meeting and webcam recording, Camilla attempted to communicate with and began forming a friendship with Stacy. The video lasts only four minutes, but it sets a baseline for Stacy's English communication and the hesitancy she demonstrated through her behavior. In Camilla, we can see a strategy developing to connect relationally as she incorporates the use of technology as a tool to facilitate spoken communication skills. The video opens with Stacy's flat affect. Camilla is off to the left side of the camera, trying to start conversation with Stacy.

Fig. 17.4 A still shot of Camilla's webcam footage after inking. Stacy sat back to look

Camilla: "What's your favorite color?"

Stacy keeps looking at the screen. There is no response. She moves forward reaching toward the color pallet on the screen. Her lips slightly purse forward as if the beginning of a 'b' is waiting to emerge but she sits back and says nothing.

Expressionless.

A second question from Camilla: "You like this—Do you like this color?"

An aqua blue squiggle appears to the left of Stacy's face. Figure 17.4.

Stacy sits back, away from the computer, presses her lips tightly together, turning the corners of her mouth in a slight downward curve, but her eyes are beginning to smile. It appears she is trying not to smile. She momentarily looks in the direction of Camilla and back at the screen, nodding her head "yes" Camilla lets out an, "oooohhh." The squiggle disappears from the screen and this catches Stacy's attention and she immediately reaches to point again, but this time there is an obvious visible articulation of her lips pressing together forming the "pi" combination, as the "i" vowel is elongated into a smile. She bounces back away from the screen and toward the screen again, leaning in so close all that is visible is now a wide-mouthed smile. A pink squiggle appears where the aqua once was. A soft sound comes from Camilla's direction, "Pink. Do you like pink?" she asks Stacy.

Camilla is engaging Stacy in multiple tasks. She starts a conversation and through questioning introduces color vocabulary and voice inflection while building relationship by showing she has an interest in what Stacy likes. At the same time, she is modeling how to use the stylus and the webcam software's draw on screen feature. Rogoff's [35] model speaks of apprenticeship as a metaphor for the relationship between the expert and the novice, guided participation by the expert during hands-on involvement in a shared activity, and the concept of participatory appropriation, referring to how the individual changes through his or her involvement with the activity, which may prepare the individual for later involvement in related activities. More skilled people (experts and more advanced apprentices) assist apprentices in their learning by involvement and communication.

Camilla continues through a series of questions that result in increasingly open responses from Stacy: "What, what is [sic] your other favorite colors?" Stacy no longer shows hesitation responding through pointing, indicating she comprehends the question. This time, her flat affect is gone and her eyes smile so much that her irises nearly disappear. "Oh, purple. Do you like purple also?" Camilla asks from off screen.

Camilla takes note of the progress she is seeing in Stacy and switches activities to try to get Stacy to vocalize rather than just point.

"Can you say your…Do you know your A, B, Cs?"

Stacy nods "yes." [The accuracy of her non-verbal acknowledgement was confirmed by her preschool teacher. Stacy did know the alphabet]. Camilla makes sure she does not ask something of Stacy that she is incapable of doing and once she receives confirmation, she proceeds.

"Can you say-Can you sing your A, B, Cs" [Both faces are out of view for a moment before Stacy leans back in, tilts her head to the right and averts eye contact by looking down]

There is still no verbal response. Camilla tries again, but offers scaffolded assistance:

"Can you sing your A, B, Cs with me?"

There is a smile this time, but still no response. Camilla reassures her,

"It's okay" She pauses for three seconds and says again,

"It's okay. Why don't you try?"

Eight seconds of silence pass. Stacy's face moves back in view, but now she's looking around behind her at the other buddy partnerships. Three more seconds pass. Camilla tries again, decreasing the task,

"Can you sing a little bit to me?"

There is a pause and Stacy moves her hand up to her mouth. She looks over at Camilla and a smile starts spreading across her face as she hears Camilla begins the song on her own, laughing at herself when she gets to "H, I, J, K" and speaks out:

"L, M, . . . N-O?"

Stacy looks down and away from Camilla as Camilla picks up singing, "Q, R, S.."

Stacy looks up and smiles at Camilla. For the first time, Stacy starts mouthing the rest of the words to finish the song with Camilla, in mime. I can see that Camilla rotates the screen housing the webcam because it tilts up to capture Stacy's face better. This shows me Camilla is aware of the importance of capturing Stacy's facial expression as a clue to intention and inner thought. Stacy's smile is very broad with both hands over her mouth, gradually reforming the curve of both hands into semi-circles cupped around her mouth as if she is telling a secret, but her mouth isn't moving from the upward curved position. Camilla finishes with, "Now I know my…"

and Stacy's hands drop, she purses her lips in a smile and looks back at Camilla. Stacy shrugs her shoulders, reaches for the stylus and tries drawing on her own.

It should be understood that "expertise is a relative term; experts are more skilled than novices and have some degree of vision regarding the organization of a skill, but they are not finished developing themselves" ([35], p. 350). The experts make decisions how to divide the activity into smaller subgoals on a scale the apprentice can handle, while also providing helpful advice on how to handle the tools [5] and skills required [35].

Camilla tries another topic revolving around drawing a turtle:

"Do you know what's your favorite animal?"

Still no response, but Stacy points to something on the computer. Camilla says,

"Turtles? Do you like turtles? Can you draw a turtle for me?"

Stacy selects the aqua color. Camilla first squiggled on the screen while asking her favorite color and draws a narrow vertical ellipse filling most of the screen with the top part left unconnected at first, but fills in most of the shape. The image disappears. Stacy reaches back and her voice is audible saying, "color green" with a smile on her face. Camilla asks,

"Can you try to draw a little bit of a turtle?"

Stacy moves in and the concentration and focus in her eyes makes her look very serious as she draws an image that happens to show up in the screen right around her eye, emphasizing the expression without her realizing. She jumps back with a gigantic smile on her face and looks at what she just created. In a very un-clear articulation, says what sounds like "I remumturt-lie" [which, when left to stretches of the imagination, appears to translate: I don't remember what a turtle looks like]. Camilla reassures her again,

"It's okay."

Camilla picks up the stylus and places a dot to look like an eye inside Stacy's organic form and exclaims cheerfully:

"It's a happy turtle!"

Stacy smiles again. Camilla says,

"and then…"

The color red becomes visible on the screen as Camilla transforms Stacy's shape into the head by drawing the shell in red. Stacy's affect looks like she's concentrating, her eyes widen as she sees the image and bursts back into a smile. Camilla:

"There's a turtle!"

[end webcam video].

Camilla and Stacy co-created meaning. The conception of the *zone of proximal development* [40] is extended by Rogoff [35] within the apprenticeship model and is termed *guided participation*. Guided participation "involves subtle communication between people as to what new information is needed or appropriate and how it can be made compatible with current levels of skill and understanding" ([35], p. 351). Children are assisted by their partners to varying degrees, while providing and seeking guidance. This guidance may take on many forms such as "distal arrangements based on practical considerations," "explicit face-to-face interaction," "casual conversation that is not explicitly didactic," and "subtle nonverbal and verbal forms of interaction" ([35], p. 351). When children are involved in active observation or joint skilled decision making through guided participation, they may transfer acquired skills for later individual performance in similar problems: "I see the process as one of appropriation [35] in which through participation, children transform their understanding and skill in solving the problem" ([35], p. 362), rather than simply internalizing information. Participatory appropriation suggests that the expert is not only in the position of the instructor, but also becomes a learner through the process of guided participation. This acquired learning may be used in future applicable learning situations.

Furthermore, Camilla became an English language instructor for Stacy. Enright [9] talked about the distinct types of languages used for everyday interactions compared to the type of language used within classrooms and specialized professions. According to Enright [9], language for everyday interactions called basic interpersonal conversation skills (BICS) developmentally comes before cognitive academic language proficiency (CALP). There needs to be a foundation of "well-developed interpersonal languages (BICS), generally with the help of formal instruction" ([9], p. 83) before CALP can become solid. Camilla was simultaneously helping Stacy develop BICS and CALP skills through conversation and literacy strategies.

Technology helped Camilla facilitate human interaction and English dialog. She began from a relational standpoint in getting to know what Stacy liked, disliked, and her demonstrated level of skill. She got to know how Stacy thought [11]. From there, Camilla encouraged Stacy when she hesitated and provided further scaffolding. When she met resistance, Camilla either increased support, or transitioned to a new activity. Technology allowed a basic, blank canvas for Camilla and Stacy to draw on shared knowledge and co-create meaning. Technology helped provide a space where Camilla could help Stacy develop BICS and CALP skills, as well as motor development through drawing and writing. Camilla helped introduce Stacy to technological tools, and created a documented record of the process. A simple tool of a webcam and on-screen drawing program allowed Camilla the flexibility to create an individualized plan based on Stacy's needs.

Lacina [22], points out that isolated drill and practice is not an effective way to improve academic achievement:

> During the 1980s and 1990s, the focus was on the cognitive and language proficiency needs of ESL students, in which content-based teaching became a widely accepted means of teaching English. Today's instruction emphasizes students constructing meaning with computers, reminding us of the work of Vygotsky and Piaget (p. 113).

In addition, Lacina [22] suggests that as new technologies develop and further research demonstrates effective teaching methods in promoting language acquisition, the field of computer-assisted instruction (CAI) will continue to change. Through this, students are able to construct their own knowledge, as teachers scaffold students' learning. ([22], p.113). Enright [9] mentions broad social approaches to academic literacy that acknowledge a perspective of "multiple literacies," of which academic literacy is only one part "of an individual's repertoire of literacy practices, with critical, personal, or community literacies also informing one's understanding text and of the world" ([9], p. 85). In mentoring with technology, both the mentor and apprentice have the opportunity to develop multiple literacies.

It was a joy to watch the relational bond develop between Camilla and Stacy from their initial meeting, through the dance practices, the high fives, the shared reading, to one of the last webcam videos of the 2009–2010 school year. In that recording, Stacy looked directly at the camera, answered questions immediately, spoke in phrases, and drew a picture all on her own. Then Stacy narrated a short story to go with the picture she drew. In the following dialog from this video, there was a notable difference in the interaction between Camilla and Stacy, as well as Stacy's ability and willingness to communicate verbally with Camilla. Camilla came up with interview questions for Stacy, one of which was the same as her initial question from months earlier. This time, however, Stacy actually articulated her favorite animal:

CAMILLA: What's your favorite animal?
STACY: Aaaa Panda
CAMILLA: You like Pandas?
STACY: Yeah [big smiles this whole time, looking at Camilla as the question is being asked, then directly at the camera for her response. She appears very confident]
CAMILLA: What else? What else? That's it?
STACY: Um. Dragons [bursting into a smile again]
CAMILLA: Ok, you like dragons?
STACY: And I love pony and pig
CAMILLA: You like pig? What does a pig say?
STACY: oin, oin, oin
CAMILLA: Oink, oink, oink, yah! Do you have any animals at home?
STACY: No, but I hab dog
CAMILLA: Oh, you have a dog? What's the dog's name?
STACY: a Mocha
CAMILLA: You're dog's, "Mocha"? Well how old is Mocha?
STACY: A girl
CAMILLA: Well, how old is she?
STACY: [smile fades, looking around, she softly repeats] A girl
CAMILLA: [hesitation sounding like she doesn't know where to go with that response and in a barely audible low tone, Camilla says: "ok." Then with a renewed enthusiasm in her voice, she continues] Who's your favorite princess?

The conversation continued with mermaids and Dora and a drawing on screen. There is evidence in a couple of Stacy's responses to Camilla's questions that there was still a language barrier, but the progress was astounding. Even more astounding was that even as she spoke with such ease to her big buddy, Camilla, Stacy still hardly spoke in class. Watching Camilla's webcam video was the first I ever witnessed either Stacy or Camilla speaking and interacting in that manner within class time. I literally laughed for joy several times–not just for Stacy's progress in verbal and non-verbal expressiveness that I would not have seen in such depth otherwise, but also the persistence and technique Camilla demonstrated throughout the process. I had not seen that level of determination, passion, or persistence in other aspects of Camilla's school work as I did during her interaction with Stacy. For instance, Camilla jumped up and down after running over to me to exclaim how excited she was that Stacy was so excited that the book she picked out was her favorite and Camilla did not even know before she chose it for Stacy on our library field trip. Camilla figured Stacy might like it based on her research data and analysis. Her assertion was accurate. Figure 17.5 is a photo Camilla took of Stacy because she was so excited that her research led her to Stacy's favorite characters without even knowing. Stacy felt such a strong connection with Camilla, she asked Camilla to meet her mom after school. Her mom spoke little English, but could see her daughter was excited.

In a final example for Camilla and Stacy, I will present evidence of Camilla's developing strategies and methods as an instructor and her role in facilitating Stacy's developing English literacy continued through partner reading. This dialog occurred during the literacy project where Camilla selected books for Stacy based on the data she collected learning about Stacy over the year. Camilla brought a selection of books from which Stacy could choose. Camilla captured Stacy's facial expressions on the webcam as Stacy saw the books. Camilla also used the webcam to document which book Stacy reached for first. Camilla hypothesized in advance that this gesture would indicate intentionality and possibly favorite or first-choice book. Camilla and several

Fig. 17.5 Stacy holds the books Camilla selected for her during the library field trip

other students decided to use this method to give their buddy choice and control in the reading process even though they were the ones to select the books at the library for their buddies. After they were in the midst of reading, Camilla said, "I'm going to read some of them and she reads after me." Stacy enthusiastically pointed to the book saying: "I like this! I like this!" Camilla tilted the screen down to capture the images Stacy was pointing toward. They were drawings of ballerinas in fourth position relevé.

STACY: "I like this, and this, and this and this" [pointing to various aspects of the drawing as Camilla tilts the camera back up to Stacy's face]

STACY: [looking at the camera smiling] "I like all of it."

CAMILLA: I will read some. Ok? I will ask you some questions. "My aunt Gena is a ballerina… taking me back stage before the show." Can you find Gena?

I assume Stacy's identification is incorrect because Camilla's voice is first heard saying, "no," then there is a brief pause, followed by, "Yes! Good job."

STACY: [*reading the words in the book*] Some of the dancers are [*After each word she reads, Stacy pauses and looks up to Camilla for reassurance. Another pause Camilla helps her with the word,*] "practicing," [*and Stacy repeats after Camilla.*]

Figure 17.6 shows what literacy buddy sessions can look like. Notice some mentors sit on the floor with their buddies, top left, and there are multiple books, webcams

Fig. 17.6 Mentors guide literacy and record progress with webcams each session

running, and mentors also had mobile devices or digital cameras to record additional data.

Stacy's preschool teacher is seen in the webcam as she came by to check on Stacy's progress and also model a technique for Camilla of reading a few words and letting Stacy fill in a few words. Stacy's preschool teacher concluded her check-in with positive reinforcement by saying, "Good job! High five!" Although the "high five" was originally intended for Stacy, Camilla looked up from tracking the sentences on the page during the modeling, and she held her hand up for a "high five" from the preschool teacher. When Camilla noticed the gaze and hand orientation was directed toward Stacy, Camilla giggled and said, "oh." It showed me that Camilla felt accomplished in the work she was doing with Stacy and realized her efforts were worth acknowledgement also. The preschool teacher saw this and said how both of them were doing a great job, and gave them each a "high five." The preschool teacher continued on to the next pairing and out of view of the camera. Stacy continued reading quickly:

STACY: I do my…[reading next sentence followed by a pause]
CAMILLA: plié
STACY: Plié. What's plié?
CAMILLA: It's like this. When you're bending down. [demonstration visible]
STACY: [smiled] yeah
CAMILLA: Do you wanna try? Yeah. Come over here. Let's try that

They both get up and are part way out of view of the camera. Camilla's hands are on Stacy's arms guiding her in a downward motion. She moves the camera screen to document the vocabulary word as it is defined and enacted through Stacy after she modeled it. Then Camilla said, "Let's try that again. Can you do a plié?" Stacy bends her knees and Camilla says, "Good job!"

Camilla again switches the reading strategy by going back to reading one word and having Stacy repeat after her. When she notices Stacy look up at the camera, she refocused Stacy's gaze to the book by pointing out something she knows will catch Stacy's attention:

CAMILLA: How many ballerinas are there? Count. [Stacy counts while pointing] Good job. [Camilla turns the page] Here, I'll read. [Camilla reads a section of the text modeling fluency and expression]
STACY: [pointing to a picture] Oh those are make up!
CAMILLA: Do you like make up?
STACY: Yeah!

Camilla continues modeling fluent reading of the text with expression.

STACY: [repeating the novel sounding phrase she just heard] Cheeks. Look like a pink apple. [Camilla finishes the sentence: "make-up on my cheeks."]
STACY: Cheeks. Yeaaah. No! Pink apple? No. Apples are red!

Stacy noticed that the author's description of "pink apples" did not match her understanding and meaning she has associated with the color for apples. This is a distinct difference in Stacy's response and reaction from when Camilla asked Stacy the age of her dog, Mocha, and she responds "a girl." When Stacy says, "No. Apples are red!" it indicates a level of English language understanding and reading comprehension through first repeating the novel phrase she heard Camilla read, then by making sense of the text. Reading continues and Camilla asks Stacy if she would like to read. Stacy begins, but quickly becomes stuck. She looks to Camilla for help. Stacy wants Camilla to understand that she can identify some letters in the word, but not the word itself:

STACY: Some letter I know. Some letter I know
CAMILLA: That's okay. I'll help you. [Camilla and Stacy read in chorus]

Schmidt et al. [40], have a wiki with resources to link K-6 literacy learning activity types with ways technology can be used as a tool to support literacy goals. I am using their tables, specifically Tables 2, 5, and 6, to help locate some of the types of literacy learning seen in the evidence I presented above. Although I am not providing the images of the tables, I will refer to them by number for reference purposes. Table 2 identifies "The During-Reading Activity Types." These include reading aloud while the student listens to an oral reading of a book, students asking questions about what they are reading, directed reading/thinking activity (DR-TA), and discussing the text being read. The goal of the during-reading activity types is to "develop readers who check their understanding as they read, integrating their new understanding with existing knowledge" ([40], Table 2). One example of this in Camilla's work with Stacy was demonstrated when she was not familiar with the vocabulary word, plié, she asked what it meant, and Camilla verbally described the action in words, demonstrated the word, and had Stacy enact the movement with her. Another during-reading activity was when Stacy wanted to make sense of "pink apples."

Table 5 identifies "The Comprehension Activity Types." A goal of this type of literacy activity is to ascertain a reader's understanding of a text passage. Camilla utilized something similar to the Cloze Technique where she let Stacy insert words that were omitted as she read a few words, and let Stacy read a few words. The goal is to complete and construct meaning from text.

Table 6 describes "The Fluency Activity Types" where the goal is to improve a reader's speed or rate of reading and ability to read expressively. Modeling is a method where a student listens to a reader whose words are fluent and automatic. Storytelling is another strategy to improve student fluency. A student tells a story or narrative through improvisation or embellishment. Camilla worked through storytelling with Stacy as she drew pictures recorded by the webcam, utilizing the on-screen drawing feature.

Stacy received excellent literacy instruction from her preschool teacher throughout the year. Typically one-half, to three-fourths of this preschool teacher's four-year-old class is reading anywhere between a first- and third-grade level before they reach kindergarten. Many of the students are English language learners and primarily speak a language other than English at home. The excellent literacy instruction was supported by individual instruction and documentation with the help of a sixth-grade teacher-researcher, Camilla [24]. Camilla helped provide Stacy with "a richly responsive interpersonal world" ([33], p. 105) and helped Stacy learn how to communicate better. Pressley says that children who engage with literacy in such environments "are going to be cognitively far ahead of agemates who do not" ([33], p. 105).

Camilla demonstrated both of their learning by creating a 30 min Windows MovieMaker documentary. This chronicled Stacy's progress as an English language learner, her social and emotional development, command of a stylus and emergent writing skills with sounding out words and invented spellings, even noticing the missing "l" in a word that she wrote on the screen to identify an aspect of her illustration. Figure 17.7 is webcam with inking data Camilla collected.

The relationship between Camilla and Stacy grew so that they ran to each other every time one saw the other. Stacy, like most of the other preschoolers, voluntarily requested her parents meet her "big kid." The documentary produced by Camilla included Stacy's digital drawings and paintings, videos, scrolling transcribed story, a message she wrote to Stacy's parents asking if they ever heard Stacy read as a transition into video footage of Stacy reading, a message to Stacy, and rolling credits listing Stacy as the star of the movie, and Camilla as the designer.

In December 7 of the 2010–2011 school year, I asked the mentors to free-write memories of their mentoring experience during the previous, 2009–2011, school year. Here are excerpts from what Camilla wrote about her time with Stacy a year after mentoring her:

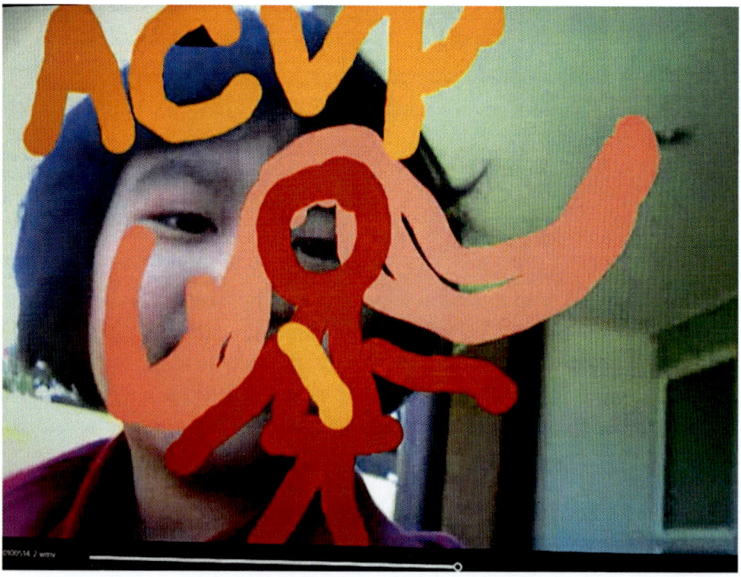

Fig. 17.7 This still image of Camilla's webcam recorded video and inking is clear evidence of progress in speaking, storytelling, inking, writing and spelling by the end of the school year in May

> "My buddy is Stacy. She used to come here to school, now she's gone...I also liked how our pre-K partners first tried on our webcams in our computer; she would laugh when she sees her face distorted on the webcam. Stacy really likes drawing. When I ask her what to play, she would always ask to draw. She likes to draw princesses and doggies; the best thing I like about her that she would tell a background story of her picture. I think she would be a great writer when she grows up...Stacy likes to be tickled, and her laugh is really cute.The one thing that was challenging with Stacy was that when I read with her, she would not listen that much and ask if she can just play...I really miss Stacy! She was a really good partner!"

Camilla truly became an architect of learning, displaying the qualities of a teacher-researcher, a relational bond, and showed evidence of an individual using technology for the public good [12] and influencing a little life. I was able to see skills develop in Camilla that I would not have seen emerge through the other typical learning activities directed just toward her own class and with her peers. Camilla identified progress in Stacy's literacy writing development and asserted that she thinks Stacy "would be a great writer when she grows up." Although some same-age peer interactions show similar dynamics, there is another level of competition or comparison among peers and the dynamic appears to take on a different nuance than in my observations of cross-age mentoring. Jeff is one such example.

17.3.4 The Unexpected: Jeff and Greg

Jeff was also a sixth grade student in Camilla's class, but unlike Camilla, he hardly ever showed non-verbal expression. This may at first be considered a cultural construct. His family is Korean. However, his parents showed concern for anti-social behavior at home, school, outside of school, and how they could not get him to communicate with them. They were concerned that he did not have any friends. They said he would do nothing other than play games on his computer when he got home. His parents were called in for meetings several times during the 2009–2010 school year, along with email and phone communication to discuss academics, lack of engagement, missing assignments and failing grades in most subjects, as well as concern for showing signs of under-cover bullying behavior toward his classmates, both physical and verbal. I described all of the strategies, both behavioral and academic, that I tried with Jeff before calling them requesting any insight they might have. I explained reasons for the strategies I chose and how they had worked with other challenging students in the past, but did not seem to be effective with Jeff. I worked with his parents to try to determine any clues or insight. All of us felt at a loss as to how best we could proceed. I was quite hesitant to pair him as a mentor and knew I would need to watch carefully. I paired him with Greg, a quiet four-year-old. Recall that the initial pairing was for dance instruction and from there branched off into various other mentoring activities, including literacy, as described in this paper.

I do not have data collected by Jeff last year, from his perspective. Even during group projects exploring webcam use with peers in September, Jeff deleted all of the group work files his group decided to store on his computer for presenting the next day, frustrating the other students in the group for lost work. Even though I do not have Jeff's own thoughts, chronicling his mentoring journey from the beginning, I observed changes in him through the mentoring process that I did not expect. The changes rippled out and began to influence the way he viewed himself, and this year, I am seeing glimmers and little sparks that give me hope—despite the failure of all of the other strategies I employed.

Jeff's little buddy, Greg, looked up to him and smiled every time Jeff came into the room. Jeff did not seem to notice until I pointed it out to him. The first time, Jeff did not even look up right away, but then, I saw what appeared to be a double-take as Jeff took notice that Greg was happy to see him. He successfully taught Greg to swing dance the basic steps with a girl and through the mentoring interactions and the progress he saw enacted through his little buddy, I saw Jeff smile for the first time. He showed interest in getting to see Greg again and showed persistence in helping Greg when he was having a hard time with particular movements. Jeff mentioned being proud of his little buddy.

By February, the school engaged in a study of the 2010 Winter Olympics in Vancouver. My class used their computers to research historic similarities and differences from the original Olympics in Greece, as well as research on countries participating in the 2010 Winter Olympics. Each student or pairs of students in my class selected a country to learn about and follow and then became the lead of a team comprised of several children from each grade from Kindergarten through fifth. Jeff spoke with confidence as a group leader, interacted with the younger children, smiled throughout the time. The observable difference was so great that three other teachers of different grades came to me to point him out and ask if I noticed. To anyone else who did not know Jeff prior, it would appear as nothing out of the ordinary. For my colleagues and even more for me, a seemingly small movement like that was an enormous victory.

December 9, 2010, on the same day this year that Camilla reflected on her memories of the experience with Stacy, Jeff wrote as well. I received his typed response via email:

> "Last year, the whole year; my partner's name was Greg. He was always excited when seeing me this year. He calls me a big brother. Greg is very fun to work with; even I would enjoy working with him! Greg was my first partner to ever work with me for the whole year when I came to [this school]. To improve our [w]righting experience for our projects, we use computers. The computers helped us in many stuff. If it's research on our buddies, we record and write that down. For the dance with our little buddies, the recording part was kind of hard. I had to keep switching around almost every time my partner keeps moving around. The difficult part is when it comes to teaching them a simple rock-step. I know their brains did not improve yet but it was pretty difficult. When we read to them, we would see if they can read the words by themselves. My partner Greg is still learning his alphabets. It can get pretty hard when it's teaching. First I read the word then he would repeat the word that I say. Well, it was very fun to work with Greg last year. I hope to work with him again this year!"

The reflective component is an important aspect of teaching, learning, and researching. Mirrors of ourselves in our students sometimes help us see things in ways we did not see them before. Teaching students like Jeff can be frustrating at times when I feel powerless in my efforts to break through and make any observable positive change. I see mirrors of myself in Jeff's words how he felt at times when he worked with his buddy: "I know their brains did not improve yet but it was pretty difficult. It can get pretty hard when it's teaching." And yet, with the smallest glimmer of positive change in my own students brings a renewed enthusiasm and a passion to keep going. Page [28] agrees with Goswami and Stillman's (as cited in Page, 1994) assertion that teachers who research "become reflective, thinking teachers," they "become theorists who find connections with practice," and "the concept of 'I can't wait to get back into the classroom' resurfaces" ([28], p. 53). Jeff said, "I hope to work with him again this year!" I saw that in myself when I wanted to loop with my students and be their teacher for a second year during 2010–2011. I wanted another chance to continue and build on what I started. I think when a teacher researches and learns from her own students, it allows a glimpse into even more possibility than what is seen if she simply expects her students to learn from her.

Mentoring Greg was one thing in school for which Jeff demonstrated enthusiasm and passion that carried over to this current school year. Jeff demonstrated through action that he has the capacity to develop nurturing behavior through training and when given a chance to practice those skills in an environment somewhat removed from his peers, those skills can actually increase. Although Jeff has a long way to go and does not give the appearance of focusing in class most of the time, or being passionate about other academic subjects, he is showing a passion for his newly developing skills in digital art production, periodic high scores on assessments when he studies, and is turning in most of his homework. Jeff has made some friends in his peer group this year, and talks and laughs with them.

Along with specifically working with behaviors, and pointing out the unacceptable bullying behaviors, there have been major strides, as small as they may appear to an outside observer. Jeff's confidence and self-concept increased, especially after returning to the classroom one day last year, only to get called back to the preschool room because Greg said he wanted his parents to meet Jeff. I watched the smile spread across Jeff's face. I watched Jeff smile during the times Greg reached up to take his hand or when Greg leaned in closer to Jeff when they read together. I like to imagine how these experiences could possibly affect the future of my students' relationships.

Mentoring does not fix all problems. Mentoring, when paired with explicit instruction and technology, can provide a vehicle for allowing other skills to be developed and expressed that may not be otherwise observed. These skills go far beyond literacy, scientific inquiry, or dance. In a discussion during the 2010–2011 school year, I asked my students why they thought we were continuing mentoring this year. Jeff raised his hand. I was surprised, first because he does not volunteer to speak in class. Second, Jeff was actually focused on the conversation. Not just any conversation, it was a conversation regarding mentoring. His response to my question of "why mentoring?" was simple. Not even a full sentence, and yet it provided me with a window into which I could view the way Jeff saw the experience. Jeff responded: "Help you improve on your work."

Through this process, the social-relational component of mentoring that I have observed can be a powerful thing. Greg loved Jeff like a big brother and helped break down Jeff's walls separating him from human interaction. I still have not been able to identify the source of Jeff's non-resourceful behaviors, but if a strategy is working to make a difference in his emotional and social health filtering into his behavioral choices, then I find it very worthwhile to continue. On December 9, 2011, Jeff wrote in a reflective response about mentoring a new student this year: "I am going to use a lot of thinking to get this all right. This is really hard to work with a new partner who just came to [this school]." He expressed that he hoped he would have been able to mentor "someone who knew my name and I knew his" and how Greg was a good buddy. The relational connection persisted across the summer when they did not interact or communicate with each other. I replied in email to Jeff on that same day I received his: "Jeff, do you know that I chose you to be Jefferson's partner because I saw that you did a really good job with Greg? You will get to work with Greg again this year after the dance program is over." The following year's dance program was on February 18, 2011. We continued with reading buddies and because of so many requests from both the big kids and last year's little buddies to reconnect.

Jeff used technology before the mentoring experience. He played games for countless hours. Once I introduced the class to digital art, he had been developing his talents in that area with quite impressive results, and his peers commend him for the quality. Prior to introductions of positive uses of technology, he only knew how to be a consumer, primarily through online gaming. The question becomes, how do we as practitioners and researchers, teach students to utilize technology for making a positive difference in their own lives and the lives of someone else—for the public good. What environments can we create to develop human connection and a solid foundation for a love of learning and experience produced knowledge and research produced knowledge? Even if schools do not have the flexibility to implement a mentoring program to this extent, individual teachers can start on a small scale and collaborate with other teachers in their building and start with one project—even if there is little to no access to technology. Again, technology can enhance the process and I have outlined additional benefits of introducing technology, but teaching the core skills can still be done regardless of technology, because the core to all of this is humanity [43, 44].

17.4 Where Next?

Technology is part of society, and it is now requiring us to look at alternate modes of education that will prepare our young people for the different world in which they will live, while holding true to a solid foundational core and utilizing the tools available to them with the purpose of making a positive impact on society. Several students have voiced that this experience will help them know how to teach their own kids someday. A child's family is their first teacher. Although shaping a child's behavioral choices cannot rest squarely on the shoulders of educators, we can work toward creating environments that support and allow children opportunities for knowledge acquired through experience and research. In some cases, schools do have the ability to educate children and young adults about how they should behave online and it can be done in the context of how to behave responsibly and ethically in the real world. Camilla and Stacy's story is not unique within this environment. Boys, like Jeff, even the ones who have difficulties socializing with their peers, have responded positively when they are placed in a mentor position and realize that a younger child is looking up to them as a role model. They speak in words of "pride," "excitement," "time is up already?" When someone feels a relational connection to another person and an increased opinion of self, they tend to more often encourage and uplift than tear down and destroy. There is evidence of social and emotional growth and development.

This study shows what is possible in one classroom. This was a small school and there was flexibility to re-arrange class structure and shift paradigms. Not all schools have that option. Additionally, there are many challenges in planning and training for the integration of a 1:1 program. There is cost involved and time, especially if you do not have someone on site specializing in tech support. There is a major shift in thinking that needs to occur in the parents and teachers who are used to traditional factory model systems. Traditional assessments and grading scales no longer adequately reflect the actual teaching and learning results when implementing this educational approach. Commonly accepted alphabetic and numeric systems based on a 100 point scale no longer make sense for assessing creativity in developing research, the process of solving problems, or ingenuity for identifying and locating tools for a problem with no known solution. I would envision practitioners and educators collaborating on possible ways of assessing leaning and providing multiple ways of assessing. I would also challenge teacher education programs to review their methods for training teachers. What they need to teach teachers is to learn how to set as goals for their students: "Oh! I get it! You teach the big kids, the big kids teach the little kids, and the little kids teach the grown-ups!" I am not advocating for eradicating memorization of core content. On the contrary, I see the necessity for children possessing a knowledge base to provide a foundation for synthesizing, solving, and innovating. Working memory can only hold so much information. But, what I am advocating is a shift in the way we evaluate and assess education.

My hope is to ignite the social imagination and start conversations about what other scenarios may be imagined utilizing a similar foundational concept with touch and inking capable devices. Are there applications for special education, ELL, and world languages with inking and touch devices? What other content combinations may work well? The development of specific programs for training students in digital citizenship? Teaching children digital citizenship needs to begin with humanity in real life before it can be transferred to a screen that hides faces and divides people in the digital realm. These "type[s] of 'deep learning' are more compatible with the needs of the knowledge-based economy and the development of the network society than are conventional models of learning" [38] (p. 266).

The call for educational reform transcends merely being prepared to be globally competitive. It must incorporate educating children who are prepared to reach out and make a positive social change in humanity. This requires skills that include the development of empathy, compassion, creativity and a sense of moral value. Learning should focus on "moral purpose and process of teaching and learning, not only on the structure and the content of education" ([38], p. 284). Learning as a cultural process includes complex aspects of development representing a larger human experience regardless of gender, class status, racial, or ethnic group membership [5]. Effective learning design in the classroom supported by touch and inking technology can enhance these learning goals and may cultivate learning environments that foster the development of social, emotional, and creative thought processes resulting in a love for humanity and for learning how to help someone else succeed and grow. These questions were core of the WIPTTE 2015 high school design challenge to envision the possible for inking and touch as a game in the classroom.

17.5 Additional Resources

This study provided the foundation of further iterations of design based research that was established from grounded theory. In essence, the continuation is partly my response to my own call for future work. The underlying concept in learning design has remained solid across time. However, these concepts have been established and expanded to all grades Pre-K through 10th grade (being 1:1). And because of this study, I have led professional development to train many educators. Here is where we have come since:

An Office Mix (Mixes within the Mix allow the viewer to see device applications in a range of grades by clicking on the image of the Mix on the slide; drawing a blind contour on a blank slide with the rear-facing camera allows the video to be superimposed with the drawing after recording stops to check for accuracy of line, proportion and shape when the still life is set up behind the rear facing camera. This was inspired by Camilla and Stacy. Architects of learning were also inspired by Project Base Learning with Kindergarten [48].

Students designing learning is expanding to not only the ability to envision something much bigger for education where kids lead the teaching [47], but also youth leading the way for a University-level research proposal with Surface Hub for collaboration, human interaction, and inking. And, yes, the big kids teach the little kids and the little kids teach the grown-ups, now, professional development for educators to become teacher-researchers, designing learning with inking and touch devices down to Pre-Kindergarten.

Acknowledgments The author thanks Dr. Juli Lorton for essential feedback through early stages of research.

The support of Amazing Grace Christian School and Renton Preparatory Christian School, allowed the author to simultaneously teach full time and conduct research, implement findings for new iterative designs and study further implementation through design based research. Their flexibility and support have allowed for much research and innovation to be realized in practice across the past 10 years.

Portions of this study have been presented at the Workshop on the Impact of Pen and Touch Technology on Education, Redmond, WA, on April 29, 2015.

References

1. Argrelo M (2005) Mad hot ballroom [Documentary Film]
2. Bigozzi L, Biggeri A, Boschi F, Conti P, Fiorentini C (2002) Children scientists know the reasons why and they are poets too. Non-randomized controlled trial to evaluate the effectiveness of a strategy aimed at improving the learning of scientific concepts. Eur J Psychol Edu 17(4):343–362
3. Butler DL (1998) In search of the architect of learning a commentary on scaffolding as a metaphor for instructional interactions. J Learn Disabil 31(4):374–385
4. Charmaz K (2006) Constructing grounded theory: a practical guide through qualitative analysis. Introducing qualitative methods series. SAGE, London
5. Cole M (1989) Cultural psychology: a once and future discipline? In: Bergman JJ (ed) Nebraska Symposium on Motivation, vol 37, p 279
6. Cotton D, Gresty K (2006) Reflecting on the think-aloud method for evaluating e-learning. Br J Edu Technol 37(1):45–54
7. Counts GS (1978) Dare the school build a new social order?, vol 143. SIU Press, Illinois
8. Cuban L (2003) Why is it so hard to get good schools?. Teachers College Press, New York
9. Enright KA (2011) Language and literacy for a new mainstream. Am Edu Res J 48(1):80–118
10. Erickson F (2006) Definition and analysis of data from videotape: some research procedures and their rationales. In: Handbook of complementary methods in education research, vol 3. Taylor & Francis, Hoboken, pp 177–192
11. Fair C, Vandermaas-Peeler M, Beaudry R, Dew J (2005) I learned how little kids think: third-graders scaffolding of craft activities with preschoolers. Early Child Develop Care 175(3):229–241
12. Feinberg T, Robey N (2009) Cyberbullying. Edu Dig: Essent Read Condens Quick Rev 74(7):26–31
13. Gibbs M (2010) Digital citizenship and the real world. Netw World 27(19):34 www.networkworld.com
14. Glaser B, Strauss A (1967) The discovery of grounded theory: strategies for qualitative research. Aldin pub, Chicago
15. Harris J (2001) Virtual vantage points-using webcams for teleresearch. Learn Lead Technol 28(6):14–17
16. Hew KF, Brush T (2007) Integrating technology into k-12 teaching and learning: current knowledge gaps and recommendations for future research. Edu Technol Res Develop 55(3):223–252
17. Houge TT, Peyton D, Geier C, Petrie B (2007) Adolescent literacy tutoring: face-to-face and via webcam technology. Read Psychol 28(3):283–300
18. International Society for Technology in Education (2002) National educational technology standards for teachers: preparing teachers to use technology. ISTE (International Society for Technology in Education). Accessed 15 Mar 2011
19. Inan FA, Lowther DL (2010) Laptops in the K-12 classrooms: exploring factors impacting instructional use. Comput Edu 55(3):937–944
20. Jacobsen DM, Lock JV (2004) Technology and teacher education for a knowledge era: mentoring for student futures, not our past. J Technol Teach Edu 12(1):75–100
21. Juvonen J, Gross EF (2008) Extending the school grounds?-bullying experiences in cyberspace. J Sch Health 78(9):496–505
22. Lacina J (2004) Technology in the classroom: promoting language acquisitions: technology and English language learners. Child Edu 81(2):113–115
23. Lamont, K.: The relational nature of mentoring gifted children using desktop videoconferencing. Ph.D. thesis, University of Southern Queensland (2004). Unpublished
24. Langhout RD, Thomas E (2010) Imagining participatory action research in collaboration with children: an introduction. Am J Community Psychol 46(1–2):60–66
25. Moran MJ, Tegano DW (2005) Moving toward visual literacy: photography as a language of teacher inquiry. Early Child Res Pract 7(1):1–20

26. Oken-Wright P (2001) Documentation: both mirror and light. Innov Early Edu: Int Reggio Exch 8(4):5–15
27. Oppenheimer T (2003) The flickering mind: the false promise of technology in the classroom, and how learning can be saved. Random House, New York
28. Page, E.: Does real research mean teacher research? Engl J pp. 51–54 (1994)
29. Palincsar AS, Brown AL, Martin SM (1987) Peer interaction in reading comprehension instruction. Edu Psychol 22(3–4):231–253
30. Paris SG, Paris AH (2001) Classroom applications of research on self-regulated learning. Edu Psychol 36(2):89–101
31. Pelling CB (1988) Plutarch on sparta. In: Plutarch: life of Antony. Cambridge University Press, Cambridge, pp 28–35
32. Pitri E (2006) Teacher research in the socioconstructivist art classroom. Art Edu 59(5):40–45
33. Pressley M (2006) Reading instruction that works: the case for balanced teaching, 3rd edn. Guilford Press, New York
34. Robinson K (2010) Challenging education paradigms [Oral Presenattion]. Accessed 9 Mar 2011
35. Rogoff B (1991) Social interaction as apprenticeship in thinking: guided participation in spatial planning
36. Rosenshine B, Meister C (1994) Reciprocal teaching: a review of the research. Rev Edu Res 64(4):479–530
37. Rutledge D, Duran J, Carroll-Miranda J (2007) Three years of the new mexico laptop learning initiative (NMLLI): stumbling toward innovation. AACE J 15(4):339–366
38. Sahlberg P (2006) Education reform for raising economic competitiveness. J Edu Chang 7(4):259–287
39. Sawyer CF, Butler DR, Curtis M (2010) Using webcams to show change and movement in the physical environment. J Geogr 109(6):251–263
40. Schmidt D, Harris J, Hofer M (2011) K-6 literacy learning activity types
41. Soder R (2004) The double bind of civic education assessment and accountability. In: Sirotnik A (ed) Holding accountability accountable: what ought to matter in public education. Teachers College Press, New York, pp 100–105
42. Strauss AL (1987) Codes and coding. In: Qualitative analysis for social scientists. Cambridge University Press, New York, pp 55–81
43. Vygotsky L (1978) Mind in society. Harvard University Press, Cambridge
44. Vygotsky L (1987) Thinking and speech. In: The collected works of LS Vygotsky. Volume 1: problems of general psychology. Plenum, New York, pp 37–285
45. Wertsch J (1987) Mediated action in social space. In: Mind as action. Oxford University Press, New York, pp 109–140
46. Yang JC, Chen CH, Jeng MC (2010) Integrating video-capture virtual reality technology into a physically interactive learning environment for English learning. Comput Edu 55(3):1346–1356
47. Zimmerman M (2015) Microsoft presence. ISTE 2015 [Online presentation]. 28 June– July 1, 2015
48. Zimmerman M (2015) Office mix with students and teachers: once upon a stem classroom [video file]. April 2015

Part V
Research in the Wild: Classroom Perspectives

Chapter 18
Personalizing Student Learning Using the MyEduDecks Application Through Teacher Supervision and Peer-to-Peer Networks

Radhir Kothuri, Samuel Cohen, Nicholas Wilke, and Aileen Owens

Abstract The MyEduDecks application is a pen-based digital flashcards program coded by several students at South Fayette High School over a development period of three years. Here we describe the results of the MyEduDecks platform when used to aid a third-grade Technology Literacy class in the South Fayette Intermediate School. The results show that the MyEduDecks application is well received by students and is an effective teaching tool for elementary instructors. Our results also show that the MyEduDecks application provides the ecosystem for an individualized learning environment.

18.1 Introduction

The MyEduDecks application is designed for pen-based computers to recreate the feel of traditional paper-based flashcards [2]. It includes a game-like mode, which allows students to play flashcards, just as one would while using conventional methods. Furthermore, the interface also incorporates pen recognition features that allow for instant gratification of students work. In addition, teachers are responsible for creating decks consisting of individual cards. Each deck may contain cards covering individual student's focus area needs or an entire range of class material. In order to encompass the diversity of decks, cards are marked based on the content. Figure 18.1 shows children actively learning with the MyEduDecks platform during a beta test. Figure 18.2 shows a number of screenshots from the application. For K-12

R. Kothuri
University of Illinois at Urbana-Champaign, Champaign, IL, USA
e-mail: kothuri2@illinois.edu

S. Cohen (✉) · N. Wilke · A. Owens
South Fayette High School, 3640 Old Oakdale Road, Mcdonald, PA, USA
e-mail: samuel.lawrence.cohen@gmail.com

N. Wilke
e-mail: nick.wilke26@gmail.com

A. Owens
e-mail: amowens@southfayette.org

T. Hammond et al. (eds.), *Revolutionizing Education with Digital Ink*,
Human–Computer Interaction Series, DOI 10.1007/978-3-319-31193-7_18

Fig. 18.1 A student using the MyEduDecks platform during a beta test

education, standards-based learning has become the indicator of each cards specific content area. Our application is poised to have deep standards integration by making it easier for the teacher to identify problem areas for students based on their level and national standards.

In this paper, we offer the effect of this application in a third grade Technology Literacy classroom where students are taught Computational Thinking and Global Citizenship as part of the existing curriculum. Based on the data collected, this study reveals insights into how MyEduDecks application can be used to foster and encourage a personalized learning environment. Specifically, we surmised that improvements to MyEduDecks application, that allow students to create a peer network of flashcard decks that can be shared, will promote and support peer learning networks.

18.2 Problem Statement and Context

Conventional paper-based flashcards have been a staple learning tool for student self-study of classwork concepts for many years, and the advantages of flashcards for reasons such as their accessibility, convenience, simplicity, and so on has encouraged researchers to develop digital interfaces that expand upon their advantages while alleviating their disadvantages such as the lack of dynamic feedback and the burden

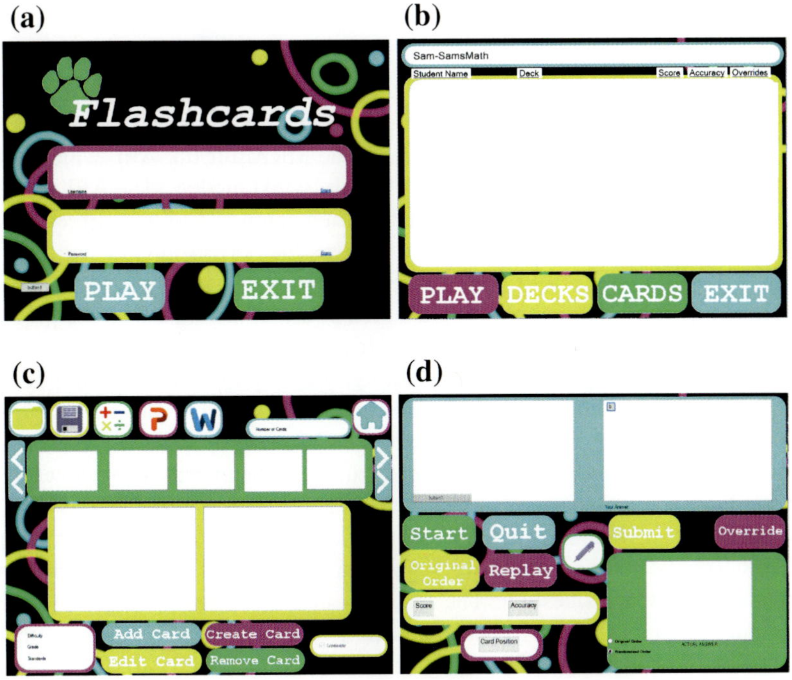

Fig. 18.2 Screenshots of the MyEduDecks platform. **a** MyEduDecks login screen. **b** MyEduDecks menu screen. **c** MyEduDecks create deck screen. **d** MyEduDecks play screen

of transporting them as the amount of self-study content expands (e.g., [1]). Other researchers have taken a different response to flashcards and provide an alternative form of learning interaction to flashcards through writing practice (e.g., [6, 7]), writing review (e.g., [8, 9]), or sketching design (e.g., [10]) instead of reading review of individual concepts. While these two different types of approaches developed ways to either expand upon or provide alternatives to flashcards for improving their functionality, the former approach focus on a specialized domain while the latter takes alternative approaches that do not consider existing advantages inherent with flashcards.

The most current, popular versions of traditional flashcards are retail sets that have the same questions and answers for every consumer. The questions are not tailored to meet the specifications and learning curves for each individual student.[1] As a result, MyEduDecks aims to fix this disparity by personalizing student learning [3–5]. Specifically through a standards-based feature, MyEduDecks can see the areas in which the student is struggling and then notify the instructor accordingly so that he/she can hone in on those specific skills for the particular student. In general, enhancing personalized learning is our main vision for this application.

[1]Ultimate Ink Flashcards. https://apps.microsoft.com/ultimateinkflashcards.

18.3 Methods Employed

MyEduDecks is a pen-based application that allows students and teachers to create decks of cards that have either writing or pre-formatted text as an answer and question. The basis of the application revolves around the Microsoft Ink API, which allows user to draw out their decks, and includes an ink-to-text module. The API interprets the writing into a plain text format, which is then compared to the correct answer. If the answer is not correct, that author receives the correct answer and the card is moved back to the deck to be played again. Teachers can create decks through word documents by following a simple bulleted format included with the program. Decks can also be created by an AutoMath feature, which gives teachers the ability to create random math problems incorporating, addition, subtraction, multiplication, and division. The problems are put together into a deck that can be assigned to students, so that the teacher does not have to spend time writing out simple equations. When a teacher assigns a deck to a group of students, the menu screen shows which students have completed the deck and that student's score on the deck. There is a built-in anti-cheat system as students can override the computer if it did not interpret the text correctly, but the teacher gets a notification of how many times each student used it and on which question. The teacher can use the program to test relative understanding of the topic by checking each individual student's scores compared to those of the entire class. The program has the functionality to allow students to create and share decks among themselves, creating a peer network to aid their learning. All of this functionality comes together allowing teachers to evaluate each student compared to a class, while creating a peer-to-peer network so that students can share and help each other through creating new and unique decks.

The process we used for beta testing the MyEduDecks application was relatively simple, starting with the main focus group of 3rd grade students. We contacted the third grade technology literacy teacher, Mr. Shad Wachter. We explained that we were creating the beta test for MyEduDecks to target specific goals: (1) to evaluate the ability to develop card decks to help teachers differentiate learning by assigning decks to address teaching standards, (2) to investigate the opportunity for students to personalize their learning, (3) to identify benefits and challenges of using MyEduDecks in South Fayettes future 1:1 initiative using the HP Revolve Notebook-to-Tablet PC, (4) to gather information on how students respond to the pen-based modality, and (5) to evaluate the ease of use for teacher development of card decks. We gave Mr. Wachter the program and a tutorial of how exactly to make a good deck of flashcards using the MyEduDecks application. For this test we used the Word feature to turn a document of questions into flashcards, since it is currently the easiest and fastest way to create a deck. Mr. Wachter created three separate decks to address teaching standards used in his classroom. Figure 18.3 shows students actively studying with the digital flashcards. The next iteration of MyEduDecks will include options for selecting standards, so the beta test on Fig. 18.3 was designed to investigate future opportunities. The question deck on Cyberbullying addressed National Educational Technology Standards for Students (NETS), published by the International Society for Technol-

Fig. 18.3 Students studying flashcards in MyEduDecks platform during a beta test

ogy in Education (ISTE). The second question deck, on Computational Thinking concepts, addressed Pennsylvania Common Core Math Standards and NETS. The third deck addressed Pennsylvania Common Core Standards in Math.

After Mr. Wachter created the decks we scheduled the beta test for February 27, 2015. MyEduDecks application was tested on a class of 12 students. The 12 students were divided into three equal groups. While students worked with MyEduDecks our team observed and guided them throughout the process and recorded what we saw and the children's feedbacks during the test. During this process we collected data based on student interviews, observations, and a post survey. After each group of students completed their first experience with MyEduDecks, we rotated students through a short online survey and then to live interviews, to collect their input on the process. The data from the survey is also included within this report. From the three student groups we videotaped two groups of students responding to interview questions as they reflected on their experience. From the data recorded, we have identified issues and are using this information to create an improved application for the future.

18.4 Results and Evaluation

After analyzing the data, it is evident that the use of MyEduDecks supports a personalized learning environment for students. Students were divided into three learning teams, and each team was assigned a separate card deck created by the teacher. After the students completed their assignment using Flashcards, they completed an online survey and then participated in a group interview to offer additional insight about the use of MyEduDecks on their learning. The survey questions that pertain directly to the results of the study are discussed below. *To avoid confusion, please note: This product was formerly known as Flashcards. The name was recently changed to avoid confusion with the traditional flashcard method. The survey questions refer to the product by its earlier name, Flashcards, because that is the name previously introduced to the students.*

Ninety-two percent of students said that they enjoyed using the MyEduDecks application and completing the assignment that the teacher created for them, see Fig. 18.4. Despite the occasional bugs in the program, and the difficulties some students had using the pen, they almost unanimously liked using MyEduDecks. Several students stated that MyEduDecks would make it easier for them to learn new words. Another student declared that he would use MyEduDecks to work on topics that he had trouble with until he understood them.

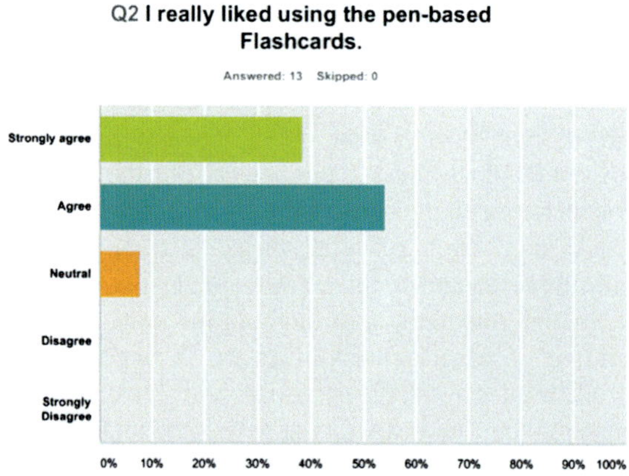

Answer Choices	Responses	
Strongly agree	38.46%	5
Agree	53.85%	7
Neutral	7.69%	1
Disagree	0.00%	0
Strongly Disagree	0.00%	0
Total		13

Fig. 18.4 Survey results for question 2

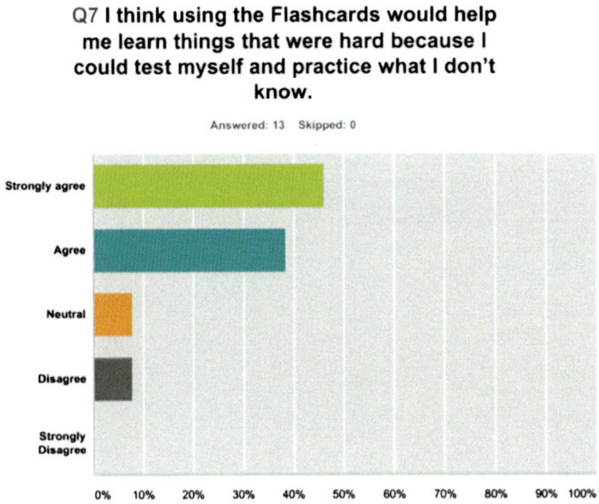

Answer Choices	Responses	
Strongly agree	46.15%	6
Agree	38.46%	5
Neutral	7.69%	1
Disagree	7.69%	1
Strongly Disagree	0.00%	0
Total		13

Fig. 18.5 Survey results for question 7

The vision for MyEduDecks is that students will be able to make their own decks, and practice the decks created by their teacher, as many times as necessary for students to fully understand the concept. It personalizes the education of every student to fit individualized needs. According to student surveys, 85 % believe that using MyEduDecks will help students learn, see Fig. 18.5.

The pen tablet aspect is an important part of MyEduDecks. In post interviews, multiple students stated that they preferred to use the pen over a keyboard, since it is faster and easier than typing. The data collected through the survey indicated that 85 % of the students liked writing with the pen on the tablet, see Fig. 18.6. Typing is unnatural for most young children, almost as strange as learning a new language. To be fast at typing, one must have large enough hands and good fine motor skills to hit the small keys, and most young children lack these two qualities. A pen, however, is natural to children, as they first learn to create words by writing the letters with a writing utensil. It allows students to complete the same assignment in much less time than if they were to type.

As seen in Fig. 18.7 and Table 18.1, 69 % of students stated that they would use the program to further their personal learning, and the remaining 31 % remained neutral on the topic. In the interview that was conducted after the beta test, several students declared that they would use the program to advance their learning. Others thought

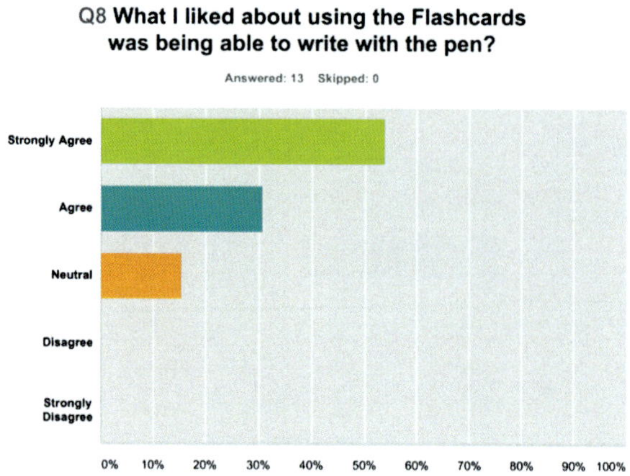

Answer Choices	Responses	
Strongly Agree	53.85%	7
Agree	30.77%	4
Neutral	15.38%	2
Disagree	0.00%	0
Strongly Disagree	0.00%	0
Total		13

Fig. 18.6 Survey results for question 8

MyEduDecks would be more effective in helping to learn information than using already prepared paper flashcards from a store, since the purchased flashcards would not be as tailored to their needs as the electronic variety.

In addition to students enjoying using the program, Mr. Wachter, the teacher who participated in the beta test, spoke highly of the program in an interview after the test. He explained that teachers would want to use the program, since students enjoy it and it could prove to be an effective teaching tool. Also, Mr. Wachter was impressed with how easy it was to create cards with the Microsoft Word function. He also believed that teachers would be more willing to use the program with the Word function, for several reasons. Most importantly, teachers already have their assessments, lectures, and handouts created as Word documents. It is a simple process to copy from their existing documents into the MyEduDecks format. In addition, this new iteration of MyEduDecks has created a timesaving method by allowing the Microsoft Word function to exist. In the first iteration teachers had to write directly onto the screen to create dozens of individual flashcards per deck. The first iteration presented a learning curve for the teachers, since they were not highly skilled at using the pen-based modality on a tablet. Microsoft Word is a familiar program that most teachers use already for their lesson plans.

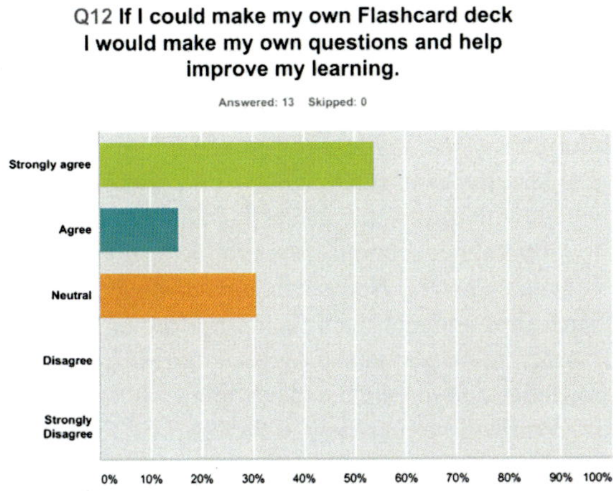

Answer Choices	Responses	
Strongly agree	53.85%	7
Agree	15.38%	2
Neutral	30.77%	4
Disagree	0.00%	0
Strongly Disagree	0.00%	0
Total		13

Fig. 18.7 Survey results for question 12

Table 18.1 Illustration depicting partial survey summary results for all 12 student participants

	I really liked using the pen-based flashcards (%)	I think using the flashcards would help me learn things that were hard because I could test myself and practice what I don't know (%)	What I liked about using the flashcards was being able to write with the pen (%)	If I could make my own flashcard deck I would make my own questions and help improve my learning (%)
Strongly agree	38.46	46.15	53.85	53.85
Agree	53.85	38.46	30.77	15.38
Neutral	7.69	7.69	15.38	30.77
Disagree	0	7.69	0	0
Strongly disagree	0	0	0	0

18.5 Future Work

For future iterations and deployment, we will be recoding the application entirely, incorporating information and suggestions gathered by the previous beta test. The previous version of MyEduDecks referenced in this publication is comprised of three years of development with three separate development teams. Since this project was initially meant to be purely educational, the product is not correctly formatted, and includes many redundant errors. Newer versions of the MyEduDecks program are coded with a fourth development team including former team members currently engaged in their undergraduate studies and new students from the high school. With the advanced knowledge and foresight to developing a full project, a much improved version of the program will be presented at the 2016 CPTTE conference if all goes according plan. As for future research the South Fayette School District has implemented a one-to-one policy, with all of the laptops having touchscreens. The available pool of beta testers has increased from one class to over four hundred students. Such a large increase in the reach of the program will provide us with significantly better data than previous tests.

As for actual major changes to the program, the new version will improve upon the Automath and Word functionality, add the capability to save pictures onto cards, close the separation of cards and decks, and complete reconstruction of the User Interface and Graphical elements.

Acknowledgments The production of this application was not possible without the acknowledgement of several key individuals. Particularly, Dr. Ananda Gunawardena, Associate Professor of Computer Science at Carnegie Mellon University, and Mr. Shad Wachter, Technology Literacy Teacher Grades 3-5, South Fayette School District, were pivotal in aiding us. The expertise and guidance that Dr. Gunawardena provided was very much appreciated by the group. His knowledge and expertise allowed us to go beyond the existing curriculum offered at South Fayette and through his mentorship, we were able to keep the project on task. While Dr. Gunawardena aided us in the technical aspects of the development process, Mr. Wachter was instrumental in helping retain the educational component, particularly with the standards-based education information. We are also very thankful to Superintendent Dr. Bille Rondinelli, the South Fayette Board of Education, and the South Fayette Foundation for Excellence, for providing necessary resources and their enthusiastic support for this project over the last two years. We are also grateful for the teachers and administration of South Fayette Township Elementary School for being actively involved in beta testing the MyEduDecks application. We appreciate the time they invested to help us with this project.

References

1. Chien ME, Jheng CM, Lin NM, Tang HH, Taele P, Tseng WS, Chen MY (2015) iCAN: a tablet-based pedagogical system for improving communication skills of children with autism. Int J Hum-Comput Stud 73(1):79–90
2. Jeong Y, Gunawardena A, Koedinger KR (2010) Designing a pen-based flashcard application to support classroom learning environment. In: CHI '10 extended abstracts on human factors in computing systems, CHI EA '10. ACM, New York, pp 4695–4698

3. Li JT, Fan YN (2015) Using iPad to make e-flashcards and sharing the e-cards through doceri. In: Hammond T, Valentine S, Adler A, Payton M (eds) The impact of pen and touch technology on education. Springer International Publishing, Switzerland, pp 249–257
4. Raymond D, Liew J, Hammond TA (2015) A vision for education: transforming how formal systems are taught within mass lectures by using pen technology to create a personalized learning environment. In: Hammond T, Valentine S, Adler A, Payton M (eds) The impact of pen and touch technology on education. Springer International Publishing, Switzerland, pp 355–363
5. Solberg VS, Phelps LA, Haakenson KA, Durham JF, Timmons J (2012) The nature and use of individualized learning plans as a promising career intervention strategy. J Career Dev 39(6):500–514
6. Taele P, Hammond T (2015) Enhancing instruction of written east asian languages with sketch recognition-based "intelligent language workbook" interfaces. In: Hammond T, Valentine S, Adler A, Payton M (eds) The impact of pen and touch technology on education. Springer International Publishing, Switzerland, pp 119–126
7. Taele P, Hammond T (2016) An intelligent sketch-based educational interface for learning complex written east asian. In: Hammond T, Valentine S, Adler A (eds) Revolutionizing education with digital ink: the impact of pen and touch technology on education. Springer International Publishing, Switzerland
8. Taele P, Barreto L, Hammond T (2016) Maestoso: an intelligent educational sketching tool for learning music theory. In: Hammond T, Valentine S, Adler A (eds) Revolutionizing education with digital ink: the impact of pen and touch technology on education. Springer International Publishing, Switzerland
9. Valentine S, Lara-Garduno R, Linsey J, Hammond T (2015) Mechanix: a sketch based tutoring system that automatically corrects hand-sketched statics homework. In: Hammond T, Valentine S, Adler A, Payton M (eds) The impact of pen and touch technology on education. Springer International Publishing, Switzerland
10. Wetzel J, Forbus K (2015) Increasing student confidence in engineering sketching via a software coach. In: Hammond T, Valentine S, Adler A, Payton M (eds) The impact of pen and touch technology on education. Springer International Publishing, Switzerland

Chapter 19
Inking Pedagogy

Dale Pokorski, David Okoth, Vaishali Nandy, Julaine Fowlin, Catherine Amelink, and Glenda Scales

Abstract Technology-enhanced instructional delivery is increasingly becoming the norm in the delivery of the engineering curriculum. Electronic inking is one such technology that has proven to afford enhanced learning experiences such as supporting note taking and sharing, including real-time distributed conversation. However, despite its proven benefits including other classroom technologies, several institutions still struggle with university-wide implementation or department-wide adoption. We review the key developments that some signature engineering schools have undertaken to foster the use of inking technology in the last two decades. We also examine the different aspects of inking as a classroom tool that makes learning in the 21st Century more enriching. While there are a plethora of studies that highlight computer use or other novel technologies in education, we demonstrate a couple of success stories and best practices for implementing inking technology in science and engineering disciplines. Findings from the review indicate that effective integration of inking pedagogies in delivering instruction spurs higher student engagement with content which in turn contributes to better learning outcomes/gains.

D. Pokorski · C. Amelink · G. Scales
College of Engineering, Virginia Tech, Blacksburg, VA, USA
e-mail: dpokorsk@vt.edu

C. Amelink
e-mail: amelink@vt.edu

G. Scales
e-mail: gscales@vt.edu

D. Okoth (✉) · V. Nandy · J. Fowlin
Learning Sciences and Technologies, Virginia Tech, Blacksburg, VA, USA
e-mail: okoth@vt.edu

V. Nandy
e-mail: vnandy@vt.edu

J. Fowlin
e-mail: jfowlin@vt.edu

T. Hammond et al. (eds.), *Revolutionizing Education with Digital Ink*,
Human–Computer Interaction Series, DOI 10.1007/978-3-319-31193-7_19

19.1 Introduction

Learning in the classrooms has not seen a significant revolution since the introduction of textbooks. Today, the millennial generation pride themselves in a vast array of technology including smartphones, tablets, gamification, 3D printing, and consistently working internet, among others. But engineering educators are yet to tap into the mainstream that drives the passions of the millennial, especially with regards to instructional technology.

Electronic inking, whether on tablets or smartboards, is one area of instructional technology yet to be fully utilized in the engineering curriculum [22, 34]. If we look at today's change in the delivery of the engineering curriculum and the role of technology in it, the growth is significant. The pervasiveness of technology in society and its role in economic development is becoming harder and harder to ignore [28, 29]. Electronic inking is fast becoming a norm in today's technology-enhanced classrooms, almost surpassing the chalkboard in terms of presenting dynamic and complex pedagogical content [12]. According to Maclaren, Singamemni and Wilson [21], integrating pen-enabled technology in teaching engineering classrooms is facilitating a rapid transformation of how content is delivered. Technology-enhanced teaching and learning research unceasingly point to the need for more interactivity and student engagement. Classrooms and laboratories all across the nation have been witnessing the need for additional tools that support exploration, discovery, collaboration, and invention [7, 10]. Shulman [29] adds that digital and online technologies present an opportunity to re-examine the fundamentals of traditional pedagogy.

While there are a plethora of studies that highlight computer use or other novel technologies in education [28], we will particularly emphasize a couple of success stories and best practices for implementing inking technology in engineering courses. The general prediction from several research groups point to a continued use of innovative technology to improve teaching and learning; for example, the Gilfus Education Group[1] predicts a surge in tablet use as a means of implementing content delivery.

We present a case for technology in engineering, together with case study findings from Virginia Tech, Georgia Tech, and University of Southern California, which are among the signature engineering schools that have rigorously researched the implications of inducting inking technology as a teaching tool in their engineering curriculum. We trace the development of inking technology and cite the findings of the selected case studies. Finally, we cross-referenced such literature with other scholarly views on the role of technology, especially the instructional affordances inking presents in the learning process.

The outlook of inking technology in engineering has been laid bare in order to predict the most probable trend taking shape in similar degree granting programs across most engineering schools and colleges. The positive effects these trends pose are discussed in the concluding section of this review.

---

[1]Gilfus Educational Group, Education strategy, research and implementation; http://www.gilfuseducationgroup.com/.

19.2 Theoretical Framework

The researchers applied a dialectical perspective as a theoretical framework in analyzing the content data.

Noting that issues and perspectives are mutually defining, the studies cited herein have been taken to presuppose the existence of particular ideas, theories or biases to the extent of their systematic analyses [3]. This manuscript serves as a literature review summarizing the results of several studies while discussing their possible implications as explanations to the phenomenon under study [4].

19.3 Method

The study investigates the phenomenon in a qualitative approach, which is a post-positivist naturalistic method of inquiry [6].

Through content analysis technique, thorough evaluation and discussion of the text and context allowed for conclusions to be drawn about the characteristics of the phenomena. Conclusions were based on the presence or absence of their ideation, researchers' knowledge, and published evidence. Using the inductive method, key themes are identified and discussed as evidence of effective implementation of inking pedagogy. The emergent reconstruction and analysis of the texts provides new insights of the problem under discussion [18].

19.4 Making the Case for Instructional Technology in Engineering

In a fast-paced world where technology is defining almost every aspect of life, many colleges worldwide have also turned to technology as tools to deliver their instruction.

This is because learners will soon apply to universities and online learning centers "expecting a transformative form of education" [29]. Today's learners have access to so many technology-enhanced media that they tend to prefer flexibility in their learning. Although flurries of technological discovery continually float around us, the challenge is to harness their potential with the right tools, strategies, and practices.

Factoring particular technology properties and gearing them to the learning objectives is one critical and tough approach. Melding the social and psychological dimension of new devices into traditional lecture/learning modes is another approach. But, the caveat has always remained that for technology to enhance learning, there needs to be a balance between instructional strategies, the technology, and the learning goals as opposed to settling for trade-offs for one, two or none at all [15].

At the turn of the millenium, mobile learning became a phenomenon that was sure to transform education. Many institutions of higher learning quickly embraced the development of the Information and Communication Technology (ICT) infrastructure to support interactive learning content, multimedia learning resources, and collaborative learning [19]. An example of such technology integration was elaborated by Iding and Crosby [14], who conducted a study to gauge the impact of the affordances technology tools would have on online education in Hawaii and the Pacific Islands. The two researchers found that computer-based resources and ICT instruction enriched or facilitated the learning experience among the studied population. They also showed that technology could be universally used to communicate to multiple audiences with variant cultures and socio-economic status (SES) as well as "improve access to higher education" [14]. In another study, Zammit [33] noted that a society with complex technology basically shifts the traditional definitions of literacy. In the 21st Century economy, literacy will not only mean an ability to read, write and do basic arithmetic. The new literacy basics will have to include an ability to read, write code, as well as utilize a programing language or two. Zammit carried out a case study research on how three teachers utilized technology to engage students in learning instructional content. He noted how one science teacher used a whiteboard as a projection screen to enable two planes for concurrent virtual display and actual use for manipulating course content. The study found that using technology in the classroom engages students in "thinking, feeling and acting at higher levels" as well as "providing positive messages about their knowledge, ability to think, share and exchange" ideas [33]. Information technology and its applications is fast becoming the currency in the 21st century education economy, or so it is perceived. A study by Lam and Tong [20] on digital devices in the classroom could not come up with a conclusive list of pros or cons for technology in the classroom; however, they recognized that there was a hesitation on the teacher's part to integrate technology in their instructional deliverables. While comparing guided use of technology versus free use of the same, Lam and Tong found that the devices were capable of facilitating engagement and interactivity between teacher-student, student-student, and student-content, making learning rich and active. The researchers also noted that the distraction caused by the technology was equally potent concluding the issue as complicated and "controversial" [20].

19.4.1 Inking Pedagogies

Unprecedented infiltration of technology in the education sector calls for an accreditation of new teaching methodologies. When the textbook was introduced in classroom pedagogy, it was a novel idea.

Inking and note taking is a big selling point for Tablet PCs and the DyKnow related software, but they seem not to be the only educational affordances that drive innovation or the use of technology in the classrooms. DyKnow is an interactive classroom presentation software. The progression of inking in the classroom discourse is now being researched proactively. Although the technology has been around since the *early 60s* [32], it has become more ubiquitous especially in digital devices that today sell touch-computing and pen/stylus as novel features.

In examining the competition; traditional paper has been in use for over 2,000 years because it is still cheap, light, portable, foldable, and content can be read from a wide range of angles. Paper, in an economy agitating conservancy, has its limits. When the world switched to the digital era; electronic paper promised a limitless landscape. This feature was well demonstrated by Ivan Sutherland's classic Sketchpad system [31].

As technology turns to touch-computing, the stylus (though not marketed well among the Tablet PC manufacturers) is becoming a preferred input device compared to the keyboard, mouse or joystick. The stylus allows its users to directly draw, write or move objects in unlimited multi-dimensional ePlanes or ePaper, thus allowing pen-based technologies to become the best choice for engineers. Inking has an effect of immersing students into a virtual learning environment [1, 12] with unlimited resources to work out solution or possibly branch out new discoveries. In the science and engineering disciplines, any good strategies that will create a flipped classroom effect is highly desirable because it allows more time to solve complex problems collaboratively and the learning environment becomes better suited for students to engage in innovative thinking skills, praxis, among other learning outcomes. Such flipped or inverted classroom strategies [11, 22] inspire new thinking in instructional delivery that in turn transforms the students' expectation of their own learning. Inking technology's biggest advantage is the extensible graphical and symbolic presentations that allow users to guide learning in any direction whilst allowing the adjustment of the lecture pace, tone, or complexity depending on everyone's reaction [13]. By way of education generally moving from the lecture approach—where students were expected to be passive listeners and active 'transcriber' of all the 'lecturer' said in class—the inking capability enables students to contribute to the knowledge by appending additional thoughts to their PowerPoint presentation, DyKnow notations, or shared PDF document [11]. Such a strategy also creates more time for critical thinking and better engagement with presented content [22, 27].

Unprecedented infiltration of technology in the education sector calls for an accreditation of new teaching methodologies. When the textbook was introduced in classroom pedagogy, it was a novel idea. Only the instructor had access to it and therefore the lecture system was born. Lecturing enabled students to capture the dictated content from the instructors so that they could have the learning material for their review after class. Since then, instructors have habitually lectured even in an age where students already have electronic access to the course content. Inking technology goes further to allow instructors and students to freely annotate, transform, or reformulate existing course content to better fit the current social times in terms of solving 21st Century problems. Engineering schools need to carefully align the technologies with new learning objectives, learning outcomes as well as assessment methods. Such benchmarking tasks lie with Accreditation Board for Engineering and Technology (ABET), which is recognized by the Council for Higher Education Accreditation. ABET is the body charged with providing engineering guidelines to educators and stakeholders. The body has indeed noted the potentials of technology and what it can accomplish in the broader spectrum of engineering programs, but the technology affordances must first be perceived by instructors as beneficial before they can be effectively integrated [30]. From the discussion above, it is clear that inking technology used effectively as a classroom tool presents various opportunities for active learning and transformative educational practices that meet desirable 21st century outcomes. We will now move on to give an overview of several Tablet PC research studies done at the selected institutions.

19.4.1.1 The Tablet PC Case Study in Virginia Tech

Over the years, Virginia Tech has been known to be a frontrunner in terms of embracing learning innovations and inventing new technologies, especially the ones that enhance teaching and learning [1].

The Tablet PC initiative was started at Virginia Tech in 2006 and currently Virginia Tech College of Engineering (COE) requires that all incoming freshmen have a Tablet PC that meets predetermined requirements. COE also offers technical software support services along with specialized faculty training in various classroom technologies and software. There are now various projects and longitudinal studies being done to gauge the importance and effects of these initiatives.

> Rather than institute a blanket ban for pervasive technology in classrooms, it would do most tech savvy instructors good to incorporate structured computer use to elicit best practices [23].

In one of the studies, Mohammadi-Aragh and Williams [23] investigated the effect of structured computer use in classrooms and reported on their observed experiences. Using the action research methodology, the two researchers set to find out the effect of the Tablet PC on instructional strategies for structured computer use in classrooms. The researchers then documented the instructors' experiences and student perceptions in one of Virginia Tech's engineering courses. The research found that there are best practices that can be nurtured to realize the full potential of classroom technologies. Among the best practice examples were; collecting student generated content and classroom polling questions, which positively contributed to higher student engagement.

A number of other studies have also looked into the pedagogical approaches that have been used in tandem with the technologies. In a study by Amelink, Scales, and Tront [1], a positive impact on student learning behavior was noted where inking pedagogy was incorporated in classroom technology. In total, 560 respondents from first- to senior-year undergraduate students answered various questions about their experiences while using Tablet PCs during class sessions and outside the course schema. When the study was conducted, Virginia Tech College of Engineering (COE) was four years into the process of using mandatory Tablet PC requirement for all freshmen. COE had also ensured that supporting software and network infrastructure allowed students to participate in class activities and presentations. Through this study, the three researchers found that overall; there was statistical significance and a positive relationship when student use of the Tablet PC was correlated with their learning behavior. The study also revealed that peer collaboration, metacognitive self-regulation, organization, and critical thinking were among the learning behaviors that were enhanced through exposure to inking technology in instruction.

19.4.1.2 The Tablet in Georgia Tech

At Georgia Tech, there was a study conducted with the Tablet PC to evaluate students' attitudes about technology in pedagogy.

Prior to introducing Tablet PCs in research initiatives between 2006 and 2008, Georgia Tech had already been experimenting with other digital inking and presentation tools such as the Elmo, SmartBoards, Classtalk, ClassinHand and WIL/MA which are technologies geared to improve student learning [25]. Thus, the Tablet PC initiative was just another tool that may be used to develop novel educational pedagogy.

Moore and Hayes [24] exposed Georgia Tech instructors and students to classroom technology to investigate whether the Tablet PC and the DyKnow software would foster active learning or greatly improve instructor-to-student or peer-to-peer interactions. The researchers also intended to gather useful insight that could be used to improve distributed learning in synchronous and asynchronous environments. While admitting that it is a challenge to evaluate the impact of classroom technology on students in general, the researchers factored in wild card effects of novelty and differences between groups to get a fair assessment from the respondents. The results indicated that interaction in class improved with the use of the technology whereby instructors made heavy use of the inking technology especially in assessing student submitted panels which they found to be an "essential feature" [25]. The students' assessment of the Tablet PCs averaged 'Very Good' and 'Excellent' especially citing how the DyKnow software enabled them to scroll back previous slides and interact/annotate the presentation as well as play-it-back after class [25].

It is noteworthy that there was overall agreement that students engaged in active learning despite the frequency for note taking during class dropping from 5.41 pre-survey, to 3.76 mid-survey, and 3.70 post-survey. The researchers also found that students preferred digital inking to solving classroom exercises and performing other input operations on their Tablet PCs. The feature seemed to have solved an earlier challenge in the basic management of other classroom assessment activities such as in-class polling, interactive snap quizzes and exams [25].

19.4.1.3 Use of Inking Technology in California State University

Inking in education has all the features traditional paper has and one poignant advantage: interactivity. It is this feature that researchers at California State University investigated.

Price and Simon [26] investigated how three physics instructors integrated digital inking in their lectures. The researchers looked at how the instructors organized their materials, and the ways in which they inked and interacted during a typical classroom activity. They evaluated the final forms of the slides that were later posted on the web for student references and drew conclusions from post-hoc discussions with the instructors on their classroom activity sessions. The research picked up general educational affordances that inking provided the students, among them: spontaneous augmentation of prepared material, guided attention, natural pacing, and finally electronic archiving.

In this California State University study, it is clear that inking technology appraised the manner in which classroom activity flowed with the technology and at times augmenting active learning. The instructors in this study integrated the traditional contents of their introductory physics lectures with technology to effectively deliver instruction. Yet the pedagogical rationale remains to be drawn for the usage of such technology in advanced engineering classes. Pedagogical traditionalists are still determinedly using their tried-and-tested methodologies while innovators cannot seem to push through the perceived benefits of re-engineered classroom technology. The fundamental issue therefore boils down to pre-existing conditions, instructional activities, and program goals to capture the transformational aspect of technology in education [20, 21].

However, questions have been posed as to the real nature of the problem. According to Moore and Hayes [24], among the issues still sticking out include:

- Poor delivery of lecture
- Need for instructors to unlearn traditional teaching methods
- Lack of adequate technology infrastructure and support
- Technology-instructor-student needs mismatch
- Lack of time and incentives for student and instructor innovators …

From the schools examined, though their contexts varied, all the studies indicate that the effectiveness of how the instructors used the inking technology depends more on how they deployed the technology affordance in accordance with their pedagogy. Student learning has been noted to have improved or become more active with a promise of better learning of complex science and engineering content using alternative or innovative teaching methods.

19.4.2 *Examples of New Pedagogies Using Inking Technologies*

Polling features, level of student understanding status query, or group activities are some of the added strategies instructors can use to quickly conduct a formative assessment of student knowledge of the content.

19.4.2.1 Northern Arizona University

Because of inking technology's instantaneous multi-directional input capabilities (i.e., from both teachers and students); classroom activities and instruction can be designed in such a manner that allows for collaborative effort on learning.

Co-creation of knowledge is an emergent format in pedagogy especially with the constructivist school of thought. Inking technology allows for both instructors and students to create knowledge and drive learning content as they experience it. In this new school of thought, the traditional role of teacher-student interaction is flipped to include enhanced student-student, teacher-student, and student-content interaction whereby even the students can initiate and direct their learning independent of classroom expectation using all manner of technology tools [11, 20]. Because of inking technology's instantaneous multi-directional input capabilities (i.e., from both teachers and students); classroom activities and instruction can be designed in such a manner that allows for collaborative effort on learning. Using modules created with Tablet PCs and Camtasia Studio—which is a screen capture and recording software, Frolik et al. [11] conducted a study and assessed a hybrid, online/in-class course developed at multiple universities. The study was carried out in Northern Arizona University and University of Vermont where wikis were utilized in the flipped classroom format. The researchers set to find out how students would gauge the quality of the learning content, its delivery, and their engagement levels. Wikis, for example, had been built into the modules and implemented in the flipped classroom to also allow students capture their ideas on the go. The study found that student engagement improved because they had more time to interact with the content, while the instructors appreciated the wiki flexibility which allowed for the generated content to support, supplement, or provide new viewpoints to the core course material [11].

Inking-capable classroom technologies such as DyKnow, Centra, eLectureTools, and Classroom Presenter have been transforming how instruction is delivered with very positive results in terms of active engagement while fostering meaningful learning [9, 22]. They are best placed to allow instructors deliver content dynamically without the common rigid and time-bound traditional lectures that limit adequate inquest of complex content. Pre-canned formula derivatives, or complex diagrams, can be presented with these eLecture tools while affording the instructors with an ability to annotate additional information. The dynamic nature of such flipped lectures also allows for appropriate assessment and active learning activities to be embedded in their design. Polling features, level of student understanding status query, or group activities are some of the added strategies instructors can use to quickly conduct a formative assessment of student knowledge of the content. Misconceptions and existing knowledge gaps can be identified and dealt with in real time. While discussing digital lofts as a means of gaining formative feedback in learning environments, Easterday et al. [9], contend that by developing scalable, efficient, and innovative design-based learning, today's technologies can transform the learning process. Such authentic assessments also enable meaningful instructions and reflections that enrich the learning experience.

19.4.2.2 University of North Carolina Case Study

Dr. Russell Mumper from the University of North Carolina flipped a first year course by offloading his lectures to online self-paced videos using Lecture Capture—a component tool developed by echo360.

He then dedicated the rest of the class meetings for active engagement exercises using one of the inking-capable classroom technologies; the eLectureTools—also packaged with echo360. The prevailing argument was that such colossal course remodeling was informed by the "desire to transform the educational experiences" of his students [22]. The result was that the students were fully engaged throughout their learning experience and were afforded sufficient time to activate higher-order thinking skills in their problem solving activities. Effective implementation enabled learning to occur as we see knowledge being co-constructed by the students when they engage in solving problems through their own experiences with the teacher, the content, and the technology [8]. Research has continuously suggested that design-based, autonomous or semi-autonomous instructional experiences create better opportunities for self-directed learning and innovation [16]. Re-inventing the class exercises and activities while tailoring the course content to accommodate inking, among other technologies, is a brave way to break old lecture habits such as the use of the chalkboard or stoical hour-long PowerPoint presentations.

19.4.3 Innovating a Way Forward

In addition to trying out innovative pedagogies, assessment and evaluation methods need to change for effective implementation of inking technology.

> Zhao et al. [34] directly ask: why don't teachers innovate when they are given computers? There are numerous factors that have been listed to answer this question; from technology incompatibility, to traditionalist versus progressive wars, to disruptiveness and unreliability of technology, or mismatched instructional goals with institutional policies, and so forth [21].

The reality in most colleges and universities is that technology is slowly creeping into the classrooms [2, 17]. From the cases reviewed, it is apparent that inking pedagogy can enhance and add value to the delivery of the engineering curriculum, more so, when both instructors and students take great advantage of the multi-directional content transaction. In the cases examined, the successful implementation of inking was due to system wide cultural changes. For example in the case of Virginia Tech, there was a mandatory Tablet PC requirement with support services.

While investigating the role organizational culture and usability have on instructional technology acceptance, Kothaneth [17] found that the general barriers such as technological complexity, lack of time among other resources, and lack of perceived values have been cited in numerous studies over an extended period of time. Key among Kothaneth's recommendations was to encourage faculty to align their teaching methods with the institutions long term planning processes, redesign training modules in professional development, and provide ample incentives that would encourage technology experimentation in the classroom.

Other initiatives should also be considered which may mitigate perceived barriers to using technology, or increase the early adopter quota and drive ubiquitous technology use in education [1, 12, 17]. Rather than institute a blanket ban for pervasive technology in classrooms, it would do most tech savvy instructors good to incorporate structured computer use to elicit best practices [23]. While discussing the success factors that impact classroom technology innovations, Zhao et al. [34] directly ask: "why don't teachers innovate when they are given computers?" There are numerous factors that have been listed to answer this question; from technology incompatibility, to traditionalist versus progressive wars, to disruptiveness and unreliability of technology, or mismatched instructional goals with institutional policies, and so forth [21]. Many also attribute the lackluster uptake of inking technology into instructional design to old habits dying hard whereas Zhao et al. [34] argue that such factors are mostly never related to other operationalizing precedents; or cross referenced with the inter-dependability and relationships the factors imbue on all the key players. It is high time engineering educators addressed all issues holistically.

In addition to trying out innovative pedagogies, assessment and evaluation methods need to change for effective implementation of inking technology. Along with emphasizing interactive dialogue between the student-content-teachers and technology; educators need to be cognizant of several success factors including but not limited to technology affordances, learner predispositions, and instructional design [13, 17, 30]. Authentic assessment, portfolios, reflective journals and wiki questions are among the diversified assessment methods that need to be integrated with the classroom technologies whereby instructors and students will see the need for inking in such classroom activities [11]. Most engineering schools are leaning toward a learner-centered approach where inking technology will be integrated into active learning involving complex science problem solving, collaborative interaction and team work, and innovative thinking skills. Knowing that learning and retention is related to the depth of mental processing [5], it would make better sense to actively engage engineering learners with instructional content integrated with the 'language' millennials understand best; technology, and in our case, inking as an instructional technology strategy.

Acknowledgments This work is based on research supported by the National Science Foundation Grant #1140425, funding the Transforming Undergraduate Education in Science, Technology, Engineering, and Mathematics (TUES) research in Virginia Tech's College of Engineering. The opinions expressed in this article are those of the authors and do not necessarily reflect the views of the National Science Foundation.

References

1. Amelink CT, Scales G, Tront JG (2012) Student use of the tablet PC: impact on student learning behaviors. Adv Eng Educ 3(1):1–17
2. Barber DA (2012) 5 higher ed tech trends for 2012 [Online Article]. Campus Technology Digital Magazine. Accessed 14 Jan 2016
3. Berg BL, Lune H (2004) Qualitative research methods for the social sciences. Pearson, Boston
4. Cooper H, Dorr N (1996) Conducting a meta-analysis. In: Leong FTL, Austin JT (eds) The psychology research handbook. Sage, Thousand Oaks
5. Craik FI, Lockhart RS (1972) Levels of processing: a framework for memory research. J Verbal Learn Verbal Behav 11(6):671–684
6. Creswell JW (2013) Research design: qualitative, quantitative, and mixed methods approaches. Sage Publications, Thousand Oaks
7. Dodds K, Callender D, Henry C (2012) Making a case for technology in academia. Coll Res Libr. pp crl12-380
8. Driscoll MP, Driscoll MP (2005) Psychology of learning for instruction. Allyn & Bacon, Needham Heights
9. Easterday M, Lewis DR, Gerber E (2013) Formative feedback in digital lofts: learning environments for real world innovation. In: AIED Workshops. Citeseer
10. Fons J (2010) A year without paper: tablet computers in the classroom. Phys Teach 48(7):481–483
11. Frolik J, Weller T, Flikkema P, Haden C (2010) Implementing an inverted classroom using table pcs for content development. In: Reed RH, Berque DA (eds) The impact of tablet PCs and pen-based technology on education: going mainstream. Purdue University Press, West Lafayette, pp 21–29
12. Galligan L, Loch B, McDonald C, Taylor JA (2010) The use of tablet and related technologies in mathematics teaching. Aust Sr Math J 24(1):38–51
13. Garrick RD, Koon M (2010) Using tablet PCs and pen-based technology to address poor student performance in an engineering technology class. The impact of tablet PCs and pen-based technology on education: going mainstream. Purdue University Press, West Lafayette, p 176
14. Iding M, Crosby ME (2013) Going beyond access: on-line education in Hawaii and the Pacific islands. Educ Inf Technol 18(2):245–252
15. Kadiyala M, Crynes BL (2000) A review of literature on effectiveness of use of information technology in education. J Eng Educ 89(2):177–189
16. Kettunen J et al (2011) Innovation pedagogy for universities of applied sciences. Creat Educ 2(01):56–62
17. Kothaneth S (2012) The relationship between organizational culture, usability, and instructional technology acceptance. Ph.D. thesis. Retrieved from Virginia Tech ETD database
18. Krippendorff K (2012) Content analysis: an introduction to its methodology. Sage, Thousand Oaks

19. Lam J, Duan CG (2012) A review of mobile learning environment in higher education sector of Hong Kong: technological and social perspectives. Hybrid learning. Springer, Heidelberg, pp 165–173
20. Lam P, Tong A (2012) Digital devices in classroom-hesitations of teachers-to-be. Electron J e-Learn 10(4):387–395
21. Maclaren P, Singamemni S, Wilson DL (2012) Technologies for engineering education. In: Global congress on manufacturing and management, GCMM2012
22. McLaughlin JE, Roth MT, Glatt DM, Gharkholonarehe N, Davidson CA, Griffin LM, Esserman DA, Mumper RJ (2014) The flipped classroom: a course redesign to foster learning and engagement in a health professions school. Acad Med 89(2):236–243
23. Mohammadi-Aragh M, Williams C (2013) Students' perceptions of tablet PC interaction techniques. Comput Educ 23(2)
24. Moore E, Hayes M (2008) Enhancing distributed learning environments with tablet PC technology and software. In: Proceedings of the 2008 American society for engineering education annual conference and exposition
25. Moore E, Utschig TT, Haas K, Klein B, Yoder P, Zhang Y, Hayes MH et al (2008) Tablet PC technology for the enhancement of synchronous distributed education. IEEE Trans Learn Technol 1(2):105–116
26. Price E, Simon B (2009) Ubiquitous presenter: a tablet PC-based system to support instructors and students. Phys Teach 47(9):570–573
27. Romney C et al (2011) Tablet PC use in freshman mathematics classes promotes stem retention. In: Frontiers in education conference (FIE), 2011. IEEE, pp F1J–1
28. Salomon G (1990) Cognitive effects with and of computer technology. Commun Res 17(1):26–44
29. Shulman LS (2005) Signature pedagogies in the professions. Daedalus 134(3):52–59
30. St. Clair S, Baker NC (2003) Faculty use and impressions of courseware management tools: a national survey. J Eng Educ 92(2):123–131
31. Sutherland I (1963) Sketchpad: a man-machined graphical communication system. Ph.D. thesis, University of Cambridge. Demonstrated on MIT's Lincoln Lab
32. Sutherland IE (1964) Sketch pad a man-machine graphical communication system. In: Proceedings of the SHARE design automation workshop. ACM, pp 6–329
33. Zammit K (2013) Using information and communication technologies to engage students in the later years of schooling in learning content and literacy: case studies of three teachers. Educ Inf Technol 18(2):205–214
34. Zhao Y, Pugh K, Sheldon S, Byers J (2002) Conditions for classroom technology innovations. Teach Coll Rec 104(3):482–515

Chapter 20
Impact of Undergraduate Tablet PC Use on Retention in STEM Majors

Carla A. Romney

Abstract Educational institutions face unrelenting pressure to incorporate the latest technology into their classrooms. U.S. higher education has been adopting computers to augment the in-class learning experience. Anecdotally, computers (PC and Mac architectures) and tablet devices (iPads, smartphones, and tablet PCs) have been used in a myriad of settings for interactive polling as means to increase student participation and engagement. To date, other uses of computers and tablet devices have taken hold in project-focused or problem solving-oriented small classes rather than in large lecture classes. Undergraduate mathematics classes seem to be a natural fit for introducing tablet devices as many students find it easier to handwrite mathematical notation than to use a keyboard. This study investigates the impact of a tablet PC implementation in undergraduate college algebra and trigonometry (CAT) on student performance and retention in science, technology, engineering, and mathematics (STEM) majors. This longitudinal project explores the effect of Tablet PC use in an important gateway course for freshmen who intend to major in a STEM field. Five important metrics were assessed: class attendance, class performance, instructor evaluation, retention in STEM, and persistence to graduation. The CAT course was taught by the same instructor as a conventional CAT lecture class from 2005 to 2007 using the same textbook, secure exams, and grading rubric. This structure provides a reasonably well-controlled setting in which to assess the impact of tablet PCs on retention in STEM.

20.1 Problem Statement and Context

While the K-12 world has embraced educational technology such as tablets quite readily, U.S. colleges and universities have been slower to do so. The 2014 Pearson Student Mobile Device Survey found that 45 % of surveyed students in an institution

C.A. Romney (✉)
Fordham College at Rose Hill, Fordham University, Bronx, NY, USA
e-mail: romney@bu.edu; cromney@fordham.edu

C.A. Romney
Metropolitan College, Boston University, Boston, MA, USA

T. Hammond et al. (eds.), *Revolutionizing Education with Digital Ink*, Human–Computer Interaction Series, DOI 10.1007/978-3-319-31193-7_20

of higher education now own at least one tablet device and they see these devices as valuable for educational endeavors [4]. Similarly, this report indicates that more than 60 % of college students believe that tablet computers help them to study more efficiently and perform better in their classes [4].

Several recent studies have investigated the impact of computer use on student learning outcomes. For example, Mueller and Oppenheimer reported that students who handwrote lecture notes scored better on tests containing conceptual questions than did students who typed notes on a laptop and they speculated that the extra processing required to distill the essence of spoken comments and translate it into notes may help students encode the information in a way that improves conceptual understanding [3]. Evidence for a positive impact of computers in the classroom stems from studies by Saunders and Klemming [9], Samson [8], and Zhu et al. [11], which show that students' use of computers or tablet devices in instructor-designed activities that are connected to course learning objectives can yield benefits in learning and engagement.

Despite these studies that support computer implementations in a variety of higher education settings, college faculty have not incorporated computers, and specifically tablet devices, into their teaching repertoires as quickly as might be expected based on their students' rapid uptake of these devices. Typing difficulties or note-taking (inking) challenges may have hindered the acceptance of these devices [10]. Concerns about student inattention and distraction due to competition from online lures such as social media websites, email, and games may also be responsible for the reluctance to use tablets in class [7]. Adopters of tablet devices in the classroom counter these claims by arguing that effective teaching with tablets promotes student engagement and participation [7].

This study was designed to better understand the impact of the use of tablet PCs on undergraduate performance in a gateway course for STEM majors and, ultimately, retention to graduation in a STEM discipline. Many studies have shown that retention in STEM is strongly influenced by academic performance in the introductory mathematics course sequence [1] and persistence to graduation and on-time graduation have also been correlated with performance in freshman year math classes [2]. The investigation of the role of technology-enhanced learning in promoting STEM retention and persistence is central to this project.

20.2 Method Employed

As described in earlier publications [5, 6], a dedicated Tablet PC classroom was initiated at Boston University (Boston, MA) with 16 student Tablet PCs and 1 instructor Tablet PC that used the Microsoft Windows XP Tablet PC Edition 2005/Version 2002/Service Pack 3. Classroom Presenter 3.0, a software package produced and freely distributed by the University of Washington, was used to permit real time bi-directional data transfer between the instructor and students. The instructor's Tablet PC was connected to an LCD projector to display the lecture slides. The instructor also simultaneously used Camtasia Studio 5.0 to produce videos that consisted of the instructor's annotated slides, all student work viewed in class, and completely synchronized audio that captured all instructor and student comments. The videos were produced as Adobe Shockwave/MP4 files and were posted on the class website immediately after each session.

A well-matched comparison group design was employed to assess the impact of tablet PC use in the CAT course. Specifically, 53 students enrolled in the non-Tablet PC CAT course in 2005, 2006, and 2007 and 48 students enrolled in the Tablet PC course in 2008 and 2009 took part in the study. These cohorts are well matched academically: the final GPA at graduation for the non-Tablet students was 2.76 and the GPA for Tablet PC students was 2.77 (not significant). The CAT course was nearly identical other than the use of the Tablet PCs and the posted lecture capture material. For example, the same instructor taught the course using the same textbook, same assignments and grading rubric, and same secure comprehensive final examination.

20.3 Results and Evaluation

Class attendance and class performance were the first indicators of impact that were assessed. Attendance was 96 % for the non-Tablet PC classes and 99 % for the Tablet PC classes (not significant). Class performance was slightly better for the Tablet PC classes: there were 3 withdrawals and 5 grades below C- (out of 48 students) and 5 withdrawals and 8 grades below C- in the non-Tablet PC classes (significant at $p < 0.05$ by χ^2 test).

The short term impact on student learning outcomes, while not dramatic, did persist. As shown in Table 20.1, student retention in STEM was higher and average time to graduation was lower in the Tablet PC group.

The last student in the pipeline to graduate from these study populations completed her studies in September 2014. Thus, data collection and analysis for this portion of the study are now complete.

In addition to direct assessment of grades, attendance, and retention to graduation in a STEM major, the utilization of the course website was also analyzed. While there

Table 20.1 Retention and time to graduation for non-Tablet PC and Tablet PC classes

Retention in STEM	Non-Tablet PC	Tablet PC
After 1 semester	93 %	98 %
After 1 year	49 %	74 %
After 2 years	33 %	63 %
Until graduation	33 %	63 %
Average length of enrollment until graduation	4.23 years	4.07 years

was a transition in learning management websites from CourseInfo to Blackboard at the same time as the transition between the non-Tablet PC and Tablet PC classes, both systems allowed access to posted materials with comparable ease. Interestingly, there was a difference in students' utilization of the course website in the non-Tablet PC and Tablet PC cohorts. Since the instructor used lecture capture for the Tablet PC classes but did not have access to this technology for the non-Tablet PC classes, the students in the Tablet PC classes had access to video recordings of the class sessions and could view them as desired. On average, students in the Tablet PC classes accessed the course website 4 times more frequently than did students in the non-Tablet PC classes. The reason for this difference has not been identified.

The instructor course evaluation data were additional important indicators that were examined to assess the impact of using Tablet PCs in CAT classes. The students' evaluation of the course was not significantly different. On a scale of 1 (low) to 5 (high), the course received an average score of 4.66 in the Tablet PC format and 4.83 in the non-Tablet format. This difference is not statistically significant.

20.4 Future Work

An initial barrier to the adoption of tablets in higher education was cost, but this obstacle is becoming now surmountable. Tablet devices seem to be a platform that is here to stay; mobile computing technologies provide constant connections to the world of information. Since current and prospective college students today have experienced tablets during their precollege education, the impetus grows stronger for higher education faculty to imbue their classes with these devices.

While data collection on the students who took the CAT class between 2005 and 2009 is complete insofar as they have finished their undergraduate enrollment at the University, there are several additional analyses that are planned. For example, no effort has yet been devoted to determining the post-graduation STEM and non-STEM career paths of the students who participated in this study. Additional future activities include:

1. using social media (Facebook, LinkedIn, and others) to find out the career paths of graduates;
2. surveying graduates using alumni email addresses to determine career paths and memories of their introductory math experience;
3. determining impact of CAT course in Tablet/non-Tablet format on performance in next math class.

In addition, little evaluation of the impact of teaching with tablets on the classroom instructor has been undertaken, so best practices have not been developed or shared. Since other faculty members have used this classroom technology and colleagues have launched related efforts using smartphones and iPads, it is important to study the impact on faculty workloads, professional development, and satisfaction with the classroom setting.

As technology becomes increasing prevalent in everyday life, faculty members must consider how to align their content, pedagogy, and technology use to create an optimal learning environment for their students.

Acknowledgments I gratefully acknowledge the support of Fabian Torres-Ardila, Juan Pedro Paniagua, and Cathy Lysy in developing, implementing, and assessing this Tablet PC implementation.

Many thanks to the Boston University students who participated in this study and continue to respond to inquiries about their careers. Support for this project came from the Hewlett–Packard Foundation and the Boston University Office of the Provost.

References

1. Chen X (2013) STEM attrition: college students' paths into and out of STEM fields. Statistical analysis report. NCES 2014-001. National Center for Education Statistics. Accessed 23 Feb 2015
2. Hurtado S, Eagan K, Chang M (2010) Degrees of success: bachelors degree completion rates among initial STEM majors. Higher Education Research Institute at UCLA. Accessed 23 Feb 2015
3. Mueller PA, Oppenheimer DM (2014) The pen is mightier than the keyboard advantages of longhand over laptop note taking. Psychol Sci 25:1159–1168
4. Pearson (2014) Pearson student mobile device survey: college students May 16. Accessed 16 May 2014
5. Romney C (2011) Student and instructor Tablet PC use increases retention in undergraduate mathematics classes. In: Reed R, Berque D (eds.) Proceedings of the fifth workshop on the impact of pen-based technology on education, Blacksburg, VA, 10/25-26/10. The impact of Tablet PCs and pen-based technology 2010: going mainstream, pp 121–128. Addison-Wesley series in new horizons in technology, Purdue University Press
6. Romney C et al (2011) Tablet PC use in freshman mathematics classes promotes STEM retention. In: Frontiers in education conference (FIE). IEEE, pp F1J–1
7. Sample M (2012) Best practices for laptops in the classroom. The Chronicle of Higher Education (March 20). Accessed 29 Nov 2012
8. Samson P (2010) Deliberate engagement of laptops in large lecture classes to improve attentiveness and engagement. Comput Educ 1(2):1–19
9. Saunders G, Klemming F (2003) Integrating technology into a traditional learning environment reasons for and risks of success. Act Learn High Educ 4(1):74–86
10. Weider B (2011) iPads could hinder teaching, professors say. Chron High Educ 57(28):A22–A23. Accessed 29 Nov 2012
11. Zhu E, Kaplan M, Dershimer RC, Bergom I (2011) Use of laptops in the classroom: research and best practices. CRLT Occas Pap 30:6. Accessed 23 Feb 2015

Chapter 21
Analysis of Student Perspectives on Using Tablet PCs in Junior and Senior Level Chemical Engineering Courses

Enrique Palou, Zaira Ramírez-Apud, Nelly Ramírez-Corona, and Aurelio López-Malo

Abstract The *How People Learn* framework was used to redesign one junior-level chemical engineering course entitled Kinetics and Homogeneous Reactor Design (seventh semester) as well as two senior-level courses, Catalysis and Heterogeneous Reactor Design (eighth semester) and Process Dynamics and Control (ninth semester). Our goal was to improve chemical engineering teaching and learning by creating high-quality learning environments that promote an interactive classroom while integrating formative assessments into classroom practices by means of Tablet PCs and associated technologies. In order to examine how students perceived the use of Tablet PCs and associated technologies, we conducted semi-structured interviews with students that had completed the course sequence. The analysis indicated a number of themes that consistently appeared within the interview sessions and were addressed by students from different viewpoints. Five overall themes emerged: student experience in using Tablet PCs, impact on learning, potential of Tablet PCs and associated technologies, formative assessments, as well as advantages and disadvantages of using the Tablet PC in studied classrooms. This paper reports upon the themes identified in the analysis of the results from the semi-structured interviews.

E. Palou (✉) · N. Ramírez-Corona · A. López-Malo
Department of Chemical and Food Engineering, Center for Science, Engineering, and Technology Education, Universidad de las Americas Puebla, San Andres Cholula, Puebla 72810, Mexico
e-mail: enrique.palou@udlap.mx

Z. Ramírez-Apud
School of Biology, Benemerita Universidad Autonoma de Puebla, Edificio 112a, Ciudad Universitaria. Boulevard Valsequillo y Avenida San Claudio, Col. Jardines de San Manuel., Puebla 72570, Mexico
e-mail: tajaza@hotmail.com

N. Ramírez-Corona
e-mail: nelly.ramirez@udlap.mx

A. López-Malo
e-mail: aurelio.lopezm@udlap.mx

T. Hammond et al. (eds.), *Revolutionizing Education with Digital Ink*, Human–Computer Interaction Series, DOI 10.1007/978-3-319-31193-7_21

21.1 Problem Statement and Context

Universidad de las Américas Puebla (UDLAP) is a Mexican private institution of higher learning committed to first-class teaching, public service, research and learning in a wide range of academic disciplines including business administration, the physical and social sciences, engineering, humanities, and the arts. Since 1959, the Southern Association of Colleges and Schools Commission on Colleges (SACSCOC) has accredited UDLAP in the United States.

21.1.1 Description of the Studied Courses

The studied course sequence consisted of a junior course entitled Kinetics and Homogeneous Reactor Design (seventh semester) as well as two senior courses, Catalysis and Heterogeneous Reactor Design (eighth semester) and Process Dynamics and Control (ninth semester) for the chemical engineering undergraduate program at UDLAP, which is accredited by the *Consejo de Acreditación de la Enseñanza de la Ingeniería* (CACEI), which is the Mexican peer-accrediting agency to the USA ABET. Due to the small class size involved in our study (three students were the entire cohort), we were able to give each student a Tablet PC, and so they were using the tablets not only in the Tablet PC based learning experiences in the redesigned courses but for their everyday activities and other courses during three semesters.

Our goal was to improve chemical engineering teaching and learning by creating high-quality learning environments that promote an interactive classroom while integrating formative assessments into classroom practices by means of Tablet PCs and associated technologies [10, 15].

In the studied courses, we mainly utilized three Tablet PC associated technologies, *OneNote* [18], *InkSurvey* [14], and *Classroom Presenter* [4] to gauge student learning in real time, provide immediate feedback, and make real-time pedagogical adjustments as needed, especially in the redesigned problem-solving learning environments [11, 13]. Many specialized software packages were installed on the Tablet PCs. Detailed information is available elsewhere [10, 11, 15].

21.1.2 Redesign of the Studied Courses

The studied courses could be improved by taking into account technological advances and recent research on human learning and cognitive processes that underlie expert performances [10, 11, 15]. An organizing structure used to redesign the courses was the *How People Learn* (HPL) framework [6, 7], which suggests that we ask about the degree to which learning environments are: (a) *Knowledge centered*, in the sense of being based on a careful analysis of what we want people to know and be able to do when they finish with our materials or course and providing them with the foundational knowledge, skills, and attitudes needed for successful transfer; (b) *Learner centered*, in the sense of connecting to the strengths, interests, and preconceptions of learners and helping them learn about themselves as learners; (c) *Community centered*, in the sense of providing an environment, both within and outside the classroom, where students feel safe to ask questions, learn to use technology to access resources, and work collaboratively, as well as being supported to develop lifelong learning skills; and (d) *Assessment centered*, in the sense of providing multiple opportunities to make students' thinking visible so they can receive feedback and be given chances to revise [6, 7, 10, 11, 15]. These four overlapping lenses are useful for analyzing the quality of various learning environments. Balance among the four lenses is particularly important to create high-quality learning environments [6, 7, 15].

We also needed to understand the kinds of skills, attitudes, and knowledge structures that support competent performance. Thus, for the redesigning of studied courses, similarly as previously described [10, 11, 15] we "worked backwards" as suggested by Wiggins and McTighe [19] taking into account Jenkins model [12] as well as the HPL framework [6, 7]. Our redesigns involved a transformation of studied course from a lecture-based format to a "challenge-based" format. We use the term "challenge-based" as a general term for a variety of approaches to instruction categorized as inductive learning that many have studied such as case-based instruction, problem-based learning, learning by design, inquiry learning, and anchored instruction. There are important differences among these approaches, but important commonalities as well [15]. We used the HPL framework as a set of lenses for guiding the redesign of the lessons, development of our challenges but also the overall instruction that surrounded the challenges [6, 7, 10, 11, 15]. As described elsewhere [10, 11, 15], particularly important were opportunities to make students' thinking visible and give them chances to revise; we also noted the importance of provided opportunities for "what if" thinking, given variations on the challenge and for new problems that also involved the lessons' concepts. Detailed information is available elsewhere [10, 11, 15].

In an increasingly collaborative, mobile and globally inter-connected environment, UDLAP envisions ubiquitous computing as a natural, empowering component of every teaching, learning, and research activity. UDLAP is committed not only to adopting and adapting technologies to all its scholarly endeavors, but also to playing an active role in their development [10]. Tablet PCs combine a standard notebook computer with a digitizing screen and a pen-like stylus device to produce a computer that allows ease of input of natural writing and drawing. Pedagogically, applications for the Tablet PC include lecture/presentation enhancement, problem-solving demonstrations, active learning support, guided brainstorming, reading, commenting, marking-up (providing feedback), and grading of student work.

A review of the current literature [4, 10, 11, 14, 15, 18] supports the following advantages in using a Tablet PC: First, digital ink enables instructors to write "on the fly" during class as one would write on a chalkboard or on a transparency. This is especially meaningful for engineering and science courses where examples and explanations are often mathematically and graphically intensive. Second, the freedom of marking-up significantly changes the way students and teachers interact. It facilitates bidirectional sharing of information, moving students beyond merely observing presentations to interacting with the material, the teacher, and each other. In addition, the use of Tablet PCs supports more efficient management of information. Dynamic working notes can be saved in a searchable format, while lecture notes with vivid annotations become available for students' online viewing.

Vast amounts of educational and psychological research support the efficacy of both active learning and frequent real-time formative assessment in improving learning [10, 11, 15]. We utilized *InkSurvey*, a web-based tool developed specifically to allow an instructor to pose open-ended questions to students during class and receive real-time student responses [14]. Students utilized Tablet PCs to respond to these questions with their own words/sentences/paragraphs entered manually via the keyboard, or with digital ink that allows handwriting, sketches, equations, graphs, chemical structures, derivations, etc. Confidence level can be included if desired (as was our case). The instructor received an instantaneous compilation of web-based student responses [10, 14, 15].

A variety of Tablet-PC-compatible tools are being utilized to facilitate communication within the classroom, such as *Classroom Presenter*. We identified classroom assessment techniques (CATs) appropriate to each section of the courses and then adapted them into the Tablet PC/*Classroom Presenter* environment. The instructor also made use of CATs that are already features within *Classroom Presenter*, like the polling features [4]. Instructor utilized CATs to gauge student learning in real time and made real-time pedagogical adjustments as needed. *Classroom Presenter* can broadcast the presenter's screen content to the entire class using wireless networking [4]. In this mode, students were able to receive the application output and instructor's annotations as well as add their own notes to every course presentation [4, 10, 11, 15].

One type of sequence of the activities realized by the students using the Tablet PCs was that the teacher using *InkSurvey* or *Classroom Presenter* posted a question (from a previous semester quiz or exam) about a particular topic. The questions were asked mainly: (i) before class began, in order to reveal the students' prior knowledge about a specific topic and/or (ii) at the end of the class, to know how much they learned about a topic. Once students received the questions on their Tablet PCs, they wrote their answers and then sent them back to the professor's Tablet PC. Students utilized Tablet PCs to respond to the challenging questions (posed by the instructor) manually via the keyboard or with digital ink. The instructor received an instantaneous compilation of web-based student responses. Then she displayed selected responses to the rest of the class on the classroom presentation screen to make students' thinking visible and give them chances to revise, as well as to provide opportunities for "what if" thinking, given variations on the challenging question [10, 11, 14, 15].

Further, in response to students' answers (and sometimes students' questions), the instructor and/or the students would provide feedback, comments, and/or change instruction accordingly. The objective of such exercises with *InkSurvey* and

Classroom Presenter was to (by means of these formative assessments) enable students to acquire skills and knowledge that would be useful for their formal summative assessments, because finally, the questions asked in these exercises were very similar to those that would appear in quizzes and exams during the semester, which had a direct effect on their final grade [10, 11, 15].

21.2 Method Employed

In order to examine how students perceived the use of Tablet PCs and associated technologies, we conducted semi-structured interviews (lasting on average 40 min each) with students (one man and two women) that had completed the course sequence. These students were the original class size at the beginning of the study. Audio recordings were transcribed and then analyzed. We developed codes inductively through the data and based on relevant literature [5, 9, 17]. At the beginning, broad codes associated with responses from graduate students in a previous work [11] were utilized, and then a set of finer-grained codes emerged from the data. Examples from this subset of fine-grained codes will be presented in the following sections.

21.3 Results and Evaluation

Comparison of student performance with and without Tablet PCs by using studied courses' historical final grades (in our university grades are on a scale from 0 to 10 with a minimum undergraduate pass grade of 7.5) for the previous five years as control indicated an increase from 8.12 ± 0.16 to 8.95 ± 0.45 for the first studied course (Kinetics and Homogeneous Reactor) and from 8.22 ± 0.19 to 8.84 ± 0.49 for the three studied course sequence. In other undergraduate and graduate courses, the formative assessment exercises performed with the Tablet PCs and associated technologies had a positive impact on the grades of summative assessments [10, 15]. Qualitative analysis indicated a number of themes that consistently appeared within the interview sessions and were addressed by students from different viewpoints. Five overall themes emerged: student experience in using Tablet PCs, impact on learning, potential of Tablet PCs and associated technologies, formative assessments, along with advantages and disadvantages of using the Tablet PCs in chemical engineering classrooms as well as in other courses. Results obtained previously from graduate students are available elsewhere [11].

Table 21.1 Selected phrases from students' quotes about their experience using Tablet PCs

Before	After
At first I took my notes in my notebook and did not use the Tablet…sometimes it is hard	*It helped me a lot to visualize the things that the instructor was trying to convey*
At first I did not like to use it, even didn't turned on the Tablet	*I liked so much that nowadays I do not want to return it*
It was hard, I actually used my laptop	*I can say that in the end it really was a very useful tool*
At first it was a bit tricky, because we were not used to working with the subtleties of the Tablet	*It was more dynamic…In the end it was a very enriching experience for me*
At first it took a bit of work to adapt especially to specific software, being able to manage several software and take notes with the tablet	*It was very convenient because you could have your files, you could write in many apps and save all your files and have them for study…*

21.3.1 Student Experience

The undergraduate students expressed having at first, some difficulty (or reluctance) to use the Tablet PCs (Table 21.1), but later commented that based on the experience gained during the time they used it (three semesters), they found it not only very useful, but most of the comments consider that it was a very enriching experience that enhanced their learning as can be observed in the selected quotes presented in Table 21.1.

Our undergraduate student participants noted that the use of a Tablet PC in class leads to greater participation, due to the interaction with the teacher and peers; similarly, students mention that using the Tablet PC encouraged participation in the studied classrooms and allowed them anonymity that gave them confidence to respond without fear of being embarrassed for not giving a "correct" answer. A recurrent theme was how they developed Tablet PC and associated technologies' expertise over three consecutive semesters.

21.3.2 Impact on Learning

Undergraduate students commented that using the Tablet PC affected how they managed and obtained information during class to favor their learning. They think that using the Tablet PC in the classroom had a favorable impact on their learning, especially when comparing themselves to students that didn't have a tablet in other courses (than the redesigned). Further, they mentioned that taking notes in addition to the information provided by the instructor supplemented the ideas taught in the course. Those ideas were then easier to remember because the technology allowed them to record important cues to help them learn. Selected words or attitudes expressed by students taken from their actual quotes are presented in Table 21.2.

Table 21.2 Selected words/attitudes and quotes related to students' perception about Tablet PCs' impact on learning

Words/Attitudes	Fragments from students' quotes
Easier	*...it was easier to learn...*
	...the easiness to work with so many software that the Tablets have...
Helpful	*I am very visual so I understand by means of images and formulas, so it made it easier and helpful for me.*
	...you become skillful
Quicker	*...you are able to understand more than from a whiteboard*
Dynamic	*...because of the software installed in the Tablets ...*
Work faster	*I do not know if I learned better ...but it felt that my learning was much faster*

21.3.3 Potential of Tablet PCs

It is important to remember that the undergraduate student participants utilized the tablets not only in the Tablet PC based learning experiences in the redesigned courses but for their everyday activities and other courses during three semesters. Thus, within this category, several comments were made with regards to the software, whether it was useful for courses other than the redesigned, or if they consider any other use for tested software in redesigned classrooms. It was observed that the students tried to potentiate the uses of their Tablet PCs, using software that was already installed in the Tablet PCs as well as some others that they asked to be installed for both academic and recreational aspects. Being able to develop formulas, chemical structures, make notes, solve cases, exercises, etc., in any of the software used in class (*OneNote*, *InkSurvey*, and *Classroom Presenter*) both individually and in teams, allowed for a greater understanding of the topics discussed in class.

On the other hand, graduate students that only had the Tablet PCs in a particular course [11], noted that the use of the Tablet PC in the classroom increased their motivation and participation, however, they thought Tablets have not been "exploited" enough. They considered the potential of the Tablet PC as great, as long as its use is maximized and similar activities are implemented in most courses. Undergraduate students mentioned that collaborative work and communication is streamlined using the Tablet PCs and associated technologies as can be observed (Table 21.3) in the fragments of student quotes that arose from the interviews.

21.3.4 Formative Assessment

Undergraduate students commented that Tablet PCs and associated technologies offer the possibility of real-time feedback, which allowed them to make their thinking visible and had the opportunity to revise their ideas immediately. Real-time

Table 21.3 Selected fragments from quotes related to students' perception about the potential of Tablet PCs

Potential	Fragments from students' quotes
Had on hand required software	*All the tools you need for class were in the Tablet PC*
Performed many simulations using different software	*Used OneNote for all my notes*
	It was easy to learn new software, you just needed time to try it
	All the exercises that I did by hand then I simulated them by means of the Tablet PC
	Solving exercises and then many software such as Excel ...also used MATLAB, polymath, and Aspen
Able to use it in exams or exercises	*It was useful to perform more examples*
It was very convenient *It has tools like colors* *It takes less to write something as a formula*	*We could even write on the same screen as a team* *The thing that you can find your mistakes or your assertions in a problem was very helpful to me* *Activities were easier*
It really works as a library or as your notebook	*You can have all your books, your notes and everything*

Table 21.4 Selected fragments from quotes related to students' perception regarding formative assessments by means of Tablet PCs

You can compare with responses from classmates and see if you were wrong... *I had the actual examples, then no detail escaped me*	*Teacher made us see our mistakes.* *Helped me to learn better* *Studying was much easier*
I understand better when someone is telling where to look, here is wrong!	*Very helpful, we could see all the answers*
You can make notes that are easier to study	*You can see what the other classmates did*
I feel that learning is individual ...Tablet facilitates learning	*You develop many skills*
Feedback was one of the parts that I very much liked of the Tablets	*You can easily find your mistakes in a problem*

feedback on the exercises performed in redesigned classes was very helpful for them. Anonymity gave them more confidence to participate in the processes of formative assessment. Selected fragments from student quotes are presented in Table 21.4.

21.3.5 Advantages and Disadvantages

Undergraduate students mention as advantages of Tablet PCs, the stylus pen to take notes on the teacher's slides and that the screen can be rotated in order to take notes more comfortably. Software available in the Tablet PCs was also mentioned as an advantage. Among the disadvantages, students mentioned that in some cases, being connected to the network could divert attention (check their e-mail, check social networks, etc.), causing them to lose sight of the class and teacher comments.

One of the students mentioned that prior to using Tablet PCs she felt "fear of being embarrassed for not giving 'correct' answers". With the anonymity provided by Tablet PCs and associated technologies, she mentioned her level of participation increased and indicated feeling much more confident after the three course sequence. Similar results have been reported for courses with many more students involved than in our case [4, 10, 11, 15]. In general, student participants indicated that tended to work faster and felt they were learning better. This was more evident as they progressed in the three-course sequence.

21.3.6 Redesigned Learning Environments "HPL-ness"

Carney [8] identified goals and sub-goals of each lens of the HPL framework as well as classroom practices associated with every one of them. As many practices can serve multiple goals, she further described their possible relationships. We will try to explicitly tie the HPL framework with the results of student interviews (Table 21.5). Results from graduate students' interviews have also been reported [11].

Learner-centered classroom. The goal of learner-centered instruction is to help students build on the conceptual and cultural knowledge that they already have and to help them develop better skills and practices for future learning. This was evident in the undergraduate student interviews (Table 21.5) through a variety of specific learner-centered classroom practices (that also served the purpose of formative assessment) fostered by the use of Tablet PCs and associated technologies [8]. Undergraduate students were given ample opportunities to do this in a social or learning community context due to the very small class-size. Under these circumstances, every one of these practices can be learner-, knowledge- and community-centered [8], thus they will be additionally promoted by means of Tablet PCs and associated technologies in following semesters when students will be using Tablet PCs only in the studied courses (will not have them all the time).

Knowledge-centered classroom. A goal of a knowledge-centered classroom is to create flexible, adaptive understandings of the ideas, skills and important information of a given domain [8]. This was evident (Table 21.5) in the undergraduate student interviews through a variety of specific knowledge-centered classroom practices (that are also assessment-centered) fostered by the use of Tablet PCs and associated technologies [8]. Some specific practices that support knowledge-building (activities that lead to an understanding of the discipline) but are also community-centered were not evident in the undergraduate interviews, although part of the studied course sequence offering. Thus the following will be enhanced in the following semesters: students will clearly be told that they are participating in designs, investigations, or

Table 21.5 How People Learn (HPL) framework [6, 7] relationship to selected classroom practices and activities

HPL framework	Classroom practices
Learner-centered	Observation, questioning, conversation, and reflection on student activities and products
	Open-ended long-term problem solving activities that force students to deeply examine a phenomenon, discussing misconceptions, presenting situations/problems that will provide cognitive conflict, and enabling students to readjust their thinking
	Fostering student reflection on their own understandings and thinking, self-assessment, reflection on own growth and change over time, and discussing the nature of misconceptions and their role in understanding
Knowledge-centered	Encouraging students to formulate questions about their understanding, classroom activities that help students practice reasoning with concepts, classroom activities that relate facts to concepts, practicing transfer or extension to other problem contexts or kinds of activities, as well as classroom activities that call for students to articulate their explanations or reasoning
Assessment-centered	Designing activities that can be used to make student thinking visible, using day-to-day student activities and work products to provide formative assessment feedback continually, assessments are integrated with instruction rather than separate from it
	Providing formal and informal feedback, provide feedback about how the student does tasks in addition to whether he or she does them correctly, assess students' abilities to relate content to other parts of the curriculum and their life experiences while feedback given encourages and helps students to revise their thinking
Community-centered	The creation of a learning community in the classroom in which every student feels that he/she has a stake in the knowledge construction process
	Establishing a classroom climate in which students have freedom to make mistakes, as well as establishing a classroom climate in which students feel free to ask questions as well as explore new questions and hypotheses
	Classroom practices that value student sharing and critique of each other's work

other domain-authentic activities; further, students will be asked to reflect on how their work relates to domain or professional activities [8].

Assessment-centered classroom. The goal of assessment-centered instruction is to provide ongoing insight into students' knowledge construction so that classroom activities can be tuned [8]. This was evident (Table 21.5) in the undergraduate student interviews through a variety of specific assessment-centered classroom practices [8]. Relating content to other parts of the curriculum and their life experiences while giving feedback, which encourages and helps students to revise their thinking, was clearly fostered by the use of Tablet PCs and associated technologies in the studied course sequence as stated in the undergraduate interviews. A specific practice relating to the assessment-centered goal not clearly evident in the undergraduate interviews was assessing the student's ability to discern whether and when to apply facts or procedures to novel situations (transfer) [8], therefore this concept should be included in the next course sequence offerings. Because of the anonymity afforded by Tablet PC technologies, students felt comfortable sharing their ideas with classmates, which enabled instructors to assess student understanding frequently during the processes of instruction, problem solving, and peer evaluations to quickly identify the most common difficulties, provide immediate feedback, redirect classroom activities, and/or refine instruction based on feedback received as previously described for other undergraduate and graduate courses [10, 11, 15].

Community-centered classroom. The goal of community-centered instruction is to connect students' knowledge construction to the multiple community contexts in which the knowledge is situated. These contexts include the school and classroom community, the student's larger social community, and a community of practice in which the knowledge is used [8]. These were evident in the undergraduate student interviews (Table 21.5) through a variety of specific classroom practices [8]. Several community-centered specific practices that were not clearly evident in the undergraduate interviews, which should be taken into account in the new sequence course redesign are: establishment of relationships between classrooms and the community in which UDLAP is settled, classroom tasks in which students are explicitly asked to report on or reflect on the relationships between their home life and classroom undertakings, activities in which persons from the community share their practices or knowledge with the students, activities in which students share their work with persons from the community, curricular foci that encourage making connections between outside and in-school learning, outside expert practitioners are consulted in order to help students understand the community of practice in which the knowledge is used, tasks engaged in are similar to those practiced by experts, and experts are a resource for students, among others [6–8].

21.4 Future Work

Since the subject size was very small (n = 3), we need to be very careful of overgeneralizing and making conclusions regarding other undergraduate students' Tablet PC experiences based on this study as reported by other authors [1–3, 16]. However, our findings demonstrated that the studied undergraduate students thought that using Tablet PCs and associated technologies: increased their motivation to participate in class as well as their scores in graded work-products; made the Tablet PC based learning experiences and studied classrooms more active and kept them constantly thinking, thus learning with understanding increased; that UDLAP should implement these type of learning environments into other courses; enable the teacher to provide a great deal of real-time feedback to students that made their thinking visible and gave them chances to revise.

Among the disadvantages, students think that teachers should be advised of the possibility of checking their e-mail and social networks while using the Tablet PCs.

Tablet PC associated technologies generated possibilities for self-assessment, making it possible for students to anonymously analyze their own and classmates' results. Another positive result of Tablet PC use was a visible increase in student motivation to participate in class discussions and problem-solving activities mediated through technologies (*OneNote*, *InkSurvey*, and *Classroom Presenter*) associated with Tablet PCs.

Students' initial conceptions provided the foundation on which more formal understanding of the subject matter was built. Further, frequent formative assessment helped make students' thinking visible to themselves, their peers, and their instructor. Facilitated by Tablet PC technologies, feedback (in studied courses) that guided modification/refinement in thinking increased.

Furthermore, a new re-design of the course sequence should take into account suggestions presented above while asking with more detail what would the course sequence new learning environments look like if they operate at the intersection of the four lenses of the HPL framework?

Acknowledgments We acknowledge financial support from HEWLETT-PACKARD (HP), through the HP Catalyst Grant Initiative for the project "Critical Support Systems to Enhance the Development of 21st Century Expertise in Engineering Students: Using Tablet PCs and Associated Technologies, the *Framework for 21st Century Learning*, and Guidelines from Research on *How People Learn*". Author Ramrez-Apud acknowledges financial support for her PhD studies from the National Council for Science and Technology of Mexico (CONACyT) and *Universidad de las Americas Puebla*.

References

1. Adler A, Davis R (2007) Speech and sketching: an empirical study of multimodal interaction. In: Proceedings of the 4th eurographics workshop on sketch-based interfaces and modeling, SBIM '07. ACM, New York, NY, pp 83–90
2. Anderson R, Anderson R, Simon B, Wolfman SA, VanDeGrift T, Yasuhara K (2004) Experiences with a Tablet PC based lecture presentation system in computer science courses. In: Proceedings of the 35th SIGCSE technical symposium on computer science education, SIGCSE '04. ACM, New York, NY, pp 56–60
3. Anderson R, Hoyer C, Prince C, Su J, Videon F, Wolfman S (2004) Speech, ink, and slides: the interaction of content channels. In: Proceedings of the 12th annual ACM international conference on multimedia, MULTIMEDIA '04. ACM, New York, NY, pp 796–803
4. Anderson R, McDowell L, Simon B (2005) Use of Classroom Presenter in engineering courses. In: Proceedings of the 35th annual conference on frontiers in education, FIE'05. IEEE, pp T2G–13
5. Bardin L (2002) Análisis de contenido. Ediciones Akal, 3rd edn. Madrid, Spain
6. Bransford JD, Brown AL, Cocking RR (1999) How people learn: brain, mind, experience, and school. National Academy Press, Washington, DC
7. Bransford J, Vye N, Bateman H (2002) Creating high-quality learning environments: guidelines from research on how people learn. In: Proceedings of the knowledge economy and postsecondary education: report of workshop, National Academy Press, Washington, DC, pp 159–198

8. Carney K (2005) Toward a definition of HPL-ness. Center for the study of learning, instruction, and teacher development. University of Illinois, Chicago, IL
9. Creswell JW (2012) Qualitative inquiry and research design: choosing among five approaches. Sage, Thousand Oaks
10. Cuba G, Judith V, Lopez-Malo A, Palou E (2011) Using Tablet PCs and associated technologies to reveal undergraduate and graduate student thinking. In: Proceedings of the ASEE annual conference. American Society for Engineering Education., Vancouver, BC, https://peer.asee.org
11. Cuba G, Judith V, Lopez-Malo A, Palou E (2012) Graduate student perspectives on using Tablet PCs and associated technologies. In: Proceedings of the ASEE annual conference. American Society for Engineering Education. San Antonio, TX, https://peer.asee.org
12. Jenkins JJ (1979) Four points to remember: A tetrahedral model of memory experiments. In: Cermak LS, Craik FIM (eds) Levels of processing in human memory. Erlbaum Associates, Hillsdale, NJ, pp 429–446
13. Jonassen DH (2010) Learning to solve problems: a handbook for designing problem-solving learning environments. Routledge, New York, NY
14. Kowalski F, Kowalski S, Hoover E (2007) Using InkSurvey: a free web-based tool for open-ended questioning to promote active learning and real-time formative assessment of tablet pc-equipped engineering students. In: Proceedings of the ASEE annual conference. American Society for Engineering Education. Honolulu, HI. https://peer.asee.org
15. Palou E, Gazca L, García JAD, Lobato JAR, Ojeda LGG, Arnal JFT, Munguía MTJ, López-Malo A, Garibay JM (2012) High-quality learning environments for engineering design: using Tablet PCs and guidelines from research on how people learn. Int J Food Stud 1(1):1–16
16. Prasad M, Hammond T (2012) Observational study on teaching artifacts created using Tablet PC. In: Proceedings of the CHI '12 extended abstracts on human factors in computing systems, CHI EA '12. ACM, New York, NY, pp 301–316
17. Raigada JLP (2002) Epistemología, metodología y técnicas del análisis de contenido. Socioling Stud 3(1):1–42
18. Tofan DC (2009) Using a Tablet PC and OneNote 2007 to teach chemistry. J Chem Educ 87(1):47–48
19. Wiggins GP, McTighe J (2006) The understanding by design. Expanded 2nd edn, Merrill Education/ASCD, Upper Saddle River, NJ

Chapter 22
Student Demonstrations of Learning: Making Thinking Visible Using Pen and Touch

Richard Kassissieh and Jeff Tillinghast

Abstract Teachers seek to create moments when students demonstrate their understanding of knowledge or skills and teachers provide feedback, known as formative assessment. Pen and touch input, in combination with apps that support digital ink and virtual manipulation, allow students to express their knowledge in more varied and natural ways, improving formative assessment and subsequent differentiation of instruction. Teachers and students at University Prep (Seattle) have used digital ink and virtual manipulation to increase the flexibility of formative assessment in a variety of subject areas. General purpose apps for writing, drawing, and making explainer videos have gained adoption more quickly at U Prep than subject specific learning apps that use a very specific pedagogical model. This paper describes the conceptual basis for our work with formative assessment, shares examples of student use of digital ink and virtual manipulation, and identifies themes among these examples.

22.1 Introduction

In the past three years, University Prep has made wholesale changes to how technology supports instruction. The most visible of these changes has been the introduction of a 1:1 student device program: iPads for middle school students and touchscreen laptops for upper school students. When designing this program, we had the benefit of learning from the experiences of schools that have been running student laptop programs for up to 14 years. Introducing devices is only one piece of the change in our educational ecosystem, and arguably not the most important one. A clear theory of action for how device capabilities amplify and extend good education practice is the most important quality of U Prep's technology initiative.

R. Kassissieh (✉) · J. Tillinghast
University Prep, 8000 25th Ave NE, Seattle, WA, USA
e-mail: rkassissieh@universityprep.org

J. Tillinghast
e-mail: jtillinghast@universityprep.org

T. Hammond et al. (eds.), *Revolutionizing Education with Digital Ink*,
Human–Computer Interaction Series, DOI 10.1007/978-3-319-31193-7_22

Our theory of action includes (1) clear and frequent expression of the reasons for the initiative, (2) learning environment design grounded in education research and contemporary practice, (3) horizontal and vertical alignment of school support for the change, (4) professional development linked to individual teacher improvement goals, and (5) design for student responsibility and leadership. A full explanation of these ideas exceeds the scope of this article, so we focus our discussion on one key aspect of the model: how tablet computing enables students to make their thinking visible to the teacher and thus demonstrate their understanding of appropriate material or skills. Our teachers, with the support of instructional technology specialists, create opportunities for students to demonstrate their learning and receive essential formative feedback.

Formative assessment is the evaluation of student mastery of knowledge and skills for the purpose of informing further instruction. In contrast to summative assessment, formative feedback occurs throughout, not after the learning process. It helps the student make further progress toward mastery of knowledge and skills, whereas summative assessment represents the final measurement of a student's proficiency on selected topics. At University Prep, we use the terms "formative" and "summative" with students in order to help them develop understanding and ownership of their learning process, and only summative assessments determine semester grades.

High quality formative assessment is timely, actionable, and specific [1, 2]. The assessment occurs after students have engaged in learning activities for the topic, but before they move on to another topic, thus it is timely. Feedback focuses on observable qualities of the student work, not immutable characteristics of the student, and thus it is actionable. The assessment focuses on discrete learning objectives, whether concrete or abstract, and thus it is specific. Effective formative assessment therefore provides feedback to the student while the subject is memorable, focuses on what the student did, and specifies a small enough component of the overall work that the student can handle.

Timely, actionable, and specific feedback invites a response from the student, the ideal moment for a teacher to differentiate instruction and provide the specific next steps for that student to improve mastery in identified areas. The variation of learning activities for individual student needs is one form of differentiation [4]. However, even the most skilled teacher cannot always provide an effective response to each student's learning needs on the spot. The effective teacher prepares in advance a diverse collection of learning activities designed to redress the typical obstacles encountered by students and is therefore ready to direct each student to the appropriate activity based on the results of his or her formative assessment. Ideally, students are not only repeating prior learning activities but also approaching the material in different ways that will allow them to learn what they did not master the first time through.

22.2 Pen and Touch Examples

Pen and touch technologies provide students with additional means beyond conventional laptop computers to demonstrate understanding. At one level, the device simply adds two input modalities to the previous set. Conventional laptop computers can capture type, audio, and video. Today's mobile devices can also capture pen and finger input. However, the technical enhancement represents much more than just greater variety of input. While laptop computers have the capacity to capture audio and video, for example, mobile devices have additional design considerations (e.g., multiple cameras, portability, weight, ease of software use) which make those capacities more accessible to students. The greater the number of supported digital modalities, the more varied and effective methods teachers may design to enhance the qualities of the digital learning environment.

One simple example comes from U Prep's middle school math classes, see Fig. 22.1. Tablet devices, course web sites, and digital ink allow students to work at their own pace and at the appropriate level of challenge. U Prep's math teachers make sets of leveled problems available to students as downloadable PDFs. Students access these worksheets on the class web site, write directly on their copy of each document in digital ink, and then return them to the teacher via electronic dropbox. This provides both teacher and student with a digital record of the demonstration of understanding and an opportunity for both to keep copies of submitted work.

An example of a newer form of tablet app, Dragon Box may leverage kinesthetic learning to provide students with opportunities to build and demonstrate understanding of algebra, see Fig. 22.2. As students drag symbols from one part of an equation

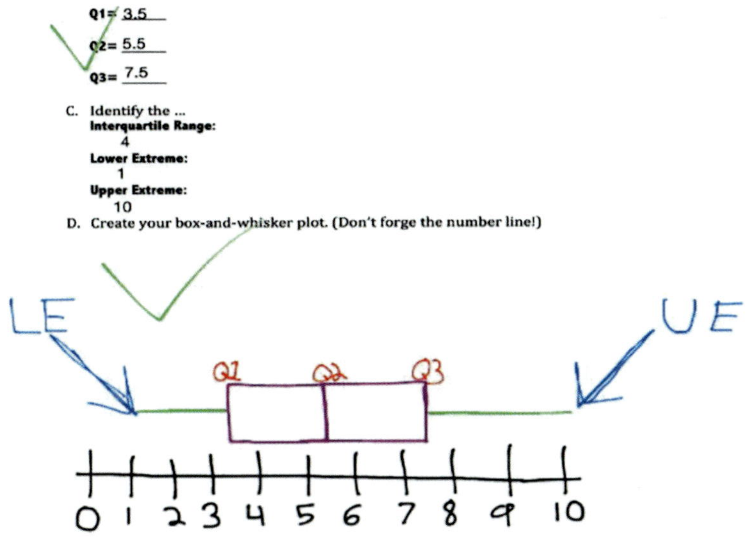

Fig. 22.1 Sixth grade mathematics assignment with student and teacher notations

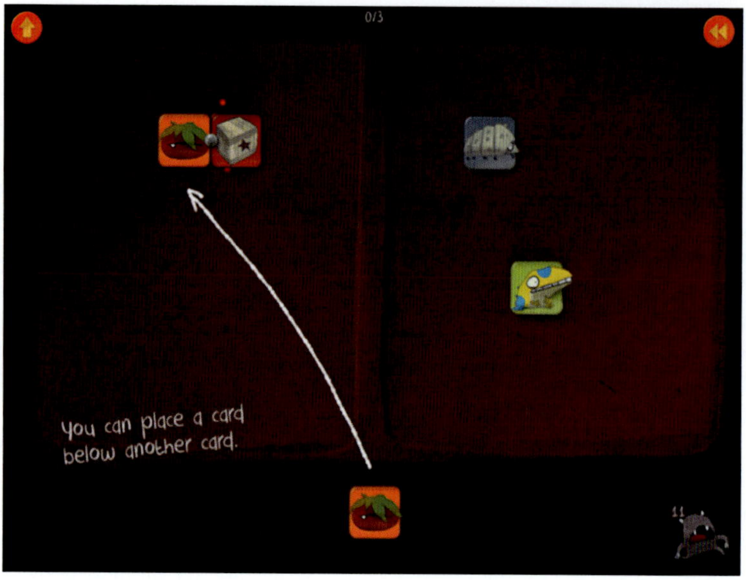

Fig. 22.2 Dragon Box instructions for how to move virtual objects

to another, they may be using visual and motor neural pathways to help establish both understanding and memory of algebraic processes. Since Dragon Box assesses continually and records student progress through discretely defined learning objectives, students, teachers, and parents may view evidence of mastery, including quality of solutions.

How do you know whether someone knows something? One common strategy is to ask the person to explain it. A number of apps for constructing explanations have appeared in recent years, increasingly integrating the use of pen and touch. U Prep students use Explain Everything, Prezi, iMovie, and other apps to explain concepts and arguments and thereby express their understanding in multimedia, storable, shareable form, see Fig. 22.3.

Tablet notetaking apps such as OneNote and Notability allow students to record information in class more naturally than keyboard alone. Teachers who present information both orally and visually can create a notetaking problem for students who have limited options for recording information. With a paper notebook, the content is difficult to search or reorganize later. With a conventional laptop, the student only captures words, missing essential information communicated visually or audially. In addition, disciplines such as math and science rely heavily on notation which is not immediately accessible on a standard keyboard. Some U Prep students have learned to quickly switch between keyboard and stylus (or finger!), with the support of an app that can change modes with equal speed.

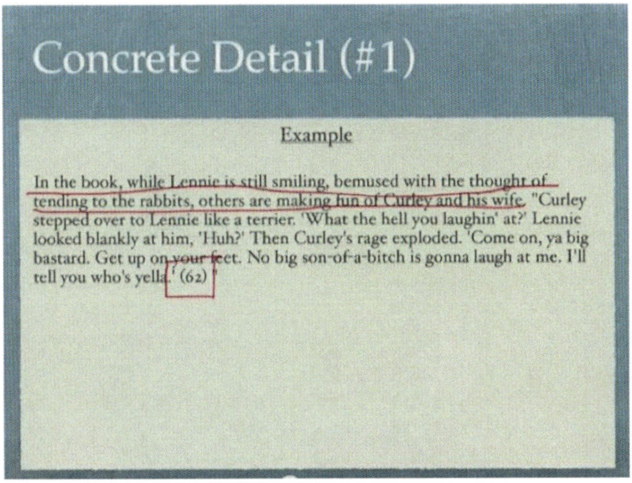

Fig. 22.3 Student explanation of the writing process (still frame from video)

The cognitive value of taking notes exceeds just the act of recording information. The most learning takes place when the student reviews notes, a process of reorganizing the information, identifying connections among related ideas, and thinking of questions about the recorded content. Digital, mixed media notes provide the student with the opportunity to perform these important learning acts without having to rewrite all of the content, see Fig. 22.4. Sharing the electronic notebook with the teacher makes it possible for the student to make this thinking visible to the teacher, who then gains a better understanding of the student's content mastery and can also provide the student with valuable feedback in the moment.

Language students create flashcards that mix illustration with text, both serving as useful practice and making the quality of their thinking visible to the teacher, see Fig. 22.5.

What of comprehensive apps such as Khan Academy, which recently added handwriting recognition to the iPad app? Interestingly, these have largely not caught on among U Prep teachers, and the reason has become increasingly clear of late. While the Khan Academy app boasts advanced technical capabilities, its learning environment relies on a specific pedagogical model of a repeated cycle of demonstration and practice, see Fig. 22.6. A teacher who disagrees with an app's pedagogical model is unlikely to use it much with her students. This may help explain why general-purpose, multimedia productivity apps have grown in popularity in our school while subject-specific, narrow-purpose apps have been used only sparingly.

Do writing and speaking, two classic forms of making thinking visible (or audible) take a back seat in a mobile world? In our experience, students have learned to type on glass more quickly than the adults in our community expected. While a number of students have chosen to use an external keyboard with their tablet device, the school has not required it, and many students have gotten by just fine typing on glass.

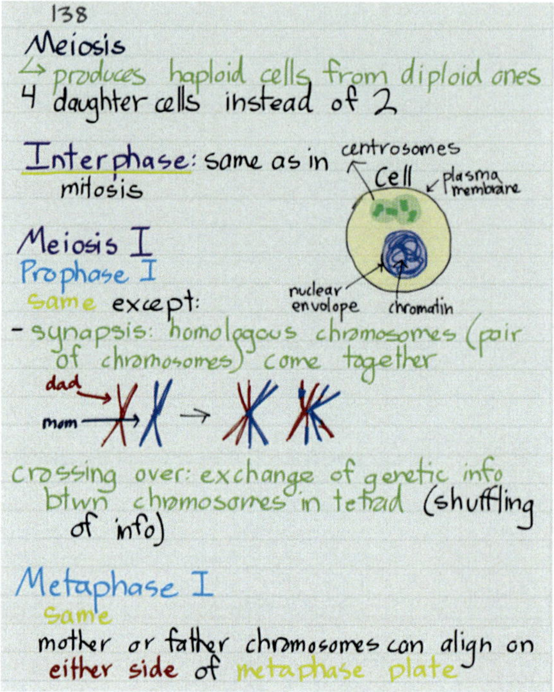

Fig. 22.4 Student mixed media notes

Fig. 22.5 Student-illustrated flashcards for language study

With regard to speaking, plenty of time continues to be available in class for class discussions, group work, and student presentations. In addition, tablet devices continue to be as powerful as their laptop predecessors for recording audio, submitting it to an assignment drop box, and incorporating audio within multimedia presentations.

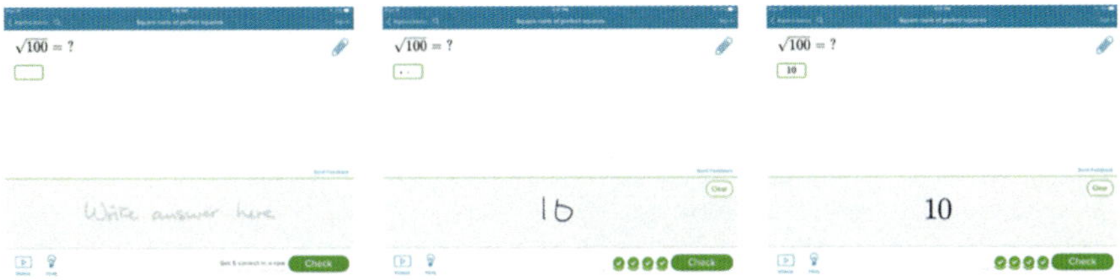

Fig. 22.6 Handwriting recognition in Khan Academy for iOS

22.3 Conclusion

In an online article [3], Baylor education professor Tony Talbert describes how he took time away from the university to rediscover life in the high school classroom. He was surprised to find that electronic devices are not just tools but actually a context within which students live and work. Thanks to digital ink and tactile virtual environments, this context now includes additional modalities for capturing and expressing ideas in forms that both peers and adults can view and respond to. The examples in this paper speak to the potential that University Prep teachers have identified for pen and touch to make student thinking visible more quickly and accurately. At the same time, our teachers have more swiftly adopted general purpose tools, avoid subject-specific tools with narrowly defined pedagogy. The coming years hold great promise as teachers continue to deepen their practice with general purpose digital ink tools, and subject specific apps diversify in their pedagogical approaches and learn from teacher expertise.

Acknowledgments The authors wish to thank David Denton at Curriculum in Context and the Seattle Pacific University School of Education for feedback and review on the early stages of this work. In addition, we thank the faculty of University Prep for sharing their work developing innovative uses of technology in their classrooms, and the students whose work is featured herein.

References

1. Black P, Wiliam D (1998) Inside the black box: raising standards through classroom assessment. Granada Learning, London
2. Busick KU, Stiggins RJ (1997) Making connections: case studies for student-centered classroom assessment. ERIC, Portland
3. Talbert TL, Trumble J (2014) An education prof. goes back to high school, finds technology is no longer a tool but a context. In: The Hechinger report: covering innovation and inequality in education. Accessed 23 Feb 2015
4. Tomlinson CA, Imbeau MB (2010) Leading and managing a differentiated classroom. ASCD, Alexandria

Chapter 23
The Integration of Inking, Touch and Flipping Within the Mathematics Middle School Classroom

Leslie Williams

Abstract This article discusses the benefits of access to a stylus and Microsoft OneNote in teaching seventh-grade math to students at Cary Academy. While the research presented is based upon the experiences of one teacher in a single classroom environment over an eight-year period, the results of this preliminary exploration suggest that changes to the classroom format facilitated by these technologies produce a richer, and more efficient teaching and learning experience. This article explores advantages of inking for both the teacher and students, including the ability to create videos, resulting in videos tailored for this course to be used when flipping the classroom. With the release of Office 8.1, students and teachers are also using touch input, allowing a more enhanced educational experience. Surveys help to describe the student and adult experience. Microsoft OneNote videos capture the teacher using her resources, stylus input and OneNote with students.

23.1 Introduction

As an Instructional Technology Facilitator and seventh grade math teacher in a one-to-one laptop school, I have had the opportunity to explore both useful and ineffective technology in the classroom. Because of my primary role as a teacher, I am always looking for ways to be more efficient with my time, including the time it takes to teach content, as well as the time it takes to help my students learn effectively and cooperatively. The use of inking, touch, and flipping the classroom have become integral in my teaching not only because they create an efficient learning environment [5, 6], but also because these tools help keep my students engaged and allow me to evaluate that engagement.

L. Williams (✉)
Cary Academy, NC Cary, USA
e-mail: leslie_williams@caryacademy.org

T. Hammond et al. (eds.), *Revolutionizing Education with Digital Ink*,
Human–Computer Interaction Series, DOI 10.1007/978-3-319-31193-7_23

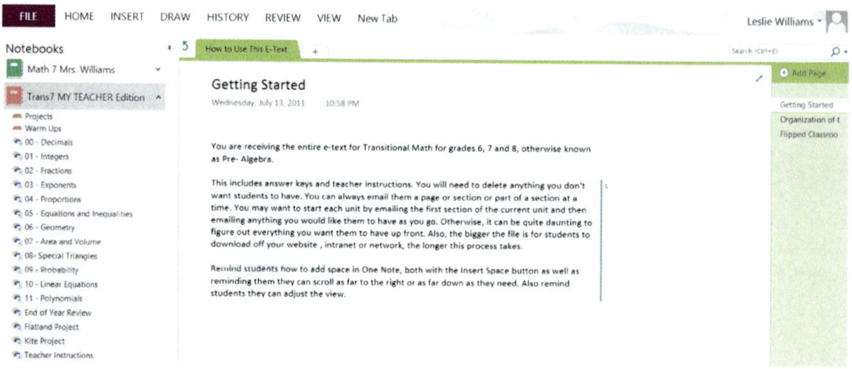

Fig. 23.1 OneNote digital format of converted textbook, notes, and practice activities

My students and I use these technologies daily for notes, video creations, collaboration, and to build organizational and study skills. In addition, we are now able to incorporate applets, apps and other programs into the teaching of mathematics. This changeover from desktop computers, textbooks and pencil and paper classrooms to tablet laptops and their concurrent technologies began when, as part of a 2008 grant, I converted a textbook to a digital format. Using OneNote [1], Smart Notes and other software, I replaced twelve weeks (one trimester for our school) worth of notes, practice, extra practice, and activities (Fig. 23.1). Videos [2, 3] show how the teachers at Cary Academy in Cary, North Carolina, seamlessly integrate OneNote into their classrooms to elevate the education of students through presentation, organization, and real-time collaboration with both students and other educators. Major benefits included the organization of all materials in one well-structured place that any instructor or student could easily use, and allowing students the tactile experience of writing in a versatile textbook.

23.2 Classroom Methods: Inking

Over the course of three summers, the electronic textbook and other resources were created, including one wiki for videos (Fig. 23.2) and one for discovery based activities (Fig. 23.3). The combination of these resources created new paths to explore pedagogy using inking and touch interface within the classroom. Inking was used throughout the e-text as I completed problems with verbal explanation while screencasting to create the videos.

Now, students use inking daily in my classroom and at home, taking notes and completing practice questions. They also create their own videos, capturing work through stylus and touch input. When screencasting, students must be able to write their steps and explain them, allowing opportunities for increased metacognition, as well as demonstration of mastery. They also collaborate with shared OneNote

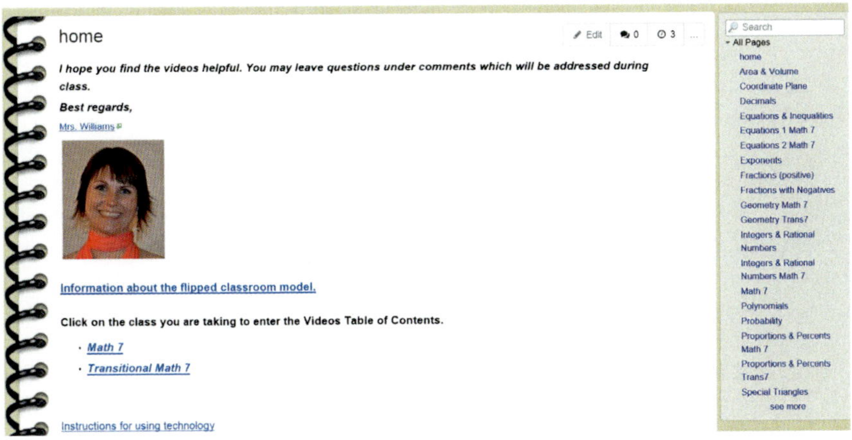

Fig. 23.2 Wiki page for video resources

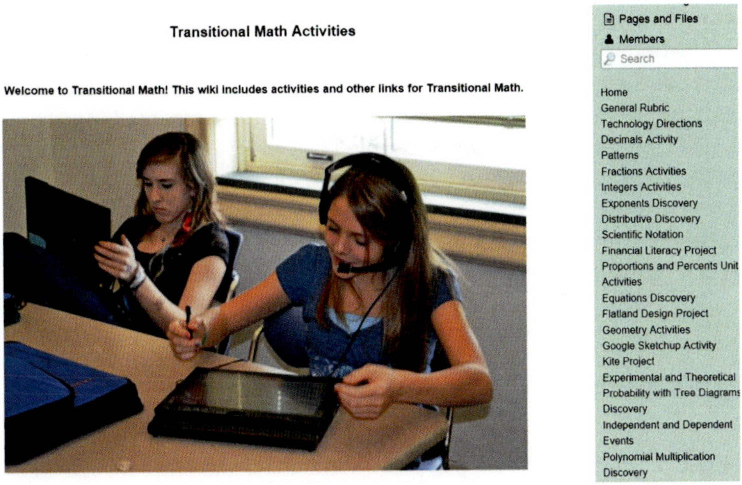

Fig. 23.3 Wiki page for discovery based activities

notebooks, using inking when writing symbols. Without inking, electronic devices would only be used for researching, typing papers, or using Microsoft programs and apps, which is a minor part of what we do in math. With inking, resources are now dynamic and are replacing more static learning modalities.

Most of our school community cannot imagine a world without stylus and touch technologies as part of their daily experience with computers. Cary Academy asked students and faculty, in a survey they took midway through the academic year, such questions as "How often do you use your stylus in the course of your studies?" and "How would you feel about giving up a touch screen?" hoping to gauge not only their comfort-level with using a stylus and touch screen, but also how important they find these features in the learning environment. From 449 responses received, the results showed the success of the technological integration: 83 % use a stylus daily, 87 % want a stylus to be available, and 77 % want the touch interface to exist on their computers. These results mean not only that students and faculty have become familiar with the technologies, but that they would miss them if taken away—demonstrating they would find their learning environment depleted by their absence.

At this point, I was curious about our school's integration of these technologies into the classroom. Microsoft interviewed me, along with other faculty at our school, about our use of OneNote. They also videotaped my classroom, my e-text and the students' use of my e-text. Two of the videos they made are included at the end of this article [2, 3].

Now that we have a touch screen and Lenovo Yoga TabletPC, the students can turn their screen over completely, creating a tablet. This technological flexibility allows the use of inking and touch to complete almost all of their work in math. In other classes, inking is used extensively in subject areas that require a great deal of annotation and/or specific writing skills- such as the sciences and world languages (Mandarin Chinese, Pinyin). The touch capability integrates nicely with inking, so that, while working in tablet mode, students can use the virtual keyboard, stop and start videos, navigate the screen with touch, use swiping to adjust multiples windows, and interact with applets. Between touch and pen input, a computer that can be used as a tablet, and cloud computing, students truly have an all-in-one device, and we have replaced the need for other physical materials. Not only have we reduced the need for paper and other, more traditional learning materials, but also the combination of touch screen, inking, and the Lenovo Yoga TabletPC has prepared the way for exciting changes in how students learn as well.

23.3 Classroom Methods: Flipping

For example, I have used the flipped classroom model and other aspects of blended learning with these resources, along with traditional lecture-based teaching [4]. During the fall of 2011, I began using my videos to flip my classroom. I received some strong indications that home-based learning of these sections through watching videos that could be paused, rewound, and replayed offered at least some students a better absorption rate. My first year using the flipped classroom, students achieved the highest scores on assessments ever throughout the four units taught. Although test scores were higher, there were some unforeseen obstacles. Mainly, some of our parents were not ready for this approach, as flipping the classroom was new and the perception was that I was not teaching. So, over the next few years, I incorporated the videos in smaller increments as a way to be more efficient with time, allowing me to cover the material more thoroughly. I always use the flipped method at the beginning of the year for review, allowing students to work at their own pace when covering basic topics. Whenever the students take a quiz or test during class, I often assign a video for homework to introduce the next topic, in this way making the best use of our time. Students can also learn my expectations around watching the videos: they must take notes and show all work; they also often work on a few problems that can be self-checked upon completion. As the year progresses, students become accustomed to using videos as part of class.

23.4 Results

This year, I used the flipped classroom for the first part of our equations unit, since equation answers are easy to self-check. Halfway through the unit, students took a survey about their experience. Some of the questions included a scale, such as, "On a scale of 1–5, rate how much you liked the flipped method of blended learning." I also asked open-ended questions. This combination of scaled and open-ended questions revealed the students' likes and dislikes, measurable against each other, as well as opening up discussion for topics I had not anticipated.

Although the evidence of better test scores indicated an increased absorption rate of the material when using the flipped classroom, the open-response feedback for flipping was mixed. Some students indicated that the absence of a live teacher could be challenging because they were unable to ask questions immediately. Other students found taking notes tedious, especially when they felt they had already mastered the concept. When students chose to use completed notes or watching the videos without taking notes, without notes or feedback, some students miss content. Students almost unanimously liked that they could rewind and pause the videos and use them as a reference.

For the scaled responses, out of 45 students, 28 (62 %) rated the flipped classroom with a 4 or 5 out of 5 (5 representing that they "loved" the method). 20 out of 45 (44 %) would like me to continue using it for the remainder of the unit. The year I utilized flipping the classroom for the first four units I had very similar feedback. Therefore, the scaled responses revealed that while some students responded well to the flipped classroom format, others seemed to prefer the more traditional teacher-led structure.

23.5 Summary

Overall, I have found a mixture of flipped and traditional pedagogies to be in my students' best interest. This mixture of teaching methods permits me to offer my students more freedom to pace their learning in ways that work best for them, while also adhering to traditional pedagogy to preserve the question-and-answer format with which students are most familiar. Also, my students are twelve and thirteen and still learning how to collaborate, work at their own pace, and learn without constant supervision. My goal is to help them develop effective strategies for the different types of learning to which they are exposed. This goal can be partly achieved by becoming used to learning from videos on a student's own time, and collaborating with other students using all available technologies.

In my experience, the incorporation of inking and touch input has revolutionized both teaching and learning. At this point in my career, I cannot imagine my classroom without either of them.

Acknowledgments The author thanks Joselyn Todd for her support in the creation of this document.

References

1. Hammond T, Valentine S, Adler A (eds) (2015) Using shared Microsoft OneNote "Binders" to create a school environment for sharing, continual formative assessment, and information organization. The impact of pen and touch technology on education. Springer International Publishing, Switzerland, pp 241–248
2. Office videos: OneNote in education: teachers using OneNote in the classroom (video file) (2014). Accessed 1 July 2014
3. Office videos: OneNote in education: transforming learning via technology and e-textbooks (video file) (2014). Accessed 1 July 2014
4. Roshan S (2015) The flipped classroom: touch enabled, academically proven. In: Hammond T, Valentine S, Adler A, Payton M (eds) The impact of pen and touch technology on education. Springer International Publishing, Switzerland, pp 215–222
5. Valentine S, Field M, Hammond T, Smith A (2011) A shape comparison technique for use in sketch-based tutoring systems. In: Proceedings of the 2011 intelligent user interfaces workshop on sketch recognition, vol 11, Palo Alto, IUI
6. Valentine S, Lara-Garduno R, Linsey J, Hammond T (2015) Mechanix: a sketch based tutoring system that automatically corrects hand-sketched statics homework. In: Hammond T, Valentine S, Adler A, Payton M (eds) The impact of pen and touch technology on education. Springer International Publishing, Switzerland, pp 91–104

Chapter 24
DYKNOW as a Tool for Differentiation: Exploring Alternative Ways to Assess in the Middle School Social Studies Classroom

Sara Mata

Abstract In this study, we evaluated the use of DYKNOW software for assessment in a middle school social studies classroom. DYKNOW software is a tool that can be used to differentiate for students' learning needs by providing them with several multimedia options that allow them to utilize their computers to read, annotate, record, type, and ask for feedback from the teacher. It allows teachers to monitor students' progress in the class, monitor and limit Internet usage, as well as engage in teacher–student communication during the class without making disruptions. The digital ink feature proved to be very beneficial as it provides clear immediate feedback about a students' written piece. As a result, students had a very positive experience as they took the final exam. Their learning needs were differentiated and students felt more confident and positive about their performance.

24.1 Introduction

As teachers, we assess every day in our classrooms through formative or summative measures. Assessment guides us by informing us on the learning that has taken place. It also informs us by helping us make instructional decisions for the future based on the learning that has already taken place. This research paper summarizes the process of administering a summative assessment in a middle school social studies classroom while using the DYKNOW software, which incorporates digital ink and tablet technology.

Educational Goals: Students will complete a summative assessment, which will provide them with the ability to: (1) demonstrate their understanding of a concept in multiple ways, including voice recording and in a written format, (2) better understand the Declaration of Independence, the Constitution, and the meaning of citizenship in the United States, (3) have access to print and audio versions of articles, (4) encourage critical thinking, and (5) obtain specific and meaningful digital feedback within minutes of taking their assessment.

S. Mata (✉)
Whitfield School, Creve Coeur, Mo, USA
e-mail: sara.mata@whitfieldschool.org

T. Hammond et al. (eds.), *Revolutionizing Education with Digital Ink*,
Human–Computer Interaction Series, DOI 10.1007/978-3-319-31193-7_24

24.2 Problem Statement and Context

I teach at an independent, coeducational college preparatory day school that caters to students in grades 6–12. It is located in suburban St. Louis. Whitfield's mission is to "cultivate ethical, confident, and successful students in a community of innovation, collaboration, and trust." I teach 8th grade Social Studies to a group of 51 students, with 15 of those students having diagnosed learning disabilities. As I got to know my students throughout the fall, I noticed that not only did they need more choice when it came to reading and writing, but they also needed a better system of accommodations when it came to showing their understanding through assessments. This is when I began the journey toward utilizing DYKNOW software as a tool for assessment in Social Studies.

The Essential Questions for my course are:

- Why do we need a government?
- What does it mean to be a citizen?
- How do citizens influence government policy?
- How is power gained, used, justified, and lost?
- Can an individual make a difference?

24.3 Method Employed

As a reading/literacy specialist, I have learned that one of the most important aspects of teaching reading and writing is being able to provide students with choice. According to Chris Tovani [4], author of "So what do they really know? Assessment that informs teaching and learning," students need to have choices available when it comes to reading and writing. Students' assessments need to be a reflection of the style that is being taught in your classroom. Assessing student understanding does not equate giving everyone the exact same prompt questions. Thus, as I began to design my assessments, I utilized an assessment structure known as "Tic Tac Toe." This assessment format is based on a 9 box grid, which contains different prompts, all which may assess the same topic, but in different ways. In order to complete the assessment, students need to pick out three boxes in a row, vertical, or diagonally. When created carefully, a Tic Tac Toe guarantees that a student will be utilizing certain skills in their three prompt choices. For example, one prompt may require you to read and annotate, another prompt may require you to watch a video and respond to a question in a constructed response format, and the last prompt may require image analysis and a verbal podcast to answer a question. Since my final exam was going to be on the Declaration of Independence, the U.S. Constitution, and the meaning of U.S. citizenship, my final exam Tic Tac Toe grid assessed students' understanding of all three of these topics.

I created writing prompts that addressed these Civics and U.S. Government topics. However, each of the options enabled students to access information and compose their responses in different ways. Students thrive on having choice when it comes to assessment. It gives them a higher sense of ownership in their learning. However, no matter which way they choose, they will have a reading/annotating passage. The following are three sample prompts that I provided my students with for their winter final exam:

- Watch the Boston Tea Party video and take notes as you watch. Then, read and annotate the text from the website. After watching the video and reading, respond to the following question: Why is the Boston Tea Party such a noteworthy event in American History?
- After reading and annotating the excerpts from the Declaration of Independence, respond to the following question: What ideas about government did Thomas Jefferson discuss in the Declaration of Independence? How was the Declaration of Independence an inspiration to our nation?
- Analyze the cartoon about the Articles of Confederation. What idea was the cartoonist expressing when he titled the cartoon "Rough Sailing Ahead?" Audio record your response.

As you can see in Fig. 24.1, the combination of prompts in a Tic Tac Toe assessment is very easy to follow, whether it is completed on paper or electronically. However, DYKNOW software makes multimedia information for the assessment more easily accessible, it enables students to annotate readings, and it allows for a smooth system

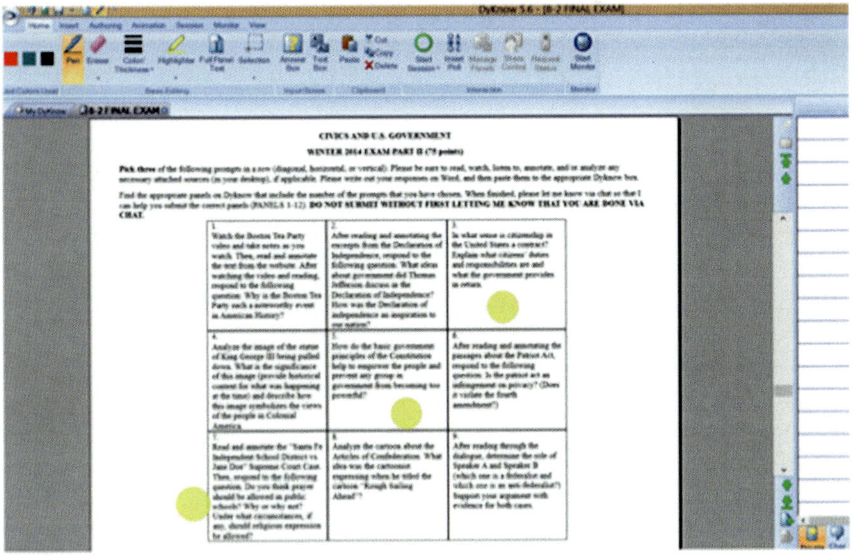

Fig. 24.1 The combination of prompts in a Tic Tac Toe assessment is very easy to follow, whether it is completed on paper or electronically

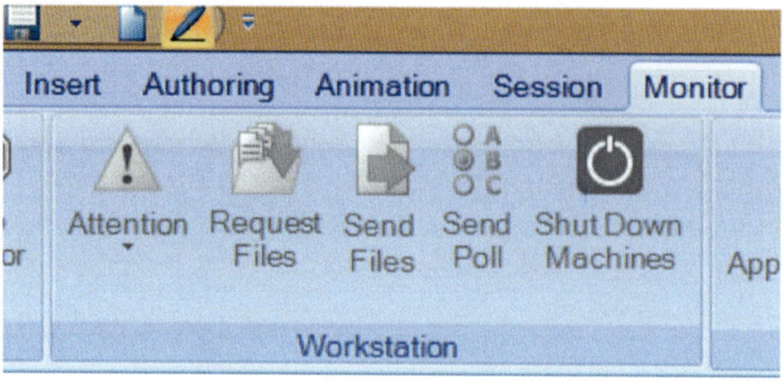

Fig. 24.2 The 'send files' feature

of turning in work, which automatically gets placed into an e-folder for the teacher to grade, provide feedback, and send back to the students. The 'send files' feature (Fig. 24.2) allows teachers to upload multimedia files for students to have access to throughout their assessment. The files are automatically downloaded to students' desktops. This makes it easy for everyone to have the information that they need without having to download it or browse for it themselves.

Something that often makes teachers less susceptible to using technology for summative assessments is the fact that plagiarism can become an issue when students have access to the internet and their electronic notes on One Note. DYKNOW software allows teachers to monitor which websites a student may open while taking an assessment. For example, for my winter final exam, I included a link in one of the Tic Tac Toe prompts that took students to a history website. I was able to block all other internet access, yet leave this particular site open for students to open. Other security measures of DYKNOW include the screen monitor feature, which allows you to see all the screens during the session. I see this as a great tool during an assessment because you can be monitoring student progress and even answer student questions via chat from your own screen. In addition, a teacher can send reminders out to the whole class while in a DYKNOW session, and students can respond to you and to one another's questions without speaking out loud and making disruptions on the quiet learning environment of an assessment [2, 3].

Figure 24.3 illustrates another great asset of DYKNOW, which is the ability to build in panels that include self-assessment checklists that students need to utilize before submitting their final work to the teacher. The particular example in the above image shows the same checklist three times, one for each of the three Tic Tac Toe prompts chosen for the assessment. DYKNOW gives students the opportunity to use digital ink to self-reflect as they check off each item that they have completed in their written assignment. By having electronic copies of checklists, it makes it easier for students to access these and fill them out as they write their responses.

The digital ink feature of DYKNOW is very beneficial, especially for the teacher to provide clear and written feedback about a students' written piece. The following picture below shows what it looks like for a teacher to provide feedback to a student on a DYKNOW written response. What I most enjoy about this tool is that it allows

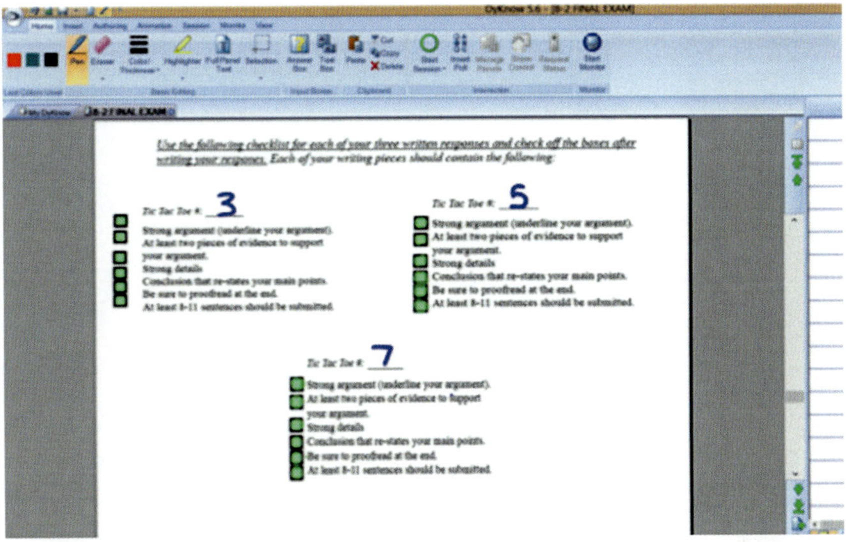

Fig. 24.3 DYKNOW provides the ability to build in panels that include self-assessment checklists that students need to utilize before submitting their final work to the teacher

for the student to receive that immediate feedback. Once a teacher makes corrections on an assessment, the 'submit' button allows him/her to send a student the graded assessment, not only with written feedback throughout the panels, but also with written feedback on the rubric, which is also included in a students' final exam e-packet.

Once the teacher receives the assessments, it is very powerful to be able to make comments on students' work by utilizing digital ink (Fig. 24.4), as it enables the teacher to send the feedback to the student right away. DYKNOW places students' feedback into a folder that they can easily access in order to read the teachers' comments in order to apply their feedback.

Having a successful DYKNOW assessment with my students was a result of multiple previous 'practice' sessions with them. Students need to first become familiar with the software by using it for in-class activities and for smaller, formative assessments [1]. I learned how to use DYKNOW by literally just trying it out one day at the beginning of the school year with my classes. There is no way to learn how to use this program on one's own. A teacher must have students logged into the session in order for the session to work. My students used DYKNOW on a weekly basis since the beginning of the school year in mid-August until December. All of this time and preparation helped them figure out what the software's features were and how to effectively navigate it.

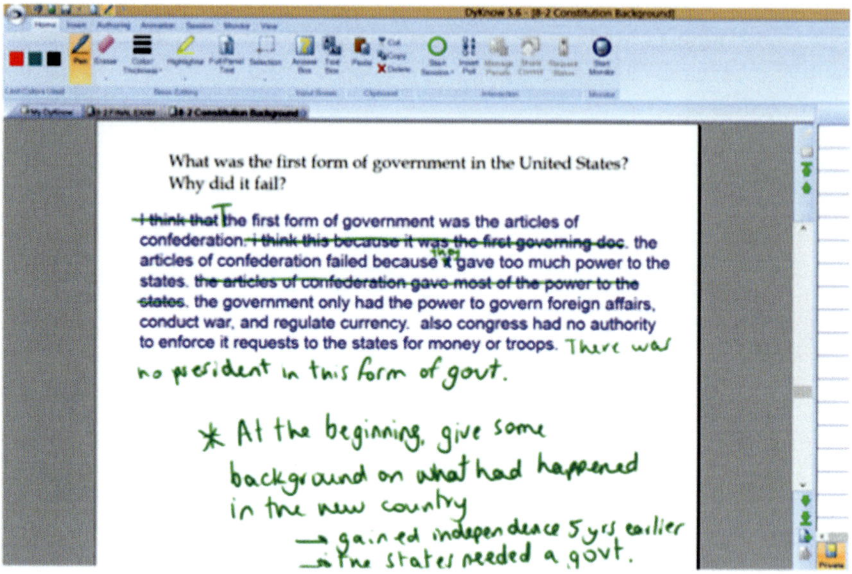

Fig. 24.4 Teachers can digitally ink on student assessments and return the feedback to the student immediately

24.4 Results and Evaluation

Taking a final exam on the DYKNOW software allowed students to not only have immediate feedback, but it also allowed them to utilize multiple tools in order to show their understanding of the concepts in the exam. Thus, DYKNOW software is a tool that can be used to differentiate for students' learning needs by providing them with several multi-media options that allow them to utilize their computers to read, annotate, record, type, and ask for feedback from the teacher. While many of the students chose to type their responses, some students chose to use digital ink to annotate their readings and to write out their responses. In addition, students were able to access multi-media information in order to write about it during the exam. Attached to the DYKNOW exam were multiple video links, audio links, as well as digital articles. Students were able to self-assess while taking the exam by utilizing their writing checklist. Students were able to ask questions throughout the exam without disrupting their peers, as they were able to utilize the "chat" feature of the software, which allows students and teacher to chat back and forth about questions they might have.

Students had a great, positive experience as they took this final exam. While the idea of taking a final exam can be stressful and overwhelming, many of my students walked out my classroom feeling confident and positive about their performance on my final exam. By providing students with the opportunity to utilize the DYKNOW resource as a tool to demonstrate understanding, their learning needs were differentiated and students were able to show their progress in a meaningful and creative manner.

24.5 Future Work

After having developed the first DYKNOW Social Studies exam at Whitfield, I am looking forward to utilizing DYKNOW for ongoing formative/summative assessments throughout my units. In addition, I would like to continue to explore the idea of using DYKNOW for multi-draft writing pieces in the classroom, as it is a great tool that allows students to receive meaningful instant feedback.

In the coming months, I also hope to explore the pros/cons of utilizing DYKNOW versus Google Classroom for daily work that students turn in. I have found Google classroom to be extremely effective when it comes to keeping student work organized and also when it comes to providing feedback on students' writing. However, DYKNOW allows students to utilize digital ink, which makes it possible to annotate/handwrite written responses, while Google Classroom does not. I look forward to learning about which types of lessons/assessments DYKNOW will help maximize my students' collaboration, meaningful feedback, and authentic learning.

Acknowledgments I am very thankful for all the help, guidance, and patience that Matt DiGiulio and Mark Payton provided me with. Their help has made it possible for me to provide my students with countless digital experiences that have enriched their learning. They served as mentors throughout the school year and offered extensive support as I prepared to administer a DYKNOW final exam.

References

1. Berque D (2006) An evaluation of a broad deployment of DYKNOW software to support note taking and interaction using pen-based computers. J Comput Sci Coll 21(6):204–216
2. Carruthers C (2015) An interactive learner-centered classroomm: successful use of tablet computing and DYKNOW software in foundational mathematics. In: Hammond T, Valentine S, Adler A, Payton M (eds) The impact of pen and touch technology on education. Springer International Publishing, Switzerland, pp 315–322
3. Read JC, Horton M (2015) Studying digital ink technologies with children—methods and insights for the research community. In: Hammond T, Valentine S, Adler A, Payton M (eds) The impact of pen and touch technology on education, Springer International Publishing, Switzerland, pp 23–34
4. Tovani C (2011) So what do they really know?: assessment that informs teaching and learning. Stenhouse Publishers

Part VI
Voices of the Future: Student Perspectives

Chapter 25
WIPTTE 2015 High School Contest

Stephanie Valentine, Hannah Conrad, Cassandra Oduola, and Tracy Hammond

Abstract The WIPTTE High School Contest was held on the first day of the WIPTTE conference on the Microsoft Campus in Redmond, Washington. The High School Contest is an annual event originating in the Department of Computer Science and Engineering at Texas A&M University, which extended into the WIPTTE conference. 2015 marked the second year of the WIPTTE High School Contest. During the contest, high school students participate in an intense day of brainstorming, design, prototyping, and presentation to compete against top schools across the United States. Nineteen high school and middle school students combined into four teams from two different schools: Renton Prep from Renton, WA, and University Prep from Seattle, WA. The high school students participated in many elements of WIPTTE throughout the Contest, including watching and commenting on the opening keynotes and presenting for the entire WIPTTE audience. Additionally, many students were able to participate in all three days of the conference. The students were active and engaged in the WIPTTE community, particularly while providing valuable feedback during the You-Try-It sessions.

25.1 Introduction

The WIPTTE High School contest serves to give high school students a chance to be innovative and apply science, technology, engineering, and mathematics (STEM) learning techniques. High School students are given the challenge to develop a new

S. Valentine (✉) · H. Conrad · C. Oduola · T. Hammond
Sketch Recognition Lab, Computer Science & Engineering Department,
Texas A&M University, College Station, TX, USA
e-mail: valentine@cs.tamu.edu

H. Conrad
e-mail: haconrad@tamu.edu

C. Oduola
e-mail: catoyin82@tamu.edu

T. Hammond
e-mail: hammond@tamu.edu

T. Hammond et al. (eds.), *Revolutionizing Education with Digital Ink*,
Human–Computer Interaction Series, DOI 10.1007/978-3-319-31193-7_25

tool for revolutionizing education. WIPTTE 2015 High School Contest students were given the prompt to create a tablet or mobile game about a topic taught in elementary, middle, or high school. Through collaboration with a team, participants had to present a seven-minute pitch that included a paper demonstration of their game.

25.1.1 History of the High School Contest

Virtually all universities and educators agree that STEM are important to student learning. However, it can be difficult to spark student interest in core STEM subjects in high school, let alone at the higher education levels.

For almost ten years, the Computer Science and Engineering Department at Texas A&M University has hosted a contest for high school students interested in pursuing an education and career in computer science. Each contest was held on a single Saturday and consisted of nine to 16 teams comprised of students from high schools across the state of Texas. A new topic was presented to the teams with a specific problem to be solved on the day of the contest. The main purpose of the contest is to spark interest in STEM, as well as generate new ideas in regard to future technology.

Thus, each topic chosen had to be in direct relation to STEM, but also be relevant and interesting to the students competing. This delicate balance between focus and intrigue makes the selection of the subject for each contest an important process in and of itself. Each year, teams are motivated by the topic's relevance to their lives while also intrigued by the relation it has to STEM.

The first year of the conference was in 2006. In 2006, faculty member Dr. Rick Furuta and coordinator Kourtney Gruner provided the topic of human computer interfaces for the competing teams to consider. In 2007, the topic of computer games was presented to 12 high school teams. In subsequent years, coordinator Theresa Roberts and various faculty members ran the competition with the topics of graphics (2008), computational thinking (2009), texting (2010), Internet privacy (2011), and intelligent fabrics (2012 run by Dr. Tracy Hammond, Ph.D. student Manoj Prasad, and the Sketch Recognition Lab).

Each year, working alongside the head faculty member and coordinator were five to six contest judges, available staff, and between 20 and 30 Texas A&M University student volunteers. Many of the student volunteers were past recipients of TAMU Computer Science and Engineering scholarships. Others were members of various TAMU groups, such as AWICS (Aggie Women in Computer Science) who volunteered to help make a difference and engage high school students in STEM.

A regular attendee of the Texas A&M University Computer Science and Engineering high school contest remarked: "This is my favorite computer science contest I do with my students. I believe it does more to show students what computer science truly is than all the programming competitions do. I would like to bring more teams so I can expose more students to the terrific opportunity."

Theresa Roberts, who acted as the head coordinator of the event when it was still strictly a part of Texas A&M University, stated that there is a possibility of the contest returning to the university. She also commented that "There is a lot of work involved [in the event], but once the students get here on that Saturday morning, I am so excited to see them that the work disappears."

25.1.2 History of WIPTTE Involvement

In 2014, in order to engage high school students in sketch and education research, the high school contest was integrated into the WIPTTE conference.[1] The WIPTTE conference has been known for integrating a diverse cohort of participants, providing perspectives from university professors, deans, IT administrators, and high school teachers. The inclusion of high school students provided another level of user perspective that can help drive the field forward.

Connecting the contest to the workshop allowed students to be introduced to the conversation about pen and touch technology in present and future educational settings. It also allowed students to directly interact with university and industry professionals in the field of computer science and technology. In 2014, high school students were paired with academia and/or industry leaders at a mentoring lunch to converse with one another.

In 2014, the involved schools were all local schools from Texas. In 2015, we had two schools from Washington state. In 2015, WIPTTE was able to find a number of sponsors to provide scholarships for many of the participating high school students.

25.2 Contest Logistics

The 2015 High School Design Contest was held on the first day of the three day WIPTTE conference at Microsoft in Redmond, WA and organized by TAMU Sketch Recognition Lab Ph.D. students Stephanie Valentine and Cassandra Oduola.

By participating in the contest on the first day, the high school students were able to participate in the second and third day of the conference with a solid introduction to tablet research, as well as experience thinking creatively about the topic. It also provided them with familiarity with a cohort of high school students to share the rest of the conference with. Additionally, their presentations at the end of the contest provided an introduction to the entirety of the conference participants.

The high school contest centered around the topic of educational games facilitated by pen and touch interaction. Teams were challenged to create an idea for an educational game application for a commonly taught K-12 subject. The application

[1]The 2014 WIPTTE conference was described in the Introduction of [2].

created should adequately teach the chosen subject while making use of pen and touch. It also should effectively attract users long-term, for example, for a semester.

25.2.1 Schedule

The team schedule for the 2015 WIPTTE High School contest is in Table 25.1. Students started with an introductory meeting to get students excited about the day. Students were then fortunate enough to watch two keynote talks by two famous researchers, Sharon Oviatt and Pam Mueller. Following the talk the contest organizers led a high-school specific talk to ensure the students effectively understood the implications of the research performed and discussed by the two keynote speakers.

25.3 Reflecting on the Keynotes

Both in 2014 and in 2015, students started off the contest by watching the morning's insightful keynote (Barbara Tversky's [7] in 2014, and Pam Mueller and Sharon Oviatt's [5] in 2015). Both talks discussed the value of sketching in education. After the talks, the students reflected upon and discussed the conclusions from each of the talks and their implications.

Pam Mueller's talk presented evidence that students learned and remembered more from a lecture when taking handwritten notes then when they were taking notes on a computer [4]. The students first discussed why this might be the case, followed by the implications of the work. They mentioned how it is impossible to hand-write as fast as they can type. It is possible to type almost word-for-word what the teacher says. However, when hand-writing notes, one must abbreviate the contents of the lecture. The act of shortening the content causes them to focus on including only what it most important. This requires actively listening to the lecture and parsing it for its important contents. They discussed the implication of the work, recognizing that not only is it important for them to take hand-written notes in their own classes, but that it is also important for them to ensure that any future pen-based educational applications encourage active learning and thought.

Sharon Oviatt's talk discussed the advantages of traditional and digital pens over typing [5] as shown in the recent literature. Hand-drawn diagrams help students view and interpret information, but they also help students communicate more non-linguistic content. Students using pens produce both a greater number and a greater variation of ideas and scientific hypotheses. Students show greater fMRI activity when hand-drawing than when type-writing. Not only is the traditional pen better than the keyboard, but the digital pen is better than the traditional pen. When comparing the two, the digital pen encouraged people to draw more diagrams, to draw a greater percentage of correct diagrams, and to make a greater percentage of correct interpretations than a regular pen. The strength of the traditional and digital pen is

Table 25.1 WIPTTE 2015 high school contest schedule

Time	Activity	Details
7:00–8:15	Registration/Sign-in	Participants visited the sign-in desk to pick up names tags and program information packet. The packet included rules and expectations, emergency contact information, and general information. After participants checked in, they were directed to enjoy breakfast and beverages before the Welcome/Introduction and Contest Overview
8:15–8:30	Welcome/Introduction and contest overview	Program Coordinators welcomed and made staff/volunteer introductions. The presenters discussed the Contest conduct rules and information
8:30–10:00	Keynote speakers: Pam Mueller and Sharon Oviatt	The keynote speakers gave the students background information regarding the impact of pen and touch technology on education
10:00–10:15	Short break/Move to contest workspace	A student volunteer escorted the teams to the contest workspace
10:15–10:30	Contest instructions	Program Coordinators presented the specific Contest topic, rules, and other information
10:30–11:45	Worktime	Teams worked in their individual workspaces on the Contest topic
11:45–1:00	Lunch	Teams/students shared lunch with professionals in the tablet computing and educational software industries
1:00–4:15	Worktime	Teams/students worked in their individual workspaces on the Contest topic
4:15–4:30	Work stops, teams prepare to present	A student volunteer escorted the teams back to the Queen Anne Room
4:30–5:00	Team presentations	Each team gave a seven-minute presentation in front of the judges, WIPTTE attendees, and the other participants
5:00–5:15	Closing ceremony and awards	First place, second place, third place, and fourth place team winners were announced. Each individual team member received a prize along with a prize for his or her school. At this time, the Contest was over and the teams could returned home if they chose
5:50–6:00	Sign-out	Group leaders consulted the registration desk to sign out before heading home after an exciting day!
5:50–6:00	Social event and poster session	Teams and teachers were invited to attend the WIPTTE social event and poster session at the Westin Bellevue

interesting when compared to the fact that students claim to prefer the keyboard significantly over the pen, even when their grades are shown to drop a full grade point when using the keyboard instead of the pen. The students were quite surprised by these conclusions and thought about the impact on their own classroom experiences.

The two keynote talks served as a framework for the rest of the contest discussions.

25.4 Contest Details

After discussing the keynote talks, the students were motivated through a presentation delivered by the contest organizers Stephanie Valentine and Cassandra Oduola. A snapshot of Valentine and Odoula presenting the Contest Instructions can be seen in Fig. 25.1.

Valentine began the presentation with a back and forth discussion about games, both educational and not. The students were asked to think about their favorite electronic game, and ponder what about it makes it so compelling and fun. There are many different types of electronic games available, each with a different type of base platform driving the play:

FIRST OR THIRD PERSON: shooter, Halo, Call of Duty, Battlefield, etc.
ACTION/ADVENTURE: usually 3rd person with some exceptions, The Legend of Zelda, Uncharted, God of War
PLATFORMING: Mario, Prince of Persia, Psychonauts
REAL-TIME STRATEGY (RTS): Civilizations, Command and Conquer, all "4X" games

Fig. 25.1 Valentine and Odoula presenting the contest instructions, prompt, and example paper prototype

DRIVING/FLYING SIMULATORS: Forza, Need for Speed, Ridge Racer, Ace Combat
ROLE-PLAYING GAMES: The Elder Scrolls, World of Warcraft, Runescape
"CASUAL GAMES": Nearly anything made for the iPad or iPhone
EXERCISE GAMES: Wii Fitness, etc.
EDUCATIONAL GAMES: Math Blaster!, nearly any "game" on your school's computer lab computers. Games meant to teach math, science, and history.

The topic of the contest focused on educational games meant to teach core skills, like math, science, and history, which are also often causal. Casual games include puzzle games (e.g., Candy Crush, maze solving), farming simulators (e.g., FarmVille, CityVille, PetVille), social multiplayer (e.g., Words with Friends, Draw Something, Mafia Wars), Sidescrollers (Flappy Bird), and Tower Defense (e.g., Plants vs. Zombies, Bloons).

The discussion transitioned into why people play casual games, for example, mobile applications, and why they are so addictive. Answers to the query included social components (connecting with friends), illusions of progress (just one more level until...), upgrades (e.g., Pokemon evolving), rewards for exploring (such as gold coins in Mario), and others.

25.4.1 The Contest Topic

The gaming discussion led into the official presentation of the contest topic.

The 2015 WIPTTE High School Contest Prompt

"Choose a topic commonly taught in elementary, middle, or high schools and design a 'gamified' pen or touch tablet application. You should design your application such that it adequately teaches your chosen topic, makes explicit use of tablet touch & gesture functionality, and strategically attracts users for long-term use (over many months)."

YOUR TASK:
Create a 7-minute presentation to 'pitch' your game.

Students were supplied with materials to use however they thought best describes their idea, including poster boards, popsicle sticks, construction paper, modeling clay, rubber cement, markers, pipe cleaners, pens, and colored pencils.

25.4.2 Introduction to Paper Prototyping

The high school students were given the challenge to design a paper prototype of their applications. They were given a tutorial and an example demonstration by the contest organizers.

Fig. 25.2 A high school student "swipes" the iPad calculator paper prototype

Oduola talked to the students about the use of paper prototyping in software development. She covered what paper prototyping is and the benefits to software engineers of creating such prototypes to test out user experience as well as possible designs. She employed a paper-based demo of the iPhone's calculator app to demonstrate how paper prototyping works.

Oduola: "What program did Stephanie use to create this talk?"
Students: "Microsoft Powerpoint."
Oduola: "How many of you have used Powerpoint?"

Most if not all of the students raised their hands.

Oduola: "All of you? Okay, How easy is it to use?"
Students: Shrugs. "Easy."
Oduola: "Pretty easy? Okay, somewhere on this campus there is testing going on. And there, they bring in people who use Powerpoint everyday. And those people evaluate the changes before they role it out to the market."
Oduola: "And before they actually build a new application, they design the app on paper, building a paper prototype, and evaluate it initially using that paper prototype with others."
Valentine: "Creating a paper prototype can take five minutes, whereas creating an entire demoable application with all the bells and whistles can take weeks."

Odulola and Valentine brought out a paper prototype of an iPad calculator application. A student came up to the front to demonstrate how he would use the app using the paper prototype. Figure 25.2 shows a student "swiping" the paper prototype as if it were an iPad or SmartPhone. Students marvelled how they can evaluate a user interface without actually spending hours upon hours implementing the user interface.

Fig. 25.3 Stephanie Valentine introducing "our lovely friend 'Print-A-Costume', a paper prototype of a 3D printer for Halloween and super hero costumes"

Valentine then further introduced the concept of paper protoype experiments with a 3D demo created by Valentine and Oduola (see Fig. 25.3).

25.4.3 Introduction to Wizard-of-Oz Experiments

As part of the lecture on evaluating user interface, Valentine also introduced the concept of Wizard-of-Oz (WoZ) experiments with a short lecture using a 3D paper prototype created by Valentine and Oduola. Figure 25.4 shows Valentine and Oduola using their paper prototype in an attempt to describe the concept of Wizard-of-Oz experiments (with Oduola acting out the part of the wizard behind the curtain).

In the story of the "Wizard of Oz," a man behind a curtain projected the face of a great and powerful wizard to all who asked for an audience with him. However, when the curtain was pulled back, his trick was revealed to the main characters of the story and they were able to see all the intricate workings of his technology. A WoZ demonstration, similarly, is a presentation of the inner working of a design or piece of technology, with a human (called the wizard) modifying the demonstration behind the scenes to reflect user interactions.

WoZ experiments are crucial to the development of artificial intelligence applications and are considered to go hand-in-hand conceptually with the Turing test. In an

Fig. 25.4 A high school student modeling the "grumpy cat costume" produced by the "Print-a-Costume" paper prototype, operated by Cassandra Oduola behind the curtain

ideal WoZ experiment, the lines between the computer and the human operator are blurred such that the user may assume that all of the operations are in fact performed by the computer. In this way, the designers can see how a user would respond to such as system if they did in fact build the system.

In the case of the high school design contest, the students will not have the resources to build a completely convincing WoZ protoyping tool, but they were encouraged to use their understanding of Wizard-of-Oz experiments to develop and present an effective paper prototype. Teams had to demonstrate and act out how their proposed game would work using only the materials given to them: poster board, popsicle sticks, construction paper, modeling clay, rubber cement, markers, and pipe cleaners.

25.4.4 Designing!

At this point, the students assembled in teams. They were given four hours to design their novel pen and touch application.

25.5 Student Teams and Projects Designed

The four participating teams in the event consisted of three teams from Renton Prep in Renton, Washington, and one team from University Prep in Seattle, Washington.

25.5.1 *Team 1*

The first team consisted of five girls from Renton Prep, in Renton, WA. Their proposed game, Live and Learn, functioned as a means of experiencing and learning languages and cultures from around the world by means of touch technology. Overall, Live and Learn would allow students to virtually visit a culture and language which they want to learn more about.

In a digital age where everyone can connect to everyone else, the world can sometimes feel like it is shrinking. Language barriers are being built and broken down as the digital world expands. Because it is difficult to understand and remember a language from a book, Team 1 (shown in Fig. 25.5) wants to aid in language learning using visual learning and handwritten means (Fig. 25.6).

Fig. 25.5 Team 1 giving their presentation and game pitch to the judges at the 2015 WIPTTE high school design event

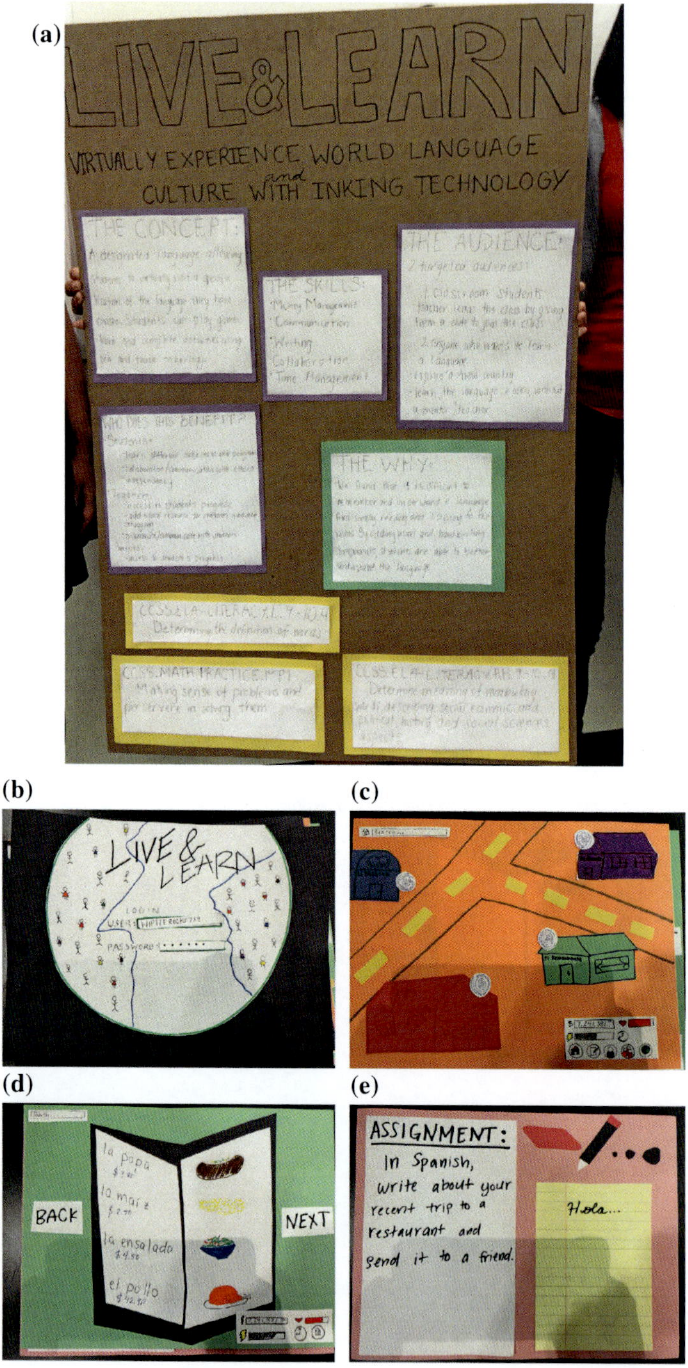

Fig. 25.6 Live and learn paper prototypes

Fig. 25.7 Team 2 presenting their game idea at WIPTTE 2015

25.5.2 Team 2

Team 2 consisted of four high school students from University Prep, in Seattle, WA. Team 2 pitched a game, The Exploration, that would take students on a step-by-step story game about specific historical events. Much like a choose-your-own-adventure game, Team 2's concept would allow for students to immerse themselves in the world of the past (shown in Figs. 25.7 and 25.8). Together, Team 2 sought to solve the issue of disinterest in history seen in middle school students. While there are games involving history already in circulation, current middle school students are not interested in them.

25.5.3 Team 3

Team 3 consisted of five students from Renton Prep (shown in Fig. 25.9). Their game, RenaLaunch, aimed to teach scientific inquiry in a way that is both pleasurable and entertaining to younger audiences. The poster prototype is shown in Fig. 25.10.

Team 3 argued that scientific inquiry in the classroom is not taught in a way that is entertaining to younger audiences. While educators have combated this by creating specific scientific procedures, such as a baking soda volcano experiment, the usable experiments have become repetitive.

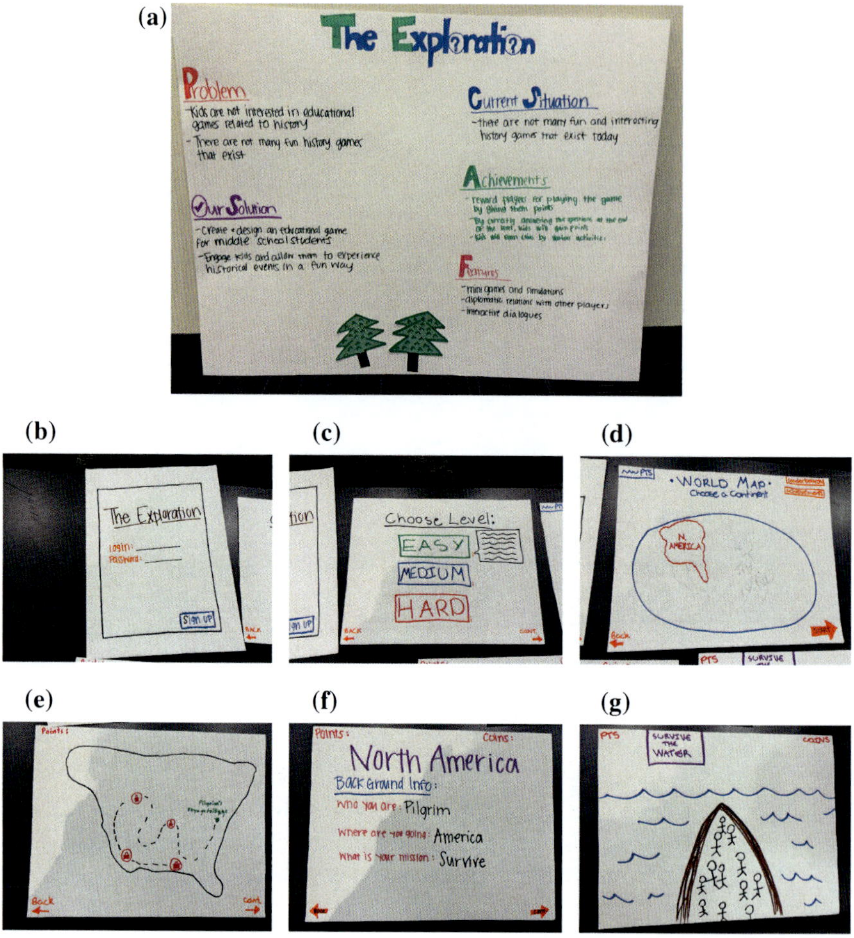

Fig. 25.8 The exploration paper prototypes

RenaLauch places students in the middle of the Renaissance as a character who is an apprentice to Leonardo DiVinci. Upon selection of the game level, students would be sent to a 3D location to build different projects to complete level objectives. They would then proceed to another section of the level to complete challenges with their newly designed project, such as flying through hoops with a glider. Ultimately, the game would allow students to create their own procedures involving scientific inquiry, test them, and upload their creations for others to interact with and compete against to see which fulfills the objectives better. This would allow for student cooperation and team learning while still allowing for individual work and experimentation.

Pen and touch technology is an important aspect of this game design because touch technology would allow for more control in the environment of the game. It would also simplify the building of 3D objects in the game. Team 3 suggested using

Fig. 25.9 Team 3 after their initial pitch to the WIPTTE high school event judges

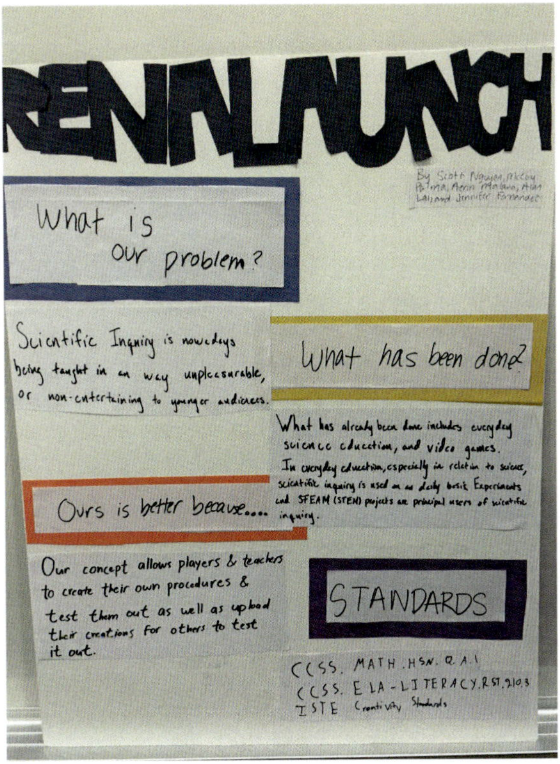

Fig. 25.10 Team 3's poster prototype

Fig. 25.11 Team 4 presenting their game idea at WIPTTE 2015

gesture recognition to control the constructed objects in the game. For example, a glider would be controlled by hand motion rather than just tapping a touch screen.

25.5.4 *Team 4*

Team 4 (shown in Fig. 25.11) was also made up of five students from Renton Prep. Similarly to Team 1, this group pitched an idea for a game revolving around the idea of learning how to write and speak a new language (Fig. 25.12).

Team 4's proposed game did not take a player to a virtual village, but instead showed them how to write in different languages in a stroke-by-stroke process. The game also gave students a phonetic spelling of the word, so that learning pronunciation would be straightforward and easy. Ultimately, their proposed game aimed to aid in a student's learning about cultures, communication, literacy, and vocabulary, but to still feel in control of their desired learning goals.

25.6 Judging and Awards Ceremony

The judges were members of the WIPTTE community, volunteers included members of the organizing committee, keynote speakers, sponsors, and presenters. After the

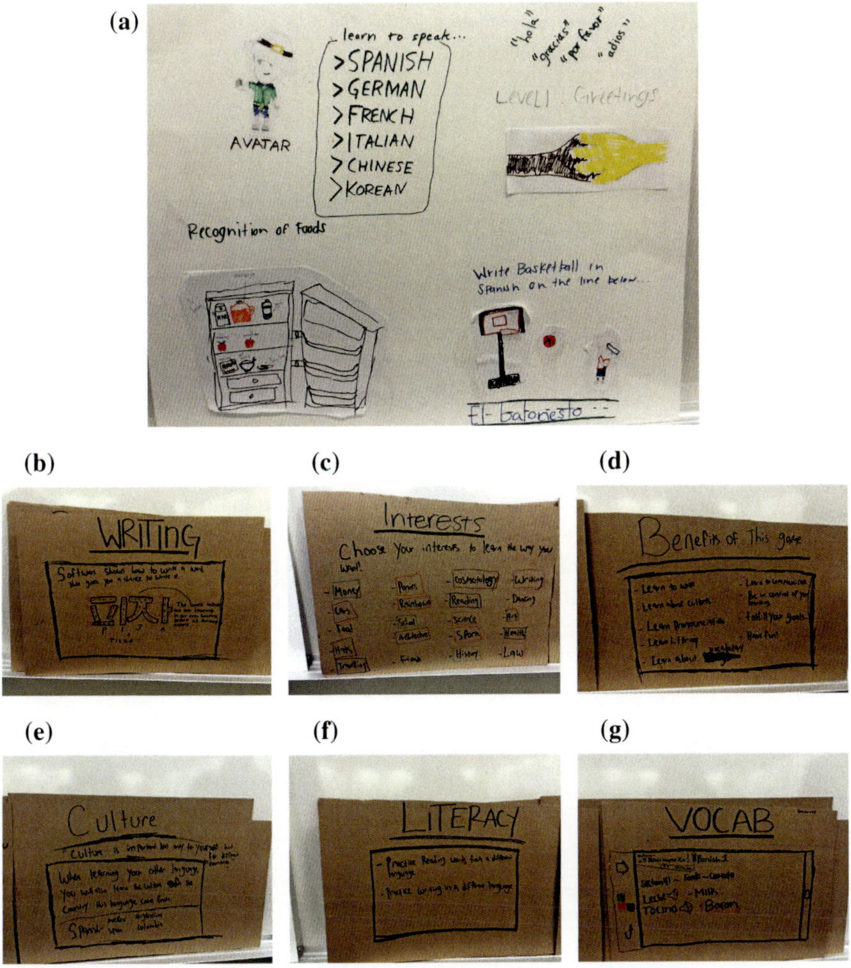

Fig. 25.12 Team 4's language learning paper prototypes

games were pitched, the judges deliberated and ranked the teams. Teams were judged on function, design, novelty, appropriateness, and presentation. Table 25.2 shows the proportion of points given each category.

Teams that ranked in the top four received gifts ranging from slingshot monkeys and Lego products to LittleBits student sets. In both 2014 and 2015, there were four teams that participated in the contest, making it so that each team left WIPTTE with an award.

Table 25.2 WIPTTE high school contest judging rubric

Category	Description	Max Points (%)
Function	Will it Work?	30
Design	Is it well-thought out?	10
Novelty	Is it cool, creative, new, and interesting?	20
Appropriateness	Does it solve the given problem?	30
Presentation	Are the students excited and well-spoken?	10

25.7 After the Contest

After the conference three of the teams were able to remain for the rest of the conference. They participated in all of the You-Try-Its on the second and third day [3, 6, 8, 9], many Keynotes during the rest of the conference, and provided fantastic feedback to all of the presenters. Figure 25.13 shows Stephanie Valentine presenting her You-Try-It on the children's social network, KidGab, to the high school students and their teacher Michelle Zimmerman [8].

Fig. 25.13 Participants at the KidGab You-Try-It complete their True Colors personality test

25.8 Student Reflections

Upon the completion of the 2015 contest, four 2015 high school contest participants aged 13 through 15: Kayla Gonzalvo, Tiffany Dinh, Scott Nguyen, Jasmine Fernandez, and their teacher, Michelle Zimmerman, Ph.D. chose to write about their experiences in the following chapter [1]. Rather then focus on the projects they created, the students reflected on various ideas for technology innovation in learning. They did not constrict their thoughts to the classroom, but rather the lessons that can be learned by hands-on and immersive experiences. The students presented the idea of learning tools beyond lectures and textbooks. They cited current methods as "outdated" and lacking "collaboration and interaction." The conference helped them realized the value in "the student voice" as they realized they are the market for certain educational advances.

25.9 Conclusion

Science, technology, engineering, and mathematics are increasingly important in a world that is constantly being digitalized. However, it can be difficult for students at the high school level to be interested and motivated in courses involving STEM topics. Furthermore, it is also challenging for those interested in STEM to meet experts and professionals in the field until they are at the university or post-university level. The WIPTTE High School Design Contest allowed high school students to become involved in futuristic innovation, interact with professionals, and kindle an interest in topics related to STEM. Overall, this allows participants to become more and more embedded into the research field relating to pen and touch technology. While obstacles, such as funding, arise in the process of hosting high school events, the success of bringing technology and enthusiasm into important topics that normally would be uninteresting or unrelatable to the masses outweighs the challenges. In conclusion, like the high school students stated in their reflection, technology and innovation are the future of education—and the students themselves possess the voices that will inspire and direct technological innovation in the future. Listen for them.

Acknowledgments The authors extend special thanks to Jonathan Grudin and Mark Payton as well as the conference sponsors for including the High School Contest within the 2015 WIPTTE conference. Additionally, the authors thank members of the Sketch Recognition lab for their help in the contest conception and implementation both before and during the contest.

References

1. Gonzalvo K, Dinh T, Nguyen S, Fernandez J, Zimmerman M (2016) Youth re-envisioning the future of education. In: Hammond T, Valentine S, Adler A (eds) Revolutionizing education with digital ink: the impact of pen and touch technology on education. Springer International Publishing, Berlin
2. Hammond T, Valentine S, Adler A, Payton M (2015) The impact of pen and touch technology on education. Springer International Publishing, Berlin
3. Lara-Garduno R, Hammond T (2016) Smartstrokes: digitizing paper-based neuropsychological tests. In: Hammond T, Valentine S, Adler A (eds) Revolutionizing education with digital ink: the impact of pen and touch technology on education. Springer International Publishing, Berlin
4. Mueller PA, Oppenheimer DM (2014) The pen is mightier than the keyboard advantages of longhand over laptop note taking. Psychol Sci 25(6):1159
5. Oviatt S (2016) Computer interfaces can stimulate or undermine students ability to think. In: Hammond T, Valentine S, Adler A (eds) Revolutionizing education with digital ink: the impact of pen and touch technology on education. Springer International Publishing, Berlin
6. Polsley S, Ray J, Nelligan T, Helms M, Linsey J, Hammond T (2016) Leveraging trends in student interaction to enhance the effectiveness of sketch-based educational software. In: Hammond T, Valentine S, Adler A (eds) Revolutionizing education with digital ink: the impact of pen and touch technology on education. Springer International Publishing, Berlin
7. Tversky B (2015) Keynote address: tools for thinking. In: Hammond T, Valentine S, Adler A, Payton M (eds) The impact of pen and touch technology on education, Springer International Publishing, Berlin, pp 1–4
8. Valentine S, Leyva-McMurty A, Borgos-Rodriguez K, Hammond T (2016) Kidgab: a sketch-based social network for teaching healthy social networking habits. In: Hammond T, Valentine S, Adler A (eds) Revolutionizing education with digital ink: the impact of pen and touch technology on education. Springer International Publishing, Berlin
9. Williford B, Nelligan T, Taele P, Li W, Linsey J, Hammond T (2016) Persketchtivity: an intelligent pen-based educational application for design sketching instruction. In: Hammond T, Valentine S, Adler A (eds) Revolutionizing education with digital ink: the impact of pen and touch technology on education. Springer International Publishing, Berlin

Chapter 26
Youth Re-envisioning the Future of Education

Kayla Gonzalvo, Tiffany Dinh, Scott Nguyen, Jasmine Fernandez, and Michelle Zimmerman

Abstract The locus of discussion on empowerment through student voice often rests in refined adult writing. Here, four students were given the opportunity to offer perspectives of the future of education as a result of attending the ninth Workshop on the Impact of Pen and Touch Technology on Education. The authors, three females and two males ranging in age from 13–15, were part of two teams in the High School Design Challenge during WIPTTE in 2015, now known as the Conference on Pen and Touch Technology in Education (CPTTE). This contribution provides insight into the process students took to design concepts for original games leveraging gesture, pen and touch technology that "strategically attracts users for long-term use (over many months)." They discuss their designs for game concepts they named Live & Learn, and Plumbum and Touch. They conclude with their vision for the future of education. The experience allowed them to realize the power of student voice in education. Their writing provides a glimpse into formal and informal learning environments they have lived within. Evidence of blended learning allowing for the intersection of human connection, experiential learning, lecture, and cross-age mentoring have been transferred into this culminating piece that originated from complex, real-world design challenges, failure, redesign, redrafting and communicating ideas.

K. Gonzalvo · T. Dinh · S. Nguyen · J. Fernandez · M. Zimmerman (✉)
Renton Preparatory Christian School, Renton, WA, USA
e-mail: m.zimmerman@agcschool.org

K. Gonzalvo
e-mail: kayla.marie.gonzalvo@gmail.com

T. Dinh
e-mail: tiffany.lynn.dinh@gmail.com

S. Nguyen
e-mail: scott.n9862@email.com

J. Fernandez
e-mail: jasawn2019@gmail.com

T. Hammond et al. (eds.), *Revolutionizing Education with Digital Ink*,
Human–Computer Interaction Series, DOI 10.1007/978-3-319-31193-7_26

26.1 Introduction

One of the goals of the Workshop on the Impact of Pen and Touch Technology on Education is to increase innovation and dialog in the education space. This goal was accomplished through inviting a younger generation into a setting with researchers to be part of the conversation. In this way, students had the opportunity to experience role models in technology and research fields. They were able to attempt putting theory into practice with a goal of creating a game that could be developed in the near future. At the end of the contextual introduction, you will read the thought process of some of the students who were part of this experience. At WIPTTE, students took the role of apprentices to expert researchers and developers.

Rogoff's [17] work speaks of apprenticeship as a metaphor for the relationship between experts and novices, guided participation by the expert during hands-on involvement in a shared activity, and the concept of participatory appropriation, referring to how individuals change through co-created involvement with an activity. There exists evidence that the combination of apprenticeship, guided participation, and participatory appropriation can facilitate the learning in a novice individual for later involvement in related activities. It can be argued that in the area of being teens of this generation, the students were the experts and the developers and researchers were novices learning from them as much as the students were novices in research and the technical aspects of developing for gesture and touch devices. Scaffolding [26] can provide the necessary structure for novices to reach higher or deeper and more complex thought and, in turn, action, than they could have alone [4, 27]. Developers have verbalized the benefit of hearing target audience perspective early on rather than waiting until development is complete and needing to redesign based on later feedback. This shift in perspective provides a variation on the traditional perspective of adults scaffolding the learning of youth. The future of education lies in a new architecture of learning, including the razing of artificial age boundaries for only learning among same-age peers and the divide that still exists in cultural landscapes. In Who Owns the Learning?, Alan November [14] uses his Digital Learning Farm model to show teachers how technology allows students to take ownership of their learning, create their own learning tools, and participate in meaningful work. In his model, every student is a teacher and a global publisher.

To become a global publisher creates a new level of responsibility that students in prior years did not need to grapple with. The factory model system of education did not place that responsibility in the hands of youth. Published work was vetted. An expert produced content that students were not to question. Children did not have the same access as they do now to publish content with a global reach or have their voice heard while experiencing multiple perspectives. Democratic, free societies allow voices to be heard. Technology has the power to amplify who we are and how we think. More than ever, "civic education—teaching students their moral and intellectual responsibilities as critical and informed citizens in a democracy" [20] (pp. 100–101) is important in the discussions of technological innovation. Part of that responsibility is to train students to be curious, to question, to see multiple perspectives, to understand that humanity is at the core of our interaction [8] with technology, and to have reasons for choices they make. This is all the foundation of education the students invited to WIPTTE have received in their school and was reinforced through their experience.

WIPTTE is on the cutting edge of bridging a cultural divide in considering the voice of children from very diverse backgrounds, both ethnically and socioeconomic status [3, 5, 10]. There was a dedicated effort made to break stereotype threat [21] and value student voice so highly that WIPTTE made students a valuable group of contributors and part of the story told [23] through a design challenge and publication at a point in history where pen and touch technology is emerging. They provided students who would not otherwise have the means or access to these conversations the ability to fully participate. WIPTTE is creating change with purpose. As a result, several students who never considered a career in technology have begun to pursue technology driven career paths. Others who were interested, have pursued with a renewed passion that is exciting to observe as an educator.

In 1932, George Counts, an influential education theorist and educator, called for a change in the architecture of education [6]. He called for change in traditional Euro-American 19th Century school design in favor of progressive education that is most known for experiential learning, collaboration, problem solving, and social responsibility. He identified that there will be calls for change without purpose or direction, but change for the sake of change is ineffective. Removing the date on his writing, one could mistake his call to action as in the same cry for change in a 21st Century publication. Action and change for the sake of change is ineffective, just as is a construction without a solid foundation. In this way, as researchers, we see the wisdom in looking back to those that have gone before us and what they have learned [7] as we envision the future and push the boundaries of what is currently possible. There are concepts and theories that have continued to demonstrate strength and integrity in multiple contexts and throughout the ongoing development and change in the technology landscape, because the foundation of their work lies in the human condition [27] and cognition [22].

Theory and research in publication can spark academic conversations and competition. For students, a high school design competition served a similar purpose. They responded to a challenge, a call to action, worked under constraints, investigated then communicated their ideas to achieve an end goal. This meant, the challenge required students to identify a gap in the gaming market, develop something intrinsically motivating [18] that would also benefit students in an educational way, and incorporate multiple modalities for learning and documenting their understanding.

For students to be able to take on this task in teams, they would need to understand the purpose of the challenge, research what already exists in the market, gaps in education that could benefit from new methods or gaps in gaming, the capability of pen and touch at this point and envisioning what could be in the future. To make a compelling case, they would need to identify and present a twist to capture multiple audiences, educators and students, so both could see the value in the final product. This meant students needed to know something about pedagogy. Some students had previous experience with designing, testing, implementing gaming and conducting small-scale research studies on gaming in the classroom. The WIPTTE challenge allowed students to practice research skills, identify a topic of focus, review what currently exists, answer a question and the challenge of designing.

WIPTTE High School Design challenge allowed them to take that knowledge and imagine what it would be like to envision and design a marketable product and pitch it to a group of experts. Prior to the challenge, students studied Common Core State Standards and team members imagined what type of standards could apply to a range of education settings or digital media. They had those in mind as goals to help form the direction of their challenge.

This process was not automatic. It took time for students to practice. The next section gives students voice in the conversation to help adults understand their process at the challenge and what skills they learned in school to help prepare them. This was their contribution to a broader conversation. It allowed a new generation to be empowered to see how their voice sparked thought and innovation. As teams chose names for the competition, the first team to write showed they saw value in examining the past, the present, and future while maintaining their cultural identity. Team R.A.P. wrote the first section collaboratively.

26.2 Respice, Adspice, Prospice: Examine the Past, Examine the Present, Examine the Future

A group of five girls attending Renton Preparatory Christian School were part of team they called R.A.P (Respice, adspice, prospice). This team wanted to reflect their cultural identity in their team name and the goal of their World Language focus in their game design. Their team name became part of the inspiration of their game, much like a language to decipher. Each girl comes from a different ethnic background and wanted to capture a historical richness in the game they designed to reflect the past, present, and future of World Language Learning. They chose Latin to represent scientific language, and its acronym reflected a modern music genera. They are all students of color within the 13–16 age range. Their inspiration for a game using pen and touch technology came from an interest in World Language learning. They could easily acknowledge the hardships of attempting to learn a language with only one resource available for use. With a limited amount of reference tools, it can be quite difficult for one to effectively learn a language, or any subject matter, in a fulfilling and efficient manner. So when the group, otherwise referred to as Team R.A.P., were informed of an upcoming game design contest revolved around the teaching of a school subject, they saw this as an opportunity to put their ideas into action.

The contest was held on April 29, 2015 at the Microsoft campus in Redmond, Washington, as part of the ninth annual Workshop on the Impact of Pen and Touch Technology on Education (WIPTTE). The challenge's designated target audience consisted of high school students, and in groups, they were asked to create a concept for a "gamified" touch screen application that could teach a topic typically learned in

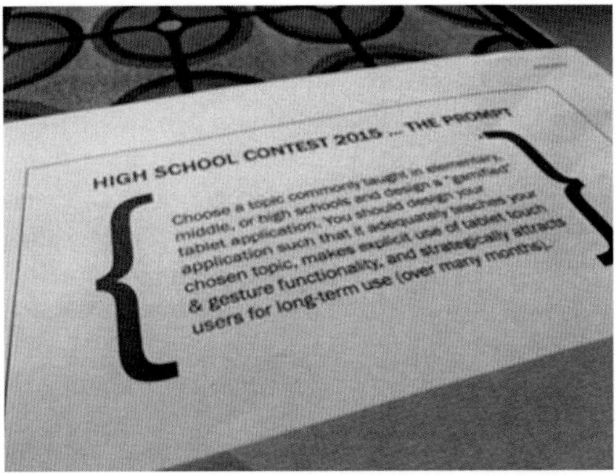

Fig. 26.1 Reviewing what exists

either elementary, middle, or high school. The learning could happen for students in school or outside of school. Restrictions set in place were the explicit incorporation of tablet touch and gesture functionality, as well as the attraction of users for long-term use (Fig. 26.1).

To prepare for the event, the team worked alongside their classmates at school to start forming potential game concepts. Since the prompt for the challenge could not to be released prior to competition day, the students worked on developing ideas for games under the broad category of "educational game designs."

The group thought like designers: reading various articles online, searching on app stores to see what already existed and what was yet to be developed, and asking one another what tools they wish they had to help them learn. Along the way, they also researched Common Core State Standards, as well as standards for World Languages.

All students in the group expressed the difficulties they had with learning a world language successfully through an online course. "We weren't getting the conversation component that was crucial for learning a language, and even though we had some images, we weren't getting a visual component that was also needed" said one student.

Naomi, one member of the group, came up with a concept loosely based off Sims (in terms of economy, virtual avatars, as well as virtual reality) that allowed students to experience the life of the country of the language they were learning. A player could get directions to a movie theater, go inside and watch a film in the language they were learning with or without subtitles. They could write letters to friends about the movie. They could learn to purchase groceries and learn the currency of the country, exchange rates and cultural norms as part of learning about global economy in the context of learning a language. They could purchase clothing and look at style trends that would get updated. Drawing through inking could be part of exploring careers in those countries that required design. For example, if a student was learning Italian, they could go to Milan, and explore how a fashion designer works with technology and the engineering with pattern design, sketch their own designs and see them work. They could interact with clients and learn colors and shapes. At restaurants, students would practice ordering food and paying according to local customs. Game players could learn about history and context of culture through exploration of towns, cities, villages, and communities and learn the geography as they walk and travel. Music and artists work could be part of interactive components. Other players could add their own music or favorite things from their area so others can experience it.

Characters comprising World Languages from Asian countries are much better to practice with inking than trying to keyboard type. There could be places to learn calligraphy and other forms of art. People can upload photographs from actual travels and tag them. Writing things correctly could unlock other features as a student learns to communicate better verbally and in written digital ink. There already exists ink recognition to make this possible.

To make the experience real and collaborative, it could be a Massively Multiplayer Online Role-Playing Game (MMORPG). where avatars could interact with others and get a chance to talk with native speakers in different countries or connect with teachers in different countries. Teachers could connect with classes and swap the ability to score other student's work, like an exchange program for teachers and share learning ideas. Teachers could have access to student accounts if they wanted to make the game part of blended learning, or students could learn independently.

To make it a STEM game, students could practice going to medical facilities and asking for help in case of emergency. While at a hospital, they could learn about viruses, broken bones, medical reactions and other medical or legal practices. This would help prepare people for emergencies if they end up studying or living abroad. Some of these components could also inspire careers or study abroad.

Live & Learn, a program concept formed by five girls, focused on helping others learn a language in a fun and collaborative way utilizing inking technology to learn to write the language. There exist language learning apps and games, but to our knowledge, there does not yet exist a game that teaches students to correctly form letters or characters in the language they are learning, practice writing for accuracy and communicate with inking. In Live & Learn, users can virtually visit a country, learn about its culture and geography with interactive activities and practice writing skills when completing assignments. Student competencies can be recorded and documented and scores in the game can be translated to competency and standards mastery.

In pitching the idea at WIPTTE, the team members each took a section to talk about and practiced their pitch during the time they were designing. One of the students, Jasmine, watches Shark Tank and decided to model her introduction after the pitches that had effective and persuasive elements. Their team took 1st place in the design challenge. Several of the team members in this team and one in the Plumbum and Touch team were so inspired by the experience they spent a large part of the summer drafting a research proposal for the Surface Hub. They learned how to develop research questions, investigate knowledge in published literature, construct a design, and identify a budget. WIPTTE inspired a call to action. Two students, Kayla, and Tiffany entered college early as a Junior in high school since the experience at WIPTTE and have sought out internships in the technology field. Kayla opted to take a research writing course her first year of college because she was inspired. This team also went on to submitting their design as a proposal for International Society for Technology in Education and presented in Philadelphia, PA in June 2015, and then was asked to present for the Los Angeles Unified School District Redefining Learning conference. They also presented at iNACOL (International Association for K-12 Online Learning) in Orlando, FL in November 2015.

26.3 Plumbum and Touch

For the design game concept called, Plumbum and Touch, our team decided to create a concept for a STEM game where the objective was to create 3D objects using touch in order to complete certain tasks, such as getting a plane to fly through a hoop, or a catapult to destroy a tower. To see a student created media presentation on a mobile device or computer go to: https://doc.co/jRszUA/nTs872 or scan Fig. 26.2.

To set our idea in motion, we decided to use our group's favorite subjects, and we ended up with History, Science, and Art. To our knowledge, after searching games for education on the market, we found no other concept like it that included inking and touch. No other time in history beside the Renaissance would fit our concept as well to combine these subjects and achieve the look and feel of a game that we wanted to create. We developed our concept by placing the player into the time of the Renaissance, where the player would be commissioned every week by a digital contractor to create machines to contractor's liking.

From there, we looked at the components of STEM and identified learning inherent in the process that pushed creativity and innovation. It is essential to learn from mistakes and redesign. We decided to implement this into the concept by having the player test his mechanism and have a questionnaire that a teacher could read. The questionnaire would be a type of hidden formative assessment to ask questions such as, what failed? What worked? What would you do differently if you had another chance? The player would be given more chances to build on what they learned from failure. This was the first round of brainstorming.

We also decided to take inspiration from one of the biggest video game companies in the world, Valve Software. Their product, Steam, is a program where people can buy games, connect with friends online to play games, and upload different artworks or concepts that can put added to a game. To incorporate this into our concept, we decided to allow the game player to share contraptions for the weekly job presented by the contractor. There is power in peer review and feedback. If a player is playing

Fig. 26.2 Scan the QR code to see student created media

the game at home and does not have a built-in classroom community, they can share what they built on the internet with a global community of builders. It could also be adapted for classroom use and help teachers who are new to teaching STEM projects. The game could serve as a guide to support them in helping their students design, fail, redesign, and provide feedback to others based on what they learned. The contraptions could be evaluated and rated by the community online. The community would rate the contraptions by downloading other people's contraptions and testing it.

Our team discussed multiple potential ways of testing. The first way would be to have a game mechanism that would allow virtual testing with authentic physics responses. This would bring in another element of physics learning that could be expanded later. Second, we thought about blending physical Maker Space concepts with virtual Maker Space concepts. Designs could be sketched with digital ink. The program would help generate patterns that people could use to create objects in real life. The challenge of identifying materials that would work, and getting feedback from a community of builders could also increase critical thinking and collaboration skills. When people build their design or contraption they could record it being tested in a real-world environment and upload a video to the community for review, feedback, and votes.

After building the main concept of the game, we started working on how we can start making the game relevant to our target audience, of being for all ages and ability levels. For lower levels, we wanted to include the basics, such as just the structure of a contraption, with controlled choices. This could let children as young as kindergarten see cause and effect and basic science concepts while practicing sketches. This could also be basic level for adults. Basic templates could be provided and simpler designs for building would be available. For children who advance through those levels or for the high school or college grade level, contraptions would require additional constraints, more technical knowledge such as aerodynamics or gravity, and potentially computer drafting and up through architectural programs, coding and virtual or augmented reality like HoloLens or Vive. Digital inking and touch could expand to haptic feedback as the designs transition from a mobile device to virtual or augmented space.

Part of our school design as students trains us to look at learning process and learning goals. We already started looking at Common Core State Standards for other projects. We investigated what they meant and how people could demonstrate that kind of knowledge. Going into the WIPTTE high school design challenge, each of our team picked Common Core State Standards we thought could apply to whatever the challenge could be and figured ways to draw on ideas that would help meet those goals of learning, even if the learning was implicit. We learned about implicit and explicit knowledge from research we did in gaming with Portal 2 with our teacher across several years. Learning can happen in games when people do not know they are learning. We want them to transfer learning [2, 19]. Building and reflecting can help with that. Inking and touch allow for that process in a different way than not having that ability.

After we finished the concept of our game, created the visuals, user interface, and models to display the concept, we practiced the presentation hoping to win first place, and made the presentation to the judges, and made the presentation to the judges. We were awarded fourth place. We learned from feedback what part of our pitch was not clear. We were grateful for a second chance to show our idea at ISTE and now this publication.

26.4 Reflections from a Teacher

In 2011 during the Microsoft Innovative Educator U.S. Forum, high school teacher Michelle Zimmerman took a tour of the Home of the Future in the Envisioning Center on the Microsoft Redmond Campus with a team of educators. The tour guides asked them to imagine what their classrooms might be like in the next 5–10 years if homes had the capabilities they imagined. At the time, she wished that someday she would be able to share that experience with her students. Four years later that desire became a reality as they participated in and experienced WIPTTE 2015 at Microsoft.

The students participated in the entire conference, from the keynotes [11, 15] to the You-Try-Its [12, 16, 24, 28], and interacted with influential researchers and designers; Jonathan Grudin and Michel Pahud from Microsoft Research; Chris Pratley for reaching out to the Sway team and David Jones for the students to experience the Envisioning Center.. Microsoft's Robyn Hrivnatz invited the high school students to the Global Educator Exchange colocated with WIPTTE and encouraged high school student Scott Nguyen to boldly speak directly to Microsoft CEO Satya Nadella during the Fireside Chat at the Global Educator Exchange. 2014 WIPTTE chair Tracy Hammond offered the students an opportunity to document their experience through this publication. Each of these people exemplified a group of exceptional adults who find value in students' voices and purpose.

Across those five days, her students experienced a shift in understanding about education and its possibilities. There, the students did not just envision, they acted. They provided feedback to the Sway development team, and experienced the power of voice. Figure 26.3 shows Zimmerman's students during the design process of the challenge on site during WIPTTE. One of the talks emphasized how the designer observed hands in detail as he was designing a digital pen so writing could be natural. He looked at contact points hand made to paper. The students heard how something seemingly insignificant became crucial in design.

The effect of WIPTTE has been long lasting and impactful. Since then, her students submitted eight proposals to ISTE (International Society for Technology in Education) 2015, which were accepted at workshops, interactive lectures, birds-of-a-feather, and ISTE Ignite. Kayla, Jasmine, and Scott, inspired by WIPTTE, participated in the writing of a Surface Hub for Research proposal during their summer vacation. The students defined research questions on how to use a pen and touch device to increase communication and collaboration across a range of ages at two school sites from Pre-Kindergarten through 10th grade as well as teachers participat-

Fig. 26.3 Students during the design process of the challenge on site during WIPTTE

ing in a distance learning education program (the Virtual Enhanced Online Master's in Technology in Education).

One student was accepted to and provided college credit for The Congress of Future Medical Leaders in Boston, and noticed parallels between the future of technology in education and medicine. Two students spoke at a Los Angeles Unified School District conference. Three students are seriously considering shifting their career focus toward technology from a different field.

Zimmerman has taught all the grades from Preschool through 10th grade. She had the opportunity to watch the developmental progression of students in different grades while studying Learning sciences and Human Development through the Ph.D. program at University of Washington, College of Education. As her work has investigated learning design and the importance of human connection, motivation, and mentoring, Zimmerman has seen how technology can support increased human connection. The work on pen and touch technology is one of the most exciting areas to advance the field as it relates to education because of the ability to facilitate communication and collaboration.

The following sections are a collaborative effort across several high school students to express what they experienced between April and June 2015, as it intersected with their experience in her classroom.

26.5 The Future of Education, by Tiffany Dinh and Kayla Gonzalvo

The future is approaching quickly and technology is already becoming a part of our everyday lives. At the Workshop on the Impact of Pen and Touch Technology on Education (WIPTTE) in April 2015, we learned about the ways technology developers have already collaborated with educators to explore how technology and education can actually work together. This is true for education and training of people who are pursuing a medical career. At the Envisioning Center, we saw the vision of what types of tools could do to assist medical leaders in collaborating to solve problems across distance, ranging from diagnosis to developing parts for prosthetics. "Increasingly, you'll learn by simulations," said Dr. Stephen Ray Mitchell [13]. This relates to certain video games and how they imitate reality through the way the game is designed. A good example of gaming and simulation for solving problems in the medical field is a game called, Foldit, where "Gamers have solved the structure of a retrovirus enzyme whose configuration had stumped scientists for more than a decade. The gamers achieved their discovery by playing Foldit, an online game that allows players to collaborate and compete in predicting the structure of protein molecules" [9].

Our class has worked with gaming in the classroom from 2011 to 2015 and several of us, including Jasmine Fernandez and Scott Nguyen have presented on their work with Portal 2 in the classroom. Although the game was not made specifically for the purpose of education, there were physics and mathematical simulations as part of the game. We looked at implicit-to-explicit knowledge extraction and what happens when students are having so much fun playing a game that they do not realize they are learning. We imagine this becoming more and more part of education. We know WIPTTE imagines this as well.

During the High School Design Challenge at WIPTTE 2015, our goal was to create a game that helped students learn a concept using pen and touch technology. Students can relate video gaming to their own lives by adapting certain skills from those games and using them in their everyday lives as well as in school. Video games can be part of education for they can teach different skills and allow students to open up their minds and start thinking of how they could complete a level. Applying this to medical knowledge and training, we heard about the use of 3D printing for parts, and saw how motion sensors like Kinect could impact physical therapy. We imagine concepts could be combined with gaming for children or adults who do not want to do physical therapy on their own.

Figure 26.4 shows Tiffany Dinh taking notes connecting technology and the field of medicine.

Dr. Craig Venter stated that soon doctors and nurses may have the capability to email vaccines [25]. They were talking about coding and looking at genetic code. It would allow people in remote locations to access life-saving information that could help them create a vaccine they needed in a short amount of time, with less resources.

Since the 3D printer has already been invented, printing parts for medical equipment, prosthetics, or even surgical tools, could be a breakthrough. This would allow the medical schools to teach medical students an easy and quick way to treat their patients. If education and technology have already teamed up, other career fields such as the medical field will enhance and improve the direction education is heading. We have seen innovations in medicine through times of crisis and through necessity. Those innovations lead to more refined technologies used by the general public.

We also envision that sooner in the future children as young as Pre-Kindergarten will have access to technologies that replace textbooks and, young as they are, they

Fig. 26.4 Tiffany Dinh takes notes connecting technology and the field of medicine at the Congress for Future Medical Leaders established through the National Academy of Future Physicians and Medical Leaders held at the University of Massachusetts in June 2015

Fig. 26.5 Two high school mentors, Kayla Gonzalvo and Genesis Conyers guide younger learners in science, as they introduce them to more complex anatomy and physiology concepts

might even begin to research and discover things that could interest them at an early age. Figure 26.5 shows two high school mentors, Kayla Gonzalvo and Genesis Conyers, guiding younger learners in science, as they introduce them to more complex anatomy and physiology concepts. The future of education needs to focus on training children to think and ask essential questions, to find problems that impact their lives, the community, and globally, and a will to do something to create change. This allows little children to be able to open their eyes and see the broad perspective that adults see. We may even have children assist scientists, researchers, developers, or educators in their research since they have a perspective that we do not have and can be far more creative than we are, because they do not have all the constraints of knowing what is thought to be impossible.

An example of this is a twelve year-old boy name Carson Barry, who is currently researching about concussions and has been interested in researching the possible correlation between concussions and suicide [1]. During his talk at The Congress for Future Medical Leaders at University of Massachusetts Lowell, June 2015, he discussed using helmets with sensors that notify him whether or not an athlete would report their injuries or symptoms to an adult. If this child has already started his research, I'm sure other children, possibly younger, could start researching on their own. When we mentored little buddies in Kindergarten in our school, they were already coming up with great ideas they wanted to investigate and share with others. The future of education will look at the complexity of thought children can have and encourage it. It is never too early to start and develop new technologies and brainstorming possibilities for the future.

We believe that student voice is essential for driving the future of education [30]. From personal experiences, each student in our group has found an importance in their voice. We see that students will have more control in their education in a way so that they can guide their own learning. We believe this. We believe that what students think matters.

26.6 The Future of Education, by Scott Nguyen

26.6.1 The Absent Future

Imagine a future where students do not physically have to be at school, but learn at home. Allowing students to work at home gives them a comfortable environment rather than an unfamiliar building. Advancements in technology allow students to be inside the classroom without physically being there. Technology like holograms and the HoloLens are examples of these types of situations. Since collaboration is a key part in education, and holograms can put the students inside a virtual environment, the students can experience things with each other that they would not normally be able to experience in real life, such as environments in space. The Surface Hub mainly allows collaboration in person, however, using the Surface Hub has many features that allow the collaboration between multiple people in different areas. The virtual environments could also help each of the students learn from each other, as more collaboration can invoke curiosity, as well as having the students help each other through specific tasks.

26.6.2 Collaboration

Memories made through working with others can be retained much better than just sitting and listening to someone, and this can greatly benefit students. We see the future holds much more than different class periods with desks and rows, we see classes where students are encouraged to teach one another new things from their own experiences instead of only using textbooks and lectures. Our class already does this, but it is still new to many people. This is potentially positive as interaction between students and teachers can induce emotion and create more vivid memories of what the students are learning about. This method can also teach skills to students needed in the workplace. The factory education system, as many of us know, is becoming outdated and no longer matches the end goals for educating a society where many of those type of skills can be done by machines or computers. During the Industrial Revolution, the time that schools were being started, this system was good as it trained students to work in a factory by responding to a bell to change shifts or periods. Today, the workforce requires workers that are competent and able to collaborate with other employees and be able to adapt to varying situations.

26.6.3 Artifacting

Standardized tests are not the best ways to show what someone has learned, and many schools are beginning to realize that. Some students learn in different ways, some learn visually while others can learn hands on, which makes it hard to measure what the student has gained from school. Like in the previous section that talked about collaboration, with different group projects, such as creating short films to demonstrate learning can bring out student's strengths, and exposes their weaknesses so other students can help them become better. We do that through a process of critique and revision of multiple drafts. We create rubrics based on what we notice is most effective during draft phases and how to demonstrate clear learning. As we watched the video on Future Productivity Group projects that bring out what the students have learned can also benefit many others, as the Internet is a means to share that artifact that students have created for others to view and learn from.

26.6.4 Student Guidance

Student voice is incredibly important when it comes to education, as they are the ones learning. I see students having much more control over what they are learning in the future. We still want students to have a well-rounded education, however, we want students to be able to choose the type of content they want to learn, so that they are able to be more engaged and receive more from the information. Though students are able to choose their own classes in school, they do not typically have much control in what they learn in that class. From this, I see that teachers should be more of a guide to spark interest and questions for further learning rather than maintaining entire responsibility of course design or dissemination. Students then could teach one another what they have learned, as discussed earlier, to help one another learn about certain topics. We currently do this at my school, but with the support of new tools in the future, I imagine adaptive technologies that allow students to build their courses.

26.7 The Future of Education, by Jasmine Fernandez

Although there are schools that utilize technology for educational purposes, the majority of schools across the world have yet to come to this level of advancement within their classrooms. Many seem to overlook the positives of technology and argue that it has been brought into this world with cruel intentions: to decrease social skills. There are times that this statement can be found true, and unfortunately, many people nowadays see it that way. The point I am trying to make is that this entire way of thinking can be changed, for technology is rapidly advancing and growing in spectacular ways at this moment. Technology can have a negative effect on society, but that is not always the case, especially from my experience at my school. One day, I envision that technological devices will be found in every classroom, for both communication and collaboration purposes, ultimately benefiting students in amazing ways.

26.7.1 Envisioning

In June of 2015, two of my classmates, my teacher, and I developed a proposal in the form of a paper stating how our school could possibly use a Surface Hub to enhance learning and conduct research in the classroom setting [29]. The primary question we came up with for our paper revolved around the idea of what collaboration between students, ranging from pre-kindergarten to graduate school educational levels, in different campus sites would look like utilizing Surface Hubs to collaborate and communicate. There would be multiple levels of focus. First, we decided that students could work together on group projects within their own class. Second, students could collaborate across classrooms or campuses by using Surface Hub to mentoring younger grade levels and help teach them to use the right tools for the right job, digital citizenship with authentic projects, and collaboratively create with inking. Third, the teachers could collaborate as they are designing learning or while our classes are collaborating. It could be easier for them to harness experts from outside the classroom, and work with each other, especially the teachers working on their own Master's graduate online program while teaching us and researching how well their

Fig. 26.6 Kayla Gonzalvo and Jasmine Fernandez explain Sway to a teacher at the International Society in Education, June 2015, introducing the concept of the design challenge and their concept

designs work in class. We have learned that teachers guide students, but students also inspire learning in teachers. In this way, Surface Hub can allow for a range of skill development from handwriting in Pre-Kindergarten to solving problems collaboratively as Graduate Students who are currently our teachers and leading us by modeling what they want us to do by asking essential questions. Student collaboration + various ages and education levels + multiple locations + an ever-present use of communication and social skills, despite the fact that technology is being used = the direction that I think the education system of the future should progress in.

26.7.2 Experience

My former middle school class and the ninth grade class of Philadelphia-based School of the Future collaborated via the Internet in the 2012 and 2013 academic years. We worked as mentors in a way, but the form was through critiquing student-made video tutorials. The overall experience was great and students were given the opportunity to gain so much more knowledge in terms of how to use Movie Maker, Community Clips, as well as communication and collaboration skills to make our message clear and teach a skill to another audience. By looking at tutorials created by other students on the opposite side of the United States, we were able to see successes and failures more easily than when we just looked at our own. We could be more objective. Some of us also got slightly competitive, because we wanted to show that we could make a tutorial just as good if not better than kids who were older than us. That got us to revise our work and come to a consensus about which things were most effective and which things were not helpful. We got better at storytelling, video-editing, and conveying ideas.

However, reflecting back on this partnership, it is evident that despite the positives, collaboration could have been carried out much more effectively had it been for the Surface Hub. Students and teachers were limited to physically writing out their opinions in the form of a list, but with this device, communication could be advanced to simultaneous video, inking, and audio usage. Students would be given the ability to virtually travel and talk to students across the globe, and provide instant feedback to one another by speaking, opposed to typing.

This would have been especially helpful when the CEO of Corinth, Ondrej Homola found a team's tutorials on YouTube and their company from the Czech Republic contacted us in Seattle and formed a partnership across distance. Our teacher told us to do our best work, because we never knew who may find it somewhere in the world. None of us realized it would become a reality so soon. We also did not imagine that we would present at a conference with the CEO, the teacher from Philadelphia, and our teacher at International Society for Technology in Education in 2014. Inking could be used to write out thoughts and jot down notes regarding video critique, sketch ideas, draw plans for storyboarding, sketch designs for new products, all the more providing another effective visual aspect of collaboration. Figure 26.6 shows Kayla Gonzalvo and Jasmine Fernandez explaining Sway to a teacher at the International Society for Technology in Education, June 2015. Gonzalvo and Fernandez introduce the concept of the design challenge and their concept.

26.7.3 Interaction and Application

However, not only could the Surface Hub be found applicable to critiquing video tutorials, but to a whole range of student projects. In the 2014–2015 school year, 8th–10th grade students took an anatomy and physiology course created by Florida Virtual Schools. For one of our group projects, we were instructed to create a replica of some type of bone structure. We worked in small groups of 3–4 people, but imagine if this project was taken to a whole new level with an international school or experts in related fields. With technology, it can. Students could virtually create the bone on the device or share pictures of their physical replicas with students or experts across the globe doing the same project or observing. Models could be replicated, refined, and printed out with 3D printers. As mentioned previously, students would also have the chance to communicate via dual cameras and audio. We recently talked to a Microsoft researcher who specializes in haptic touch, and if the Surface Hub incorporated this component into its capabilities, students would then have the opportunity to actually feel the structure of the bone, crevices and all. It would give us a whole new way to practice palpation as part of that course. Our teacher blended the online course content from Florida Virtual Schools with inclass Science, Technology, Engineering, Arts and Mathematics (STEAM) project based learning. Since we helped design projects for blended learning, we imagine helping to design learning with haptic feedback, 3D printers, and other tools in the future.

This is just one scenario in the classroom where technology can be made useful. If executed properly, student interaction with electronic devices can be extremely positive and beneficial. Current traditional education is outdated; it needs something new and innovative to keep up with technological advancements. Education should not be restricted to textbooks and lectures, but expanded to interaction and collaboration across multiple platforms and modalities. Just imagine what will happen when we bring in gesture, with things like Kinect, and HoloLens.

We have already had a glimpse of learning like this with experts, other teachers and students in different locations in our same country and globally, but we envision that in the future, we will be able to break language barriers with tools like Skype with translation by speaking, connecting our ideas, visions, with people who have the expertise to help us carry it out, mutually benefiting us and the global community. At the Envisioning Center, we were able to see what this may look like in 5–10 years. When that happens, we will be able to say we saw it coming and are part of the innovation as college students or interns. This is my vision for where I see our future in education going, and one day, I hope to see it being carried out in all schools worldwide.

26.8 Biographies

All four high school students are participating in the Renton Prep High School Apprentice program that helps students gain college and career readiness experience.

Kayla Gonzalvo is a junior and was accepted to begin studying full time at Bellevue College in Autumn 2015 to obtain her A.S. Direct Transfer Agreement through Running Start. She is certified in Microsoft Office.

Jasmine Fernandez, is a freshman in high school and was requested by Microsoft to speak for Los Angeles Unified School District in August 2015.

Kayla Gonzalvo and Jasmine Fernandez recently attended the International Society for Technology in Education 2015 held in Philadelphia. (ISTE 2015 for short) Jasmine and Kayla presented 3 times with their teacher Michelle Zimmerman and was interviewed by Robyn Hrivnatz at the Microsoft Learning Lounge.

Scott Nguyen is a sophomore in high school. Scott has worked with Visual Studio and After Effects and has started a company in building computers.

Tiffany Dinh is a junior enrolled in the Running Start Program at Bellevue College for two years beginning Autumn 2015 where she will transfer to a university. She recently attended a medical conference in Boston and learned about the different sciences and technologies that relate to education and its future. It gave her ideas of where technology and education are headed.

All four students have designed learning environments and evaluated curricula with the help of Dr. Zimmerman. They have presented at conferences such as ISTE (International Society for Technology in Education), Northwest Council for Computer Education, Emerald City ComiCon, University of Nebraska–Lincoln Tech EDGE, SXSWedu (Jasmine and Scott's proposals were accepted in the same category as adults identified as having an 20 % acceptance rate) and International Association for K-12 Online Learning. (Figures 26.7 and 26.8 show Scott Nguyen, Jennifer Fernandez, and Jasmine Fernandez preparing to present their workshops.) Jasmine, Tiffany, and Kayla's team won first place in the High School Design Challenge at WIPTTE.

Michelle Zimmerman, received her Ph.D. in Learning Sciences and Human Development from the University of Washington College of Education in 2011 and has taught all the grades from Pre-Kindergarten through 10th grade, co-taught, led professional development, led the school-wide 1:1 plan, and has presented her research and work across the United States and Canada, inspiring her students to join her since 2012. She is concurrently Adjunct Faculty at Concordia University Wisconsin and is guiding a cohort of educators though a Virtual Enhanced Online Master's where they will research and refine their own practice culminating in a capstone that will benefit the entire school body.

Fig. 26.7 Scott Nguyen at SXSWedu, March 2015, preparing to present his Future 15

Fig. 26.8 Jennifer Fernandez, Michelle Zimmerman, and Jasmine Fernandez prior to presenting their workshop on gaming in the classroom at SXSWedu, March 2015

Acknowledgments Thanks to Jonathan Grudin for his efforts in securing scholarships for the participating high school students. Thanks to Michel Pahud for organizing a field trip to talk about his work as a researcher. Thanks to Chris Pratley for reaching out to the Sway team and David Jones for the students to experience the Envisioning Center. Thanks to Ari Schorr for opening speaking opportunities to students and mentoring them by telling truelife stories of discovering passion in the tech field, and bringing in colleagues as role models to talk to the students. Thanks to Robyn Hrivnatz for providing leadership in the Education team, opening opportunities to the students and encouraging Zimmerman to become part of the MIE Expert team. Thanks to Tracy Hammond and Stephanie Valentine showed students they were an important part of the conversation at WIPTTE. Thanks to Juli Lorton for her influence in Zimmerman's research design and her feedback during drafts for this chapter. To David-Paul and Gloria who made Renton Prep a reality, so many students are forever changed.

References

1. Barry C (2015) World's youngest concussion researcher. Speech presented at the congress of future medical leaders, Boston. Accessed 14 June 2015
2. Bransford JD, Schwartz DL (1999) Rethinking transfer: a simple proposal with multiple implications. Rev Res Educ pp 61–100
3. Brantlinger EA (2003) Dividing classes: how the middle class negotiates and rationalizes school advantage. Psychology Press, New York
4. Butler DL (1998) In search of the architect of learning a commentary on scaffolding as a metaphor for instructional interactions. J Learn Disabil 31(4):374–385
5. Cole M (1990) Cultural psychology: a once and future discipline? In: Nebraska Symposium on Motivation, 1989: Cross-cultural Perspectives. University of Nebraska Press
6. Counts GS (1978) Dare the school build a new social order?, vol 143. Southern Illinois University Press, Carbondale
7. de Montaigne M, Frame DM (1976) The complete essays of Montaigne. Stanford University Press, Stanford
8. de Saint-Exupéry A, Woods K (1943) The little prince. Harcourt, Brace & World
9. Gray L (2011) Gamers succeed where scientists fail [news article]. Accessed 14 Jan 2016
10. Heath SB (1982) Questioning at home and at school: a comparative study. In: Heath SB, Spindler G (eds) Doing the ethnography of schooling: educational anthropology in action. Holt Rhinehart & Winston, New York
11. Hinckley K, Buxton B (2016) Inking outside the box: how context sensing affords more natural pen (and touch) computing. In: Hammond T, Valentine S, Adler A (eds) Revolutionizing education with digital ink: the impact of pen and touch technology on education. Springer International Publishing, New York
12. Lara-Garduno R, Leslie N, Hammond T (2016) Smartstrokes: digitizing paper-based neuropsychological tests. In: Hammond T, Valentine S, Adler A (eds) Revolutionizing education with digital ink: the impact of pen and touch technology on education. Springer International Publishing, New York
13. Michell S (2015) Dr. Stephen Mitchell speaks to the congress of future medical physicians. speech presented at the congress of future medical leaders, Boston, MA. Accessed 14 June 2015
14. November A (2012) Who owns the learning?: preparing students for success in the digital age. Solution Tree Press, Bloomington
15. Oviatt S (2016) Computer interfaces can stimulate or undermine students' ability to think. In: Hammond T, Valentine S, Adler A (eds) Revolutionizing education with digital ink: the impact of pen and touch technology on education. Springer International Publishing, New York

16. Polsley S, Ray J, Nelligan T, Helms M, Linsey J, Hammond T (2016) Leveraging trends in student interaction to enhance the effectiveness of sketch-based educational software. In: Hammond T, Valentine S, Adler A (eds) Revolutionizing education with digital ink: the impact of pen and touch technology on education. Springer International Publishing, New York
17. Rogoff B (1991) Social interaction as apprenticeship in thinking: Guided participation in spatial planning. In: Resnick LB, Levine JM, Teasley SD (eds) Perspectives on socially shared cognition. American Psychological Association, Washington
18. Ryan RM, Deci EL (2000) Self-determination theory and the facilitation of intrinsic motivation, social development, and well-being. Am Psychol 55(1):68–78
19. Schwartz DL, Bransford JD, Sears D (2005) Efficiency and innovation in transfer. In: Mestre JP (ed) Transfer of learning from a modern multidisciplinary perspective. Information Age Publishing, Portland, pp 1–51
20. Soder R (2004) The double bind of civic education assessment and accountability. In: Sirotnik KA (ed) Holding accountability accountable: what ought to matter in public education. Teachers College Press, New York, pp 100–115
21. Steele CM (1997) A threat in the air: how stereotypes shape intellectual identity and performance. Am Psychol 52(6):613–629
22. Sun R, Zhang X, Slusarz P, Mathews R (2007) The interaction of implicit learning, explicit hypothesis testing learning and implicit-to-explicit knowledge extraction. Neural Netw 20(1):34–47
23. Tillman LC (2006) Researching and writing from an african-american perspective: reflective notes on three research studies. Int J Qual Stud Educ 19(3):265–287
24. Valentine S, Leyva-McMurtry A, Borgos-Rodriguez K, Hammond T (2016) The digital sash: a sketch-based badge system in a social network for children. In: Hammond T, Valentine S, Adler A (eds) Revolutionizing education with digital ink: the impact of pen and touch technology on education. Springer International Publishing, New York
25. Venter C (2015) Dr. Craig Venter speaks to the congress of future medical physicians. Speech presented at the Congress of Future Medical Leaders, Boston, MA (2015). Accessed 14 June 2015
26. Vygotsky LS (1987) The collected works of LS Vygotsky, vol 1: thinking and speech (translated by N. Minick, vol. 1). Plenim Press, New York
27. Vygotsky LS (1987) Mind in society. Harvard University Press, Cambridge
28. Williford B, Nelligan T, Taele P, Li W, Linsey J, Hammond T (2016) Persketchtivity: an intelligent pen-based educational application for design sketching instruction. In: Hammond T, Valentine S, Adler A (eds) Revolutionizing education with digital ink: the impact of pen and touch technology on education. Springer International Publishing, New York
29. Zimmerman M (2016) Surface hub for research [research proposal] (2015). Accessed 14 Jan 2016
30. Zimmerman M (2016) An aqua squiggle and giggles: pre-teens as researchers influencing little lives through inking and touch devices. In: Hammond T, Valentine S, Adler A (eds) Revolutionizing education with digital ink: the impact of pen and touch technology on education. Springer International Publishing, New York